Guiding Reading and Writing in the Content Areas

Practical Strategies

Third Edition

M. Carrol Tama
Portland State University

Anita McClain Haley
Pacific University

 KENDALL/HUNT PUBLISHING COMPANY
4050 Westmark Drive   P.O. Box 1840   Dubuque, Iowa 52004-1840

Cover art by Emily Young

Copyright © 1998, 2001, 2007 by M. Carrol Tama and Anita McClain Haley

ISBN 978-0-7575-4210-7

Printed in the United States of America
10 9 8 7 6 5 4 3 2 1

For Larry, Joe, Charles, Norb, Michael,
Allison, Truman, Calvin

CONTENTS

PREFACE

Rationale

As its title suggests, *Guiding Reading and Writing in the Content Areas: Practical Strategies* presents a host of instructional activities and strategies teachers can use to help students learn content material through reading, writing and discussion.

We have culled these activities from practicing educators who have tried these strategies and provided feedback to us; from reading what our colleagues are writing on content area reading and writing; and from conference ideas gleaned over the years from many generous professionals. The process of selecting activities and cultivating our particular approach was one we wrestled with over many rewrites of this textbook. We have made choices. *Our goal is to provide classroom teachers with instructional tools that will add versatility to the instructional approach they use in helping students learn.* This support is intended to encourage teachers in their development of a meaning-centered environment where students are motivated and can function successfully. **Another goal is to provide classroom teachers with additional scaffolding activities that enhance students' learning.**

What is the goal of this text?

Students need to know how they learn, and to be able to apply fix-up strategies when they are not learning. Scaffolding consists of providing instructional literacy skills or tools. With continued use students begin to implement these strategies to independently achieve and to move to the next level of cognition. Cognition refers to the true understanding of concepts using higher order thinking skills, inquiry and self-monitoring.

For those who wish to pursue theoretical and research questions in depth, we have indicated sources and provided references where further reading can be done.

Our Audience

This textbook is meant for preservice teachers as well as practicing educators. As a part of the workshops we have conducted in many school districts it has been an integral part of staff development.

This book serves as a useful resource for inservice teachers who want to improve their teaching of reading and writing in the content areas. The key here is the phrase "want to improve." This means that the administration, the principals, curriculum coaches and teachers believe that everybody is a teacher of literacy. When that occurred during the time we conducted our professional development workshops, we noticed a marked difference in teacher attitudes and in a number of cases student reading and writing scores improved.

In addition, we are pleased to see that the text has been useful outside the K-12 area such as in optometry classes. Optometric faculty have used it to enhance learner engagement in their coursework. For the instructors of content area read-

Strategies for all teachers.

ing courses, we've attempted to blend theory and practice in a way that is helpful for you and your students. For other practicing educators, we've highlighted many strategies that your colleagues find most useful and incorporated others that are new. For the novice teacher, we hope these strategies will serve as a template for designing and delivering content that will serve you well now and in your future. We promise you that persistence and study will convince you that the time spent developing these strategies is worth the effort. We ask you to selectively attend to what we've written. In short, we want you to decide why and when to implement the strategies you choose. Begin with activities that appeal to you. As time and conviction increase, we hope you will add to your repertoire.

How to Use This Book

*Note **Your Turn** activities.*

Each chapter begins with *Target Questions*. We ask our readers to develop questions for themselves and to keep a writing log of their reactions to their reading. An introductory *graphic organizer* demonstrates the ideas developed in the chapter as well as the relationship of these ideas to each other.

Interspersed throughout the text are exercises called *Your Turn*. These are designed to encourage educators to become involved with ideas presented and to apply knowledge of specific strategies introduced. These activity sheets also can be uses as assignments since they are easily removed from the text.

Throughout each chapter are *Teacher Talk and Student Talk* segments, anecdotes we have collected from practicing educators in response to our request for feedback to the ideas presented in this text. We have a strong belief that teachers make strategies work. When teachers talk, their colleagues listen.

Figures are featured liberally throughout the text. We have presented an eclectic mix of charts, student work, and sample strategies to illustrate what we have written.

The instructional strategies we've presented are the heart of this book. We have selected a variety of easily adapted instructional techniques to use across the curriculum. In making our choices, we have relied on both research and practice to present the most effective strategies presently in use.

For each strategy we have added an *Instructional Summary* that clarifies the focus and learning principles met by that technique. In the Instructional Summary we have indicated how the strategy supports specific state and national literacy standards, the primary focus of the strategy, when to use it, materials needed and the learning principles imbedded in the implementation of the strategy. The learning principles are the basis for sound teaching and add credence to the value of the strategies. No matter which literacy strategies teachers choose to use, they need to select these on the basis of effective teaching and learning principles. Culled from the last 20 years of cognitive and social learning research, these principles support the development of thoughtful, active readers.

Lesson Plan Models show how to implement a particular strategy. Each lesson plan includes the traditional lesson plan components and addresses clear, concise directions and explanations.

In the margins, we have included citations that credit authors for ideas we have synthesized or drawn on. Other margin notations provide questions, short definitions or highlight critical ideas in the accompanying paragraphs.

Each chapter has a section on *Inclusion Techniques* and a section on *Strategies for Second Language Learners* in which techniques are illustrated that should work for all students, but especially those with special needs. We have deliberately made the decision to interchange the terms English as a Second Language (ESL), English Language Learners (ELL) and Second Language Learners (SLL), since that is the way these terms are reflected in current research and professional writing.

A reference list of readings quoted in the text and useful for further study concludes each chapter. Finally, we have updated the websites throughout each chapter and have listed those in the reference section. We understand that websites have a very short lifespan and apologize for any inconvenience caused by their disappearance. In some instances other reference listings, such as magazines for students, appear in this final chapter section as well.

A unique section in each chapter is Inclusion Techniques.

Chapters close with *Endings: A Summary*, followed by *Expanding Understandings through Discussion*, which we hope will encourage students to discuss chapter information using a variety of strategies that can be used in middle and high school classrooms. A suggested activity list, *In the Field Applications*, is presented for instructors to use to extend practice of the material presented and for practical assignments.

Characteristics of This Book
The goals previously described served as our guide in the selection of chapter topics.

❑ Chapter One examines content area literacy. This chapter is an overview providing a rationale for content area reading and writing and examining the ways we as instructors become informed and active. The Unit Organizer is introduced as a means of organizing instruction, as well as collecting and analyzing data.

❑ Chapter Two outlines a decision-making model for selecting key words to teach as well as varied strategies for vocabulary reinforcement.

❑ Chapter Three focuses on strategies that help readers activate prior knowledge and connect these understandings to the use of study skill strategies and to the content to be learned.

❑ Chapter Four presents strategies that enable students to construct comprehension while reading, viewing, or listening to content material.

❑ Chapter Five offers several discussion strategies to foster active participation of all students in the content area class. Questioning techniques, problem-solving activities and role responsibilities are highlighted.

❑ Chapter Six argues for an increasing role for writing in the content area classroom. Strategies that support this philosophy are many and varied.

Note these topics for future reference.

❑ Chapter Seven presents a case for integrating adolescent literature with content materials. Activities are presented that move students beyond reading for information to those that also help students to sense, feel and think about the issues raised in the content area classroom.

❑ Chapter Eight compares standardized and informal assessment practices. Authentic assessment examples are demonstrated. Emphasis is on a number of informal procedures.

❏ Chapter Nine describes a literacy environment where real-world reading materials are integrated with content area materials. Included are a variety of strategies to facilitate the use of survival reading skills. Particularly important in this chapter is the inclusion of a multi-media approach to instruction that emphasizes technology such as the use of the Internet.

These chapters are intended for **all** content area teachers. The following graphic organizer presents the chapter interrelationships.

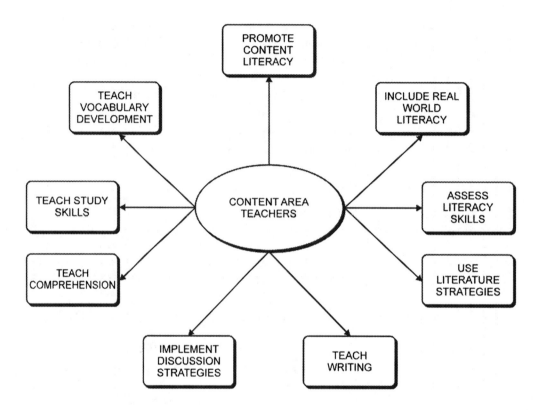

All content area teachers have the above responsibilities and we hope you choose to implement some of these strategies in your work samples or units of study. Each chapter will give you ideas and strategies to apply to your discipline.

In short, we have written a textbook that affords a basic understanding of the reading and writing process as applied to the content area classroom and provides strategies for promoting and enhancing the learning of content for all students.

Acknowledgments

First, thanks must go to each other. This book has grown out of a partnership forged through many conference presentations, workshops, and service activities in our respective professional organizations. Anita's enthusiasm, good humor, and treasure trove of never-ending activities contributed much to the text's practicality and usefulness. Carrol's perseverance, attention to pertinent details, patience, and writing abilities kept us on schedule and enabled us to write a textbook we are proud to use and to disseminate.

Second, we're thankful to our families who supported us while we cocooned with El Libro, The Book. In the extended families of both authors there is a love for learning, language and books that inspired us to share what we have learned about literacy with the intention that others will be inclined to join in the conversation.

Third, lending his expertise in formatting and graphics, Bruce Eaton has been an indispensable part of this team, transforming rudimentary sketches into crisp images and giving the pages their particular look.

Fourth, Dave Martinez, a special education professor emeritus, committed his academic organizational expertise to this project. His reading of the manuscript particularly helped us note major inconsistencies and clarify our ideas, especially in the sections *Inclusion Techniques*.

Fifth, Emily Young, art professor, has taken the title of the book and created a visual metaphor for the text. For this third edition, she used the Coquille River Lighthouse in Bandon, Oregon as a model, thereby, creating a graphic image that illuminates the meaning that we hope readers construct in their journey through these pages.

We also thank many of the mentors we have had over the years, like Harold Herber and Bill Sheldon of Syracuse University and Richard Schminke, University of Oregon, who provided their graduate students the opportunity to experience what literacy activities could accomplish K–12.

Finally, many colleagues, graduate students and teachers have influenced this book. They have uncomplainingly read rough drafts of these chapters. Their subsequent suggestions are appreciated, and many have found their way into this book. Specifically, we are grateful to teachers like Megan Owens, who has shared over the years many writing and technology activities/projects that her middle school students have found "cool" and worth exploring. Likewise, Professor Danelle Stevens has given us insights, ideas and inspiration for working with preservice and inservice teachers.

In addition, we have listened carefully to the many stories our graduate students and their students told us as they spoke about the literacy topics represented in this text. We have tried to represent these anecdotes accurately in the featured *Teacher Talk* throughout the text. Many of these are anonymous because of the time that has passed since we first heard the stories. We'd like to give those, however, who we were able to contact special thanks. They include:

- ❑ Alex Gordin, English teacher
- ❑ Brian Quinn, social studies teacher
- ❑ David Burmester, science teacher

- David Ellenberg, science teacher
- Deborah Tiusanan, language arts teacher
- Emily Gaffney, ESL/Spanish teacher
- James Fox, industrial arts teacher
- Jeffrey Sanchez, high school student
- Jim Anderson, health teacher
- Joan Flora, English teacher
- Jon Yeakey, social studies teacher
- Julie McDevitt, science teacher
- Kerry Muckleston, science teacher
- Kris Middlebusher, health teacher
- Laura Cummings, English teacher
- Mark Sprenger, math teacher
- MaryBeth Munroe, middle school teacher
- Max Chvilicek, eighth grade student
- Megan Owens, language arts teacher
- Melinda LaPore, English teacher
- Michael Connor, English teacher
- Michael McCauley, science teacher
- Nick Fenger, science teacher
- Paul Lardy, science teacher
- Phillip Neeley, English teacher
- Ramona Dauenhauer, health teacher
- Rick Morine, chemistry teacher
- Rob Massey, science teacher
- Sanjay Bedi, physical education teacher
- Simone Conley, social studies teacher
- Stacy Johnson, elementary teacher
- Stephanie Hall-Zurek, special education teacher
- Steve Becker, mathematics teacher
- Tadd Reaney, science teacher
- Terry Bennett, mathematics teacher
- Tracy Coyle, ESL teacher
- Vickie Sorenson, special education teacher

Content Area Literacy

Granny was loving and kind.... She wanted me to tell her stories then because she was interested in what I had learned. So I told her about what I had read and been taught, and she listened patiently. In turn, Granny told me her war stories, including what she knew about the Battle of Antietam, when Grandpa was killed. This was one of the bloodiest one-day battles during the war. Her stories gave me a great love for history, especially of the War between the States.
Mildred Bollinger Andrews, "My Grandmothers" (1994, p. 64–65).

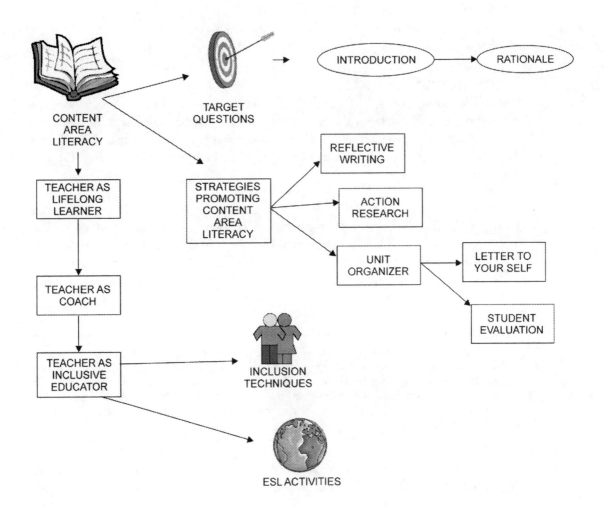

Target Questions

Target Questions

Consider the following questions before reading this chapter. Discuss these with a colleague. Check your responses when you have completed reading the chapter. Write notes in your journal and create specific questions for yourself as well.

1. What is content area literacy?
2. What do recent national assessments say about students' reading ability?
3. What are the new literacy demands facing our students today?
4. How do teachers in the content areas regard including the teaching of reading and writing in their curriculum?
5. Why is it critical to be selective in choosing literacy strategies and to study their effectiveness?
6. How could a teacher's action research on literacy be used in meeting the certification requirements of the National Board for Professional Teaching Standards?
7. What is meant by a diversity-responsive educator?
8. How can reflective writing inform your teaching?
9. What are the responsibilities of a literacy coach?
10. Describe how the unit organizer functions as a comprehensive planning strategy.

Introduction

"My child doesn't fit in and has dropped out of school." As teachers, how many of us have heard this from a clerk at the market, or the waitress at our favorite deli, or our car serviceperson, who are also parents of adolescents. Usually, we also have the opportunity to meet this young adult who appears delightful and, more importantly—able.

Why are these capable young people dropping out as well as the 3000 others that drop out daily in the United States (Biancarosa & Snow, 2004)? Why are nearly a third of high school students not graduating; or a half of the black, Hispanic and Native American students (Paulson, 2006)? The answers are myriad. The Christian Science Monitor's survey found that students' number one reason for opting out were "boring classes." However, the reasons are complex ranging from social to academic issues.

TEACHER TALK ───────────────────────────────

I met twice with the guidance counselor to consult about the attendance and progress of some of my students. One student has a disabled, unemployed mother and no money to purchase even the reduced cost student bus pass to come to class; also she has to accompany her mother to many doctor's appointments. We are looking into community resources to obtain a bus pass for her. Another student was unable to come to class part of the week because she had a series of court hearings to attend.

───

Biancarosa & Snow, 2004

Santa (2006) reports that the Alliance for Excellent Education's report, *Reading Next: A Vision for Action and Research in Middle and High School Literacy*, concludes that students who dropout "lack the strategies to help them comprehend what they read." The authors of the report (Biancarosa & Snow, 2004) report that older struggling readers "can read words accurately, but they do not comprehend what they read." They give up rather than persevere seeking that elusive diploma.

Will fix-up policies that some states are implementing like "raising the legal dropout age or limit the reasons students can leave school" work? If students aren't attending school with the current regulations, why would they attend with these new laws?

One focus that is proving effective is an emphasis on content area literacy cultivated in learning communities that are supportive and engaging.

If students can read and comprehend as well as write, we not only address their literacy needs but also provide them with the means to move on realizing their ambitions in higher education or in the workplace.

What is content area literacy?

Definition

In this text, we define content area literacy as the ability to use reading and writing to learn subject matter. Although literacy is not a discipline itself, literacy instruction cuts across all disciplines (Harris & Hodges, 1995). Content area literacy is a multidimensional process dependent on a person's prior knowledge of, attitude toward, and interest in the subject as well as the language and conceptual difficulty of the material.

How many of us remember loving English class, but dreading math class, or vice versa? Was it our attitude or was it the difficulty level of the subject matter? How many of us remember how puzzled we were by the situation, knowing that we could "call out" the words of the math problem, but couldn't make any sense of it. In many content areas, we did not know "how" to construct the meaning of the words we thought we were "reading." This "how," our strategic learning skills, were more caught than taught.

Today, the good news is that preservice and veteran teachers know much more about "scaffolding," supportive activities that help students visualize and organize content like graphic organizers, Venn Diagrams, and matrices, and that *Graves & Graves* can be removed as learners demonstrate strategic behaviors in their own literacy *(1994)* development. Not only in our literacy classes for preparing teachers, but also in our professional development workshops, we observe an increasing willingness among participants to examine their practice and incorporate more literacy activities in their subject area teaching.

Over the last few years, we have found many more teachers, who not only bring a high level of subject area expertise to their classrooms as well as a passion for the discipline they teach, but also an awareness of such content area literacy activities as K-W-L, reciprocal teaching, vocabulary building techniques, reading and writing workshops, sustained silent reading, etc. As they enhance their teaching literacy repertoire, more students are helped. But the bad news is that in reading alone, although eighth graders have improved since 1992 in reading at the basic *NAEP, 2005* level, meaning that they get the literal meaning of what they read, and they can make simple inferences, relate ideas to their own experience, and draw conclusions. But there was no significant change at the proficient level. An eighth-grader reading at this level should be able to readily provide from their reading inferential meanings, make connections from the reading to their own lives as well as from those experiences gained from other readings and analyze the author's use of literary devices.

However, the long term trends indicate that although the younger fourth grade students appear to be improving, eighth and twelfth graders are at a stalemate (Perie et al. 2005). In addition, in a typical high-poverty, urban school, approximately half of incoming ninth-grade students read at a sixth-or seventh grade level (Balfanz, 2002).

Rationale

Fortunately at this time both political and educational forces are directing their resources and research at improving the literacy of adolescents. The federal program, *No Child Left Behind* (2002), is extending its reach to establish standards for middle and high school achievement in its High School Initiative. Organizations like the International Reading Association (IRA) and National Council of Teachers of English (NCTE) as well as the Bill and Melinda Gates Foundation are promoting resources that provide members with professional development. In a recent survey of key topics in reading by the IRA, "adolescent literacy" headed the list of the 14 "Very Hot" topics (Cassidy and Cassidy, 2006).

Several elements of effective adolescent literacy programs are proving promising. Teachers are examining many of these in various combinations, implementing and studying their effects to see what works with their students. These include such instructional elements as:

U.S. Secretary of Education, Spellings, 2006

Biancarosa & Snow, 2004

1. Direct, explicit comprehension instruction	Learning strategies and processes that proficient readers use
2. Text-based collaborative learning	Interacting with one another using texts
3. Diverse texts	Using texts on varied difficulty levels with various topics
4. Intensive writing	Providing opportunities to engage in the different kinds of writing tasks required by varied content areas
5. A technology component	Using technology as a tool and topic for literacy instruction
6. Extended time for literacy	Engaging in literacy instruction and practice consistently in language arts and the other content areas

As a way of thinking about best practice, content area literacy, and professional development, we would like you to complete the following Anticipation Guide. See Figure 1.1. This is a prereading literacy strategy that can be adapted to an instructional unit in most content areas. It is typically used before reading

FIGURE 1.1. ANTICIPATION GUIDE

Directions: Before reading the rest of the chapter, read the following statements and check those with which you agree. Discuss these with a partner, providing reasons for your choices.

_____ 1. Teachers learn best when they are involved in their own learning.
_____ 2. A collaborative network among teachers builds empowerment and encourages risk taking.
_____ 3. Accomplished teachers serve as coaches to mentor their colleagues in literacy strategies.
_____ 4. There is a high resistance to implementing content area reading and writing strategies.
_____ 5. Choice and perceptions guide the selection of learning activities rather than prescription and compliance in a student-centered classroom.
_____ 6. Social, communication and problem solving skills are enhanced in a classroom community that fosters learning activities among diverse populations.
_____ 7. Satisfaction stems from active involvement in difficult enterprises.

to bridge what students know to what they are going to learn. Refer to Table 1 for a summary of the focus and use of an Anticipation Guide. At the end of the chapter we will ask you to complete the same guide again to check your understandings. Will they have changed?

Anticipation Guide

TABLE 1

INSTRUCTIONAL SUMMARY OF ANTICIPATION GUIDE

Literacy Strategy	Anticipation Guide
Primary Focus	Prereading
Learning Principle	❑ Active Involvement ❑ Building/reviewing background knowledge
When to Use	Before or after reading
Goals: National or State Literacy Standards	❑ Draw connections between reading selection and other experiences ❑ Extend and deepen comprehension by relating reading to other experiences
Materials	Teacher-made Anticipation Guide
Time	20 Minutes

What is the function of an anticipation guide?

We are living in a world where the "capacity to handle, manipulate, control, and work with text and discourses—in print, verbal, visual, and multimedia forms—

is increasingly replacing the capacity to work with our hands as our primary mode of production" (Elkins & Luke, 1999). Consequently, as adolescents, students are facing more complex and differentiated reading activities. Their literacy skills require use and refining as they face new textual cultures of online literacy and the popular and youth culture offerings of mass media. As Elkins and Luke (1999) describe:

> The kinds of reading around and of these new technologies may generate cognitive processes, sociocultural practices, and preferred "ways with words" that are unique blendings. E-mail writing combines the grammatical characteristics of written and spoken language into a new kind of electronic Creole. Surfing the Internet requires kinds of schema recognition, elaboration, and, indeed, code switching that we haven't even begun to fully describe. And constructing a Web page entails a visual, aural, and intertextual aesthetic for which we don't even have critical criteria, yet.

This situation necessitates an increase in collaborative practices that enable teachers to develop high-level literacy activities for middle and high school students as well as assume more responsibility for studying their own practice (Moje et al., 2000).

Why are content area teachers growing more interested in literacy?

In our ongoing work with teachers of adolescents we are seeing a change from teachers asking, "What do we do with students who are having difficulty with reading?" to teachers who are comfortable with raising many questions concerning their students' literacy. In seeking out the answers, they implement strategies that may help students and then study the results. In addition, they are constructing a more global view of literacy seeing it as a broader concept that demands the development of such skills as second-guessing, analyzing, and critiquing not only their school texts but also online culture. As a consequence, teachers are looking across the curriculum for opportunities to introduce and reinforce students' literacy. Each teacher, a teacher of reading, takes on more meaning in this light.

TEACHER TALK

While the reading block program is not a total solution to all of the problems and inequities facing reading instruction and getting students to benchmark, a degree of success can be measured by this action research pursuit. We plan to continue this project next fall and address other concerns regarding reading instruction. These concerns would include assessment, instructional techniques and strategies, and teaching for comprehension.

We realize teachers wear many hats, however, we believe the following three roles are critical to promoting a literacy program at the secondary level that makes a difference: teacher as lifelong learner, teacher as coach, and teacher as inclusive educator.

Teacher as Lifelong Learner

Theories of adult learning demonstrate that teachers learn best when they are active in their own learning and when their opportunities to learn are focused on their activities with students. In addition, this learning is productive when teachers ground these activities in inquiry, experimentation and reflection. Finally, this learning is reinforced when teachers have the opportunities to interact with other educators in a collaborative network that provides sources for new ideas and feedback. Teaching efficacy research also suggests that teachers are more likely to implement new classroom strategies if they have confidence in their own abilities.

Sprinthall, Reiman & Theis-Sprinthall (1996)

Most readers of this text will be taking a course on reading and writing across the content areas. As such, this creates an environment that allows for this experimentation. We encourage readers to try these activities out in microteaching simulations in the class, debrief with colleagues on presentations, and then adapt these activities to their classrooms.

Gove & Kennedy-Calloway (1992)

Teaching is an art and a craft. We believe that the more you study it as a craft, the more artful you become. In addition, the educator who approaches teaching with an experimental eye and asks "What happens when I try this?" needn't worry about getting it right the first time. Any craft improves with experience and time. In some ways, teaching is a lot like the theater. Dame Judi Dench says that in "the theatre (unlike film) you get more chances to get it right" (Hicks, p. D2). Teaching should be approached that way. Every teaching experience becomes a study to analyze, critique and change if needed over the span of one's career.

Stenhouse (1988)

As you begin to implement these literacy strategies demonstrated in this text in your own classrooms, we would suggest that you study them with a critical eye on their effectiveness and fit with the students you are teaching. We present an all-encompassing menu of literacy strategies, realizing that some strategies will suit your palate and that of your students better than others. The important question remains, however, do they help my students learn the content? In order to answer this question, we ask you to study your use of literacy strategies over a term or semester. For example, "Does the use of a K-W-L PLUS over time help my students focus on the critical elements of what they are studying, improve the quality of questions they raise, and achieve the learning goals, either the students or I have set for this unit?" The following reflection demonstrates this critical analysis:

TEACHER TALK

The students were really into these K-W-L PLUS activities over the last semester. I think it is because they took much more ownership of doing the work because of the questions they raised. They really had to put in top effort and quality thought. I think the end result is that the students are proud of their work. I found, however, that students really showed very little prior knowledge with some of the topics. I could feel their frustration when they tried to answer questions or do projects with insufficient background. Next time I teach some of these units, I intend to do some introductory lessons to build their background understanding.

As lifelong learners, teachers constantly redefine their work to maximize learning for all. We are impressed with the growing sense of empowerment that is connected with this redefining.

Polanyi (1958)

*Cardelle-Elawar
(1993)*

Teachers today see themselves as critical consumers of curriculum materials. In addition, they develop their own instructional materials and write about their experiences in implementing them. In the process of writing they learn more about their teaching. As many writers attest, they write to find out what they are thinking, what they are looking at, what they see and what it means (Murray, 1990). Our hope is that many of the strategies presented in this text provide a context for this inquiry.

*Harste, Short &
Burke (1988)*

In Wilhelm's (1997) *You gotta Be the book*, he shares his accounts of teaching language arts and remedial reading to adolescents. His reflections became a working document for analyzing and formulating his concerns, ideas and plans for teaching. Ultimately, it became a book detailing his journey, his problems and his successes. The following excerpt indicates where he started:

> What a day! What a week of days! What a year of days! The eighth graders simply hate reading, or say that they do, and they refuse to even try to do it. Whether this is a defense mechanism, a learned behavior or what, I don't know, but they won't be shaken from it. And another thing I don't know is how to help them change so they'll have a chance to become better readers. I have tried plan A, B, C, and D and I don't have a plan E! And if I don't find a parachute quickly, I believe that I am going to crash and burn and take all of my little kiddies with me. And then I will be the biggest smoking black hole in family history (p. 2).

As a teacher dedicated to studying his teaching, Wilhelm continued for the next several years to raise questions in his journals; and observe, test and adapt his teaching. He writes "Teacher-research revitalized my passion for teaching, for reading literature with students, and it helped me to both read and teach in more aware and powerful ways" (p. 8).

Rudduck (1988)

In the throes of trying to juggle undergraduate or graduate teacher education classes, plan and conduct lessons for field experiences, and deal with everyday life, this approach may seem overwhelming. Yet it is an approach characteristic of good teaching. Veteran teachers claim that finding time for action research, the natural exploration of teaching activities in one's own classroom through disciplined inquiry, is no different from the way they find time to teach because they are the same. The questions they ask as teachers are the same questions they ask as researchers: What do I know about my students? How do they learn best in my classes? And how can I enhance their learning?

What is the advantage of being a nationally certified teacher?

An emerging goal for teachers planning their own professional development is national certification. We believe that conducting research on the literacy development of students can serve as a legitimate entry in the portfolios that teachers prepare for their National Board certification. These portfolios represent an analysis of the teacher's classroom work and include selections that tap their knowledge, skills, disposition and professional judgment that distinguish their practice.

One of the five propositions of the National Board for Professional Teaching Standards (NBPTS) is that "Teachers think systematically about their practice and learn from experience." The NBPTS describes able teachers as those who stay abreast of education scholarship as well as conduct and publish it. We believe that action research is a natural conduit for fostering an experimental and problem-solving orientation to teaching. Such teachers, in turn, become models for the critical, analytical thinking that they strive to develop in their students.

A study by the National Board for Professional Teaching Standards (NBPTS) showed that National Board certified teachers (NBCTS) use more effective teaching strategies than non-certified teachers and their student assessments were more closely tied to students' learning goals (*Reading Today*, 2005, p. 4).

NB Certified teachers use more effective teaching strategies

In our work with teachers and school districts, we have found that professional educators who work collaboratively on activities designed specifically to increase reading proficiency are the most successful. Teachers and their administrators are the best facilitators of educational change in their respective environments. During workshops, we welcome opportunities for teachers and administrators to spend time together to discuss where they are going with the literacy topic under discussion. Our greatest satisfaction comes when talking with teachers about the presentations they make as teacher leaders in department and faculty meetings in their own schools. Through such activities as reflective writing, and action research, many of these content area teachers have assumed the responsibility of becoming literacy experts in their own right.

Vacca (1999)

A way of thinking about the action research process is to consider the following questions on the chart in Figure 1.2.

How does this process get translated in the classroom? For the purpose of our discussion, let us say you have identified that students in small groups are off-task frequently. You have implemented one of the cooperative discussion strategies illustrated in Chapter 5 that calls for students working in small groups, but it doesn't seem to be working. Your perceptions are that students are talking about everything except the content. After talking to colleagues and university instructors about ways to improve group process, you decide to try out implementing group roles in the discussion—an approach that has been suggested in these collegial conversations. You plan to incorporate mini-lessons that focus on roles students can take in small discussion groups. In addition, you videotape student groups after they implement the roles to see how they are working, keep an observational chart on each group's performance, give feedback to each group, and have students assess their own participation on a self-check assessment form.

How can your classroom experiences serve as research topics?

After collecting this data, you analyze your findings to plan for further instruction. This is a model of good teaching, isn't it? Some problems will entail major inquiry activities; others will involve a tweaking of an approach that may enhance students' learning.

All of these activities are a part of a student teacher's field experience. You videotape lessons, plan observations of students' work, give students feedback and ask for their feedback. The difference is that as a teacher cultivating an action research approach to teaching, you systematically focus on a problem or question that you want to address, rather than randomly conducting these activities to meet the requirements of the practicum and eventual licensure.

FIGURE 1.2.   ACTION RESEARCH GUIDESHEET

Focusing Your Question

1. What question are you interested in pursuing?

    _____

    _____

2. What do you want to accomplish by working on this question?

    For yourself:

    _____

    _____

    For your students:

    _____

    _____

3. What resources will you need to carry out this project?

    _____

    _____

4. What do you want to share with others about your project?

    _____

    _____

In Oregon, where we teach, student teachers are expected to design work samples, content-based curriculum units, that include daily lessons, pre- and post-assessment exercises, an analytical review of student gains and, finally, a reflective essay on the effect of the work sample on student learning in general. In the process of teaching these work samples, preservice teachers are collecting volumes of data. We encourage our interns to be systematic in collecting these data and use them to focus on questions whose answers lead to informed action.

How do I get started on conducting my own research? The best advice we have noted is to start watching and record your observations. For starters, we suggest implementing a few of the activities that are suggested in this text; "record what you see and don't worry about the things you do not see, and when you find something that interests you, pursue it" (Isakson & Brody, 1996).

Teacher as Coach

In the last few years the role of the "literacy coach" in the schools has grown from a grass-roots phenomenon to a national occurrence. Unfortunately, this occurrence is minimal at the middle and high school levels. In a recent survey conducted by the International Reading Association, 17% of the 186 responding literacy coaches were working at the middle school and only 7% at the high school level. Whereas 86% and 41% respectively worked at the primary and intermediate levels (*Reading Today*, 2006, p. 1).

To guide this movement and improve these percentages for adolescent students, the International Reading Association (IRA) in collaboration with national educational organizations in English, mathematics, science and social studies have published *Standards for Middle and High School Literacy Coaches* (2006).

Math literacy differs from science literacy, as these differ from social studies and the language arts—yet all definitions of literacy must include reading and writing as a means of understanding an algorithm, a lab manual, a poem and other subject area texts. As Eisner writes (1997) about the new literacy:

> In order to be read, a poem, an equation, a painting, a dance, a novel, or a contract each requires a distinctive form of literacy, when literacy means, as I intend it to mean, a way of conveying meaning through and recovering meaning from the form of representation in which it appears (p. 353).

Wouldn't it be a wondrous addition to the secondary curriculum conversation to have literacy coaches from varied disciplines who share myriad roles, vision, and responsibilities articulate their projects collaboratively. To hear the old refrain in middle schools and high schools, "Do I really have to teach reading (and often writing as well)?" become less frequent because of the focus and support of the literacy coaches would be a refreshing change. Long overdue, the recent emphasis on adolescents and their academic progress or lack of it make this an ideal time for districts and schools to select accomplished middle and high school teachers who have demonstrated in their own classrooms that they are skilled in developing and implementing instructional strategies as literacy coaches.

Who is a literacy coach?

Often coaches are accomplished teachers released from classroom duties who conduct staff in-service, provide hands-on mentoring visiting and providing feedback in classrooms as well as demonstrating instructional strategies. In addition, they help teachers with interpreting assessment to guide instruction. Frequently, these coaches have undergone rigorous training in their fields. Some coaches have received their reading specialist license, and/or a masters or doctorate in their field. Literacy coaches must be good listeners, thoughtful questioners, problem solvers and reflective practitioners. Coaching is not for the timid; coaches must be able to cultivate trust, work amidst the frequently chaotic conditions of "school," and exude the confidence in what they do that builds the skills of colleagues, and promotes increased academic achievement of students.

Roles of the Literacy Coach

TEACHER TALK

I was able to attend a literacy coach meeting. They discussed the needs of the whole district. There were mini-lessons given on writer's workshops, Lucy Calkin's curriculum, tall stories, guided writing instruction and how to implement writer's workshops as a literacy coach approaching classroom teachers. This was an awesome experience, I was able to hear from literacy coaches all over the school district and the struggles their students are having. We were able to discuss strategies that worked in many different situations and schools. This was like visiting at least 10 different schools in the district, through conversation and discussion of strategies and difficulties.

Buly, Coskie, Robinson & Egawa, 2006

A coach needs to be above all else non-evaluative. Trust building and mutual goal-setting occur when the job description of the coach does not include an evaluative component. Finally, all instructional dialogue to be effective must include not only a discussion of the "what' and "how" but more importantly, the "why" of teaching. Coaching should involve shifts in understanding about teaching and learning in addition to learning strategies that will help their students become more literate.

Why literacy coaches at this time?

Cassidy, Garcia & Boggs, 2005; Tatum, 2005

From books on why boys aren't achieving in high school, especially black adolescent males to a poor showing of minorities in colleges and to the latest NAEP (National Assessment of Educational Progress) report, the message is the same—our adolescents are in trouble academically especially in reading and writing. Furthermore, in a recent report by the nonprofit testing company ACT, it stated that "barely more than half (51%) of students showed that they could handle the reading requirements of a first-year college course. ACT recommended revised high school reading standards in core subjects and more help for struggling readers and more reading training for subject area teachers.

ACT Report 2006

How do literacy coaches' contributions change this picture?

First, more coaches need to be hired for the middle and high schools. Once they are in place they can be a tremendous asset to the busy teacher already smothered with the duties of helping over a hundred students daily to academically succeed. In addition, these coaches as colleagues are an invaluable source of intellectual and moral support.

Bacon, 2005

What if a middle school or high school does not have a literacy coach or even worse no prospects of any? If coaches aren't in the picture, other teachers can assume this role. In our work with teachers of adolescents, we have seen them conduct effective, motivating literacy presentations at faculty meetings or in-service days.

As teachers and members of a faculty dedicated to students and their achievement, they assume the responsibility to present literacy concepts and strategies they have just learned in a way that motivates their fellow teachers to try these literacy ideas out. First of all, they have examples from their own class that demonstrate how they implemented these strategies, the content material they used, and the examples of students' work—the most telling evidence of all. Their rallying cry "It really works!" motivates other teachers and demonstrates success. They have the pulse of the school; they know how quickly to go; how to sequence their training, and most importantly how to walk their colleagues through the highs and lows of trying something new. They are available for follow-up, an essential ingredient for curriculum change. Lasting curriculum change occurs when teachers collaborate and have the nurturing support of a colleague who can assist, demonstrate, mentor and discuss the art and science of literacy teaching in the school where teachers do their work (Hawley & Valli, 1999).

Teacher as Inclusive Educator

Students with disabilities drop out of high school at nearly twice the rate of non-disabled peers (Cobb, et al., 2005). In addition, 44% of Hispanic ESL students born outside the United States dropped out of high school (National Center for Educational Statistics, 2002). Why is this occurring when we know that these students can succeed academically (Erickson, 2002)? Inclusive education is a right that helps all students realize their potential. It reduces fear and rejection of those who appear different. Through inclusive education increasing numbers of students with special needs participate in the culture, curricula and community of their school. It enables students to participate in the life and work of their school to the best of their abilities, Finally, Inclusion works "when all teachers believe and practice the idea that that they will not sacrifice the many for the few" (Villa, 2000). Through teaming especially teachers are selected to meet all students needs in inclusive classrooms.

Our student teachers report increasing numbers of diverse populations in their classroom each year. This is not difficult to believe considering that one of every seven children grows up speaking a language other than English in the United States today. In addition, as a result of the Americans with Disabilities Act 1992 (ADA) and Individuals with Disabilities Education Act 1990 (IDEA) and recent litigation, increasing numbers of students with special needs are included in the regular classroom.

Who is an inclusive educator? This teacher believes that students with a broad range of backgrounds and abilities can work together in a classroom. This is a teacher who is aware and supportive of diverse populations. This diversity covers a host of differences, students with different learning needs, emotional needs, cultures, subcultures, gender, life experiences, life situations, ages, abilities, skills, strategies, language proficiency, beliefs, personal characteristics, and affectional orientation, or values.

How do you as a teacher meet the learning needs of all these students in your classroom? Recognizing that students are different is the first step. In your educational psychology courses, you've learned much about individual differences. You've learned that the knowledge of learning differences develops by attending to the sources of differences among students, and you understand how these affect learning. Now is the time to apply those understandings and learning.

How successful can I expect students with special needs and English language learners to be in achieving classroom goals? Effective educational practices for these students and teachers who are well prepared to work with them can ensure that students develop social, communication, and problem-solving skills as well as achieve learning goals.

Cruickshank and Haefele (2001) describe a type of teacher that we believe is critical for these times—diversity responsive teachers. These are educators who are "interested in and are particularly sensitive to students who are different culturally, socially, economically, intellectually, physically, or emotionally." In addition, such language arts standards as those developed by the International Reading Association and the National Council of Teachers of English (2000) suggest that all students be given the tools to comprehend, interpret, evaluate and appreciate a wide range of text. We believe the many activities suggested in this text will aid mainstreamed students in comprehending and expressing difficult ideas.

Cobb, et al., 2005; National Center for Educational Statistics, 2002

Dole & Donaldson, The Reading Coach's Corner (2006)

Schnorr & Davern, (2005)

Barringer (1993)

Who benefits from an inclusive classroom?

Anstrom (1998); O'Byrne (2001)

How can a teacher increase flow?

There is a certain satisfaction you experience in establishing an environment that says "all students are important and can learn." This is what the University of Chicago psychologist Csikszentmihalyi (1993) calls *flow*—a feeling of satisfaction achieved by being actively involved in a difficult enterprise, a task that stretches physical or mental abilities. He also outlines three principles that increase this satisfaction that mirror much of what we have studied over the years that allow all students to achieve similar satisfaction with the learning experiences. Activities should:

1. Have concrete goals and manageable rules
2. Be adjusted to student capacities
3. Provide clear information about how well students are doing.

Clearly these principles, "when implemented, communicate to your students that they are expected to learn and are treated as if they are capable of learning. In addition to skillful and artful 'pedagogy,' teacher attitude is critical in reaching diverse student populations" (D.H. Martinez, Special Education professor, personal communication, January 31, 1997).

TEACHER TALK

When asked why I was going back to a difficult school, I replied, "because of kids like Dwayne who came to my class as slow learners reading at the fifth grade level, but now, as tenth graders read literature ranging from tenth to college level."

List adaptations you have implemented or observed in the classroom.

As we have seen in the previous examples, successful teachers of students with varied abilities respond to this diversity by setting a goal of teaching differently to students. Alternate ways of learning are presented and encouraged. Some students will need visual and audio reinforcements. Taking care when planning seating arrangements as well as thoughtfully grouping students are important environmental adaptations. Others include:

O'Bryne (2001)

Anstrom (1998)

- ❏ Use pictures, tables, maps, diagrams, globes, and other visual aids to assist in comparison and contrast for comprehension of concepts
- ❏ Provide students with adaptive technology, the use of the Internet and Web
- ❏ Maintain a library of supplementary books and workbooks written in simple English which offer additional illustrations for problems
- ❏ Develop interests and arouse curiosity through hands-on lab-based methodology, the out-of-doors, pictures, newspaper clippings, and periodicals
- ❏ Allow students to collaborate with their peers, whenever possible. Heterogeneous, small groups or dyads help the process of acquisition of language and concepts
- ❏ Highlighting text for essential information
- ❏ Teach advanced organizational skills such as developing background knowledge, previewing, explicit practice, and reviewing text material. See Chapter 3
- ❏ Allowing students with limited English proficiency (ESL students) and others with special needs to have more time completing tasks or tests
- ❏ Having students complete these orally
- ❏ Giving shorter assignments than those given to regular students
- ❏ Inviting guest speakers with special needs so that kids can learn first-hand how they are succeeding.

Before we conclude this chapter, we would like to introduce a teacher-oriented curriculum design process that focuses on supporting the learning of content with literacy activities: the Unit Organizer.

Unit Organizer

TABLE 2

INSTRUCTIONAL SUMMARY OF A UNIT ORGANIZER

Literacy Strategy	Unit Organizer
Primary Focus	Unit of Instruction
Learning Principle	❏ Organizing topics & information ❏ Active involvement ❏ Building/reviewing background knowledge
When to Use	❏ Planning lessons ❏ Before, during, after lessons
Goals: National or State Literacy Standards	❏ Use a variety of strategies to increase comprehension ❏ Draw connections by relating content to other texts, experiences, issues and events ❏ Structure information ❏ Produce visual forms that enhance the impact of a product or presentation
Materials	Unit Organizer Template
Time	Allot time throughout unit

The unit organizer is a holistic planning activity that helps teachers be accountable for their students' learning.

The Unit Organizer is a visual device that graphically traces the content of a unit of study and related concepts, goals and objectives. As a graphic overview, it allows teachers to:

❏ plan a time schedule for teaching the unit,
❏ determine what content to teach that includes benchmarks or standards,
❏ show the relationship of this unit to past units and future units of study,
❏ determine which cognitive skills to teach, review or practice, and
❏ design a post-assessment.

It is a powerful strategy that "focuses attention on critical outcomes, identifies critical content features, prompts elaboration on critical points, helps make relationships concrete and is designed to enhance student organization, understanding, remembering, responses and beliefs in the value of the content" (Center for Research on Learning, 1996).

*Lenz et al.
(1995a)*

The Unit Organizer is ideal for action research in that it allows teachers to examine student learning gains. In addition, teachers are able to analyze students' participation and learning directly through the use of student self-assessment activities. The Center for Research on Learning at the University of Kansas found that teachers and researchers observed gains—10 to 20 percentage points— in student learning when a Unit Organizer was implemented.

What is the most effective way to ensure the Unit Organizer's success?

Students' learning increased significantly when teachers had: a) received instruction in the use of the Unit Organizer, b) discussed its efficacy with other colleagues, c) included student participation in the use of the organizer, d) routinely used it over time, and e) had high expectations for student learning. There are other beneficial rewards resulting from the use of the Unit Organizer as well. For example, students' participation leads to ownership of their learning. Teachers have an opportunity to study this curriculum unit and these results can be used to meet their National Board of Professional Teaching Standards, and finally, the Unit Organizer is a means of addressing individual differences in your classroom.

How does students' participation in the design of the Unit Organizer contribute to their learning? In addition to the teacher's goals and questions, they identify personal content and learning goals. Students monitor the effort they put into the unit assignments and reflect on learning behaviors that work well for them. Besides this self-assessment, they share their learning behaviors with other students. Students can keep a learning log and "evaluate the extent to which they achieved each unit goal and each personal goal" (Marzano, Pickering & Pollock, 2001, p. 154). This active engagement leads to ownership and confidence in their own learning.

For the learner with special needs, including second language learners, we believe it is one of the most comprehensive ways for students to get the information they need to study.

Procedure. Teachers are encouraged to use the acronym SMARTER (Lenz, Schumaker & Deshler, 1995b, p. 16) to design an Unit Organizer.

Planning guarantees results.

❑ Select the critical content, develop a big picture of what the course is about and create a number of questions that all students should be able to answer upon completing the unit. Ten questions are usually the maximum.

❑ Map the topics you will be covering throughout the course and design a visual that will help students see their progress through the content.

❑ Analyze what areas of the course content might be difficult to learn based on such characteristics as relevance, abstractness, complexity, student background and organization.

❑ Reach decisions about the types of learning strategies that should be used throughout the course to help students with difficulty of learning the material.

❑ Teach these strategies regularly throughout the year. Involve the students explicitly. They should be able to talk about the strategies they are using as well as the content they are studying.

❑ Evaluate mastery of the course content and the strategies students are using.

❑ Reevaluate course decisions and revise accordingly.

Student involvement includes:

❏ developing questions regarding their areas of interest in the topic. Teachers can teach different types of questions to capitalize on the cognitive skills needed to read and understand the text material.

❏ developing some of the post-assessment questions to be used in the final test.

How does this model provide a possible learning strategy for students? All students know the expectations for the work sample/unit. They can see at a glance where they have been—in this case, they finished a unit on the weather; they are starting a unit on oceanography, and a unit on topography maps is forthcoming. They have a visual of what they need to know, how it is organized and what they will be expected to do with the information. This visual becomes a working document. Teachers and students refer to it daily and adapt it as they need to; students add to it as additional information is learned. See Figure 1.3.

FIGURE 1.3.   UNIT ORGANIZER FOR SCIENCE: OCEANOGRAPHY

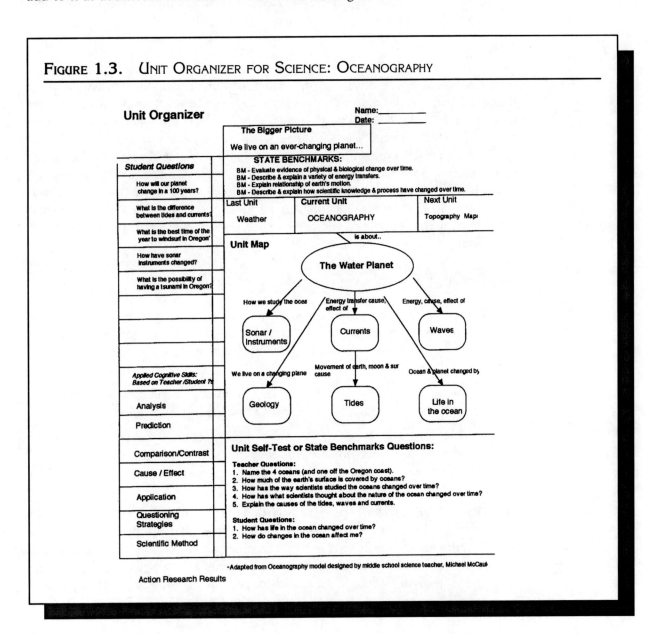

Many students with special needs frequently see their daily lessons as discrete and isolated bits of information with little connection to a unit of study. In addition, students who usually have difficulty sustaining attention have an easier time seeing the bigger picture with a visual organizer. It presents a coherent picture that they can use as a reference guide in pinpointing areas that need further explanation or areas that need to be reviewed.

Self-Evaluation Activities

The following self-evaluation activities are examples of assessment strategies that may follow the use of the work sample/unit organizer. Teachers using these organizers are encouraged to share their thinking and planning with their students. Students should know the name of the strategy being used; they should be able to explain how it will help them learn, and be able to specify what they need to do to maximize their learning using this strategy. The following activities show how teachers implement these expectations.

Letter to Yourself

In this self-evaluation activity, students write a letter to themselves about their own learning over the course of the unit. They are encouraged to congratulate themselves on specific successes and encourage themselves to improve those skills that they think they need to work on. Further, students are asked to use specifics that explain what works best for them.

As with all self-evaluation activities, students are invited to share the assessment process. Both teachers and students are engaged in recognizing needs and in acknowledging successes. As a result, students grow more articulate about their learning. They can usually provide far more specific information about their own thinking and perceived successes than the teacher notes through testing or classroom performance, as seen in this letter Beth addressed to herself.

> **Example: Science**
> Dear Beth,
> Congratulations on your last quiz—you were the only one in class to get the bonus right! And what quick thinking on the last question, you figured it out and got excused from your homework yourself as well as your whole team!
>
> Science is now your best subject, but you need to remember to check your work, write out your responses more clearly, and work on those labs!
>
> Good luck. And keep up the good work,
> Your exceptional self

Student Evaluation of the Unit Organizer

Center for Research on Learning (1996)

Opportunities for students to evaluate the strategies that are being used are essential in the classroom. If we are to be flexible and responsive to student learning needs, we need to check in on how our students are doing in acquiring, organizing and applying content information. Another evaluation technique that promotes language arts as well as metacognitive skills is the following student evaluation of the work sample/unit organizer.

> **Example: Science Work Sample/Unit**
> **Directions:** For the entire year we have used the Work Sample/Unit Organizer. Reflect on how useful it was to you. What did you like or not like about it?
>
> *It was nice to know what I would be doing in the current unit and what would be coming next. The section at the bottom helped to remind me about the different procedure and topics in the current unit.*
>
> *Maybe something that would be nice to add to the unit organizer might be a calendar of the month we were doing a particular unit.*
>
> *In short, the unit organizer makes science easier!*

In conclusion, teachers reported that "prior to using the Unit Organizer they often lost sight of the 'big picture' of the unit and frequently became bogged down with trying to cover huge amounts of information. ...the Unit Organizer helped them focus their instruction and assessment activities and that students could understand important relationships" (Lenz, Schumaker & Deshler, 1995b, p. 17). We have been awed by the adaptations of the Unit Organizer, teachers in our workshops as well as our preservice students have designed, and highly recommend its use for studying the effect of your curriculum units on your students' learning.

It is now your turn! Using the Your Turn template design a Unit Organizer and plan on how you will involve your students as part of your lesson. As you begin to use this organizer keep data regarding: a) student gains, b) student reactions to being involved in the planning, c) student reactions to their understanding of what is going on, d) their understanding of the relationships of concepts, and e) your changes to improve instruction. This action research will prove invaluable for making instructional decisions.

Notes

Your Turn

Name _____ Date _____ Subject Area _____

Directions: Using the following work sample/unit organizer, plan a unit that you will be teaching in your content area class.

❏ Identify the big picture.
❏ List key target questions.
❏ Show the progression of your units of study.
❏ Show the connecting relationship among topics.

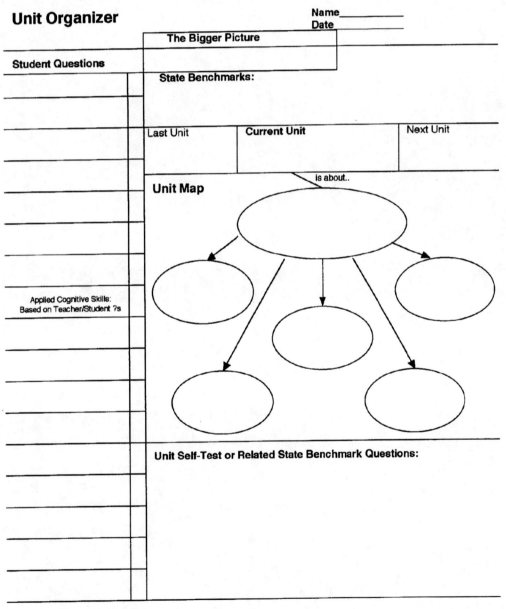

Endings: A Summary

In closing, we would like to suggest that schools adopt a state of mind in learners, in their teachers, and in their learning environment of "relaxed awareness." Our ideal schools would indeed be places where low threat exists and high challenge occurs. As we have discussed in this chapter, like the grandmother listening carefully to the child's stories and then building on what she hears, we in like manner develop an understanding of when the student can benefit from direct instruction and when he should be challenged to satisfy his curiosity and his desire for discovery and novelty.

Caine & Caine (1997)

Assuming the roles of lifelong learner, coach and inclusive educator we can cultivate that state of mind. As a consequence of these roles, we are aware, we are encouraged and we are concerned in an environment where students feel safe to try, think and make mistakes in pursuit of their goals.

Expanding Understanding Through Discussion

Directions: After completing this chapter, read the following statements and check those with which you agree. Discuss these with a partner, providing reasons for your choices.

_____ 1. Teachers learn best when they are involved in their own learning.

_____ 2. A collaborative network among teachers builds empowerment and encourages risk taking.

_____ 3. Accomplished teachers serve as coaches to mentor their colleagues in literacy strategies.

_____ 4. There is a high resistance to implementing content area reading and writing strategies.

_____ 5. Choice and perceptions guide the selection of learning activities rather than prescription and compliance in a student-centered classroom.

_____ 6. Social, communication and problem-solving skills are enhanced in a classroom community that fosters learning activities among diverse populations.

_____ 7. Satisfaction stems from active involvement in difficult enterprises.

In the Field Applications

A. If we want teachers to implement content area reading and writing strategies in the classroom, we need to change our roles as teachers. Do you agree? Why or why not? Discuss this with a veteran teacher in your field.

B. Design a unit plan for your content area. Develop an action research question that you could study based on its use.

C. Interview an educator you think who is responsive to diversity in her classroom. What are her beliefs as well as learning principles that guide her instructional activities in the classroom?

D. What questions do you have?

References ❏ ❏ ❏

Andrews, M. (1994). My grandmothers. In N. Giovanni (Ed.), *Grand mothers: Poems, reminiscences, and short stories about the keepers of our traditions.* NY: Henry Holt and Company.

Anstrom, K. (1998). *Preparing secondary education teachers to work with English language learners.* Washington, D.C.: Center of the Study of Language and Education, The George Washington University.

Bacon, S. (2005). Reading coaches: Adapting an intervention model for upper elementary and middle school readers. *Journal of Adolescent & Adult Literacy,* 48(5), 416–427.

Balfanz, R., McPartland, J. M., & Shaw, A. (2002). *Reconceptualizing extra help for high school students in a high standards era.* Baltimore: Center for Social Organization of Schools, Johns Hopkins.

Barringer, F. (1993, April 28). When English is a foreign tongue: Census finds a sharp rise in 80s. *The New York Times.*

Biancarosa, G., & Snow, C. S. (2004). Reading next—A vision for action and research in middle and high school literacy: A report to Carnegie Corporation of New York. Retrieved March 28, 2006, from http : / / www. all4ed.org / publications / ReadingNext / ReadingNext.pdf

Buly, M. R., Coskie, T., Robinson, L., & Egawa, K. (2006). Literacy coaching: Coming out of the corner. *Voices from the Middle,* 13(4), 24–28.

Caine, R., & Caine, G. (1997). *Education on the edge of possibility.* Alexandria, VA: Association for Supervision and Curriculum Development.

Cardelle–Elawar, M. (1993). The teacher as researcher in the classroom. *Action in Teacher Education,* 15(1), 49–57.

Cassidy, J., & Cassidy, D. (2006). What's hot, what's not for 2006. *Reading Today,* 23(3), 1, 8–9.

Cassidy, J., & Garcia, R., Boggs, M. (2005). The SIQ-III Test: Gender issues in literacy. *Journal of Adolescent & Adult Literacy,* 49(2), 142–148.

Center for Research on Learning. (1996). *Pedagogies for diversity in secondary schools.* Lawrence, KS: University of Kansas.

Cobb, R., Sample, P., Alwell, M., & Johns, N. (2005). Effective intervention in dropout prevention: A research synthesis—The effects of cognitive-behavioral interventions on dropout for youth with disabilities: The National Dropout Prevention Center for Students with Disabilities. Washington, DC. Retrieved May 25, 2006 from http:// research.nichcy.org/MetaAnalysis.asp?ID=41.

Cruickshank, D. R., & Haefele, D. (2001). Good teachers, plural. *Educational Leadership* 58(5): 26–30.

Csikszentmihalyi, M. (1993). *The evolving self: A psychology for the third millennium.* New York: HarperCollins.

Dearman, C. C., & Alber, S. R. (2005). The changing face of education: Teachers cope with challenges through collaboration and reflective study. *The Reading Teacher,* 58(7), 634–640.

Dole, J. A., & Donaldson, R. (2006). "What am I supposed to do all day?": Three big ideas for the reading coach. *The Reading Teacher,* 59(5), 486–488.

Eisner, E. (1997). Cognition and representation: A way to pursue the American dream. *Phi Delta Kappan* 78: 349–353.

Elkins, J. & Luke, A. (1999). Redefining adolescent literacies. Journal *of Adolescent and Adult Literacy* 43(3): 212–215.

Erickson, K. A. (2002). *All-Link: Linking adolescents with literacy.* TASH: Equity, Opportunity and Inclusion for People with Learning Disabilities. Retrieved May 25, 2006 from http : / / www.tash.org/inclusion/index.htm

Farmer, M. S. (2005). Inclusion: Where we've been, where we are, where we're going [Electronic Version]. *Electronic Journal for Inclusive Education*, 1, 1–13. Retrieved April 14, 2006 from http://www.cehs.wright.edu/~prenick/Fall Winter 05/4 MarieFarmer.htm

Getting on board (2005). *Reading Today*, 23(2), 1,4.

Gove, M., & Kennedy–Calloway, C. (1992). Action research: Empowering teachers to work with at–risk students. *Journal of Reading, 35*(7), 526–34.

Graves, M. & Graves, B. (1994). *Scaffolding reading experiences: Designs for student success*. Norwood, MA: Christopher-Gordon Publishers.

Harris, T.L., & Hodges, R.E. (1995). *The literacy dictionary: The vocabulary of reading and writing*. Newark, DE: International Reading Association.

Harste, J., Short, K., & Burke, C. (1988). *Creating classrooms for authors*. Portsmouth, NH: Heinemann.

Hawley, W. D. & Valli, L. (1999). The essentials of effective professional development: A new consensus. In L. Darling-Hammond & G. Sykes (Eds.), *Teaching as a learning profession: Handbook of policy and practice* (pp. 127–150). San Francisco, CA: Jossey-Bass.

Hicks, B. (1997, August 8). Dame Judi steps off England's stage to star in 'Mrs. Brown'. *The Oregonian*, p. D2.

International Reading Association (1996). Standards for the English language arts. Newark, DE.

International Reading Association (2006). *Standards for middle and high school literacy coaches*. Newark, DE.

IRA surveys coaches. (April/May 2006). *Reading Today*, 23 (5), 1, 3.

Isakson, M., & Brody, R. (1996). Hard questions about teacher research. In L. Patterson, C. Santa, K. Short, & K. Smith (Eds.), *Teachers are researchers: Reflections and action* (pp. 26–34). Newark, DE: International Reading Association.

Lenz, B., Bulgren, J., Schumaker, J., Deshler, D., & Boudah, D. (1995a). *The unit organizer routine*. Lawrence, KS: Edge Enterprises, Inc.

Lenz, B., Schumaker, J., & Deshler, D. (1995b). *Planning for academic diversity in America's classrooms: Windows on reality, research, change, and practice*. Joint Committee on Teacher Planning for Students with Disabilities, Office of Special Education and Rehabilitative Services, United States of America.

Marzano, R., Pickering, D., & Pollock, J. (2001). Classroom instruction that works: Research-based strategies for increasing student achievement, Alexandria, VA: Association for Supervision and Curriculum Development.

Moje, E. B., J. P. Young, et al. (2000). Reinventing adolescent literacy for new times: Perennial and millennial issues. *Journal of Adolescent & Adult Literacy* 43(5): 400–410.

Murray, D. (1990). *Shoptalk: Learning to write with writers*. Portsmouth, NH: Boynton/Cook.

National Board for Professional Teaching Strategies (2000). The five propositions of accomplished teaching. http://www.nbpts.org (2001, February 19).

NCTE/IRA Standards for the English Language Arts (2000). English Language Arts Standards. http://www.ncte.org/standards (2001, March 10).

O'Byrne, B. (2001). Needed: A compass to navigate the multilingual English classroom. *Journal of Adolescent & Adult Literacy* 44(5): 440–449.

Paulson, A. (2006). Dropout rates high, but fixes under way. Retrieved March 28, 2006 from http://www.csmonitor.com/2006/0303/pOs02 legn.html

Perie, M., Grigg, W. S., & Donahue, P. L. (2005). The nation's report card: Reading 2005. Retrieved March 28, 2006, from http://nces.ed.gov/nationsreportcard/pubs/main2005/20Q6451.asp #section2

Polanyi, M. (1958). *Personal knowledge*. London: Routledge and Kegan Paul.

Reading between the lines: What the ACT reveals about college readiness in reading.
    (2006). Iowa City, Iowa: ACT. Retrieved June 20, 2006 from http://www.act.org/
    path/policy/pdf/reading report.pdf

Rudduck, J. (1988). Changing the world of the classroom by understanding it: A review
    of some aspects of the work of Lawrence Stenhouse. *Journal of Curriculum and
    Supervision, 4*(1), 30–42.

Santa, C. (2006). A vision for adolescent literacy: Ours or theirs? *Journal of Adolescent &
    Adult Literacy, 49*(6), 466–476.

Schnorr, R. F., & Davern, L. (2005). Creating exemplary literacy classrooms through the
    power of teaming. *The Reading Teacher, 58*(6), 494–506.

Spellings, M. (2006). Fourth anniversary of *No Child Left Behind*. Retrieved March 30,
    2006, from http: / / www.ed.gov / print / news / pressreleases / 2006 / 01 /
    O1092006.html

Sprinthall, N., Reiman, A., & Theis-Sprinthall, L. (1996). Teacher professional develop-
    ment. In J. Sikula (Ed.*), Handbook of research on teacher education* (2nd ed., pp.
    666–703). NY: Macmillan.

Stenhouse, L. (1988). Artistry and teaching: The teacher as focus of research and develop-
    ment. *Journal of Curriculum & Supervision, 4*(1), 43–51.

Sturtevant, E. G. (2003). *The literacy coach: A key to improving teaching and learning in
    secondary school*. Washington, D.C.: Alliance for Excellent Education. Retrieved
    June 20, 2006 from http://www.all4ed.org

Tatum, A. W. (2004). A road map for reading specialists entering schools without exem-
    plary reading programs: Seven quick lessons. *The Reading Teacher, 58*(1), 28–39.

Vacca, R., & Vacca, J. (1999). *Content area reading: Literacy and learning across the
    curriculum*. (6th ed.). NY: Longman.

Verdaguer, A. (2005). Early intervention school-based family literacy programs: The key
    to reduced dropout rate of Hispanic ESL students. Retrieved May 18, 2006, from
    http://nces.ed.gov/

Villa, R. (2000). Inclusion: Yours mine, ours. Retrieved May 28,2006 from http://
    www.rushservices.com/indusion/what makes inclusion work.htm.

Wilhelm, J. D. (1997). *"You Gotta BE the Book"*. NY: Teachers College Press.

Vocabulary Strategies

2

HOMOPHONES

Wood you believe that I didn't no
About homophones until too daze ago?
That day in hour class in groups of for,
We had to come up with won or more.
(first stanza)
        George E. Coons (Source unknown)

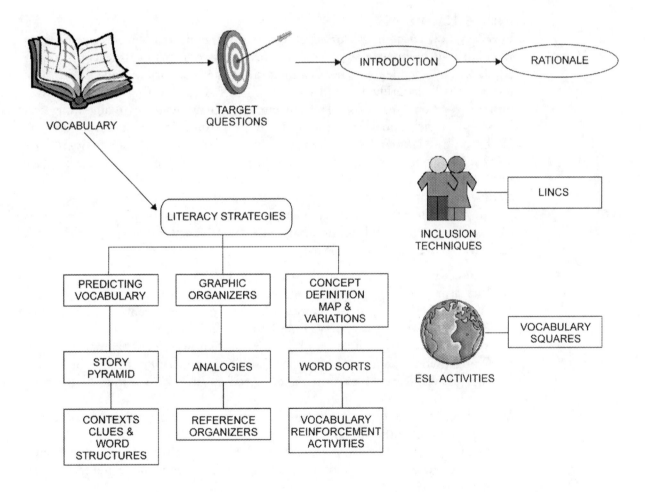

VOCABULARY

TARGET QUESTIONS

INTRODUCTION

RATIONALE

LITERACY STRATEGIES

INCLUSION TECHNIQUES

LINCS

ESL ACTIVITIES

VOCABULARY SQUARES

PREDICTING VOCABULARY

GRAPHIC ORGANIZERS

CONCEPT DEFINITION MAP & VARIATIONS

STORY PYRAMID

ANALOGIES

WORD SORTS

CONTEXTS CLUES & WORD STRUCTURES

REFERENCE ORGANIZERS

VOCABULARY REINFORCEMENT ACTIVITIES

Target Questions

Allen, 2006

Target Questions

Consider the following questions before reading this chapter. Discuss these with a colleague. Continue writing notes and develop specific questions regarding vocabulary that you want to explore.

1. Define vocabulary development.
2. Why should all content area teachers include the teaching of vocabulary?
3. How does vocabulary influence comprehension?
4. How can you increase students' vocabulary usage?
5. What is the value of implementing graphic organizers when teaching vocabulary?
6. What is a concept definition map and how can you implement it in your area?
7. Compare open and closed word sorts.
8. How does the understanding of context clues develop vocabulary?
9. How would you develop vocabulary for second language learners? For students with special needs?
10. What is the value of students knowing word structures?

Introduction

Everyday, new vocabulary words are developed to reinforce our quickly changing world. To keep abreast of the newest words and concepts is a difficult task for adults let alone students! What is a blog, a text-message or an iPod? All of these terms are still underlined in red when using WORD indicating that the word is misspelled or does not exist. There is also the phenomenon of maintaining and keeping our rich and vast vocabularies that are quickly disappearing. Stewart Holbrook in *Wildmen, Wobblies and Whistle Punks* and Ken Kesey in *Sometimes a Great Notion* reinforced and helped to keep alive woodsmen lingo that is nearly lost. Who is the whistle punk, the donkey puncher or the choker setter? What is a wigwam burner, a green chain or a donkey engine? (Terry, 2006).

To maintain rich vocabulary from the past and present, Janet Allen (2006) suggests that educators look at what makes vocabulary instruction meaningful. She suggests we capitalize on what we know:

❑ Those who know more words are better readers.
❑ Increasing the volume of reading helps readers learn new words.
❑ We can only teach a small fraction of words that adolescents need to know.
❑ Knowing a word means more than knowing a definition.
❑ Word learning is often based on background knowledge of the concept.
❑ Words used in expressive vocabulary (speaking and writing) need to be known to a greater degree than those encountered in receptive vocabulary (listening and reading).
❑ Instruction in definitions probably won't increase comprehension of a passage containing the word.
❑ Learners need vocabulary instruction that is generative so they are learning how to learn new words they encounter during independent literacy experiences, (p. 16).

Janet Allen further suggests that teachers must expose students to more reading materials that are rich in language experiences.

Definition

What constitutes vocabulary development and why is it important in the classroom? The International Reading Association defines vocabulary development as: "1) the growth of a person's stock of known words and meanings, 2) the teaching-learning principles and practices that lead to such growth, as comparing and classifying word meanings, using context, analyzing word roots and affixes, etc." (Harris & Hodges, 1995, p. 275). With current emphasis on a whole language philosophy of reading instruction, content area teachers need to reexamine their roles. Reading should be taught in all classrooms, K-12. Thus, each content area teacher is responsible for teaching students to read the materials that will enable students to comprehend specific course vocabulary. Each content area classroom will encounter vocabulary unique to the particular topic of the day.

In order to develop a meaningful vocabulary for a particular subject, teachers will need to teach each new word within the meaning of its context and relative to the use of the word in a particular content area. In other words, rote memorization of new vocabulary will not be as meaningful as students independently being able to recognize the meaning of the word in the textbook as well as use the word in writing and speaking.

We also believe that students must be able to recognize the meaning of a word in materials other than the textbook, especially outside the classroom. When students are asked to read a wide variety of materials pertinent to a content area they should begin to recognize vocabulary in many contexts. For example, DNA can be read about in textbooks. However, reading the *Double Helix* by James Watson gives a student new perspectives regarding DNA. Likewise, a student can read about the Civil War in textbooks, but it is the historical fiction books such as *Across Five Aprils* by Irene Hunt that give life to the topic and allow the student to examine the topic from new vistas.

Thus, vocabulary development applies to the exposure of students to new vocabulary in two areas—1) in the context of the textbooks, tradebooks, newspapers, pamphlets or other materials, and 2) in the use of vocabulary in speaking and writing assignments.

Whole language is the process of using tradebooks and primary sources to promote reading and writing in classrooms.

We believe that content text refers to all reading resources, not just textbooks.

Cochran (1993)

Rationale

Vocabulary distinguishes one content area from another. The uniqueness of the specialized vocabulary is something every content area teacher should confront in day-to-day instruction. Because vocabulary represents the content concepts, instruction should include the teaching of vocabulary using sound pedagogical strategies. This means that the vocabulary instruction should be meaningful by imbedding it in an integrated plan using strategies that engage students at a personal level. Ryder and Graves (1998) suggest that students need to deal with four word-learning tasks: "1) learning to read words in their oral vocabularies, 2) learning new labels for known concepts, 3) learning words representing new and difficult concepts, and 4) clarifying and enriching the meanings of known words." Vocabulary instruction in all content areas is so important that Anderson and Freebody (1981) note that vocabulary knowledge is one of the best predictors of verbal ability and that a vocabulary test might be one of the best substitutes for an intelligence test.

Vocabulary represents content concepts.

In the remainder of this chapter we will discuss ways to develop meaningful vocabulary in terms of context. We believe that to learn vocabulary one must experience the words in receptive and expressive modes. This includes reading, writing, speaking, and listening. Most importantly it means personal involvement with the words and familiarity with the words in the context of print.

TEACHER TALK

I believe all content area teachers should also be teachers of reading and writing. In my biology classroom I give spelling tests on new vocabulary. I expect students to use that vocabulary in their lab reports. For example, a student might write the liquid was "dirty." I would expect them to write the liquid was "turbid."

Literacy Strategies to Promote Vocabulary

Cochran (1993)
Herman (1979)
Ruddell (1993)

Key vocabulary defines a particular concept.

To acquire vocabulary in a particular content area means that students must comprehend words that unlock meaning required to understand a specific content field. This is referred to as **Key Vocabulary**. It has been found by researchers that all students, capable and less capable, learn more word meanings when key vocabulary is fully explained. Teachers in content areas cannot assume students can read and understand the key vocabulary that is presented. It must be taught. Vocabulary should be taught before a reading selection has been assigned. "It should focus on a few key words that have been carefully preselected by the teacher and should use actual content text as the basis for instruction" (Ruddell, 1993, p. 107). There are a number of ways students can determine what words they need to know. One is to skim the required reading for any vocabulary they do not recognize and will need to know in order to complete the reading and to ultimately comprehend it. In addition, students can work in cooperative groups to brainstorm any words (content concepts) they think might appear in the reading selection.

To teach key vocabulary there are several areas to consider. Teachers and students must understand and use 1) prior knowledge, 2) semantic and syntactic clues, 3) word structures and 4) use of reference resources. As each of these four areas is discussed, activating strategies for classroom use will be presented. The activities will include a variety of expressive and receptive modes, including independent, small group and large group organization of students and interactive discussion groups. These activities can be adapted for use prior to teaching a concept or as a follow-up reinforcement.

Prior knowledge is background information a student brings to a situation.

Conley (1993)

Barron (1969)

To construct meaning the reader must activate prior knowledge and experiences, and relate these to the new information being processed by interacting with the text and connecting relationships to help bring meaning to the concept—which includes key vocabulary. Concurrently, it is hoped that students will develop an interest, or curiosity about the topic or words. Readers who activate their prior knowledge and develop a base or foundation for the new material to be read are able to better understand concepts in the broadest sense as well as details. On the other hand, readers with little or no prior knowledge seem to concentrate on specific words and details without relating them to the broader concept. Thus recall is less efficient and effective for these readers. Clearly, a base on which to build comprehension of new materials or words facilitates an understanding of the concept presented.

That base for comprehension can be built with the activities presented in the next section of this chapter. The activities should help teachers to explain new vocabulary, to expand new vocabulary as it relates to synonyms and to help students use the new vocabulary. The activities will be categorized in terms of graphic organizers and categorization organizers. We want to reinforce that activities for developing prior knowledge can be adapted for post-reading situations as well.

Barron (1969)

Making Predictions

When students anticipate something as they read, they usually find it. This establishes a positive impact on their reading ability. Teachers need to give students enough opportunities that arriving at meaning through prediction occurs naturally. We have two suggestions for teachers to try implementing in their classrooms. First, develop a chart that allows students to predict, chapter-by-chapter, new vocabulary they think might be introduced and after reading the chapter students list the new vocabulary actually encountered in the text. See Figure 2.1.

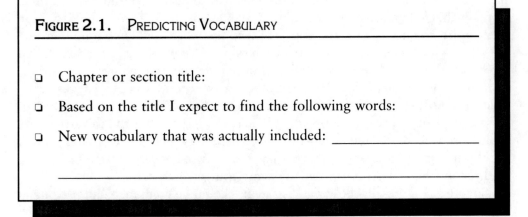

FIGURE 2.1.   PREDICTING VOCABULARY

❑   Chapter or section title:

❑   Based on the title I expect to find the following words:

❑   New vocabulary that was actually included: _____

_____

Ogle (1986)

Second, another vocabulary activity that helps students to access prior knowledge is the V-V-L. Like the K-W-L, this strategy bridges what vocabulary the students know with what they want to know and, finally, with the vocabulary they learned. See Figure 2.2.

Lastly, for making predictions see chapter 3, in which the Storyline allows students to use vocabulary before reading and during reading. This strategy is powerful in that students are writing the words, using the words and making predictions about the words. Again, in selecting the words for the storyline the teacher will want to consider words specific to their content as well as words that transcend all content areas.

Kelly Gallagher (2004) suggests another prediction strategy in which students begin class with a sponge activity that will usually take about three minutes. As students enter the classroom, on the board will be sentences that contain new vocabulary that is highlighted and taken from what they will be asked to read or to discuss. The students open their notebooks to a page that has three columns— or they could fold a paper into three columns. In the first column they copy the sentence, in the middle column they make a prediction as to the meaning of the

K-W-L is a comprehension strategy in which students identify what they know, what they want to know, and what they have learned.

FIGURE 2.2. V-V-L PROCEDURE

V	V	L
Vocabulary I know about the topic	Vocabulary I want to know more about	Vocabulary I learned after reading

highlighted word. They have a short discussion with peers regarding the meaning of the highlighted words, look them up in the dictionary and write the definition in the third column. Thus, students have read the word, discussed it and written it—all of which lend themselves to variables of current brain research discussed in chapter 3 and in keeping with what is important before reading.

The above strategy could be combined with second strategy suggested by Gallagher (2004) in which students are given a list of words and are asked to predict their definitions before reading the article. Next, they read the article and make a second prediction based on the context in which the words appeared. Finally, in a group discussion, they review their revised vocabulary predictions to find out just how close their predictions are to that of a peer.

Figure 2.3 represents how these strategies could be combined and used in an organizer for the students.

Graphic Organizers

TABLE 1

INSTRUCTIONAL SUMMARY OF GRAPHIC ORGANIZERS

Literacy Strategy	Graphic Organizers
Primary Focus	Comprehension of vocabulary knowledge
Learning Principles	❏ Talk Time ❏ Organize Information ❏ Thought-demanding Activity
When to Use	Before, during or after reading
Goals: National or State Literacy Standards	❏ Determine meanings of words using contextual and structural clues ❏ Clarify meaning of words by using graphs, charts and diagrams

Materials   Graphic Organizer definitions and
                                   examples

Time   30 Minutes

Graphic organizers are used to map the important concepts being studied by organizing and inserting phrases or representative vocabulary into a specific map. In the next section of this book we have included the structured overview, concept definition map, concept definition map variation, story map and story pyramid.

FIGURE 2.3. PREDICTING VOCABULARY

Sentences with highlighted words	Words	Predict meanings of words	Discuss the words and revise your predictions	Read the assigned reading write the words as used in context	Actual meaning as given in a dictionary
	Potential energy				
	Kinetic energy				
	Thermal energy				
The **nuclear energy** plant was closed and it was difficult to shut down the reactor.	Nuclear energy				

Structured Overviews

A structured overview is a hierarchical representation for concepts. This graphic organizer is helpful when a teacher wants to use a direct instruction approach because there is a need to develop basic information. The basic information is ordered hierarchically to show relationships among concepts and facts.

Procedure. To design such an organizer, begin with the objective of the material to be presented. One example is to place the concept at the top of the organizer.

Graphic organizers in this chapter will include the development and use of structured overviews, word maps and story maps.

Then place the major and subordinate terms in a hierarchical position to one another. See Figure 2.4.

The idea is to show a relationship of the concepts to one another and in a hierarchical order as the terms ultimately relate to the concept. Notice, also, in Figure 2.4 that the size of the print diminishes to reflect order of importance. This would be analogous to the use of chapter subheadings. It has also been found that the use of different colors to indicate the various hierarchical categories promotes better retention of vocabulary.

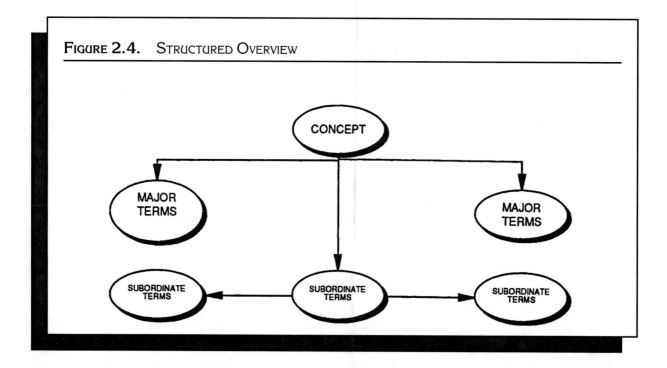

FIGURE 2.4. STRUCTURED OVERVIEW

Buzan (1983)

Structured overviews can be used in a variety of ways. They can represent a full book, a section, a chapter or one chapter subheading. A teacher might introduce the complete chapter to show the relationship of the parts to be taught daily. A daily structured overview might be used for each subordinate idea and at the end of a chapter, again, use the complete overview to bring the unit or concept to closure. It is important to select and use new vocabulary in the structured overview. See Figure 2.5 for a model for constructing content area examples.

Additionally, the structured overview can be designed with only the most critical terms. Then through discussions and reading students can add additional terms to the structure. This strategy helps students to stay on task, and promotes notetaking skills as they record the most pertinent information. Pictures and color can be used for visual associations which will help some students to more effectively recall information.

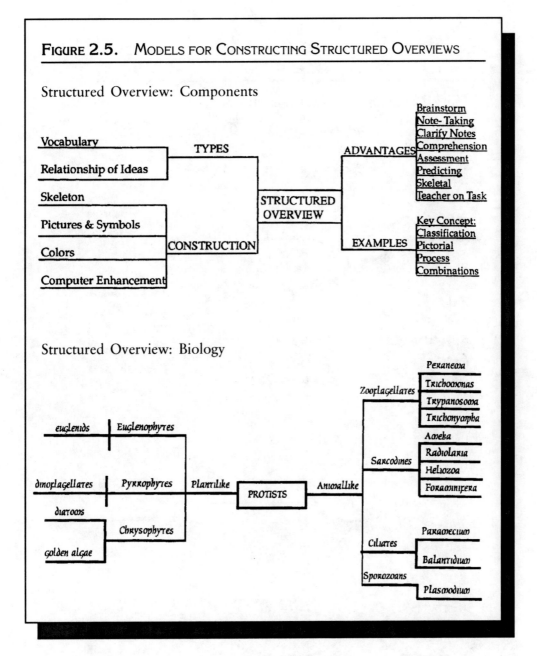

FIGURE 2.5. MODELS FOR CONSTRUCTING STRUCTURED OVERVIEWS

McClain (1987)

FIGURE 2.5.   MODELS FOR CONSTRUCTING STRUCTURED OVERVIEWS (CONT.)

Structured Overview: Physical Education

Wooden
Metal
Graphite

Grass
Clay
Synthetic
Concrete

U.S. Open
French Open
Davis Cup
Wimbledon

Pressure
Pressureless

Tennis

Jimmy Connors
John McEnroe
Martina Navratilova
Andre Agassi
Pete Sampras
Steffi Graf

Fun
Exercise
Spectator
Sport
Socializing

Singles
Doubles
Mixed Doubles

Structured Overview: Mathematics

In a structured overview the teacher directs the conceptual categories.

COORDINATE PLANE

RECTANGULAR COORDINATE SYSTEM

X-AXIS X-COORDINATE

Y-AXIS Y-COORDINATE

ORDERED PAIRS

ORIGIN

GRAPH A POINT

DETERMINE A POINT

QUADRANT

Concept Definition Map

Researchers have developed the graphic organizer called a word map. The word map elaborates and forms a broader definition for a particular term. Santa (1988) suggests that it is only logical that students be taught the "qualities of a definition." The word map elicits prior knowledge and allows students to generalize to expand their vocabularies. The word map includes three essential components for building an elaborate definition. The map could also be adapted to include antonyms or comparisons. See Figure 2.6.

Schwartz &
Raphael (1985)

Santa (1988)

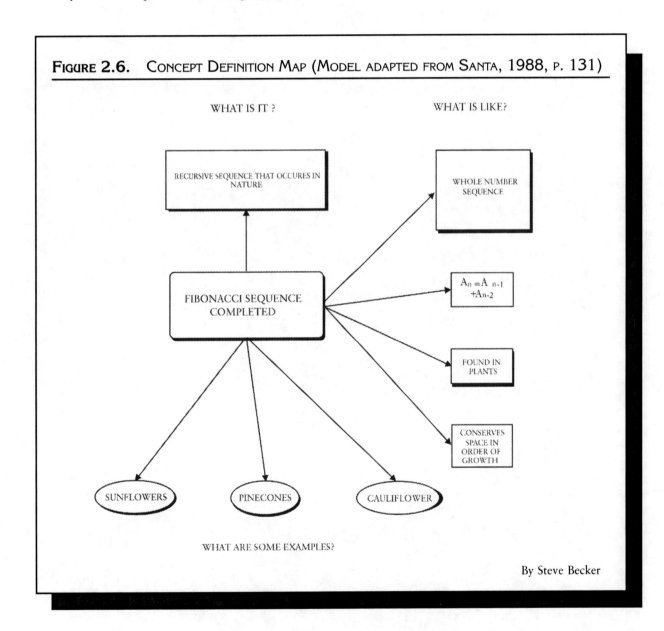

FIGURE 2.6.   CONCEPT DEFINITION MAP (MODEL ADAPTED FROM SANTA, 1988, P. 131)

By Steve Becker

Notes

Your Turn

Name _____ Date _____ Subject Area _____

DIRECTIONS: Select a new vocabulary word and complete the map.

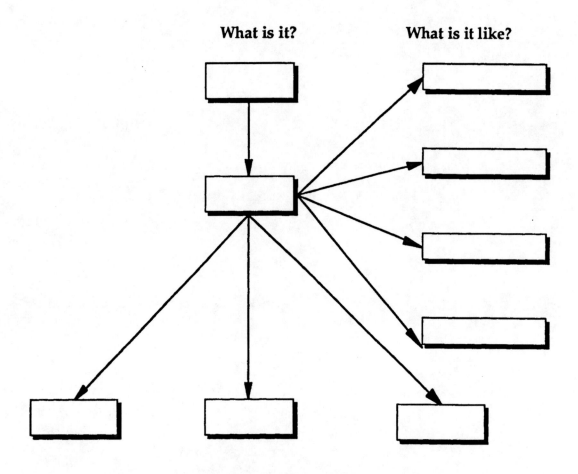

Concept Definition Map Variation

The concept definition map variation is an organizer that is more simplified than the concept definition map and incorporates the use of pictures as well as writing the selected vocabulary word in a sentence using a specific context clue. The use of pictures will better meet the learning styles of students who tend to be more tactile and/or visual. Besides including a picture for the new word, a synonym is also needed to complete the map. Because not all concept words have synonyms please note that the mathematics example has a definition rather than a synonym. If desired, one could also vary this map by changing the synonym to an antonym. Another variation would be to develop a word triangle such as the example given for music. See Figure 2.7.

The use of pictures will better meet learning styles.

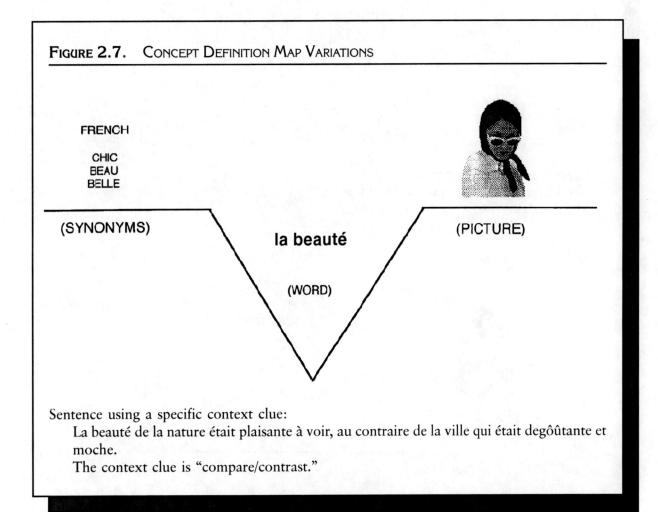

FIGURE 2.7. CONCEPT DEFINITION MAP VARIATIONS

FRENCH

CHIC
BEAU
BELLE

(SYNONYMS)

la beauté

(PICTURE)

(WORD)

Sentence using a specific context clue:
    La beauté de la nature était plaisante à voir, au contraire de la ville qui était degôûtante et moche.
    The context clue is "compare/contrast."

FIGURE 2.7. CONCEPT DEFINITION MAP VARIATIONS (CONT.)

Mathematics

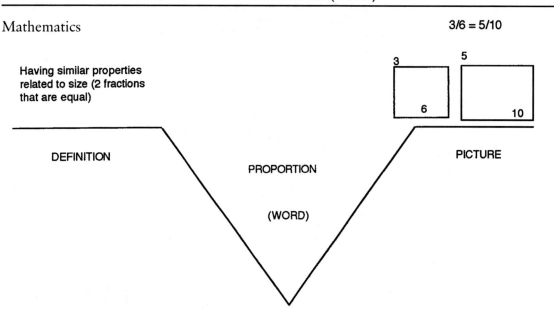

Sentence using a specific context clue:
These 2 rectangles are proportional in size, the width is ½ of the length.
The context clue is "direct description."

Word Triangle for Music

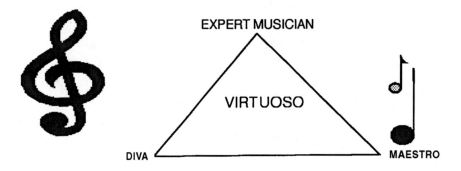

Sentence using a specific context clue:
Barbra Streisand, Bette Midler and Celine Dion, known as divas because of their singing talent and popularity, are virtuosos and maestros in their musical fields.
The context clue is "modifier."

Story Pyramid

The story pyramid is a type of story map that will help develop vocabulary. In particular, synonyms can be developed since it is likely that individual students' answers will vary. In the story pyramid students use the most descriptive words they can think of for each line in each category. See Figure 2.8.

Vacca & Vacca (1989)

The structured overview, concept definition map, concept definition map variations, story map and pyramid map are a few of the possible tools to help teachers and students to better understand vocabulary and concepts unique to a content area.

Rupley, Logan and Nichols (1999) suggest that "Instructional activities that allow for a visual display of words and promote students' comparing and contrasting of new words to known words can be a beneficial means for increasing their vocabulary knowledge." Because each is an organizer for information, each could be used as a prewriting exercise in the writing process. See Chapter Five.

Categorizing Organizers

Categorizing organizers in this chapter will include activities in which words are somehow clustered or classified to show relationships of the vocabulary or concepts. When students are asked to classify words they must arrange ideas systematically. This is an effective means to vocabulary development and reinforces the ability to conceptualize each new idea. Categorizing organizers include analogies, categorizations of words, interest/curiosity organizers, and making predictions.

Kurth (1980)

Analogies

Because they must critically think to solve relationships of words, students find this problem-solving activity to be very challenging. We suggest that teachers often demonstrate word analogy exercises in class. This could be done on the chalkboard, the overhead machine, or hand-outs as warm-up activities. Regardless of how it is accomplished, the students need to explain the relationship between the pairs of words. As students explain analogies they should do so in their own

Vacca & Vacca (1989)

FIGURE 2.8.   STORY PYRAMID

⎯⎯	Name of Character
⎯⎯ ⎯⎯	Describe Character
⎯⎯ ⎯⎯ ⎯⎯	Describe Setting
⎯⎯ ⎯⎯ ⎯⎯ ⎯⎯	Describe Main Event
⎯⎯ ⎯⎯ ⎯⎯ ⎯⎯ ⎯⎯	State Problem
⎯⎯ ⎯⎯ ⎯⎯ ⎯⎯ ⎯⎯ ⎯⎯	Describe Second Event
⎯⎯ ⎯⎯ ⎯⎯ ⎯⎯ ⎯⎯ ⎯⎯ ⎯⎯	Describe Third Event
⎯⎯ ⎯⎯ ⎯⎯ ⎯⎯ ⎯⎯ ⎯⎯ ⎯⎯ ⎯⎯	Solution to Problem

Macon, Bewell, & Vogt (1991)

words. For example, in the analogy <u>ophthalmologist</u> is to <u>eyes</u> as <u>cardiologist</u> is to <u>heart</u> the student should understand that an ophthalmologist diagnoses and prescribes for eye problems and a cardiologist diagnoses and prescribes for heart maladies.

There are eight different types of relationships in analogies that students need to be able to explain. They are:

1. Part to whole
   hoop : court :: base : (diamond)
2. Person to situation
   Ella : jazz :: Bach : (classical)
3. Cause and effect
   E-coli : disease :: Coccus : (infection)
4. synonym
   plain : ordinary :: timid : (bashful)
5. Antonym
   patrician : plebeian :: apostasy : (chauvinism)
6. Geography
   Columbia : Oregon :: Amazon : (Brazil)
7. Measurement
   quart : liquid :: pound : (solid)
8. Time
   day : week :: month : (year)

Word Sorts

TABLE 2

INSTRUCTIONAL SUMMARY OF WORD SORTS

Literacy Strategy	Word Sort—closed and open
Primary Focus	Word meanings through categorization
Learning Principles	❏ Variety of Ways to Organize ❏ Thought-demanding Activity
When to use	Before, during and after reading and for writing
Goals: National or State Literacy Standards	❏ Determine meanings of words using multiple and/or specialized meanings ❏ Determine meanings of words using the concept of categorization ❏ Expand vocabulary
Materials	Chart paper, felt markers and lists of pre-selected words
Time	30 Minutes

Procedure.

Closed Word Sort

1. The instructor pre-selects vocabulary from a content topic that can be sorted into three or four categories.
2. The instructor pre-determines the title for the concept categories. The students divide their chart paper into the number of concept categories.
3. The students decide which vocabulary words belong in which categories and list the words accordingly.

Open Word Sort

1. The instructor pre-selects vocabulary from a content topic that can be sorted into three or four categories.
2. Students must comprehend the relationships of the words to be able to determine the various categories.
3. Students then divide a piece of chart paper into the number of categories they have determined, write the category at the top of each section of the chart paper and list the vocabulary that belongs in the respective category.

It is suggested that an instructor begin with closed word sorts which are an easier challenge than the open word sorts.

The following word sort for music is called a **closed word sort** because for all of the words listed a category is also given and there is a specific place for each word.

FIGURE 2.9.   CLOSED WORD SORT FOR MUSIC

Music Terms

forte
staccato
warm
soprano
crescendo
legato
sonorous
alto
diminuendo
tenor
slur
resonant
bass
pianissimo
shrill

Articulation	Pitch
Volume	Tone Quality

The following word sort for mathematics is called an open word sort because the student must analyze the words and then determine the concept areas in which the words can be categorized. In this case—five categories: relation, linear equation, function types, graphs and statistics.

FIGURE 2.10.   OPEN WORD SORT FOR MATHEMATICS

Abs. value function	Cartesian coordinate plane	Coordinate system	Constant function	Continuous function
Dependent variable	Direct variation	Domain	Function	Greatest integer function
Identity function	Linear operation	Linear function	Mapping	Ordered pairs
Origin	Point-slope form	Quadrants	Range	Relation
X-axis	X-intercept	Y-axis	Y-intercept	Best-fit line
Slope	Slope-intercept form	Standard form	Step function	Vertical line test
Prediction equation	Regression line	Scatter plot		

Sort the terms listed above into the box or boxes below:

Relation	Linear Equation
Function types	Graphs
Statistics	

By Terry Bennet

Semantic and Syntactic Clues and Word Structures

TABLE 3

INSTRUCTIONAL SUMMARY OF CONTEXT CLUES

Literacy Strategy	Context Clues
Primary Focus	Word Meanings in Context
Learning Principles	Active Involvement in Searching for Meaning
When to Use	Before, during and after reading and for writing
Goals: National or State Literacy Standards	❑ Determine meanings of words using context clues
	❑ Determine meanings of words using syntactical clues
	❑ Determine meanings of words using affixes and roots
Materials	Context clue definition handout
Time	60 minutes

For students to develop word meanings they need to become aware of the writer's use of context clues. To be able to unlock context clues should mean that they, too, could use the same clues in their writing. This means that students must be given a variety of written materials and must read widely. The exposure to good writing gives them practice in deciphering context clues, exposure to a variety of vocabulary words and serves as a model for their own writing. Thus, we believe strongly that all content area teachers should assign a variety of reading materials to supplement and extend the textbook—if a textbook is used.

Vacca & Vacca (1989)

Semantic and syntactic clues need to be considered in studying vocabulary. Vacca and Vacca write "...grammatical relationships among words in a sentence or the structural arrangement among sentences in a passage often helps to classify the meaning of a particular word" (1989, p. 324).

Sentence structure is highly complex. Longer sentences are many times more difficult to understand. Edward Fry's Kernel Distance Theory (1977) defines a sentence kernel as having a noun, a verb and maybe a modifier. The longer the distance between the noun and the verb, the more difficult it is to comprehend. Thus, students need to be made aware of and study grammar. The placement of a word in a sentence determines its grammatical use and label as a part of speech. Students who encounter a new word can use syntactic clues to decode the word and its meaning by deciding if it's a noun, verb, adjective or other part of speech.

Fry (1977)

We believe that both semantic and syntactic clues should be studied and dealt with in text situations such as those materials that will be used for reading assignments—newspapers, magazines, trade books and/or textbooks. Furthermore, we cannot depend on English teachers to be the sole disseminators of this informa-

The use of context clues leads to students independently unlocking words.

tion. The following organizers or activity ideas are suggested to help teachers organize for instruction in all content areas.

Semantic Organizers

Tonjes and Zintz state "The exposure to a word in context may well give us a better idea of its meaning than looking it up in the dictionary, where a variety of meanings are listed from which to choose" (1992, p. 162). We, too, believe that context analysis of words, semantic or syntactic, will be more relevant when presented in sentences drawn from student reading assignments whenever possible.

Context Clues

Before one can determine which clue the author has employed in the context which includes new vocabulary, one must first understand the major types of context clues.

1. Definition

    The author defines the new word within the confines of a statement using a form of the verb *be*.

    Example: Impervious means that something cannot be penetrated.

2. Comparison/contrast

    The author contrasts the new word with a word or phrase of opposite meaning. Example: Allison's ebullience discombobulated her mom because she was usually a very laconic child.

    Note: *Because is* a clue word. Students should be able to identify words that cause one to change direction in their thinking while engaged in reading.

3. Cause/effect

    The unknown word, impenetrable, depends on the cause/effect relationship with other words.

    Example: A wall is impenetrable because it is so thick and strong.

    Note: The clue word in this statement is *because*.

4. Modifiers, examples and restatement

    The new word is further defined through phrases, appositives or clauses.

    Example: Trees that lose their leaves, such as oak or cherry, belong in the category of deciduous.

    Note: The clue is the use of examples set off by commas.

    Example: A closet, which holds brooms and vacuums, can be found in most every house.

    Note: Again, the use of examples and punctuation are the clues.

    Example: The silver bells had a mellifluous sound. In other words, their music was pleasant to hear.

    Note: This phrase restates information that defines mellifluous.

5. Antonyms/synonyms

    Opposites or similar words connote meaning.

    Example: The family lamented or bemoaned his death.

    Note: The word *or* is a clue that bemoaned is a synonym for lamented.

    Example: The man was capricious, erratic, whimsical and fanciful.

    Note: The use of commas connects synonyms with similar meanings.

Example: The prescription should ameliorate his symptoms, not aggravate them.

Note: The use of a comma and the clue word *not* help students to decipher the context clue.

6. Mood or tone

Example: The boy went down into the dark, damp cellar.

Note: The author connotes a feeling which results in the mood or tone of the word cellar.

Now that the major types of context clues have been established, how can they be implemented in the content area classroom? An example is given in Figure 2.11 and Figure 2.12.

FIGURE 2.11. SEMANTIC ORGANIZER

New Word	Write the sentence in which the new word can be found. Write your original sentence for the word.	Which content clue was used by the author? Which context clue did you use?	Write the definition, antonym and synonym, and draw a picture for the word.

FIGURE 2.12. CONTEXT CLUE ORGANIZER

Read the list of words, guess the meaning of the words, read the passage and revise your guess based on any context clues.

WORD	GUESS WITHOUT CONTEXT	REVISED GUESS

Source: Kelly Gallagher. K. (2003). Reading Reasons: Motivational Mini-Lessons for Middle and High School, Portland, ME: Stenhouse Publishers, p.55

We believe that for words to be learned well, to use them and to store them in long term memory, a variety of associations must be made so students can recall them from different encounters. These associations should be to 1) define the word, 2) develop synonyms and antonyms for the word, 3) use the word in the context of a quality sentence, and 4) make a picture of the word. A quality sentence means that the new word is fully understandable because a good context clue has been used.

> *Poor example:* I like piebalds.
> *Good example:* The horse was called a piebald because it had black and white spots. (cause/effect; clue word is *because*)

Context Clue Assignment

The following three activities are quality context clue assignments that can be adapted for any content area:

1. After thoroughly discussing the six major context clues, extract from resource materials sentences which include key vocabulary to be taught. Discuss which context clue the author had used and why.

2. Give students, in pairs, a key vocabulary word. Also, assign a context clue to each pair of students. They are to write the word in a sentence using the assigned context clue. Next, they write their sentences on the board. The rest of the class members are to decide the meaning of the word and which context clue was used.

3. Assign key vocabulary to pairs of students. They are asked to design a flashcard that on one side has the word and a picture that represents the meaning of the word. The other side has the definition of the word, synonyms and antonyms for the word and the word written in a quality sentence. These cards can be used as study cards or in word banks. Hopkins and Bean (1998/99) found in a classroom research study that the "verbal-visual word association strategy helps students to create personal associations for unfamiliar words" (p. 275). See Figure 2.13.

FIGURE 2.13.   VOCABULARY FLASHCARD

SIDE ONE	SIDE TWO
WORD: Strident	**DEFINITION:** Strident—shrill, harsh, unpleasant, irritating sound **Synonyms/Antonyms** cacophonous/mellifluous discordant/mellow vociferous/euphonious **Sentence:** The strident tone of the singer cracked the crystal goblet.

The key to unlocking the meaning of words through context analysis is two sided. Students should use both semantic and syntactic clues.

Syntactic Organizers

As teachers, we are all responsible for guiding students in reading the materials we use. Knowing our grammar helps. Grammar serves as an important clue for students to determine word meanings. The syntax or function of words in a sentence guides the student in unlocking the meaning. Knowing which part of speech the word is (noun, verb, adjective, etc.) helps students to eliminate particular words. The following instructional strategies encourage teachers to implement the use of syntax as a way of unlocking new vocabulary meanings.

1. Using a modified cloze procedure the teacher could eliminate certain parts of speech rather than the standard fifth word. For the student to supply the missing word, she must examine the surrounding text and use context analysis, in this case, syntax.

2. Select from assigned reading materials sentences that include key vocabulary. Give the students their choice of one of three words (all the same part of speech) to complete the sentence.

Conley (1993)

Taylor (1953)
Tonjes & Zintz (1992)

See Chapter 8 for a description of the cloze technique.

Word Structures

We believe that students should memorize affixes and roots in order to transfer knowledge across content areas and to simply better determine the meaning of an unknown word. Teachers readily recognize when their science, or social studies students have had this experience in their English class. The respective vocabulary of these classes does not pose a challenge to those students who have had this training. Students zero in on the meaningful parts of the word and intuit the rest from the context.

Kelly Gallagher (2004) recommends the Anaheim Union High School District "30-15-10 list" that contains the 30 most common **prefixes**, the 15 most common **roots**, and the 10 most common **suffixes**. She requires that her students memorize these 55 meanings and this is assigned as homework. Once students are familiar with these 55 word structures they can unlock many words and make educated guesses at other words by simply using one of the structures. Her example is the word "malpractice" in which the prefix "mal" is on the list which the students will know means bad and can then make an educated guess at the rest. See Figure 2.14.

Once students have an understanding of word structures teachers in any content area could have a word of the day or week in which students study the structures and together try to figure out the definition of the word. Two examples:

> Pneumonoultramicroscopicsilicovolcanoconiosis
> Pneu—lung
> Mono—one
> Ultra—very
> Microscopic—so tiny the eye cannot see it
> Silico—glass like
> Volcano—source of ash that can become glass
> Con—with
> Iosis—disease

FIGURE 2.14.   THE 30-15-10 LIST

Prefix	Meaning	Example
a, ab, abs	away, from	absent; abstinence
ad, a, ac, af, ag, an, ar, at, as	to, toward	adhere; annex; accede; adapt
bi,bis	two	bicycle; biped; bisect
circum	around	circumference
com, con	together, with	combination; connect
de	opposite; from, away	detract; defer; demerit
dis, dif, di	apart, not	disperse; different
epi	upon, on top of	epicenter
equi	equal	equality; equitable
ex,e	out, from forth	eject; exhale; exit
hyper	over; above	hyperactive; hypersensitive
hypo	under, beneath	hypodermic
In	in, into, not	inject; endure, incorrect
inter	between; among	intercede
mal, male	bad, ill	malpractice; malevolent
mis	wrong	mistake; misunderstand
mono	alone, single, one	monotone; monopoly
non	not	nonsense
ob	in front of, against	obvious
omni	everywhere, all	omnipresent
preter	past, beyond	preternatural
pro	forward	proceed; promote
re	again, back	recall; recede
retro	backward, behind, back	retroactive
se	apart	secede
sub	under	subway
super	greater, beyond	supernatural; superstition
trans	across, beyond	transcend; transcontinental
un, uni	one	unilateral; unity
un (pronounced uhn)	not	unhappy; unethical

FIGURE 2.14.   THE 30-15-10 LIST (CONT.)

Root	Meaning	Example
bas	low	basement
cap, capt	take; seize	capture; capable
cred	believe	credible
diet	speak	predict; dictionary
due, duct	lead	induce; conduct
fac, fact	make, do	artifact; facsimile
graph	write	autograph; graphic
log	word, study of	dialog; biology
mort	die; death	mortal; mortician
scrib, script	write	transcribe; subscription
spec, spect	see	specimen; aspect
tact	touch	contact; tactile
ten	hold	tenacious; retentive
therm	heat	thermostat; thermometer
ver	true	verify

Suffix	Meaning	Example
-able, -ible	able to (adj.)	usable
-er, -or	one who does (n)	competitor
-fy	to make (v)	dignify
-ism	the practice of (n)	rationalism, Catholicism
-ist	one who is occupied with	feminist; environmentalist
-less	without, lacking (adj.)	meaningless
-logue, -log	a particular kind of speaking or writing	prologue, dialog
-ness	the quality of (n)	aggressiveness
-ship	the art or skill of (adj.)	sportsmanship
-tude	the state of (n)	rectitude

Source: Kelly Gallagher (2004). Deeper Reading: Comprehending Challenging Texts, 4-12. Portland, ME: Stenhouse Publishers, p 73.

When these structures are analyzed the word definition is coal miner's black iung disease, which in this case is the disease of one lung brought on by breathing ash.

Or

Floccinaucinihilipilification
Flocci—tuft of wool
Nauci—a trifling thing
Nihili—nothing
Pili—a hair or trifle
Fication—making

When these structures are analyzed the word definition is estimating something as worthless.

Reference Organizers

TABLE 4

INSTRUCTIONAL SUMMARY FOR REFERENCE ORGANIZERS	
Literacy Strategy	**Reference Organizers**
Primary Focus	Use of Dictionary and Thesaurus
Learning Principles	Active Involvement in Searching for Meaning
When to Use	Throughout reading and writing
Goals: National or State Literacy Standards	Locate information using references
Materials	Dictionary and Thesaurus
Time	30 minutes

Students cannot and will not use reference tools if such materials are not readily available nor their use encouraged and required. Students usually prefer to take short-cuts! Finding the dictionary, finding the word, and reading the full definition take time. We suggest that teachers in all content fields allow time for students to use reference tools when developing meaningful vocabularies. We will discuss two reference tools which help to facilitate vocabulary development: the dictionary and the thesaurus.

Dictionary

Is it possible that at the high school level a student has not mastered how to use a dictionary? YES! Do your students know how to use alphabetical order to the fourth or fifth letter? Do they use guide words to locate vocabulary on a given page? Do they know how and when to use pronunciation keys and abbreviation and symbol lists? In particular, are they aware of how the various word meanings and usages are presented in a dictionary? The latter is important when key vocabulary has multiple meanings across several content areas.

FIGURE 2.15. INCORPORATING CONTEXT CLUES IN A LESSON PLAN.

How might one include a lesson for the student understanding and application of context clues in their content area? We have outlined a lesson plan to illustrate a possible scenario.

Lesson plan: Music

Grade: 10

Topic: Understanding of musical terms. (See the open word sort on page 157)

Purpose: To help students to understand basic music vocabulary.

State Content/literacy Standards: Determine meanings of words using context clues.

Student Objectives:
1. Students will be able to identify the six context clues.
2. Students will be able to demonstrate their understanding of these clues by writing music vocabulary in sentences that incorporate the six context clues.

Introduction:
1. Ask students to brainstorm what the term context clue means to them. (1 minute)
2. Introduce the six context clues with definitions. Have a hand-out of these for each student. Call on students to read the definitions, the examples and to redefine the definitions in their own words. (15 minutes)

Learning Activity:
1. Select small groups of students. Appoint a recorder and a reporter. (1 minute)
2. Explain that in small groups the students will be given a music vocabulary word such as *forte* and a specific context clue such as *comparison/contrast*. (3 minutes)
3. Referring to the handout that defines context clues each group will write a sentence using their assigned word and their assigned context clue. They should underline the word. They will use colored marking pens and butcher paper for this. If time permits they can draw a picture/s that defines their word. (15 minutes)
4. Their goal is to "stump" the rest of the class from figuring out the meaning of their word and/or the context clue that they used.
5. Each recorder will hold up the sheet of paper while the reporter reads the sentence. The rest of the class must define the word and tell which context clue was used to define the word. (15 minutes)

Closure: Students will be given a list of music terms and will be asked to select three words and to write their own sentences using a different context clue for each word. (10 minutes)

Evaluation: Students' sentences are assessed for understanding of the terms and the use of context clues.

Make sure that students are aware of specialized dictionaries for various content areas. Do they realize there is a dictionary of geographical terms, a slang dictionary, or even a dictionary of musical terms? The following instructional organizers may help teachers to incorporate dictionaries into their planning:

Physical Education
Using a slang dictionary what is the history of these words?
bullpen   three-bagger   dinger

Geography
Using a dictionary of geographical terms determine which river is the longest.
Yantze   Danube   Amazon

Music
Using a dictionary of musical terms define these words.
allegro   allegretto   andante

*Johnson &
Pearson (1984)*

Students need interesting approaches such as forming questions that require the use of a dictionary.

1. Is a lugger similar to a skiff?
2. What do raft and coracle have in common?

Finally, consider turning one of the walls of your classroom into a word wall. Keep an ongoing list of key vocabulary on large sheets of butcher paper. Use a separate piece of paper for each category of words.

Using a dictionary students find word meanings. The next step is to use the thesaurus. This reference tool gives many synonyms for those meanings.

Thesaurus
The thesaurus is a dictionary of synonyms. Students need to realize that synonyms do not have the same meaning and each is used differently. A person is not obsolete, but decrepit. An idea is not decrepit, but obsolete.

Build vocabulary through the use of a thesaurus.

The use of a thesaurus helps to expand a student's vocabulary in speaking, writing and reading. It helps students to replace redundant words with exciting words. Encourage the use of a thesaurus for the editing stage of the writing process when students want a variety of interesting words. A dictionary could not be used for this purpose. Given such assignments students realize the appropriateness and value of a thesaurus and discover the limitations of the dictionary.

Vocabulary Reinforcement

TABLE 5

INSTRUCTIONAL SUMMARY FOR VOCABULARY REINFORCEMENT

Literacy Strategy	Vocabulary Reinforcement
Primary Focus	Use of Bubblegrams and Crossword Puzzles
Learning Principles	Thought-demanding Activity
When to Use	Throughout reading and writing
Goals: National or State Literacy Standards	Increase vocabulary

Materials	Bubblegram and Crossword Templates
Time	30 minutes

Bubblegrams

In this exercise students have the opportunity to reinforce vocabulary words previously presented. The students or the teacher generate the bubblegram exercise, a puzzle format, using vocabulary from a reading assignment. The bubblegram key word should represent the theme or objective of the material read. Using key letters from each vocabulary word, students are asked to decipher the mystery word and place it in the bubblegram. See Figure 2.16.

FIGURE 2.16. BUBBLEGRAM

1. ____ O ____ ____ ____
2. __ __ O __ __
3. __ __ __ __ __ __ __ __ O __ __
4. __ __ __ __ O __ __
5. __ __ __ __ O __ __
6. __ O __ __ __ __ __ __
7. __ __ __ __ __ O
8. __ __ O __ __ __ __ __ __ __ __
9. __ __ O __ __
10. __ __ __ __ __ O __ __ __
11. __ __ __ __ __ O __

Mystery Word:

__ __ __ __ __ __ __ __ __ __ __

1. decomposes, rots
2. plant subkingdom, Thallophyte
3. to break up, to disperse
4. a kind, variety
5. soak in or soak up
6. dampness
7. colorless, odorless gas
8. degrees of hotness or coldness
9. to increase in size
10. to begin to grow, sprout
11. abnormal tissue formation

Word Choices:

dissolved, decay, fungi, germinate, oxygen, species, moisture, swell, absorbs, growth, temperature

Definition—the total of circumstances that surrounds an organism or group of organisms

Crossword Puzzles

Of course, crossword puzzles are always challenging. We have found that they can be made quite easily on the computer. You simply type in the vocabulary and a definition for each vocabulary word. The computer program will scramble them and lay out the puzzle format. Crossword puzzles are particularly good for building synonyms, reinforcement of definitions and to distinguish multiple meanings of words.

Inclusion Techniques

Increasing numbers of students with special needs are educated in the regular classroom today. Teachers adapting a philosophy of inclusive education place a value on monitoring and taking action to improve the learning and performance of all students in their classroom. These teachers maintain the integrity of their content, not watering it down, but selecting and providing instruction around the most critical concepts. These critical concepts make the facts and details hang together. If students don't understand these, they are in trouble.

Olson & Platt (1996)

Inclusion is based on the premise that students with special needs are educated in the regular classroom.

STUDENT TALK

A special needs student writes: "When I read this article on cell duplication, I couldn't understand the article or the definition, they wrote on cell duplication, because it was hard to read."

However, if we can present clearly the concepts of a unit, it then becomes easier to build on the other essential elements of the unit. Research has shown that students with special needs learn more when they are: 1) actively involved in the learning process, 2) presented abstract and complex concepts in concrete forms, 3) given information that is organized, 4) able to tie new information to previously learned information, 5) able to distinguish important information from unimportant information, and 6) presented relationships that are made explicit.

Most of the activities presented in this chapter promote these principles. See the following chart that summarizes a sampling of these:

Bulgren, Schumaker & Deshler (1994)

Research Findings	Vocabulary Activities
1. Active engagement is fostered.	Predicting Vocabulary, Fig. 2.1
2. Abstract and complex concepts are presented in concrete forms.	Word Maps, Fig. 2.6 Semantic Organizer, Fig. 2.11 Vocabulary Flashcards, Fig. 2.13
3. Information is organized.	Story Maps, Fig. 2.7 Story Pyramid, Fig. 2.8
4. New information is tied to previously learned material.	Predicting Vocabulary, Fig. 2.1 V-V-L Procedure, Fig. 2.2
5. Important information is distinguished from unimportant information.	Bubblegrams, Fig. 2.16 Structured Overviews, Fig. 2.5
6. Relationships are made explicit.	Structured Overviews, Fig. 2.5

Notice how many of these activities involve naming the concepts or key vocabulary used, provide many examples, and foster additional practice. They also specify what students need to do to learn the terms and finally, give students frequent opportunities to review these terms. All of these activities help a diverse group of students understand, master and apply key vocabulary within their content curriculum.

Even if students find their material difficult to read like the student in our example, "Student Talk," they can learn this content when it is translated into easy-to-understand formats and presented in a concrete fashion.

Bulgren, Schumaker & Deshler (1994)

We can assure you that if these activities are directly taught, and students are given opportunities to use them regularly to improve their own learning, students' ability to understand, organize and use key vocabulary will increase in your classroom.

Vocabulary Strategies for Second Language Readers

Recent research involving a study of 254 bilingual and monolingual fifth graders focused on the gap between Anglo and Latino children and it was found that it is best to teach students information about words that leads to figuring out word meanings. Strategies that were stressed were "using context, noticing words in new contexts, checking the likelihood that the word has a Spanish cognate, and analyzing morphological structure for cues to meaning." This also had a significant impact on reading comprehension. Further, second language learners should "have access to the text's meaning through Spanish, that words should be encountered in varying contexts, and that word knowledge involves spelling, pronunciation, morphology, and syntax as well as depth of meaning.

Carlo, August, McLaughlin, Snow, Dressier, Lippman, Lively, & White, 2004

This certainly reinforces the need to use a variety of strategies as stressed in the brain research discussed in Chapter 3 and the strategies presented in this chapter.

STUDENT TALK ⸻⸻⸻⸻⸻⸻⸻⸻⸻⸻⸻⸻⸻⸻⸻⸻⸻⸻⸻⸻

It's harder still when reading is a struggle, when dyslexia jumbles all the words on the page; when the kids learn you're Native American, and the slurs come hard and fast; when your mom is at work all the time, and the neighborhood is calling. There were fights. Suspensions. Thefts. Bad decisions.

Joseph Garcia (in "A teacher's gift helps him grow and pass it along")

Before selecting a strategy make sure the classroom is a safe environment and that the materials will be meaningful for a student whose background is not Anglo.

LINCS

Purpose. This vocabulary study strategy is an easy one for students with special needs to learn and to apply readily across the content areas. These students typically have either no strategies for learning or inefficient ones. As a consequence, they are frustrated and fail to learn.

Ellis (1992)

We know that if students use strategies that help them transform information or elaborate on it, they are more likely to learn through this active engagement. Creating visuals, devising mnemonics, and relating new information to their own experience have been found to be practical learning activities for all students because of the level of participation required. Students who learn the LINCS strategy are expected to 1) independently learn key vocabulary, 2) develop a sense of empowerment or control over their learning, and 3) increase their motivation to learn new strategies.

Procedure. The five steps of the strategy are:

L — List the parts
I — Imagine a picture
N — Note a reminding word
C — Construct a LINCing story
S — Self-test

What key words in your content area could you use for a LINCS lesson?

Step 1. Students create a 3" x 5" index card for the critical terms they need to study. Students are directed to first draw a horizontal line on each side of an index card. Then they write and circle the word to be learned on the top half of one side of the card. On the top half of the back of the card, they write the important parts of the definition.

Step 2. Students are asked to imagine a picture. They transform the information, such as the concept Holocaust, into a visual image. Using the word, *Holocaust,* they may create an image of people in wartime put in camps where they were encircled by guards, dogs, barbed wire fences and finally killed. Then they are asked to translate that picture into words and describe that image to a peer or to themselves.

Step 3. Students are asked to create a "reminding word," a word that sounds similar, has similar-sounding characteristics, or a word that that they already know that relates to the word they are learning. For example, the student may associate the word *holocaust* with *destruction,* a concept that students may associate with deliberately destroying.

Imaginative thinking helps students stretch their thinking and personalize their learning.

Step 4. Students generate a LINCing story that shows the association between the keyword and the reminding word. They may begin with the image created in Step 2.

For example, a student feels that in his story he sees all the kids his age who have to watch their parents and other relatives taken away by the guards. These families' lives are destroyed while all stand by waiting their turn, helpless to do anything. And he knows that he will never see them again, because he already has heard the stories of many other kids that have been in the camps longer than he has.

Students then revise the story to include the important elements of the definition in the story, e.g., "destruction of many people."

Front of card   Back of card

Holocaust	systematic, annihilation of 6 million Jews and many others by the Nazis in WWII
Reminding word: Destruction	LINCing story: **destruction of many people**

Step 5. In the self-test step, students test their memory, either going from the keyword to the definition or vice versa. Students are encouraged to use their story as a reminder of the meaning of the word.

English and second language students may find that using a dictionary will complement the use of LINCS. Gonzalez (1999) found that ESL students become more independent in their acquisition of the English language when they sharpen dictionary skills. "Persistent use of the dictionary allowed ESL learners to compensate for their deficiencies in vocabulary knowledge and become more fluent readers" (p. 269).

Vocabulary Squares developed by Hopkins & Bean (1998/99) were found to work well for students with special needs in a middle school and high school Title I program. The authors reinforced the Beck and McKeown (1991) findings that most reading authorities advocate intensive classroom vocabulary instruction to complement and support a reading program. Thus, vocabulary squares is a strategy to help special needs students to spend intensive, hands-on time with vocabulary by completing root word vocabulary squares. Note that this strategy could be adapted for various instructional needs. The students were given paper to divide into four squares. Next they were given a prefix to put in one square, they then used the dictionary to put the definition of the prefix into the next square. Using the dictionary to find a word that began with that prefix, students drew a picture of the word in the third square, and wrote it and defined it in the fourth square. See Figure 2.17.

Endings: A Summary

In this chapter we have presented vocabulary strategies which empower students to acquire and use new words. Students need to be given a number of opportunities to learn vocabulary, write with interesting vocabulary and to speak articulately using interesting and accurate vocabulary. Activities allow students to use words in different situations. However, they also need to study the use of words, contextually and structurally. Teachers in every content area need to make certain that students have studied and acquired vocabulary unique to their curriculum.

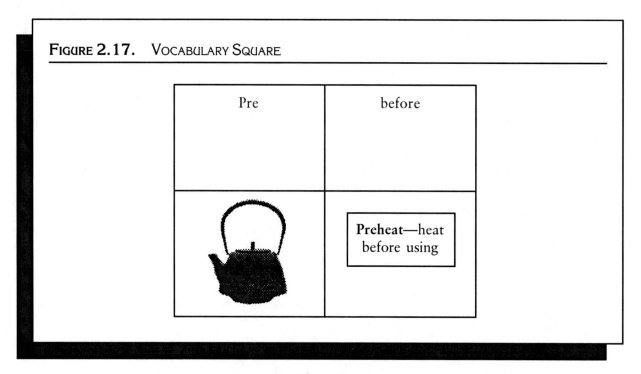

FIGURE 2.17. VOCABULARY SQUARE

New vocabulary should be related to prior knowledge. Acquisition of vocabulary can be developed through the use of a number of graphic organizers. Students can also learn to put words into categories, make predictions, and practice word usage.

We firmly believe that wide reading in all content areas should cause students to develop expanded vocabularies. In turn, their writing should also become more interesting. Lastly, key vocabulary leads to comprehension of a concept. We hope this chapter is a launching point for you. On your own, begin to expand on our suggestions to better meet the needs of your students.

Expanding Understanding through Discussion

Name _____ Date _____

DIRECTIONS: Follow the directions for each section. Be ready to report on your decisions. Be prepared to support your responses as a group.

LITERAL LEVEL—DIRECTIONS: In your small group come to consensus in your discussions. Check these statements that you agree were made explicitly by the authors.

_____ 1. All content area teachers should teach vocabulary.
_____ 2. A structured overview is a representation of terms that are related.
_____ 3. Categorizing organizers are related to graphic organizers.
_____ 4. Vocabulary journals are effective for all students.
_____ 5. Structural features of words are roots and affixes.

INTERPRETIVE LEVEL—DIRECTIONS: Come to consensus with members of your group. Check those statements that you agree were made implicitly by the authors.

_____ 1. All students can learn vocabulary.
_____ 2. ESL students need specialized help learning vocabulary.
_____ 3. The understanding of context clues will lead to more effective comprehension.
_____ 4. Context analysis involves syntactic and semantic clues.
_____ 5. Students prefer to use reference tools to verify word meanings.

APPLIED LEVEL—DIRECTIONS: Come to consensus in your group. Use your new experiences and ideas presented in this chapter to justify your choice.

_____ 1. Teachers who read widely will be good teachers of reading.
_____ 2. A person knowledgeable in using vocabulary will be a better writer.
_____ 3. Vocabulary is the key to understanding.

In the Field Applications
A. Compose a letter to parents justifying why you use student interaction in your class to teach vocabulary.
B. Your department chair is impressed with your work with special needs students, she wants you to present a few vocabulary strategies at an upcoming department meeting. Prepare a handout explaining your philosophy regarding students with special needs. In addition, prepare two lesson plans describing objectives, materials, procedures and evaluation of two subject related vocabulary strategies.
C. Generate a list of vocabulary words from your specialty area. Choose only those words critical for an understanding of the chapter. Then create the following:
1. a context clue activity
2. a structured overview.

References ❑ ❑ ❑

Allen, J. (2006). Too little or too much? What do we know about making vocabulary instruction meaningful? *Voices from the Middle*, 13(4). 16–19.

Anderson, R., & Freebody, P. (1981). Vocabulary knowledge. In J. Guthrie (Ed.), *Comprehension and teaching: Research reviews*. Newark, DE: International Reading Association.

A teacher's gift helps him grow to pass it along. (2006, March 27). *The Oregonian*, A7.

Barron, R. (1969). The use of vocabulary as an advance organizer. In H.L. Herber & P.L. Sanders (Eds.), *Research in reading in the content areas: First Report.* Syracuse, NY: Syracuse University Reading and Language Arts Center.

Beck, I. & McKeown, M. (1991). Conditions of vocabulary acquisition. In R. Barr, M. Kamil, P. Mosenthal, & P. Pearson (Eds.), *Handbook of Reading Research: Volume II.* NY: Longman.

Bulgren, J., Schumaker, J., & Deshler, D. (1994). *The concept of anchoring routine.* Lawrence, KA: Edge Enterprise, Inc.

Buzan, T. (1983). *Use both sides of your brain.* NY: Dutton.

Carlo, M., August, D., McLaughlin, B., Snow, C., Dressier, C., Lippman, D., Lively, T., & White, C. (2004). Closing the gap: Addressing the vocabulary need of English-language learners in bilingual and mainstream classrooms. *Reading Research Quarterly*, 39(2), 188–206.

Cochran, J. (1993). *Reading in the content areas for junior high and high school.* Boston: Allyn and Bacon.

Conley, M. (1993). *Content reading instruction.* New York: McGraw-Hill, Inc.

Ellis, E. (1992). *The LINCS strategy training guide.* Lawrence, KS: Edge Enterprise, Inc.

Fry, E. (1977). Fry's readability graph: Clarifications, validity and extensions to level 17. *Journal of Reading*, (21), 242–252.

Fry, E. (1987). Picture nouns for reading and vocabulary improvement. *Reading Teacher*, 41, 185–91.

Gallagher, K. (2004). *Deeper reading: Comprehending challenging texts*, 4–12. Portland, ME: Stenhouse Publishers.

Gallagher, K. (2003). Reading reasons: Motivational mini-lessons for middle and high school. Portland, ME: Stenhouse Publishers.

The graphic organizer. (2006). Retrieved August 6, 2006, from http://www.graphic.org/index.html

Gonzalez, O. (1999). Building vocabulary: Dictionary consultation and the ESL student. *Journal of Adolescent & Adult Literacy* 43 (3),264–270.

Harris, T., & Hodges, R. (Eds.). (1995). *The literacy dictionary: The vocabulary of reading and writing.* Newark, DE: International Reading Association.

Herman, W. (1979). Reading in social studies: Needed research. *Journal of Social Studies Research*, 3(2).

Holbrook, S. (2003). *Wildmen, Wobblies and Whistle Punks.* Corvallis, OR: Oregon State University Press.

Hopkins, G. & Bean, T. (1998/99). Vocabulary learning with the verbal-visual word association strategy in a Native American community. *Journal of Adolescent and Adult Literacy* 42(4), 274–281.

Hunt, I. (1964). *Across five aprils.* Chicago: Follett.

Hyerle, D. (1996). *Visual tools for constructing knowledge.* Alexandria, VA: Association for Supervision and Curriculum Development.

Johnson, D., & Pearson, P.D. (1984). *Teaching reading vocabulary.* NY: Holt, Rinehart and Winston.

Kesey, K. (1963). *Sometimes a Great Notion.* New York, NY: Penguin Press.

Kurth, R. (1980). Building a conceptual base for vocabulary. *Reading Psychology, v.1.*, 115–120.

Larkin , M. (1997). T-Tac at ODU. *The Collaborator*, 5 (2), Spring . Retrieved August 6, 2006, from http: / / www.ttac.odu.edu / articles / graphic.html

Macon, J., Bewell, D., & Vogt, M. (1991). *Responses to literature.* Newark, DE: International Reading Association.

McClain, A. (1987). Improving lectures: Challenge both sides of the brain. *Journal of Optometric Education 13*(1), 18–20.

Ogle, D. (1986). K-W-L: A teaching model that develops active reading of expository text. *Reading Teacher*, 39. 564–570.

Olson, J., & Platt, J. (1996). *Teaching children and adolescents with special needs.* Englewood Cliff, NJ: Merrill.

Ruddell, M. (1993). *Teaching content reading and writing.* Boston: Allyn & Bacon.

Rupley,H., Logan, J. & Nichols, W. (l999). Vocabulary instruction in a balanced reading program. *The Reading Teacher, 52*(4), 336–346.

Ryder, R. & Graves, M. (1998). Reading and learning in content areas. Second edition. Columbus, OH: Merrill.

Santa, C. (1988). *Content reading including study systems: Reading, writing and studying across the curriculum.* Dubuque, Iowa: Kendall/Hunt.

Schwartz, R., & Raphael, T. (1985). Concept of definition: A key to improving students' vocabulary. *The Reading Teacher, 39*, 198–204.

Solutions, N. D. (1999). Discovery's school puzzlemaker. Retrieved August 6, 2006, from http://puzzlemaker.schooldiscovery.com

Taylor, W. (1953). Cloze procedures: A new tool for measuring readability. *Journalism Quarterly*, 30, 414–438.

Terry, J. (2006, March 19). Woodsmen used lingo that is nearly lost. *Oregonian*. D6.

Tonjes, M., & Zintz, M. (1992). *Teaching reading /thinking /study skills in content classrooms.* Dubuque, IA: W.C. Brown.

Tyler, V. (1986). *Scholastics A+ guide to a better vocabulary.* NY: Scholastic, Inc.

Vacca, R., & Vacca, J. (1989). *Content area reading.* Glenview, Illinois: Scott, Foreman.

Watson, J.D. *The double helix.* NY: New American Library.

Study Skill Strategies

Study without reflection is a waste of time; reflection without study is dangerous.
Confucius

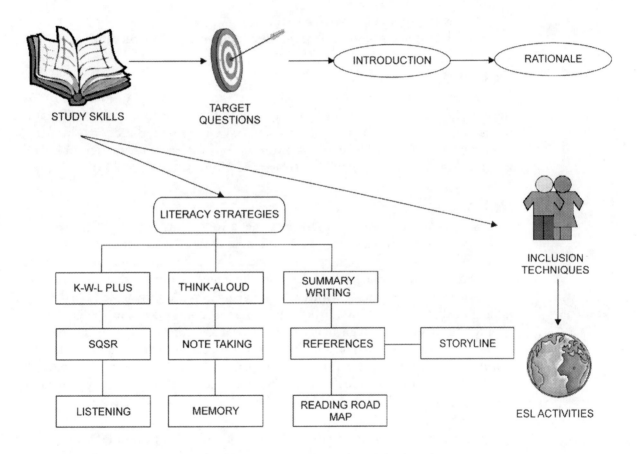

Target Questions

Consider the following questions before reading this chapter. Discuss these with a colleague. Continue writing notes and develop specific questions regarding study skills that you want to explore.

Target Questions

1. Define the phrase "learning how to learn."
2. Which strategies lend themselves best to helping to establish prior knowledge?
3. How do study skills empower students?
4. Which study skill described in this chapter best suits your content area?
5. Why should all teachers teach study skills?
6. What is the value of using a Think-Aloud?
7. What are power notes?
8. What is the value of summary writing?
9. How does current brain research affect planning for instruction?

Definition

The International Reading Association defines study skills as "a general term for those techniques and strategies that help a person read or listen for specific purposes with the intent to remember; commonly, following directions, locating, selecting, organizing and retaining information, interpreting typographic and graphic aids, and reading flexibly" (Harris & Hodges, 1995, p. 245).

Rationale

Anders & Guzzetti (1996)

"Studying is an intentional act. Students need to establish goals for studying as much as they need to have reasons for reading" (Vacca & Vacca, 1999, p. 333). Teachers cannot make assumptions regarding whether students know how to learn. Some of your students will have independent reading and study skills and will associate new learning with past knowledge, while others will need to be guided or directly told how to study and to build upon prior knowledge. In this chapter, we'll work through many techniques and strategies that guide students in setting a purpose, tapping into their background knowledge and organizing information that helps them use it. Students need to discover study strategies that best suit their individual needs. These should be skills that they can carry into adulthood. Graham and Robinson (1984) state:

> Learning how to learn on their own is more important to students than anything else we can teach them. Teaching study skills means showing students how to solve their problems—which has more to do with how they are taught than what they are taught. After all, the important differences between teachers have to do with *how* they teach, not *what* they teach.... Teachers in every classroom can provide opportunities for using study skills and strategies. The ultimate goal should be the independent use of such strategies by learners as they attempt to unlock the ideas of authors and produce ideas of their own (p. 3).

TEACHER TALK ————————————————————————————
There are too many students who truly believe that the best preparation in studying for an exam is to read the material three times. How do I get students beyond that level?

Most teachers would prefer to teach only the content of their own specialty areas. However, students cannot learn effectively or efficiently without study skills. We would suggest that teachers need to teach study skills specialized to their content areas. They should consider teaching study skills before, during, and after the teaching of content. For example, a geography teacher may want to teach map reading skills before embarking upon reading resource materials that include many maps.

Students need specialized study skills for each content area.

It takes much time, practice and exposure to many study skills before a student can establish a personal study system. Some students will need much direction before they launch out on their own. From testimony given by a few graduate students, we have heard soulful stories of the pain some felt because they knew they had few strategies if any for studying and, consequently, approached reviews and tests with anxiety and frustration. Usually in the context of these stories, one teacher has made a difference in the academic lives of these students because of the direction she provided in developing study skill habits.

Each content area teacher needs to introduce and model specific study skill strategies.

Students need to realize that a personal study system needs to be flexible and that different study skills will be applied to different learning situations. Only when a variety of study strategies are taught to students can they then discover that for them some work better than others from one content area to another. Thus, every content teacher should feel responsible to establish a variety of study skill strategies that they have found work well in their particular curricular area.

When the content instruction is presented primarily through the medium of a textbook, the content teacher provides her students with helpful skills by reviewing the textbook for the following information:
1. What study skills are necessary for grasping the content?
2. What level of proficiency is necessary for each skill?
3. Which skills are taught in the material itself?
4. Which skills are not taught adequately by the material, yet are necessary in using the textbook to fullest advantage in content study?

In addition to which study skills to use and when to use them, the classroom teacher must also recognize and deal with the current findings regarding the brain and how it works. The Association for Supervision and Curriculum Development (ASCD) has suggested that there are four research findings that affect student learning. First, teachers need to use a variety of strategies to meet the various learning styles of the students. This includes helping students to organize information. All of the strategies in this chapter include organizational skills that allow students to store information in the brain in a variety of ways.

Strategies that support brain research

Second, the brain needs immediate feedback which suggests that teachers need to make certain that students are aware of their own progress. How might a teacher give students immediate feedback? One way would be to have students correct their own work and to learn from their mistakes. Another suggestion is to use individual, small whiteboards on which students write answers to questions that arise during discussions. For example, what is the formula for finding a hypotenuse—students each write the formula on their whiteboard, hold it up and the teacher can make sure all have the correct answer. Likewise, in a chemistry classroom molecular bonds could be drawn by the students and immediate feedback given. In the language arts or foreign language classrooms, students could give tenses, verb-subject agreements, etc. on their whiteboards. Immediate feedback also means that it is important for the teacher to be timely in correcting and returning papers.

Third, the brain reacts best when learning includes active engagement of the students. Using manipulatives in the various content classrooms will help students to be actively engaged, stay on task and to store the information using a variety of learning modalities—vision, hearing, tactile and kinesthetic processing. Fourth, the brain reacts best under safe learning conditions. A student must feel safe to learn.

Brain Research Findings

Amongst the brain research findings there are a variety of theories that affect classroom teaching. Young children as well as young adults need to explore patterns and in the content area, we can reinforce patterning by implementing graphic organizers, patterns for vocabulary building such as root words and affixes. Emotions and attitudes are closely linked to the brain's normal circuits—thus, the importance of classroom environment being a safe place where students are comfortable taking risks. The hemisphericity theory has suggested that learning styles and preferences to dominance of the left or right side of the brain are related to teaching strategies and activities.

Another interpretation of brain research is based on Howard Gardner's (1991) theory of multiple intelligences. The classroom teacher should plan an array of learning opportunities. This reinforces the suggestion in the previous paragraph that teachers need to use a variety of strategies. Gerald Edelman (1992) suggests students need to be surrounded with a variety of instructional opportunities so they will make connections for learning.

In addition to the implications for teaching suggested earlier, Caine & Caine (1990) include the following:
❑ Arouse the mind's search for meaning.
❑ Present information so the learner can identify patterns and connect to previous experiences.
❑ Avoid isolating information from its context.
❑ Encourage students to reflect and review their learning.
❑ Create real world experiences.

As educators, we know that reading words three times does not necessarily mean comprehension has occurred, let alone the idea of critically thinking about the information or even application of the information. Students must be curious about the reading, make connections and apply study strategies that nurture critical thinking. They must understand and be aware of how they cognitively process. This is called metacognition.

Literacy Strategies to Promote Study Skills

Metacognition

Metacognition is the ability to control one's own cognitive processing. For students to think about and control their learning, they need monitoring strategies, study strategies, and fix-up strategies before they read, while they read, and after they read. Too many students read at a frustrational level, where decoding is less than 90% accurate and comprehension falls below 50% accuracy.

Strategic readers need a variety of techniques to use when they realize they have not understood what they just read. Too often students try to read difficult information at too fast a pace and with an attitude that this should be easy to read. Students are often mistaken in this assumption. Readers finding material easy to read are usually reading at the independent level, where they understand 99% of the words and comprehend with at least 90% accuracy. Few textbooks lend themselves to an easy read by independent readers.

As subject area teachers we must alert students to the fact that content reading requires specialized skills, and we also need to teach and implement strategies that work as good models for processing print. Through this guidance, we are helping develop their reading at an instructional level, where they decode 95% of the words and comprehend at least 75% of the material read.

Most textbooks will be written at an instructional level or the frustrational level for the average high school student. This means teachers must take some responsibility to equip students to read the assigned materials at an instructional level—meaning they need some instruction while reading. In other words, students will benefit by learning how to monitor and control their learning. A place for students to begin is with a metacognitive inventory (Miholic, 1994). See Figure 3.1. This inventory should help teachers identify "what their students know with respect to achieving higher levels of comprehension" (p. 85). From the results of the inventory, you can determine which students have strong study skills and those who will need further direction.

Since this inventory was developed to pinpoint students' understanding of their metacognitive processing, teachers would probably want to discuss their answers, rather than score them. This would help to heighten students' awareness of their need for monitoring strategies. An important area that addresses how students can make connections in their reading and strengthen their metacognitive awareness is that of applying their prior knowledge to the immediate material to be read.

Role of Prior Knowledge

Some students have background knowledge about a given topic and some have more reading skills than others. These factors make up students' prior knowledge, knowledge that stems from previous experience and determines students' readiness to read. To see how prior knowledge influences your reading, let's try an experiment. We will give you a selection to read without any discussion, which would normally activate prior knowledge. The following passage is a topic that every American student encounters a number of times throughout her school career.

*May (1990)
Baker & Brown
(1994)*

*Metacognition is the "awareness and knowledge of one's mental processes such that one can monitor, regulate, and direct them to a desired end"
Harris & Hodges
(1995, p. 153)*

*Anderson &
Armbruster
(1984)*

Prior knowledge refers to previous experience.

FIGURE 3.1. METACOGNITIVE READING AWARENESS INVENTORY

1. What do you do if you encounter a word and you don't know what it means?
   + a. Use the words around it to figure it out.
   + b. Use an outside source, such as a dictionary or expert.
   + c. Temporarily ignore it and wait for clarification.
   − d. Sound it out.

2. What do you do if you don't know what an entire sentence means?
   + a. Read it again.
   − b. Sound out all the difficult words.
   + c. Think about the other sentences in the paragraph.
   − d. Disregard it completely.

3. If you are reading science or social studies material, what would you do to remember the important information you've read?
   − a. Skip parts you don't understand.
   + b. Ask yourself questions about the important ideas.
   + c. Realize you need to remember one point rather than another.
   + d. Relate it to something you already know.

4. Before you start to read, what kind of plans do you make to help you read better?
   − a. No specific plan is needed; just start reading toward completion of the assignment.
   + b. Think about what you know about the subject.
   + c. Think about why you are reading.
   − d. Make sure the entire reading can be finished in as short a period of time as possible.

5. Why would you go back and read an entire passage over again?
   + a. You didn't understand it.
   − b. To clarify a specific or supporting idea.
   + c. It seemed important to remember.
   + d. To underline or summarize for study.

6. Knowing that you don't understand a particular sentence while reading involves understanding that
   + a. the reader may not have developed adequate links or associations for new words or concepts introduced in the sentence.
   + b. the writer may not have conveyed the ideas clearly.
   + c. two sentences may purposely contradict each other.
   − d. finding meaning for the sentence needlessly slows down the reader.

7. As you read a textbook, which of these do you do?
   + a. Adjust your pace depending on the difficulty of the material.
   − b. Generally read at a constant, steady pace.
   − c. Skip the parts you don't understand.
   + d. Continually make predictions about what you are reading.

8. While you read, which of these are important?
   + a. Know when you know and when you don't know key ideas.
   + b. Know what it is that you know in relation to what is being read.
   − c. Know that confusing text is common and usually can be ignored.
   + d. Know that different strategies can be used to aid understanding.

9. When you come across a part of the text that is confusing, what do you do?
   + a. Keep on reading until the text is clarified.
   + b. Read ahead and then look back if the text is still unclear.
   − c. Skip those sections completely; they are usually not important.
   + d. Check to see if the ideas expressed are consistent with one another.

10. Which sentences are the most important in the chapter?
    − a. Almost all of the sentences are important; otherwise, they wouldn't be there.
    + b. The sentences that contain the important details or facts.
    + c. The sentences that are directly related to the main idea.
    − d. The ones that contain the most details.

For scoring purposes, "correct" responses are marked with a (+); ambiguous or "incorrect" responses are marked with a (−). Students should be asked to select the "most correct" strategies for each item; more than one correct response is possible for each one. If photocopying for use with a class, be sure to cover the (+) and (−) row.

With Hocked Gems
Financing Him
Our hero bravely defied
all scornful laughter
that tried to deceive his scheme.
An egg, not a table typify
unexplored planet.
Now three sturdy sisters sought proof
forging sometimes through calm vastness
Yet, more often over turbulent peaks and valleys
Days became weeks as many doubters spread fearful
rumors about the edge.
At last, welcome winged creatures appeared
signifying momentous success.
Dooling & Lachman, 1972, p. 216-222.

How do you interpret the selection? Would it make a difference if we now establish prior knowledge by posing several questions for discussion and then asking you to read the passage again? For discussion and the opportunity to establish prior knowledge, examine the following questions:

1. Who was Christopher Columbus?
2. What was his mission?
3. How was the mission financed?
4. How many ships did he take on his mission?
5. What else do you know about Columbus?
6. What is symbolism? Metaphor? Simile? Where do they appear in the passage?

Go back and re-read the passage. Does it now make sense? Can you interpret it? Can you put it into perspective? This demonstration empowers students to understand the value and need to tie their prior knowledge to the topic they are about to read or study.

The following strategies will show you how to incorporate activities that tap into or build students' background knowledge.

As classroom teachers it is our responsibility to prepare students for their upcoming learning, whether it's reading a text selection, preparing for a lab, or viewing a videotape, etc. Many of the activities that help students in this preparation are discussed throughout this text:

❏ Graphic organizers to connect the selection to prior knowledge. (Chapter 2)
❏ Assignments that clarify new or specialized vocabulary. (Chapter 2)
❏ Discussion of the selection. (Chapter 5)
❏ Resources available to meet the needs of all students—real-world literacy and library books at all reading levels. (Chapters 7 & 9)
❏ Self-assessment activities that help students build upon their abilities and strengthen their areas of need. (Chapter 8)

Readers need to rely on prior knowledge before reading, during reading, and after reading. Before reading, readers should access what is already known on the topic and determine the text structure, deciding if the material is narrative or expository.

Ogle (1986)

During reading, readers use prior knowledge to make inferences, read critically, monitor comprehension, interact with the author to construct meaning and to identify the relationships of ideas.

After reading, readers use prior knowledge to summarize; to relate the new information to existing knowledge; and to evaluate, modify, reconstruct and build schemata. We believe schemata are the structures that represent the generic concepts stored in an individual's memory. Schema theory explains how these structures are formed and relate to one another as an individual develops knowledge. A reader develops schemata through experiences. If a reader has limited experience with a given topic, he or she will have limited schemata with which to build comprehension. A reader's background, or prior knowledge, greatly influences the comprehension he or she is able to construct.

Discuss the role of schema theory in learning.

We have learned that comprehension improves when students make predictions. Making predictions keeps students on task by critically relating new information with their prior knowledge. A popular strategy used by many teachers is the K-W-L PLUS.

K-W-L Plus

TABLE 1

INSTRUCTIONAL SUMMARY OF K-W-L PLUS

Literacy Strategy	K-W-L Plus
Primary Focus	Activate prior knowledge
Learning Principles	❑ Background Knowledge ❑ Talk Time ❑ Thought-demanding Activities
When to Use	Before reading
Goals: National or State Literacy Standards	❑ Connect reading selections to other texts, experiences, issues and events ❑ Draw connections and explain relationships between reading selections and other texts, experiences, issues and events
Material	Butcher paper divided into three columns
Time	30 minutes

Carr & Ogle (1987)

In this exercise students connect what is known to what is yet to be learned. Through a series of questions, the students brainstorm and anticipate what they'll learn from the unit or lesson. After they have indicated what they have learned, they are directed to map their findings, categorizing information as a prelude for creating summaries or writing extended papers. They, thereby, learn how to organize and reorganize information for clearer understanding.

Procedure. Have students complete a K-W-L PLUS as shown in Figure 3.2. In the section *What I Know,* have students brainstorm all they know about a given topic and list this information in the correct space. You will probably want to use the chalkboard or an overhead. In one classroom, we observed students preparing for a major unit on the solar system by filling in the appropriate sections of the K-W-L PLUS on a huge sheet of butcher paper stretched from one end of the back wall of the classroom to the other end.

In the space *What I Want to Learn,* students generate a list of their questions regarding the topic. Students then select which questions they want to research or simply read about if a textbook is used. The teacher may want to go back to *What I Know* and put a mark by any topics or statements that are questionable. Ask students to consider these in their selection. As students read and research their topics, they can add more questions to the *What I Want to Learn* section. Once the research is completed, have the students list what they learned by answering their previous questions and also any additional information that they learned.

After students have filled in all sections of the K-W-L *PLUS,* encourage them to categorize the content in the *What I Learned* section and then map it accordingly. In the following *K-W-L PLUS* chart, Figure 3.2, we have provided a model of a class discussion on one aspect of the solar system, the exploration of Mars.

After students complete their K-W-L PLUS charts, they can move on to mapping their findings from the third column. The following Figure 3.3 shows what this might look like.

After students have completed their maps, they are then ready to draft a summary of what they have learned or prepare a paper using the categories as a guide for structuring its layout. The K-W-L PLUS lends itself well to small group activities, facilitating peer interaction and, ultimately, increasing comprehension of the content studied. After seeing this level of discussion and interchange, can there be any doubt that students are ready to complete related projects on the subject? In the following Your Turn, design a K-W-L PLUS activity for a class you are teaching.

Using a K-W-L PLUS activity students connect what is known to what is yet to be learned.

FIGURE 3.2.   K-W-L PLUS

K-What I Know	W-What I Want to Learn	L-What I learned
❑ Mars is a planet.	❑ Why is NASA exploring Mars?	❑ NASA's Discovery Program of the solar system: 30 Years of data about Mars.
❑ cold	❑ How did the microrover get to Mars?	❑ Delta Rocket carried Pathfinder lander with Sojourner rover within.
❑ old	❑ How does Sojourner get information?	❑ Probe: Alpha X-ray Spectrometer gathers information.
❑ maybe has aliens	❑ How does Sojourner get around?	❑ Solar-generated energy fuels Sojourner.
❑ NASA interested	❑ What does the Mars landscape look like?	❑ Rocks and craters cover Mars.
❑ robot explorer	❑ Was there life on Mars?	❑ Martian meteorite, ALH 84001, may hold key to evidence of Martian life.

FIGURE 3.3.   SOLAR SYSTEM: EXPLORATION OF MARS

Notes

Your Turn

Name _____ Date _____ Subject Area _____

Directions: Design a K-W-L PLUS model to introduce this strategy to your students.

K-What I Know	W-What I Want to Know	L-What I Have Learned

Create a map from the *What I Have Learned* section of this chart:

Think-Alouds

TABLE 2

INSTRUCTIONAL SUMMARY OF THINK-ALOUDS

Literacy Strategy	Think-Alouds
Primary Focus	❑ Activate prior knowledge ❑ Understanding of the reading process ❑ Comprehension
Learning Principles	❑ Background Knowledge ❑ Metacognitive Experience
When to Use	Before reading and during reading
Goals: National or State Literacy Standards	❑ Connect reading selections to other texts, experiences, issues and events ❑ Draw connections and explain relationships between reading selections and other texts, experiences, issues and events ❑ Practice fluency to increase comprehension
Materials	Text for modeling and role-playing good reading
Time	30 Minutes

One question that many of our graduate students frequently ask is, "How do I even get students to open the textbook?" One strategy we advise early in the term is to conduct a think-aloud with a textbook. This activity "makes thinking public" by demonstrating to students how you tackle reading. You model your thinking while reading aloud a piece of content text. You demonstrate how you read, your stops and starts, the questions you raise, your skimming and scanning activity, and your puzzling over ambiguous language or inconsiderate text that hinders meaning. It is a simple but powerful technique that shows students quickly and efficiently how proficient readers work at getting meaning from text. Furthermore, there is evidence that think-alouds improve comprehension.

Davey (1983)

Procedure. Select a piece of text. We frequently take an expository piece of writing that is of high interest initially. Then we switch to a typical textbook selection. After students get a handle on the process, the textbook piece does not seem to be much of a hindrance. Read your selection over and track mentally how you are thinking about this text. Make a transparency of the text you are going to use and jot down the questions and comments you make to yourself as you read it. Then use this to model for your students how your thinking evolved while reading.

Modeling live the how of reading.

Role-play for students how you actively think your way through a piece of text. Show students that as you read, your thoughts are blazing away like the fingers on a computer keyboard—fast, furious, slow, labored—and not always going where you want them to go. Use an overhead machine so that they can read along. After you have gone through this exercise, ask students to try a few paragraphs on their own and jot down their thoughts. Have them share these with a peer. After students get comfortable with the process, you may want to role-play this activity with a pair of students. Each could take a paragraph and go back and forth between their reading and their thinking to further demonstrate the think-aloud strategy to their peers. See Figure 3.4 for an example of a think-aloud.

A chart can be made to show students typical questions that proficient readers use while reading:

Encourage students to role-play their thinking while reading.

❑ What is this going to be about?
❑ Do I know anything about this already?
❑ Do I know what this means in this context?
❑ Can I predict where this is going?

By now you have the idea. You've shown students such mental gymnastics as identifying the main idea; testing the reading against your own experience; making some hypotheses about the tone of the piece, and personalizing the reading. Have students contrast what they do when they read successfully with what they do when

FIGURE 3.4.   EXAMPLE OF A SOCIAL STUDIES THINK-ALOUD LESSON

READ	THINK ALOUD
"An 1849 diary described the burial cloths of a mother and her infant on the desert.	❑ What is this reading going to be about?
"...in this weird, long spot on God's footstool away apparently from everywhere and everybody. The bodies were wrapped together in a bed comforter and wound, quite mummified with a few yards of string that we made by tying together torn strips of a cotton dress skirt." (Catherine Haun, 1949 in *Women's Voices from the Oregon Trail*)	❑ It seems to be about hardships on a journey. ❑ One of the hardships seems to be about how the dead were handled while on this trip. ❑ Do I know anything about this already? It seems to be about a tremendous undertaking like the Oregon Trail. I already studied this in the 6th grade, although I don't remember people writing about this.
"Sanitation on the trail was even worse than it had been on the farm. Water supplies and cooking mixed with milling animals and their waste. As on the farm, the emigrants used common drinking cups. Especially in heavy migration years, crowding on the trail quickly polluted springs and shallow drinking holes along the way. Water sources became perfect breeding grounds for infectious disease—typhoid, tuberculosis, malaria, dysentery, pneumonia, measles, smallpox, yellow fever, and worst of all—cholera."	❑ Was there anything that the people liked when they were on this trail? ❑ I would like to visit one of the areas this writer talks about. I wonder if I could track down these places?

they get stuck with their reading. From this personal testimony, you are then in a better position to suggest other strategies students can use to construct meaning.

TEACHER TALK

I have always defined myself as a "slow" reader. Though I was always placed in advanced reading and writing classes and did well, I always hated in-class reading assignments or reading tests because they took me so long to complete. As the rest of the class flipped through the pages, I seemed to struggle behind. I couldn't just see the words and understand them. I needed to hear the words in my head and think about them. As I read I asked myself questions. I, in a sense, 'monitored' as I read, often repeating sentences or even paragraphs to be sure I understood.

I enjoy thinking of myself as a strategic reader. I still realize that I am a slow reader. But a slow reader does not necessarily mean a poor reader.

In a recent study Wade, Buxton and Kelly (1999) used the strategy, read-alouds, to examine reader-text interest. Too often students are assigned text readings that are not interesting and thus are not motivated to complete the assignment. Read-aloud characteristics related to interest mentioned most often by the participants of the study were "importance/value, unexpectedness, readers' connections, imagery/descriptive language, and author's connections" (Wade et al., 1999, p. 202). Humor and voice were also mentioned. "Text characteristics that were most negatively associated with interest involved problems related to comprehension such as lack of adequate explanation/background information, difficult vocabulary; and lack of coherence, as well as lack of credibility" (Wade et al., 1999, p. 202). As a teacher, you might want to have students analyze your text using the read-aloud strategy and to think about how you can support the text with interesting topics. This information would also give you insights regarding the critical reading skills that your students do or do not have while reading in your content area.

Cathy Collins Block and Susan E. Israel (2004) suggest that to make think-alouds more effective the teacher needs to consider twelve thought processes that a student should apply while reading.

1. Get an overview of the reading by thinking about the purpose and main ideas presented.
2. Determine what is the most important information.
3. Connect the most important information to the big idea that the author is presenting.
4. Activate prior knowledge.
5. The reader puts himself in the book and responds as if the reader is actually there.
6. As one reads, revise prior knowledge and make predictions.
7. Recognize the author's writing style by the depth of vocabulary introduced, the complexity of sentences, the length of paragraphs, the frequency with which big ideas are presented, and how sentences and paragraphs are connected.
8. Demonstrate the thought processing used to understand any new vocabulary.
9. Ask questions during the reading process.
10. Be aware of voice—the flavor of the reading.
11. Apply new knowledge to reader's life.
12. Be able to transfer knowledge gained in one reading to another reading.

We are very aware of the importance of electronic data gathering. Because the printed text think-aloud strategy has been effective in the past, students should apply the same technique to online text (Kymes, 2005). To increase student confidence in using online information they need instruction on how to evaluate and manipulate the information. Educators need to direct students in a way that students themselves question the accuracy and trustworthiness of online information. Participating in online think-alouds includes awareness of purpose, skimming or scanning text to determine relevance, making associations using prior knowledge, discovering new meanings and evaluating text structure and quality. Teachers can listen to students voice their thoughts as they read online text. Through the implementation of the think-aloud strategy to online text students can be self-reflective and critical thinkers. This active engagement and reflection of what is read reinforces what has been presented on recent brain research earlier in this chapter.

Strategic readers have a plan.

Before we move on to another strategy, let's discuss what good, strategic readers do when they read. First, they think about what they already know about the subject, set a purpose for reading and focus their attention on the reading selection. Next, they monitor their comprehension automatically. They use a "fix-up strategy" when they do not understand what they are reading. Another strategy that is important for students is that of summary writing. Middle school and high school teachers cannot assume that elementary level students have learned how to write a good summary. It is important for students to reflect and review information they have learned in readings or from a verbal presentation.

TABLE 3

SUMMARY WRITING

INSTRUCTIONAL SUMMARY OF SUMMARY WRITING

Literacy Strategy	Summary Writing
Primary Focus	❑ Review pertinent information
	❑ Identify main idea
	❑ Identify supporting details
Learning Principles	❑ Active engagement
	❑ Ability to condense information
When to Use	❑ After new information has been learned verbally or written
Goals: National or State Literacy Standards	❑ Become familiar with a written language structure
Materials	❑ Summary writing guide
Time	❑ 40 minutes

Make it a habit to have students summarize what they have learned. Brain research reinforces the need for reflection and review (Caine & Caine, 1990). It is a good check for the teacher to be aware of which students understand and just how well they can articulate the information. "The ability to summarize information is one of the most important critical thinking skills you can develop. Taking large quantities of information, understanding what that information means, and condensing it into a shorter version of the original allows you to have important information on hand for easy reference without having to memorize long passages or complex statistics" (Wehmeyer, Wisc-Online, 2006). According to the University of Victoria's Writer's Guide (2006), writing summaries will give the student practice in close, attentive reading, strengthen the student's understanding of the structure of writing—how a writer organizes, and develop the student's sense of what is important, and ability to distinguish between key points.

Caine & Caine, 1990

As a classroom teacher you may want to first ask students to summarize information that they have read. After this is mastered, they could then summarize verbal information such as a lecture, video/DVD, or other source material. Once students have the opportunity to write summaries the teacher can then ask them to verbally summarize information. Remember that the brain research discussed earlier in this chapter suggests that students need a variety of ways to express themselves whether it be written, verbal, drawn, or organized into graphic organizers.

Summary Writing Guide

The following guide helps students to write a summary. The teacher might consider giving this guide to students before the topic or new information is to be disseminated. This gives students an opportunity to "take notes" during class, to have the information organized and ready to be condensed into a summary of information. The biggest problem is for the student to decide what to include and what to leave out!

One way to improve summary writing might be the implementation of peer evaluations. If a student can evaluate another's summary then his/her writing of summaries will become more thoughtful. Figure 3.6 is an example that will be valuable to help students in the summary writing process.

Another creative way to improve summary writing skills might be to use what Blitz and Shelton (2004) have suggested—note-passing. Since all students love to pass notes in class, this strategy positively reinforces this typically questionable behavior! A variation of their idea might be to have pairs of students read a certain number of paragraphs or pages then using a single sheet of paper and one pencil, write back and forth to each other regarding the thesis statement and supporting details—"have a silent conversation about the reading." This could also be done at stopping points during an oral presentation. Another strategy that models these behaviors and guides students through a simulation that imitates the actions of many good readers is SQ3R.

FIGURE 3.5.   SUMMARY WRITING GUIDE

Procedure:

Draw a map or graphic organizer of the main idea and major details. To do this you need to identify key sentences—thesis statements and topic sentences. This will be easier if you underline these as you read. This is more difficult to determine when verbal information is presented.

Look for the following tasks (Cunningham and Moore, 1986) that will help the reader to determine **main idea:**

Gist: A summary of the explicit contents of a passage achieved by creating generalized statements that subsume specific information and then deleting that specific information. "Locoweed is poisonous to horses."

Interpretation: A summary of the possible or probably implicit contents of a passage. "Horses don't always know what is good for them."

Key Word: A word or term labeling the most important single idea in the passage, "horses."

Topic: A phrase labeling the subject of a passage without revealing specific content from the passage. "What happens when horses eat locoweed?"

Topic sentence/Thesis sentence: The single sentence in a paragraph or passage which tells most completely what the paragraph or passage as a whole states or is about. "Some horses are said to become loco or insane from eating locoweed."

Main Idea Task by James W. Cunningham and David W. Moore, from *Teaching Main Idea Comprehension*, James F. Bauman, editor. Reprinted by permission of International Reading Association

Read for the author's own summaries at the beginning or end of a passage. Or, listen for the speaker to summarize the information at the end of a presentation.

Finally, formulate in your own words, major points that you have read or heard. Do not interpret what is written or said; instead, report what has been written or presented. Use a format that includes an introduction, body and conclusion.

Hints:
- ❑ Highlight key sentences, phrases or words.
- ❑ Find the definition of any words you do not understand.
- ❑ Take notes or use post-it notes to remember key sentences, phrases or words.
- ❑ While reading, cross out superfluous information and underline pertinent sentences, phrases and words.
- ❑ The summary should be 15-20 percent of the original.
- ❑ Review the summary as compared to the original for accuracy.

FIGURE 3.6.   PEER EVALUATION OF A SUMMARY

Read the summary carefully and answer the following questions:

1. What do you like best about your reader's summary? Why?
2. Is it clear what is being summarized?
3. Is the thesis or the original reading or presentation clear in the summary?
4. Did your reader miss any key points?
5. Did your reader include unimportant information or personal reactions?
6. Were you lost in following the summary? How might that be improved?

SQ3R

TABLE 4

INSTRUCTIONAL SUMMARY OF SQ3R

Literacy Strategy	SQ3R
Primary Focus	❑ Activate prior knowledge ❑ Survey the material to be read ❑ Comprehension
Learning Principles	❑ Thought–demanding Activities ❑ Active Involvement in Gaining Meaning
When to Use	Before reading and during reading
Goals: National or State Literacy Standards	❑ Use a variety of reading strategies to increase comprehension ❑ Demonstrate literal, inferential and evaluative levels of comprehension
Materials	Text for modeling and role-playing
Time	30 Minutes

The SQ3R strategy is a study skill that allows students to independently learn the information they seek. However, we must remember that some students will always need direct instruction from the teacher rather than being able to apply the SQ3R independently.

Robinson (1946)

Procedure. Students need to learn the five basic steps until they can be applied automatically.

Survey the selection:

1. Study the visual aids.
2. Study the organization and presentation of the material.

Questions established about the selection:

1. Convert the chapter title into a question.
2. Convert the subheadings into questions.

Read, Recite and Review:

1. <u>Read</u> the entire selection to answer the established questions.
2. <u>Recite</u> the answers to the questions.
3. <u>Review</u> the material to verify if the answers are correct.

The key to automaticity in using SQ3R is that students are expected to continually apply this strategy in a selective and flexible manner. However, as we stated earlier, some students will need the direct instruction and modeling of this strategy each time they approach a reading selection that lends itself to SQ3R. Many students choose to adapt the SQ3R to fit their individual needs.

STUDENT TALK

As a college student looking back on my high school classes, I wish just one of my teachers would have told me about SQ3R. It seems so simple; yet, so helpful.

A variation of the SQ3R strategy is the SQRC, State, Question, Read, and Conclude as developed by Satka (1998/1999). This strategy focuses on higher level thinking skills and is based on a combination of the Directed Reading Activity, the Reading-Thinking Guide and SQ3R. "SQRC is a student-centered instructional approach, based on constructivism, which focuses on the central role of learners in creating or constructing new knowledge" (Satka, 1998/1999, p. 265). In SQRC the teacher introduces the topic and new vocabulary that is key to comprehending the topic. Next students write a position statement that is for or against the topic. During reading students read to find literal and inferential information that supports their position. The class is then divided into the position groups and student judges are appointed. The judges come to a decision regarding the strongest argument that was presented. We highly recommend this strategy when reading about controversial topics and for encouraging students to take a position and at the same time to be able to support their opinion. Too often students are opinionated without reason!

A second variation of SQ3R is Preview-Predict-Confirm (Yopp & Yopp, 2004). The first step is to preview. The teacher shows small groups of students pictures with the understanding that they will use this information in the next phase. Next, student groups predict a list of words that might be found in the reading "related" to the pictures. They, then, arrange the words into categories (like a word sort, Chapter 2 Vocabulary). Each group of students selects a word they think everyone will have and one that will be unique. These words are discussed as a class. Finally, students read the selection to confirm their predictions. This strategy gets students actively engaged and motivated and reinforces brain research in the classroom. See also, the Storyline strategy in this chapter.

Note Taking

TABLE 5

INSTRUCTIONAL SUMMARY OF NOTE TAKING	
Literacy Strategy	Note Taking
Primary Focus	❑ Framed Outline ❑ Two and Three Column Notes ❑ Semantic Feature Analysis ❑ Power Notes
Learning Principles	❑ Thought-demanding Activities ❑ Metacognitive Experience ❑ Organizing Information
When to Use	During reading and after reading
Goals: National or State Literacy Standards	❑ Use a variety of reading strategies to increase comprehension ❑ Read for information ❑ Communicate knowledge of the topic, including relevant examples, facts, and details
Materials	Variety of note taking examples
Time	30-60 Minutes

It is important for each content area teacher to give students strategies for taking notes in their particular curricular area. Note taking involves many skills such as the ability to identify the main idea, understanding of cues that signal important ideas, organization of ideas, categorization, listening, spelling, handwriting, and creating abbreviations that aid recall. Students require guidance in learning and implementing these.

Help students develop a note taking system that works for them.

A number of note taking techniques follow that can be used in your classroom. These guide students by providing a structure that enables them to use the skills mentioned previously. We would encourage you to show students various methods of taking notes, then let them choose which method works best for them. In our many visits to secondary classrooms, we have seen a number of 11th and 12th grade students receiving verbatim notes to copy from a transparency as the teacher lectures about a topic. Many of these students are headed for college in a few short years. Who will give them their notes then?

Anderson & Armbruster (1991)

I was a dropout at 16. When a counselor talked me into coming in from the cold reality of the streets and found me a place in a GED program, among the many things I learned in that caring environment was how to take notes. I couldn't believe it! Here was a way to make sense out of all that information coming at me class after class. Now, as a Spanish teacher, one of the first things I work on with my students is note taking skills. I show them my note taking from my university classes and we talk about what methods work best and check up on how we're using note taking on a regular basis.

Note Taking Framed Outlines

Use framed outlines when students need much direction.

These outlines provide guidance to students who need a lot of direction with subject matter, either because of its difficulty level or because of their inability to cull important ideas and details from text material. This framework structures the critical ideas so that the students can follow a lecture or an assigned reading, filling in the missing terms as they hear them or read about them. It provides maximum direction; however, as students become more familiar with identifying key ideas and supporting materials, they can switch to other methods of note taking.

Procedure. Teachers prepare a framed outline including the major ideas and details from a lecture they are planning to give or a reading that their students will be assigned. After explaining the framed outline, the teachers proceed to lecture on a given topic. Initially, teachers may want to have a transparency made of the framed outline. As the instructors lecture, they fill in the key terms. Once the students get the idea, they are held responsible for completing the framed outline themselves. If they are completing one that accompanies an assigned reading, the teacher would then review these in class.

For example, in the mathematics classroom one of our interns developed a note taking framework, presented in Figure 3.7. We also have added one in music history as an example from the fine arts. See Figure 3.8.

TEACHER TALK

Students should have a minute or two to familiarize themselves with the particular framed outline to be implemented. This will give them time to figure out what they should be expecting to learn from the assigned reading and to prepare themselves for that reading.

FIGURE 3.7.   MATHEMATICS NOTE TAKING FRAMEWORK

$\vec{a} \cdot \vec{b}$ = _____ where _____ is the angle when the vectors are tail to tail.

Cos 90° = _____ thus the dot product of _____ vectors is equal to _____ .

Cos 0° = _____ thus the dot product of _____ vectors in the _____ direction is equal to _____ .

Cos 180° = _____ thus the dot product of _____ vectors in the _____ direction is equal to _____ .

$$\vec{a} \cdot \vec{b} = \text{_____}$$
$$\vec{i} \cdot \vec{j} = \text{_____}$$
$$\vec{i} \cdot \vec{k} = \text{_____}$$
$$\vec{i} \cdot \vec{k} = \text{_____}$$
$$\vec{i} \cdot \vec{i} = \text{_____}$$
$$\vec{j} \cdot \vec{j} = \text{_____}$$
$$\vec{k} \cdot \vec{k} = \text{_____}$$

– > _____ $\vec{a} \cdot \vec{b}$ is _____ .

– > _____ $\vec{a} \cdot \vec{b}$ is _____ .

scalar projection –> $\vec{p}$ on $\vec{v}$ = $|\vec{p}|$ cos Θ = _____ =

vector projection –> $\vec{p}$ on $\vec{v}$ = _____

FIGURE 3.8. MUSIC FRAMED NOTE TAKING OUTLINE

1. Early Music
    a. 40,000 years ago music present.
    b. 10,000 years ago _____ from hollow bones.
    c. 1st century B.C., _____ .
    d. A.D., 1st century Romans—cymbals _____ .

2. Music and Myth
    a. Xingu men play sacred flutes—no_____ can view.
    b. Bull-roarers used by Native Americans to _____ .
    c. In Egyptian legend, the _____ beat on his belly and created_____ .
    d. The pan pipe created from_____ .

3. Voices of Instruments
    a. Nature: Woodwinds (oboe, flute, bassoon); e.g., Vivaldi's *Four Seasons*.
    b. War:_____ ; e.g., _____ .
    c. Misery: _____ ; e.g., Mozart's *Requiem*.
    d. Love: _____ ; e.g., _____ .

Source: *Musical Instruments: From flutes carved of bones, to lutes, to modern electric guitars.* (1993). (Accent on Language, Inc., Trans.) Scholastic.

Two-Column or Three-Column Notes

Pauk (1988)

We have found that our interns find the following note taking framework helpful for students. Prior to their note taking, students are asked to fold their notebook paper into halves or thirds lengthwise. The students then have either two columns or three equally sized columns for taking notes. Three-column notes are effective when students need to remember information through the use of examples. Figure 3.9 presents three-column notes for a social studies lesson.

Traditionally, two-column notes have been referred to as Cornell Notes (Pauk, 1974) in which students use the left side of a piece of paper for key words and the right for notes from reading or class discussions/lectures. Cornell Notes are particularly well suited for topics that organized with main ideas and details. Teachers will also refer to Cornell Notes as T-Notes. See Figure 3.10.

Students may need to use more than two columns. One that works well for history using the timeline as a focus for organizing information is the three-column example in Figure 3.11.

FIGURE 3.9. THREE-COLUMN NOTES: SOCIAL STUDIES

Main Idea	Detail	Example
Theodore Roosevelt	Railroad Legislation	Square Deal

FIGURE 3.10. T-NOTES, OR TWO-COLUMN NOTES

Main Idea	Details
Theodore Roosevelt	a. Railroad Legislation
	b.
	c.

FIGURE 3.11. HISTORY NOTE TAKING GUIDE

Person	Date	Event
King Henry VIII	1527	Henry VIII breaks with Church
Sir Francis Drake	1588	Spanish Armada
Oliver Cromwell	1648	Civil War
King Charles I	1649	Executed and Commonwealth established

What works well for a student taking notes in history?

A variation on the three-column notes is to use pictures for the example. See Figure 3.12.

When students reach a point where they are ready to be more independent with column notes it is a good idea to have them exchange notes in class and to analyze the variations fellow students have adapted, to discuss why one student took notes regarding a particular topic and others did not, and to see how other students used mnemonics such as color coding, underlining, use of pictures, etc. to highlight key points. Using the two column note format you might want to replace main idea/detail notes to opinion/proof (Santa, Havens & Maycumber, 1996). Using this format students develop and support arguments with evidence. They then use the evidence to develop persuasive paragraphs. See Figure 3.13.

FIGURE 3.12.   THREE-COLUMN NOTES: SOCIAL STUDIES

Main Idea	Details	Picture or Example
Theodore Roosevelt	Railroad Legislation	Square Deal

FIGURE 3.13.   OPINION/PROOF TWO-COLUMN NOTES

Pro or Con Opinion/Proof

Old growth forest should be protected.	❏ To protect the spotted-owl, an endangered species ❏ To prevent erosion ❏ To provide a natural habitat for animals, and ❏ To preserve an environment for future human enjoyment and use

A second variation on three-column notes is the Problem/Solution format (Santa, 1988) which is especially useful for math and science teachers. Students ask four basic questions. What is the problem, what are the effects, what are the causes, and what is the solution? Students then read the assigned reading to answer those questions using the Problem/Solution note taking format. See Figure 3.14.

FIGURE 3.14. PROBLEM/SOLUTION NOTE TAKING FOR BIOLOGY

Questions	Answers	Support
❑ What is the problem?	Crop soil erosion	Trenches cut into the land
❑ What are the effects?	Less crop production	Less crop production
❑ What are the causes?	Poor planning	No soil protection for conservation
❑ What are the solutions?	Conservation	Less rototilling

Adapted, Santa, 1988

Of course, all of the examples of column notes must be introduced and modeled for students during class time.

Note taking also can be done efficiently and succinctly using a Semantic Feature Analysis (Johnson & Pearson, 1984). The teacher selects a topic that has a number of critical terms and distinct features. List the key words down the side of the grid and list the key features across the top of the grid. Students are advised to use the key words on the chart as a guide and come up with descriptive features. After students complete the grid, they participate in a class discussion of the matrix that is often characterized by lively dissent as well as agreement. Again, through discussion students have the opportunity to learn from each other and firm up their understandings. A creative way to use the Semantic Feature Analysis is to have students use sticky notes to complete the grid. This can be done individually or in cooperative groups. See Figure 3.15.

Johnson &
Pearson (1984)

This exercise helps students to become concise and succinct. When modeled by the teacher, students begin to understand what information is important and what is superfluous. In the following Your Turn, develop a Semantic Feature Analysis chart for a topic in your content area.

Fill in the missing items. Check the World Wide Web using 'biome' as the keyword.

FIGURE 3.15. SEMANTIC FEATURE ANALYSIS

Biome	Temperature	Annual Rainfall	Animal Types
Desert		<10"	
Grassland	mild		Wildebeest, blesbok, eland
Forests— Temperate		30–60"	Deer, bears, cougars, wolves
Tropical	hot	60–90"	Monkeys, lions exotic birds
Tundra	cold	6–10"	
Taiga			Caribou, wolves, lemmings

When students compare their note taking system they become aware of other possibilities.

Teachers can help students become better note takers by teaching their students a system that works well in their specific content area. Try recording one of your lectures and then take notes on a transparency while you and your students listen to your presentation. Compare your notes to those of the students. Use a skeletal outline of your lecture in which students take very specific notes as demanded by the confines of the skeletal outline. Periodically, have students do a self-check of their notes. See Figure 3.16. Ask students to exchange their notes and compare note taking frameworks. Many times students simply need to be exposed to a variety of possibilities and to be able to select a combination which works best for them.

FIGURE 3.16. NOTE TAKING SELF-CHECK

Do your notes have: YES | NO

1. An organized format .... ___|___

2. Important ideas and details .... ___|___

3. Sequenced information .... ___|___

4. Underlined, starred, circled central ideas .... ___|___

5. A format easy to read and study .... ___|___

6. Abbreviations and phrases used as shortcuts .... ___|___

Your Turn

Name _____ Date _____ Subject Area _____

Design a Semantic Feature Analysis to use as a model in showing students how they can compare and contrast multiple items in a concrete and visual way.

Note Marking

It is important that students be given articles in which they can mark the most important information. Teachers might ask students to underline key phrases or to highlight them with a pen.

Procedure. Copy an article from your content area and ask students to mark the most important points made by the author. We recommend that the teacher make a transparency of the article and model the highlighting or underlining process several times until students develop an understanding of determining what is most important. Marking an article helps students to focus on key information. It stimulates thinking and learning by sifting out what is important. This sorting of concepts and the actual physical marking of the main points are ways to tell one's brain to remember. Of course, the material that is marked by students becomes material for a quick review before a quiz or a test.

Bragstad & Stumpf (1982)

As students mark an article, also encourage them to make notes in the margins. Students will need guided practice for note marking. Show them well-marked examples and discuss these. Why mark an article or book? The marking in itself helps students to focus their attention and concentration. It stimulates thinking and learning, enhances remembering and provides quick review. Students need to develop a personal code for their marks such as the following in Figure 3.17.

Why highlight text?

FIGURE 3.17.   NOTE MARKING SYSTEM

1. MAIN IDEA

2. MAJOR CONCEPTS

3. SIGNIFICANT DETAILS   A. _____ B. _____ C. _____

4. ITEMS IN A SERIES   1.   2.   3.

5. TRANSITION   (because)   (for this reason)

6. NEW VOCABULARY   Term and Definition

7. LONG IMPORTANT PASSAGE   {   }

It is important that students realize that before marking an article, it is important to first read the selection to get the big picture before making decisions as to what is important enough to mark. Too much marking is not much help. Students may also want to make notes in the margins such as important facts, impressions, questions, or major concepts. Power notes or outlining may be a strategy that is more appropriate for some students who do not find mapping, note taking, or note marking effective.

Power Notes

Power Notes (Santa, Havens & Maycumber, 1996) guide students in finding the main idea and the subordinate ideas. Unlike the typical outlining where one must follow a prescribed format, Power Notes are easier to use because students assign numbers to the main ideas and details. Main ideas are assigned Power 1 and details are assigned a Power 2, 3, or 4.

Procedure: We like to use sticky notes for this strategy. Students are assigned to find the main idea, and details 2, 3, or 4. Each is represented by a specific color of sticky note. Students write on their sticky note the information and come together in cooperative groups to "build the outline." Building the outline can be done by placing the sticky notes on the board or on butcher paper. Figure 3.18 gives an example for a music class.

FIGURE 3.18.   POWER NOTES

Power 1 Topic (Yellow sticky note)

JAZZ

Power 2 Kinds (Blue sticky note)

Easy Jazz
Traditional Jazz

Power 3 Musicians (Green sticky note)

Tom Grant
Louis Armstrong

An alternative to the use of sticky notes would be to have students make signs with the information for their assigned power and holding them, physically arrange themselves in order of the powers.

Outlining

A hands-on activity that we have found effective is to have students list all of the important information from a reading selection on a piece of paper. Cut up the phrases or words and manipulate them into an outline format using teacher developed main headings and/or supporting details. Outlining, as in webbing, requires that students recognize logical relationships of information. The outline strategy will most likely appeal to the student who thinks in a linear fashion when ordering ideas. The conventional format looks like the following:

I. Main idea
  A. Idea supporting I.
    1. Detail that supports A.
    2. Detail that supports A.
      a. Detail that supports 2.
      b. Detail that supports 2.
  B. Idea supporting I.
    1. Detail that supports B.
    2. Detail that supports B.
II. Main idea

Some students will find the outlining format to be restrictive as opposed to graphic organizers. In this book we have used a software package called Inspiration (Inspiration Software, Inc). All the graphic organizers in this book can be changed into outline form by simply clicking on a menu item. Or vice versa. Students can select whatever format works best for them. As we stated earlier, it is important for students to find what is comfortable and works best for them. We believe that to determine what works best cannot occur until a student has been exposed to a variety of possibilities.

Encourage students to select their own note taking preferences.

Reference Strategies

TABLE 6

INSTRUCTIONAL SUMMARY OF REFERENCE STRATEGIES

Literacy Strategy	Reference Strategies
Primary Focus	❑ Book Surveys ❑ Book and Library Scavenger Hunts
Learning Principles	Variety of Ways to Organize Information
When to Use	Varies
Goals: National or State Literacy Standards	❑ Use a variety of reading strategies to increase comprehension and learning
Materials	❑ Book Survey Model ❑ Library Survey Model ❑ Websites (See each chapter of this textbook.)
Time	40 Minutes

Textbooks

Textbooks are probably the most accessible reference tool students have. However, few students ever use them as such. The teacher who changes this behavior is contributing to the development of a life skill. Students also need to learn about content area specific references available in the library.

Students with good study strategies are knowledgeable about using their books as references. They know how to use book parts to help them find information quickly and efficiently. Clarification should be a natural outgrowth of using particular book parts. The following book survey alerts students to the parts of a book they can use for whatever purpose they have in mind. See Figure 3.19. If students need a definition, they should know how to use a glossary. If they want to see information summarized, they should look for the charts and graphs that analyze the information found in text, etc.

A creative and motivating way to have students survey the textbook for your class would be to develop a scavenger hunt such as the one we have developed for you as you use this text, *Guiding Reading and Writing in the Content Areas: Practical Strategies*. See Figure 3.20.

FIGURE 3.19. BOOK SURVEY

Directions: Respond to the following questions. This is not a test. I would like to know what parts of a book you are familiar with and which parts you need to learn more about. Write whatever you remember about the book part described in the question.

1. Why should you check the title and the author of a book?
2. Why is it important to note the copyright date or the date of publication of the book?
3. What does *Preface* mean, and how does it help you to understand the book?
4. What does the *Table of Contents* tell you about the book?
5. How does the *Glossary* help you?
6. What is the importance of the *Index?*
7. Why should you look at the titles, subtitles, pictures and graphs before you start to read the chapter in your book?
8. How can you make your own questions from the titles and subtitles? How can they help you to comprehend better?
9. What will you do to understand the difficult words in the chapter?
10. Why should you look at questions at the back of the chapter before reading the text?

FIGURE 3.20. TEXTBOOK SCAVENGER HUNT

❑ Consult Chapter 1 to determine what the steps are in conducting action research in your class.
❑ Peruse Chapter 3 and explain how the K-W-L Plus is different from the K-W-L.
❑ Invade Chapter 3 and explain the value of using a reading roadmap.
❑ Residing in Chapter 5 is the I-Search. What is it?
❑ Hiding in the Index is the strategy, Discussion Web. On what page is that listed? What is it?
❑ Locate formal and informal assessment in Chapter 8. Describe the difference between formal and informal assessment.
❑ Identify a topic in your content area that would be suitable for exploration using a Semantic Feature Analysis. See Chapter 2.

Library References

Students need to know about specialized reference materials for specific content areas. It would also help students to know where these materials are housed in the library. A fun activity designed as a scavenger hunt can be implemented for any content area topic.

It is important that students are aware of where to locate content area references in the library.

Halloween Scavenger Hunt

1. Consult an **Encyclopedia** and find out why we celebrate Halloween.
2. Using a **Guinness Book of World Records**, find out the weight of the world's largest pumpkin.
3. Lurking within an **Atlas** you will find the latitude and longitude of Salem, Massachusetts.
4. Residing in the **Dictionary** is the word *caldron*. Write the definition.
5. The **World Almanac** will enlighten you about the speed of a spider in mph.
6. Using the **Card Catalog**, electronic on-line or the traditional model, list the titles and authors of three books with the word *witch* in the title.
7. With the assistance of the **Junior Book of Authors**, write a short paragraph on one author mentioned in your previous list.
8. Tapping a **Thesaurus**, find all the synonyms for the word *scare*.
9. Perusing the **Periodical Guide**, find an article on flying (preferably via broom stick). Write down the name of the periodical and the title of the article.
10. Invade the **Index to Children's Poetry** and write down the title and author of one poem appropriate for the Halloween season.
11. With the help of Bartlett's Book of **Familiar Quotations**, write one line from a quotation about *bats*.

Name a topic conducive to a scavenger hunt in your subject area.

12. Wade through the audio **Music Collection** and write down the name of one piece of music with *ghost* in the title.
13. Latch on to the **librarian** and obtain from her the title of a Newberry Award book with *Rats* in the title.
14. Surf through the universe of a **World Wide Web** site and find out how other cultures celebrate Halloween, e.g., the Mexican El Dia de Los Muertos.
15. Explore an information CD, e.g., the **Grolier Multimedia Encyclopedia**, and report on the music and art used to portray the many facets of Halloween.

Complete the following Your Turn as a model for your students. You can then assign another state or a country that you may be studying for students to create their own scavenger hunt. There are many ways to adapt, this depending on your subject area. We would encourage you to take the time to allow students to search these or topics unique to your discipline. Our goal should be that all of our students have the opportunity to use these information resources. No student should leave school without these skills.

Your Turn

Name _____ Date _____ Subject Area _____

Directions: Complete the scavenger hunt using the name of your state/country. Once it is completed mount the information sheet on a piece of construction paper cut in the shape of your state/country.

Travels through Beautiful _____ **(Name of State/Country)**

1. **Atlas**   Find a map of _____ (state or country) and list the longitude and latitude of the capital.

2. **Thesaurus**   Find other words that mean beautiful.

3. **Dictionary**   What is the definition of precipitation?

4. **Encyclopedia**   Find the yearly average precipitation for _____ (state or country).

5. **Card Catalog**   Find a fiction book written by a resident of _____ (state/country), a biography of a famous resident of _____ (state), and a cookbook, featuring _____ (state's) famed foodstuffs.

6. **Almanac**   What was the population of _____ (state or country) in 1970 and 1990?

7. **National Geographic Index**   Find an article about _____ Lake (found in your state).

8. **The American Book of Days**   Look up under June and find out what year the first _____ Festival/Fair was held in _____ (city in selected state).

9. **Guinness Book of World Records**   Where is the largest _____ (state/country) tree?

10. **Dictionary of Geographical Terms**   Where is the longest river in _____ (state/country)?

Now mount this information on the shape of
your state/country cut out of colored construction paper.

Listening Strategy

TABLE 7

INSTRUCTIONAL SUMMARY OF LISTENING STRATEGY	
Literacy Strategy	**Listening**
Primary Focus	Listen with comprehension
Learning Principles	Active Involvement in Searching for Meaning
When to Use	Varies
Goals: National or State Literacy Standards	❑ Demonstrate effective listening strategies ❑ Analyze and evaluate verbal messages and the way they are delivered
Materials	Listening guide for the delivery of a verbal message
Time	40 Minutes

How often do you require students to listen during class? Keep track of the minutes per class per day. We think you will be quite surprised at the number of minutes students are asked to listen to speakers, peers, the teacher, announcements, etc. Yet, how often do we teach listening skills and strategies? To comprehend during listening is not too unlike comprehending while reading. We need to listen for 1) the main idea, 2) details, and attach meaning to these, 3) cues that signal transitions from one point to another, and finally, 4) the most critical ideas we have heard. Efficient listening requires our connecting what we hear to what we already know, questioning what the speaker is saying, and realizing that there are three levels of listening—literal, inferential and applied. See Chapter 4 for the detailed description of these levels.

If we ask students to listen then we must teach listening strategies.

Listening Guide
The following guide helps students listen for a purpose. After explaining the literal, interpretive and applied levels of comprehension, the teacher provides the students with a guide much like the following model.

Just as a good speaker at the beginning of a speech will cue her audience to the important ideas that she will address, the teacher should distribute a listening guide to students before beginning her lecture or a story. This serves to alert students to the important facts, inferences and evaluative ideas that will be made. We suggest using a story that students may know, or an adaptation as we have done as a fun starting point. Most students will be successful with this strategy if they have a schema for the story already. Then all they need to do is pay close attention to the details.

Listening includes comprehending.

Procedure. Create a three-level guide using an appropriate piece of content area material or a story. Distribute these and review the statements. If students aren't sure of what interpretive and applied thinking are, review these terms and the process that is involved. Select a statement from each section of the guide to walk students through the kind of thinking required at that level. We have selected a story appropriate for any grade level as an example. See Figure 3.21.

Students will probably want to refer to the book that you have read to check their responses. Encourage them to do this—it is the beginning of the development of another skill, checking their references.

There are a host of strategies to use to improve students' listening. Unfortunately, a comprehensive chapter on study skills limits us in referencing more. We would suggest, however, that if you want to foster this skill you may want to consider implementing a program like one that a school district sponsored—a

Develop a listening guide for your content area.

FIGURE 3.21. LISTENING GUIDE

Directions: Preview the study guide before listening to the story so you can connect what you are hearing to the ideas presented in the guide. This sets a purpose for listening and will enable you to complete the guide efficiently. Listen to the story *The True Story of the Three Pigs by A. Wolf* (Scieszka), then get into small groups and complete the following:

Part I: **Right There!** Listen carefully to the story. Check the following statements if you agree that is what you heard. Come to consensus with your group.

_____ 1. *The True Story of the Three Pigs by A. Wolf* hinges on a sneeze and a cup of sugar.
_____ 2. The wolf didn't want the food to spoil so he ate it.
_____ 3. A pigpen is a holding place for porkers.

Part II: **Think and Search!** Check those statements you can agree with based on what you think the author meant. Come to consensus in your group.

_____ 1. The big bad wolf story is a myth.
_____ 2. The pigs were selfish neighbors.
_____ 3. A wicked allergy, not a wicked wolf, caused the pigs' demise.
_____ 4. In a confrontation with a wolf, it's best to be behind a brick wall.

Part III: **On Your Own!** Check those statements you can agree upon based on your own experience and what you heard the author say.

_____ 1. In nature, there are only consequences.
_____ 2. Waste not; want not.
_____ 3. Know your neighbors.

Year of the Ear. All kinds of activities that encouraged careful listening were conducted at functions such as school board meetings to staff meetings to classrooms at every level, and giant EARS were posted on the door of those exhibiting thoughtful listening behaviors.

Ask students to design a chart of listening behaviors and post in your classroom.

If you are interested in promoting a similar activity in your classroom, the following listening behaviors could be incorporated.

Learning to Listen

1. Focus.	❏ Concentrate
2. Maintain eye contact.	
3. Get the big picture.	❏ Map out key ideas that you hear.
4. Sort out what you hear.	❏ Note main ideas, details; sort opinion from **fact**.
5. Check to be sure you heard correctly.	❏ Ask questions; paraphrase.
6. Listen for new words.	❏ Note words you don't recognize and look them up later.
7. Listen first; judge later.	❏ Underline notes that you question, and read up on that material or ask questions regarding it. ❏ Hear the speaker out. ❏ Resist distractions.
8. Use your thought time.	❏ While your brain is working faster than the speaker talks, summarize, anticipate and listen for cue words.

Another area that deserves attention is that of improving students' ability to memorize. For example, in our classes we ask students to memorize important steps in problem solving in science, key points in a piece of fiction, names of certain chemistry elements, formulae, etc. But when do we equip them with memory strategies?

TEACHER TALK

I teach my high school juniors about listening skills, but until I took your course I did not have a realistic, concrete example. I loved your idea of using *The True Story of the Three Pigs by A. Wolf!*

Memory Strategies

TABLE 8

INSTRUCTIONAL SUMMARY OF MEMORY STRATEGY	
Literacy Strategy	**Memory**
Primary Focus	Increasing memory
Learning Principles	Thought-demanding Activity
When to Use	Varies
Goals: National or State Literacy Standards	Use a variety of strategies to increase learning
Materials	Specific chains, acronyms and mnemonic devices appropriate for a particular content area
Time	40 Minutes

Organization is fundamental to memorization.

There are a number of strategies for increasing one's memory. The most important thing to remember is that whatever strategy is used, the purpose is to store, or file, the information in an organized fashion in the brain. To retrieve the information, associations must be made. It is much easier to retrieve this information if we have attached some mental structure to the information in processing it. For example, we all know that if we chunk a phone number, it is far easier to remember it than if we simply try to remember it as a list of numbers, e.g., (503) 267-3947 vs. 5032673947. We have found the following strategies work especially well. They are examples that are based on the three principles of memory: motivation, selection, and association.

Chaining
The principles of association and selection guide this activity. Ideas are linked from the known to the unknown. And all extraneous material is deleted as students examine the material to be studied and come up with a sentence or a format that incorporates the integral ideas or facts.

Develop a memory chain, acronym, or mnemonic device for a topic in your content area.

Procedure. This activity is used when a certain order is required for the information to be memorized. For example, a very common chain for memorizing the names of the planets, in order, is the following sentence: My very educated mother just served us nine pizzas. (Mercury, Venus, Earth, Mars, Jupiter, Saturn, Uranus, Neptune, Pluto – recently re-classified as a dwarf planet). Ask your preservice teachers to form small groups and have them come up with a chain sentence that will help them remember the six levels of Bloom's Taxonomy.

Acronyms
Another strategy is the use of an acronym for helping one to remember a list of information that does not have any particular order. Again, we are applying the principle of association with this strategy. For example, many of us remember the

names of the Great Lakes with the acronym "HOMES" (Huron, Ontario, Michigan, Erie, Superior). Memory principles may be remembered by the acronym SCRAM: selection, clarification, review, association, and motivation. Think of a topic area that has several terms, parts, or even steps that would fit into a neatly manicured acronym.

Mnemonic Devices

Mnemosyne, mother of muses, is responsible for our desire to recall things by inventing association techniques. "Spring forward, fall back" reminds us when to set our clocks forward or backwards. Others help us spell. For example, to remember the difference between the meaning of principle and principal tell students that the principal is a "prince of a pal." The difference between stationary and stationery is that the one that has an "e" needs an envelope. Then we all remember the ditty that has kept us from mixing the "ie" or "ei" combinations since we were in the third grade:

> I before E
> except after C,
> or when sounded like ay
> in neighbor and weigh.

Other variables that help to enhance memory are the use of color and pictures. We encourage you to be aware of what you ask students to memorize and to provide opportunities for students to brainstorm various memory strategies.

After this introduction to a number of study skill strategies, we encourage you to take inventory of your own teaching of these in your content area. Check off the appropriate descriptor that characterizes your teaching of the itemized study skill. If you are new to the profession, check those items that you are most likely to implement. Complete the following Your Turn.

Notes

Your Turn

Name _____ Date _____ Subject Area _____

Study Skills Checklist

Directions:

1. Veteran teachers: Check off under the appropriate descriptor your teaching of the following study skills.
2. Pre-service teachers: If you haven't taught yet, check those categories that indicate those study skills you most likely will implement.

I teach my students or I am planning to:

	Never	Sometimes	Frequently	Always
1. Recognize the purpose of a speaker or writer				
2. Outline				
3. Summarize				
4. Take notes				
5. Mark notes				
6. Take tests				
7. Use references				
8. Use the library				
9. Use the parts of the textbook				
10. Use SQ3R				
11. Make predictions				
12. Activate prior knowledge				
13. Use memory strategies				
14. Make graphic organizers				
15. Apply DR-TA				
16. Manage their time				
17. Play games that will reinforce content information				
18. Other:				

List those skills you think most appropriate for your curriculum:

It is always a good idea to encourage students to brainstorm and to talk about what they use as "trade secrets" to help them better study. Figure 3.22 is an example of how to implement this. Encourage students to complete the right column with study material most conducive to the type of study strategy suggested in the left column.

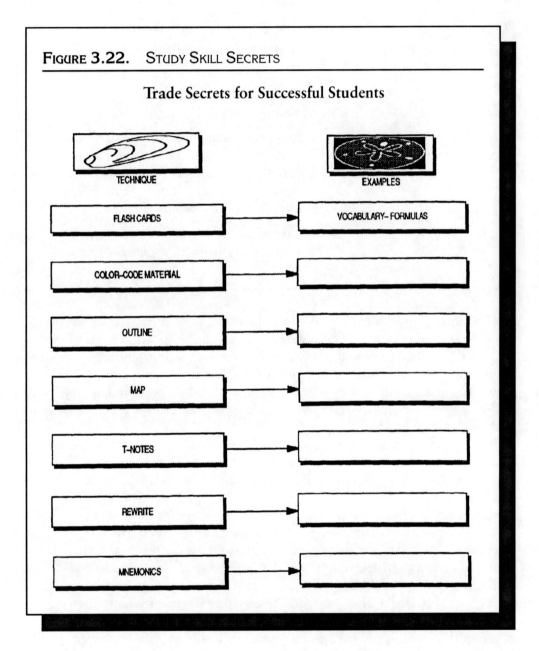

FIGURE 3.22.   STUDY SKILL SECRETS

Trade Secrets for Successful Students

TECHNIQUE	EXAMPLES
FLASH CARDS	VOCABULARY– FORMULAS
COLOR-CODE MATERIAL	
OUTLINE	
MAP	
T–NOTES	
REWRITE	
MNEMONICS	

Complete the chart with appropriate study material.

Storyline

Table 9

Instructional Summary of Storyline

Literacy Strategy	Storyline
Primary Focus	Activate prior knowledge
Learning Principles	❑ Active Involvement in Searching for Meaning ❑ Talk Time
When to Use	Before reading
Goal: National or State Literacy Standards	❑ Connect reading selections to other texts, experiences, issues and events ❑ Draw connections and explain relationships between reading selections and other texts, experiences, issues and events
Materials	List of key words or phrases taken sequentially from an assigned reading
Time	40 Minutes

Use a storyline to activate prior knowledge.

The following lesson plan should help students to further understand the value of activating prior knowledge before reading assigned materials. In this activity, the students are asked to create as accurate a story as possible from the words listed. If you are making a point of the value of activating prior knowledge before beginning to study a new unit or topic, do not provide students with any lead-in materials or activities on the Vietnam War—let them dig from their own background experiences.

What is a storyline?

In completing this storyline, many of your students probably experienced some stress and frustration, even though they were told there was no right or wrong way of creating a narrative. The facts of the Vietnam War are not easy to recall.

If you had prefaced this activity with a discussion on America's early involvement in Vietnam and brainstormed what students knew about this war, this may have been an easier task. Furthermore, if you were to cluster these terms, drawing the connections of one term to another using a semantic organizer (see Chapter 2), this activity would expedite the writing of the storyline immeasurably.

Having warned you, however, don't be surprised when students have a good time completing a storyline. The creativity of their products—even though a far cry from the actual historical account—appeals to their adolescent interests. We have found it to be a motivating activity in starting up a unit.

LESSON PLAN: **SOCIAL STUDIES**

Grade: 8

Topic: Vietnam War

Purpose: To help students to activate prior knowledge regarding the Vietnam War.

State Content/Literacy Standards:
1) Understand and represent chronological order, sequences and relationships in history;
2) Structure information in clear sequence, making connections and transitions among ideas, sentences and paragraphs.

Student Objectives:
1. Students will be able to sequence dates and chronological events in history.
2. Students will demonstrate organization by developing a paragraph(s) with a beginning, middle and ending as well as a clear sequencing of ideas and transitions.

Introduction: Students will be given a list of words taken from the selected reading in the sequential order in which they appear. The teacher should read each word **aloud** so the students know how to pronounce each one. This also helps students to develop recognition of the words as they begin their reading. This could also be done in the language spoken by the ESL students. One list could be in English and the other in the most represented second language.

America
Vietnam
1945
War
Ho Chi Minh
Vietminh
Democracy
Domino Theory
Eisenhower
Geneva Accord
Ngo Dinh Diem
Freedom
Hanoi
Viet Cong
Saigon
Johnson
Death
Gulf of Tonkin
Gulf of Tonkin Resolution

Learning Activity: Students are divided into small groups of about four. The teacher assigns one student to be the scribe and one to be the presenter. The task of the group is to write a paragraph or two or a story using the list of words in sequential order. If they do not have any understanding of a word they make a guess and use it. Each presenter reads the paragraphs or story to the rest of the class. The class decides which story seems to be the most

LESSON PLAN: SOCIAL STUDIES (CONT.)

accurate and why. The students are now ready to read the selected reading. They have read the words, pronounced the words, and used the words in their writing. They have ownership of the story and are anxious to assess how closely their story aligns to the information given in the selected reading. Teachers will find that the first thing the students will want to do is to find any of the vocabulary words they did not know to see how close they were with their description. After reading the selection each student group discusses the accuracy of their writing as it relates to the reading as well as the information, in general.

Closure: All groups reconvene and decide which group story was most accurate and why.

Alternative: Write a second paragraph using the terms in sequential order.

Evaluation: Credit could be given for the most accurate original story or the best written second story.

Inclusion Techniques

Explain SAM.

One of the authors attended a workshop recently on learning strategies for diverse populations. While there, a participant shared the following acronym, SAM, with her. It seems an appropriate one for keeping the needs of all students in the class in the forefront of our instructional decision making.

Sensitivity
Adjustment/Accommodation
Modeling

This holistic way of looking at learning seems especially appropriate for a chapter on study skills. The degree of flexibility and responsiveness we bring to our students' learning needs characterizes the sensitivity we demonstrate. How well we troubleshoot students' needs that are not being met determines the level of adaptation or accommodation we construct, and our modeling of a variety of ways to distinguish important from unimportant information provides students with the guidance they need to achieve their goals.

Teaching study skills at the beginning of a term prepares students for success.

Teachers who include a study skills unit at the beginning of the term are sensitive to the needs of learners with special needs, who require specific learning strategies in order to realize their potential. Many of the strategies outlined in the first part of this chapter can be a part of this curriculum. In addition, we would like to examine specifically how to foster the competencies associated with study skills such as the acquiring, recording, organizing, synthesizing and using information and ideas by learners with special needs.

What are some ways that a teacher can maximize her classroom environment for these competencies to be realized?

First, we believe that teachers who have worked on adapting and accommodating instructional conditions in their classrooms provide an ideal environment for learning to occur. As Ponyboy reminds us in *The Outsiders,* one can't ignore students who need this attention:

It amazed me how Johnny could get more meaning out of some of the stuff in there than I could—I was supposed to be the deep one. Johnny had failed a year in school and never made good grades—he couldn't grasp anything that was shoved at him too fast, and I guess his teachers thought he was just plain dumb. But he wasn't. He was just a little slow to get things, and he liked to explore things once he did get them. He was especially stuck on the Southern gentlemen—impressed with their manners and charm (Hinton, 1967, p. 67).

We have included a chart in Figure 3.23 that summarizes the adaptations that the Center for School and Community Integration has identified as critical for

FIGURE 3.23.   NINE TYPES OF ADAPTATIONS

Adaptations	Kinds	Examples Observed/Initialed
1. Size	Adapt the number of items that a learner is expected to learn or complete.	
2. Time	Adapt the minutes, hours, or days you allot and allow for task completion on testing.	
3. Input	Adapt the way information is delivered to the learner.	
4. Output	Adapt the way the learner can respond to instruction.	
5. Difficulty	Adapt the skill level or problem type according to the learner's need.	
6. Participation	Adapt the extent to which a learner is actively involved in the task.	
7. Level of support	Increase the amount of human interaction with a particular learner.	
8. Alternate goals	Adapt the outcome expectations while using the same materials.	
9. Substitute curriculum	Provide different curriculum and instruction to meet a learner's individual goals.	

Fill in your examples.

effective and efficient inclusion programs. We would encourage you to note in the third column those activities that you have observed in your field placements or in your own classes that are examples of that particular adaptation.

SCAN and RUN Strategy

TABLE 10

INSTRUCTIONAL SUMMARY OF SCAN AND RUN STRATEGY	
Literacy Strategy	**SCAN and RUN Strategy**
Primary Focus	Monitor comprehension
Learning Principles	Active Involvement in Searching for Meaning
When to Use	Varies
Goals: National or State Literacy Standards	Use a variety of strategies to increase learning
Materials	Reading Materials
Time	40 Minutes

A reading strategy that has been recommended for students with special needs is SCAN and RUN (Salembier, 1999). SCAN and RUN is a mnemonic device that has seven cues to help students plan and monitor their comprehension before, during and after reading a selection. Before reading, SCAN helps a student to activate prior knowledge. During reading, RUN assists a student to monitor comprehension. After reading, student understanding is extended by answering questions. SCAN and RUN is similar to SQ3R but is more concrete for a student who needs step-by-step procedures. Students follow the following format. See Figure 3.24.

It is important that the teacher model this entire process using a think-aloud strategy so that students know how to implement it. This might sound like the following:

> After previewing the chapter using the **SCAN** cues, the teacher then reads aloud the text selection using the final three **RUN** cues. For example, the teacher continues the thinking-aloud process by saying, 'Now I am going to read the selection using the **RUN** cues, and try to remember what I've learned from the **SCAN** cues to help me understand the meaning. First, each time I come to a sentence or section which I don't understand I will use the cue **R**, Read and Adjust Speed and I will slow my reading down. Also, when I come to a word I can't pronounce I need to use the **U** cue: Using Sounding It Out Skills, looking for other clues in the sentence or breaking words into parts to help identify the unknown word. Next, I will use **N**, Notice and Check Parts I Don't Understand and Reread or Read On...' (Salembier, 1999, p. 390).

FIGURE 3.24.   SCAN AND RUN STRATEGY

S	Survey headings and turn them into questions.	**R**	Read and adjust speed for better understanding.
C	Capture the meaning by trying to understand if the caption or visual conveys a message.	**U**	Use word identification such as sounding it out or breaking it into meaningful parts to help identify an unknown word that is difficult to understand.
A	Attack boldface words to understand the main ideas and details.	**N**	Notice and check parts you do not understand by placing a check mark in the margin. Try to reread that section or skip it and go back to it after you have completed reading the selection.
N	Note and read the chapter questions to focus student reading.		

Adapted SCAN and RUN task by George B. Salembier (1999), from SCAN and RUN: A Reading Comprehension Strategy that Works.

Thus, when working with students with special needs, one needs to remember that "chunking," or working in small segments, should be most beneficial for understanding and for remembering. In addition to the information presented in Figure 3.23 classroom teachers who are working with special needs students need to consider classroom environment—ways to reduce distractions, give the students extra breaks, and use a checklist to keep the students organized. In the area of assessment provide oral response tests, give small sections of the test rather than the complete test at one time, grade spelling separately from content, avoid timed tests, permit retaking of the test, and change the percentage of work required for a passing grade. Lastly, be aware that the teacher should consider behavior issues—avoid power struggles, provide peer role models, develop a system to let the student know when his/her behavior is not acceptable, develop an intervention plan and provide immediate reinforcement and feedback. This is probably a practical list of strategies for all students not just those who are inclusion students. (Special Education: Practical strategies for the classroom), see website in references. Second language learners also need to apply special strategies some of which will be discussed in the next section.

Study Skills for Second Language Readers

The Bilingual Education Act of 1967 helped schools to receive federal monies for minority students who were non-English-speaking. Changing populations in our schools has caused teachers to adapt their instruction to meet individual needs. ESL is one of those areas where there are huge population changes. These changes require that teachers learn how to engage ESL students in reading and writing assignments in their particular content area. Perez and Torres-Guzman (1996) recommend that ESL students be given a solid grounding in study skills as they relate to reading and writing in a content field. "Literacy development must be integrated in the teaching of subject matter" (Perez & Torres-Guzman, p. 154).

Rather than focus on learning of the language, second language teachers can help students learn to think about what happens during the language learning process. The teaching of metacognitive skills is a valuable use of instructional time for the content area teacher and second language teacher. When learners reflect upon their learning strategies, they can improve their learning. Which strategies might one consider? According to Anderson (2002) second language students should help to prepare and plan for their learning—think about what they want to accomplish and how to implement the process. Second language students should select and use learning strategies that work for them and to teach them to know when to apply these strategies. Students should monitor their use of learning strategies; should know how and when to orchestrate various strategies: and, second language learners should be able to evaluate their strategy use by asking four basic questions: What am I trying to accomplish? What strategies am I using? How well am I using the strategies? What else could I do?

Judie Haynes (2006) recommends the following helpful hints:
1. Teach students to study actively—write it down or say it.
2. Make sure they understand the material.
3. Assess prior knowledge so you can tie the new material to something they already know.
4. Have students create their own examples.
5. Ask students to visualize what they are learning.
6. Teach students how to determine the most important concepts.
7. Set reasonable goals for ESL students.
   The following lesson plan should help ESL students increase vocabulary development and summary writing using a graphic organizer.

LESSON PLAN FOR ESL

Grade 8

Topic: President Jefferson's Instructions to Lewis and Clark, specifically Meriwether Lewis

Purpose: To help students to study new vocabulary and to write summaries. State Content/Literacy Standards:
1. To write a summary statement.
2. To increase vocabulary.

Student Objectives:
1. Students will be able to define vocabulary and determine the part of speech.
2. Students will be able to write summary statements for paragraphs read.

Introduction:
Students will read a given number of paragraphs and complete a graphic organizer that requires that the students define basic vocabulary and write a summary for the paragraphs.

Learning Activity:
From the reading below read paragraphs and complete the following organizer. Give the part of speech of each vocabulary term and define the word. Answer each question and write your summary.

Paragraphs 1 & 2 ascertaining: celestial	What preparation has been made? SUMMARY: (Your summary of what President Jefferson wanted to have accomplished.)
Paragraphs 3 & 4 ceded: sovereign allegiance:	Why do they need a passport? SUMMARY:
Paragraph 5 Communication: Commerce:	 SUMMARY:

Closure: All students convene to discuss the reading, their definitions, part of speech of each word, and their summaries.

Alternative: The teacher could jigsaw the reading so students read and respond to less material.

Evaluation: Credit given for accuracy of vocabulary assignment and for each summary.

READING: Paragraphs 1 & 2 (adapted)
June 20 1803
To: Captain Meriwether Lewis
From: President Thomas Jefferson

On June 18,1803 the United States Legislature passed an act that appointed you, Meriwether Lewis, to proceed on your journey of discovering some of the uncharted country beyond the United States. You will need to include in your supplies instruments for <u>ascertaining</u> the geography of the country. <u>Celestial</u> observations have been provided to help you find your way.

In addition, you will need to include articles for bartering, presents for Indians, boats, tents, rifles and other arms for the men who accompany you, ammunitions, medicine, surgical instruments, and provisions. The Secretary of War will help you to assemble these items. In addition, the Secretary of War will provide you with men from our current troops who volunteer to accompany you. You will serve as their commanding officer and will be invested with all the powers of the laws to carry out your mission.

Paragraphs 3 & 4 (adapted)
When your group is within the limits of the U.S. you will be expected to communicate with me. Once you depart from the United States you should be aware of the following: The ministers from France, Spain and Great Britain and their governments have been alerted about your trip. We trust they are satisfied about the objective this trip. That objective is to learn as much as you can about the geography of this uncharted land—map the land, keep a journal of the vegetation, the people, the animals and anything else you discover.

Because Louisiana has been <u>ceded</u> by Spain to France, the passport you have is from the minister of France. The French minister is the representative of the present <u>sovereign</u> of the country of Louisiana. The passport will be a protection for you. The passport from the minister of England will entitle you to the friendly aid of any traders with <u>allegiance</u> to England.

Paragraph 5 (adapted)
The object of your mission is to explore the Missouri river and the course it takes for <u>communication</u> with the waters of the Pacific ocean. We are most interested in the Columbia, Colorado or any other river that may offer the most direct & practicable water communication across this continent for the purposes of <u>commerce.</u>
www.ncces2009.org/histroy/unit 3 overview.doc
Jefferson's Instructions to Meriwether Lewis with Key Vocabulary and Guiding Questions

AS THE READING CONTINUES ADD VOCABULARY AND SUMMARIES TO THE ORGANIZER.

Endings: A Summary

Study skill strategies have been presented in this chapter as a means of helping students locate, select, organize and retain information. They help students specifically learn to read flexibly, adjusting their pace as dictated by purpose and their own skill level. An underlying bias supports this chapter, namely, that learning how to learn is a life skill that serves students long after they leave our classrooms.

This chapter begins with strategies that enable students to assess their own prior knowledge such as K-W-L PLUS, Think-Aloud, Summary Writing and SQ3R. Study skill strategies are then introduced to provide students exposure to different methods of studying information as well as practice until they elect to design a personal mode of study that is efficient and effective.

Note taking, note marking, outlining strategies and power notes are described as well as illustrated with examples. In addition, activities for maximizing the use of reference materials in the content area classroom and listening, memory skill building and Storyline are demonstrated.

Finally, we have included study strategies targeted for diverse populations, inclusion students and second language learners. These activities are the outgrowth of research studies that show that all students succeed as a result of these practices.

In a classroom where the how of learning is as important as the what of learning, students, through practice, experience confidence and a belief in themselves, as well as studying as an investment that can help them meet future challenges.

Expanding Understanding through Discussion

Using the following Reading Road Map model, work with a partner to review Chapter 3 of this textbook. Pay attention to the following parts of the map.

Wood, et al (1992, p. 63)

1. On the left side, the location markers point out important topics in the chapter as well as starting and stopping signs.
2. In the center are road signs representing the reading process. For example, one sign may tell you to slow down because this section is especially important. You may even want to slow down and discuss the topic with your partner.
3. On the right, questions that are a combination of literal, interpretive and evaluative are used during reading for discussion and as a check for understanding.

Students who have a difficult time finding information when a large unit of text is reviewed or read find this visual map easier to navigate than simply reading the text. Students appreciate and enjoy using the map to find their way to understanding.

This highly motivating activity is a model that you can adapt to guide students through your content area by directing them to adjust their reading rate to correspond to the questions asked.

Reading Road Map

Directions: With a partner, or in small groups, review this chapter by following the reading road map. Use the road signs as cues for locating chapter material.

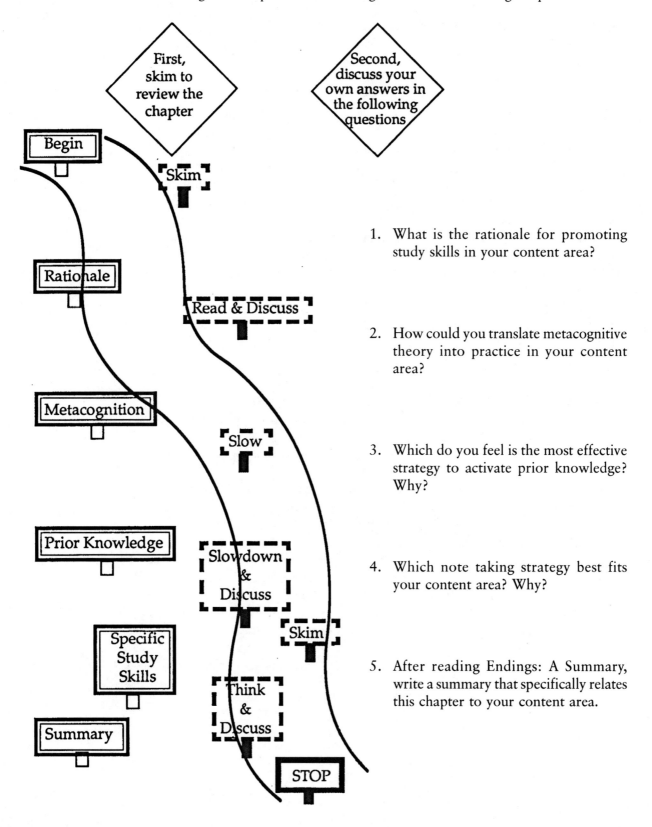

1. What is the rationale for promoting study skills in your content area?

2. How could you translate metacognitive theory into practice in your content area?

3. Which do you feel is the most effective strategy to activate prior knowledge? Why?

4. Which note taking strategy best fits your content area? Why?

5. After reading Endings: A Summary, write a summary that specifically relates this chapter to your content area.

In the Field Applications

A. React to the statement: Students who do the following will succeed in their classes:

McCutcheon (1985)

   1. attend class and sit in the front row
   2. analyze their strengths and weaknesses
   3. analyze their teacher's strengths and weaknesses
   4. are creative in their work
   5. use the many resources of the library
   6. refine their test taking techniques
   7. budget their time accordingly.

B. Develop a library scavenger hunt for students to get acquainted with available library references for your content area.

C. Create a storyline as a means of activating prior knowledge and implement it. Describe your reflections on the results of this activity. What instructional decisions will you make on the basis of your reflection? Write up these reflections.

References ❑ ❑ ❑

Anders, P., & Guzzetti, B. (1996). *Literacy instruction in the content areas.* NY Harcourt Brace College Publishing.

Anderson, Neil J. (2002). The role of metacognition in second language teaching and learning. April, Retrieved May 18, 2006 from www.caLorg/resources/digest/ 0110anderson.html

Anderson, T., & Armbruster, B. (1984). Studying. In P. D. Pearson (Ed.). *Handbook of reading research* (pp. 657-679). NY: Longman.

Anderson, T., & Armbruster, B. (1991). *The value of taking notes during lectures.* In R. Flippo & D. Caverly (Eds.). *Teaching reading and study strategies at the college level (pp. 166–194).* Newark, DE: International Reading Association.

Baker, L., & Brown, A. (1984). Metacognitive skills and reading. In P. D. Pearson (Ed.). *Handbook of reading research (pp. 353-394).* NY. Longman.

Blitz, W. & Shelton, K. (2004). Using written conversation in middle school: Lessons from a teacher researcher project. *Journal of Adolescent & Adult Literacy* 47(6), 492–507.

Block, Cathy Collins & Israel, Susan E. (2004). The ABCs of performing highly effective think-alouds. *The Reading Teacher.* 58(2). 154–167.

Bragstad, B. & Stumpf, S. (1982). *A guidebook for teaching study skills and motivation.* Boston: Allyn & Bacon.

Butruille, S. (1993). *Women's voices from the Oregon Trail.* Boise, ID: Tamarack Books, Inc.

Caine, R.N. & Caine, G. (1990). Understanding a brain-based approach to learning and teaching. *Educational Leadership* 48(2), 66–70.

Caine, R.N. & Caine, G. (1991). *Making connections: Teaching and the human brain.* Alexandria, VA: Association for Supervision and Curriculum.

Carr, E. & Ogle, D. (1987). K-W-L PLUS: A strategy for comprehension and summarization. *Journal of Reading,* 30, 626–631.

Community College of Southern Nevada. English Department. (2006). Retrieved May 18, 2006 from http://www.ccsn.nevada.edu/english/sumguide.htm

Cunningham, J. & Moore, D. (1986). The confused world of the main idea. In James Baumann (Ed.,) *Teaching main idea comprehension.* Newark, DE: International Reading Association.

Davey, B. (October, 1983). Think-Aloud: Modeling the cognitive process of reading comprehension. *Journal of Reading,* 44–47.

Department of English, University of Victoria Writer's Guide. (1995). Retrieved May 8, 2006 http://web.uvic.ca/wguide/Pages/SumHelpYou.html

Dooling, R. & Lachman, R. (1972). Effects of comprehension on retention of prose. *Journal of Experimental Psychology,* 88, 216–222.

Edelman, G.M. (1992). *Bright air, brilliant fire: On the matter of the mind.* New York: Basic.

Eisner, E.W. (1997). Cognition and representation: A way to pursue the American dream. *Phi Delta Kappan,* 78 (5), 348–353.

Gallaudet University guide to summary writing. (2001). Retrieved May 18, 2006 from http://depts.gallaudet.edu/englishworks/writing/summaries.html

Gardner, H. (1991). *The unschooled mind: How children think and how schools should teach.* New York: Basic.

Gorman, J., Junkala, J., Mooney, J., & Morrison, K. (1996). *Teacher implementation: A true story.* Boston College and Brown Middle School. Unpublished manuscript.

Graham, K., & Robinson, A. (1984). *Study skills handbook: A guide for all teachers.* Newark, DE: International Reading Association.

Greenlaw, J. (2001). English language arts and reading on the internet: A resource for K-12 teachers.
<http://www.occdsb.on.ca/~ered/htrm/scaven.htm> (2000. September 25).
<http://www.scholastic.com/instructor/curriculum/index.htm#langarts>
<http://www.ldonlie.org/ld_indepth/teaching_techniques/understanding_textbooks.html>

Harris, T., & Hodges, R. (Eds.). (1995). *The literacy dictionary: The vocabulary of reading and writing,* Newark, DE: International Reading Association.

Haynes, Judie. (2006). Study Skills for ELLS. Retrieved May 18, 2006 http: // everythingESL.net

Herrell, A. (2003). *Fifty strategies for teaching language learners.* New York: Prentice-Hall.

Hinton, S. (1967). *The outsiders.* NY: The Viking Press, Inc.

Johnson, D., & Pearson, D. (1984). *Teaching reading vocabulary* (2ⁿᵈ ed.) NY: Holt, Reinhart and Winston.

Jamieson, S. (1999).Drew University On-line resources for writers: Summary writing Retrieved May 18, 2006 http ://users .drew.edu/~sjamieso/Summary.html

Knox, Andrew. (2006). NCCES ninth grade history, Class of 2009. Retrieved fMay 18, 2006 from www.ncces2009.org/history/unit_3_overview

Kymes, A. (2005). Teaching online comprehension strategies using think-alouds. *Journal of Adolescent & Adult Literacy* 48(6), 492–500.

May, E (1990). *Reading as communication: An interactive approach.* Columbus, OH: Merrill.

McCutcheon, R. (1985). *Get off my brain: A survival guide for lazy students.* Minneapolis, MN: Free Spirit Publishing Inc.

Miholic, V., (1994). An inventory to pique students' metacognitive awareness of reading strategies. *Journal of Reading,* 38(2), 84-86.

Musical instruments. From flutes carved on bones, to lutes, to modern electric guitars (1993). (Accent on Language, Inc. Trans.) Scholastic.

New York Times. Special Education, Teaching Strategies and Best Practices - Articles. Special Education: Practical Strategies for the Classroom, (2006). Retrieved May 18, 2006 from http://specialed.about.com/cs/teacherstrategies/a/Strategies.htm

Ogle, D. (1986). K-W-L: A teaching model that develops active reading of expository text. *Reading Teacher,* 39, 564–570.

Pauk, W. (1988). *How to study in college.* Boston: Houghton Mifflin.

Pauk, W. (1974). *Critical thinking: How to prepare students for a rapidly changing world.* Santa Rosa, CA: Foundation for Critical Thinking.

Perez, B., & Torres-Guzman, M. (1996). *Learning in two worlds: An integrated Spanish/English bi-literacy approach.* White Plains, NY: Longman.

Robinson, A. (1946). *Effective study.* NY: Harper & Row.

Salembier, G. (1999). SCAN and RUN: A reading comprehension strategy that works. *Journal of Adolescent & Adult Literacy,* 42(5), 386–393.

Santa, C. (1988). *Content reading including study systems: Reading, writing and studying across the curriculum.* Dubuque, IA: Kendall-Hunt.

Santa, C., Havens, L. & Maycumber, E. (1996). *Creating independence through student owned strategies.* Dubuque, IA: Kendall-Hunt.

Satka, C. (1988/1999). SQRC: A strategy for guiding reading and higher level thinking. *Journal of Adolescent & Adult Literacy,* 42(4), 265–269.

Scieszka, J. (1989). *The true story of the three pigs by A. Wolf.* NY. Viking.

Scruggs, T., & Mastropieri, M. (1992). Effective mainstreaming strategies for mildly handicapped students. *The Elementary School Journal,* 92(3), 389–409.

Spangenberg-Urbschat, K. & Pritchard, R. (1994). *Kids come in all languages: Reading instruction for ESL students.* Newark, DE: International Reading Association.

Southwest Educational Development Laboratory. 2006). http://www.sedl.org/scimath/compass/vQ3n02/brain.html

Study Strategies Homepage (2001). University of Minnesota Duluth. Retrieved May 28, 2006 from http://www.d.umn.edu/student/loon/acad/strat

Sylwester, R. (1997, Oct.). How emotions affect learning. *Educational Leadership*: 60–65.

Vacca, R., & Vacca, J. (1996). *Content area reading* (3rd ed.). Boston: Little, Brown & Company.

Vacca, R., & Vacca, J. (1986). *Content area reading*: Literacy and learning across the curriculum (6th ed.). NY: Addison Wesley Longman.

Wade, S., Buxton, W. & Kelly, M. (1999). Using think-alouds to examine reader-text interest. *Reading Research Quarterly, 34*(2), 194–216

Wehmeyer, D. (2006). Wise-Online. Retrieved May 18, 2006 from http://www. wise-online, corn/objects/index_ti. asp ?objD_TRG2603.

Wood, K., Lapp, D., & Flood, J. (1992). *Guiding readers through text: A review of study guides.* Newark, DE: International Reading Association.

Wood, K.D. (1988). Guiding students through information text. *The Reading Teacher, 41* (9), 912–920.

Yopp, H. & Yopp, K. (2004). Preview-Predict-Confirm: Thinking about the language and content of informational text. *Reading Teacher 58,* 1, 79–82.

Young, C. (June 23,1997). Study Skills at Northport Middle School. <http://www.northport.k12.ny.us/~nms/young.html> (2000, September 25).

Comprehension Strategies

4

Little Clara read all the time. Her interest in books was indiscriminate. She was as happy to read the magic books from her Uncle Marcos's enchanted trunks as she was to contemplate the Liberal Party documents her father kept in his study. She filled innumerable notebooks with her private observations . . .

Allende (1986), *The House of the Spirits*, p. 75

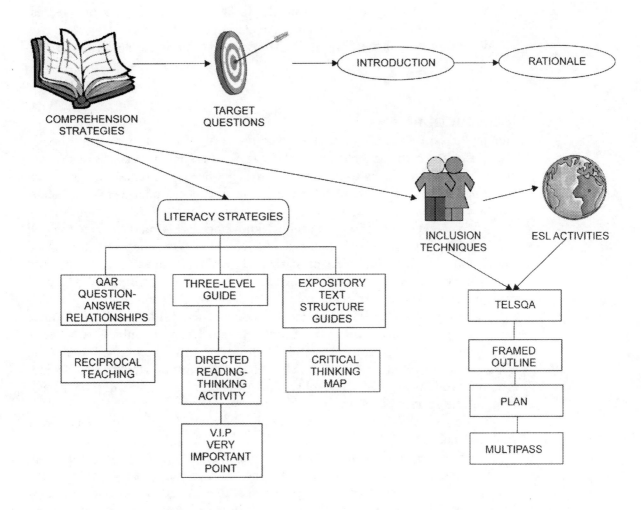

Target Questions

Target Questions

Consider the following questions before reading this chapter. Discuss these with a colleague. Continue writing notes and develop specific questions regarding comprehension that you want to explore.

1. Define comprehension.
2. Why does the use of literacy strategies in the classroom help students learn?
3. What is meant by "reading the text?"
4. Identify and describe a comprehension strategy that enables students to increase their awareness of types of questions and develop their higher level thinking skills.
5. Identify and describe comprehension guides that enable students to recognize a variety of text structures that are found in their texts.
6. Compare and contrast the use of the Reciprocal Teaching Guide and a Directed Reading-Thinking Activity.
7. At this moment in our history, why is promoting critical thinking among our students imperative?
8. What are some key learning principles to keep in mind when designing lessons for the students with special needs in your content area classroom?
9. What elements of the Framed Outline meet the academic needs of the ESL learner?
10. Other:

Introduction

Comprehension is a lot like cooking. For the cook, there is preparation before and during the cooking. Afterwards, there is clean-up and an analysis of the success of the meal. Let's say for a barbecue, the chef needs to prepare the grill, plan his courses, make sure there are skewers, brightly-colored vegetables, meats, condiments, dessert, plates, utensils, napkins and a plan for seating arrangements.

When everything goes well, a chef, we know, brings his guests over to the grill showing off the skewers with their red and yellow peppers, cherry tomatoes, and onions intermingled with pieces of marinated sirloin as well as the asparagus and corn roasting on the side. As the brochettes sizzle and deepen in color, he educates his guests on the art of his culinary endeavors. Our senses are bombarded by smells, sights, and tastes of the meal to come. This chef knows how to entice his guests preparing them for the feast to come. Eating is enhanced. Taste is heightened and enjoyment is ensured. "Oohs" and "Ahs" accompany each bite. Would the same effect occur if the chef hadn't drawn our attention to his art? After everyone is finished, the chef strolls through the group eliciting their feedback on the success of the meal.

In similar fashion, the process of comprehension demands this same attention to detail.

Tovani, 2001

Like the chef, students need to prepare for the reading by checking out chapter headings, pictures, charts, questions, and sidebars before they start reading. During the reading, they simmer together what they already know and what they are reading. They separate the details from the main ideas. They monitor, gauging meaning, questioning themselves to clarify ambiguity. They whisk together sensory images to enhance comprehension and visualize the reading. Finally, they check on where they end up—how well-done is their understanding?

Definition

One has only to consult the International Reading Association's *The literacy dictionary: The vocabulary of reading and writing* (1995) to see the attention comprehension has received over the years, and the myriad definitions developed depending on the informed thinking of the time.

Specifically, comprehension is viewed as a complex process. Many mental operations are going on simultaneously when a reader reads. Readers must recognize words and associate them with concepts stored in memory. They must develop meaningful ideas from groups of words (phrases, clauses, sentences), draw inferences, relate what is already known to what is being read, and more. Comprehension involves ongoing development as experience expands our horizons, allowing us to connect to something broader than the text itself. In short, comprehension is a constructive process of exploring and making meaning.

Harris & Hodges (1995)

Beck (1986, 1989)
Anderson et al. (1985)

Rationale

In this chapter we will explore several literacy strategies that promote comprehension and the learning principles that inform their use. Our goal is for you to understand these principles because they are critical to the instructional decision- making we use to select the appropriate literacy strategy in our classrooms. Finally, the literacy strategies presented are designed to help the reader with the comprehension process before, during, and after reading.

Literacy Strategies to Promote Comprehension

In the past few years we've been fortunate to work with middle school and high school teachers who are concerned not only with developing a strong curriculum but also with helping students understand the cognitive and metacognitive processing needed to complete academic tasks. Teachers have told us that literacy strategies work because they match the process skills students need for both instruction and assessment, the students enjoy them, and that most are adaptable across the content areas. They also provide students with a simulated experience of the cognitive activity needed in order to "read" text. Unlike Clara in Allende's *The House of the Spirits*, many of our students aren't well acquainted with deliberately "reading the text," particularly, when the text is expository.

Simpson & Nist (1999)

What is meant by "reading the text"? Wilhelm (1997) in his delightful *You Gotta Be the Book* asked middle school students this question for a number of years and consistently found that students believed school reading is being able to answer the questions at the end of a text chapter or story. Real reading is done at home with their favorite, personally-selected books or magazines.

According to students, what is the difference between school reading and personal leisure reading?

Reading as a critical activity, a socially significant, or a personally relevant way of making meaning were rarely mentioned. One anecdote, he cites, dramatically demonstrates the difference in how students approach reading.

John: I can't believe you do all that stuff when you read! Holy crap, I'm not doing...like nothing...compared to you.

Ron: I can't believe you don't do something. If you don't, you're not reading, man.... It's gotta be like wrestling or watching a movie or playing a video game...you've got to like...be there! (Wilhelm, 1997, xii)

What is the purpose of literacy learning strategies?

We've selected the following learning strategies because teachers have told us that they help students "be there" while reading. **These strategies are techniques or activities that enable students ultimately to function independently in working out their understanding and learning of content material.** They are precise external guides that students use on a regular basis. We believe that these literacy strategies activate students' background knowledge, develop students' abilities to monitor their own understanding, and infuse a sense of the organization of the written or spoken material—areas critical to comprehension.

The following literacy strategies will be described and illustrated: Question-Answer Relationships (QAR), Three-Level Guide, Expository Text Structure Guides, Reciprocal Teaching, Directed Reading-Thinking Activity (DRTA), Critical Thinking Map, and the VIP-Very Important Point. Content-related literacy activities for students with special needs and the English language learner (ELL) will conclude the chapter. Each will be illustrated with models from various content areas.

QAR – Question-Answer Relationships

TABLE 1

INSTRUCTIONAL SUMMARY OF QAR

Literacy Strategy	QAR: Question-Answer Relationships
Primary Focus	Comprehension
Learning Principles	❑ Active Involvement ❑ Talk Time ❑ Thought Demanding
When to Use	After reading
Goals: National or State Literacy Standards	❑ Promote comprehension ❑ Increase awareness of question types ❑ Refine question answers
Materials	❑ QAR definitions ❑ QAR practice Sheets ❑ Reading selection
Time	30 Minutes

TABLE 2

SUMMARY OF CRITICAL ELEMENTS OF A QAR STRATEGY

PROCESS	QAR GUIDE WORDS	EXAMPLES
Locate the information.	RIGHT THERE	How many ships did Columbus command?

Integrate ideas by putting together different pieces of text to answer the question.	THINK and SEARCH	Why did it take Columbus so long to get support for his trip?
Look for the answer outside the reading by combining what is known with what is in the text.	AUTHOR and YOU	What kind of person was Columbus?
Look for the answer from experience and background knowledge.	ON YOUR OWN	Who is your favorite explorer?

Example 1: Language Arts Model

Student Discussion Guide: Cannery Row and Marine Life

Directions: After reading the passage on marine life in the book *Cannery Row* (p. 30-32) by John Steinbeck, work with members of your group and answer the following questions. Create a question at each level as well as your response to it.

I. RIGHT THERE! The answers to these questions will be in the text and are easy to find. The words used to make up the question and words used to answer the question are RIGHT THERE in the passage.
   1. What tide level is most of this passage about?
   2. Who are the "hurrying, fighting, feeding, breeding animals?
   3. Your question:

II. THINK and SEARCH! The answer is in the reading, but you need to put together different parts of the reading to find it. You need to THINK about the question and SEARCH for the answer. Words for the question and words for the answer are not found in the same sentence. They come from different parts of the text.
   1. Why would you call the creatures in this text selection, "predatory"?
   2. How does the author create a picture of the octopus as a hunter?
   3. Your question:

III. AUTHOR and YOU! Respond to the following questions by combining your own experience with the ideas and information you have read in the text.
   1. Why is the octopus usually portrayed as a frightening sea creature?
   2. Explain how harsh realities could exist in a calm tide pool.
   3. Your question:

IV. ON YOUR OWN! The answer is not in the selection. You need to use your own background knowledge and experience to answer the questions.
   1. How are a community and a tide pool alike?
   2. In nature, which creatures are most likely to survive?
   3. Your question:

QAR : A Lesson Plan

As teachers, you will need to design units and lesson plans incorporating these strategies. What does a QAR look like in the context of a lesson? We have outlined a typical lesson plan illustrating how to incorporate this literacy strategy.

This lesson plan has been designed for a traditional 50-minute class period. The learning activity, however, probably takes the whole period. The introductory part of the lesson and student reading may be conducted in one class period and the QAR learning activity scheduled for the following class. For those teachers having the luxury of a 90-minute block period, the entire lesson can be conducted in one class period.

For helping build students' awareness and ability for recognizing and responding to different levels of questions, the QAR remains for us and the teachers we work with one of the most useful literacy strategies.

Many of the teachers we have worked with highlight the definitions of these literacy terms on classroom posters. They hang these in their classrooms as constant reminders to the students of the kind of thinking to shift to as they construct their own understanding of text.

How does the QAR contribute to better understanding?

One of our favorite observations is to watch students discuss their QAR guide. Knowledge becomes useful when it is transformed by the student. Something has to happen to the facts. By emphasizing, nurturing and reinforcing comprehension through activities which do something with facts, students will have the opportunity to see through simulation how facts are transformed into the larger picture of ideas, values and opinions. As they move into the interpretive (Think & Search level) we frequently see them advise their peers, particularly those still in the "Right There" mode, that they need to switch to "reading between the lines and searching for the answer." Ultimately, this frequent simulation of thinking at various levels transfers to students doing it independently on their own without benefit of artificial structures.

Example 2: Mathematics Model
Student Discussion Guide: Classifying Triangles

Directions: After reading the section on classifying triangles in your geometry book, work with other students in your group answering the following questions. Come up with a question of your own for each section. Write your answers on another sheet of paper. Be prepared, students from each group will be asked randomly to respond to these questions.

FIGURE 4.1.   QAR LESSON PLAN

Lesson Plan: Integrated Science and Language Arts

Grade: 10

Topic: Marine Biology and *Cannery Row* by John Steinbeck

Purpose: To help students gain knowledge of tide pools and interpret universal ideas of nature described by writers.

State Content/Literacy Standards: 1) Identify interactions among parts of a subsystem; 2) to infer meaning by identifying implicit relationships such as comparisons, and generalizations.

Student Objectives:
1. Students will be able to identify, compare and contrast the elements of a tide pool by completing a QAR Discussion Guide and reaching consensus in their responses.
2. Students will be able to draw analogies between the universal concept, "Survival" and tide pool information by completing a QAR Discussion Guide and reaching consensus in their responses.
3. Students will be able to demonstrate their understanding of a tide pool and its relationships by illustrating it.

Introduction:
1. Ask students to brainstorm the concept, "Survival." (1 minute)
2. Summarize students' ideas with a concept map. (2 minutes)
3. Introduce topic. (1 minute)
4. Show transparencies of tide pools. (2 minutes)
5. Link science with language arts—mini-lecture on writers like Steinbeck who use nature as a backdrop for their ideas (3 minutes).

Learning Activity:
1. Distribute and explain Question-Answer Relationships (QAR) Discussion Guide. (5 minutes)
2. Randomly select groups of five students. Appoint facilitator, recorder, reporter, gatekeeper, and encourager for each group. (2 minutes)
3. Direct students to respond to four levels of questions. (20 minutes)
4. Reporters present their responses as the instructor calls randomly on groups. (10 minutes)

Closure:
Students illustrate pictures, symbols or images of what John Steinbeck has described in his account of the tide pool. In addition students write an explanation of the drawings that they chose to include in their illustration. (5 minutes with option to continue as homework)

Evaluation:
Students' drawings are assessed for: a) accurate understanding of significant supporting details as well as subtle and obvious inferences, b) interconnectedness of tide pool inhabitants, and c) integration of concept, "Survival."

I. RIGHT THERE! The answers to these questions will be in the text and are easy to find. The words used to make up the question and the words used to answer the question are right there in the passage.
1. What is a triangle?
2. What is a polygon?
3. What is an acute triangle?
4. What is an obtuse triangle?
5. What is a right triangle?
6. What is a scalene triangle?
7. What is an equilateral triangle?
8. Your question:

II. THINK and SEARCH! The answer is in the reading, but you need to put together different parts of the reading to find it. You need to THINK about the question and SEARCH for the answer. Words for the question and the words for the answer are not found in the same sentence. They come from different parts of the text.
1. Can a scalene triangle be an acute triangle? If yes, give an example.
2. Can a right triangle be a scalene triangle? If yes, give an example.
3. Can an isosceles triangle be a scalene triangle? If yes, give an example.
4. Can an isosceles triangle be equilateral? If yes, give an example.
5. Your question:

III. AUTHOR and YOU! Respond to the following questions by combining your own experience with the ideas and information you have read in the text.
1. Look around your classroom to find an example of each: scalene triangle, right scalene triangle, isosceles triangle, obtuse triangle, equilateral triangle and acute scalene triangle. Write the name of each object.
2. Triangle ABC is isosceles with the congruent sides as marked. Name each of the following: sides, angles, vertex angle, base angles, side opposite angle B, congruent sides, and angle opposite segment AB.

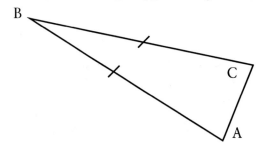

3. Draw and label triangle DEF using the given conditions:
   a) measure of angle D is less than 90°, segment DE is the hypotenuse.
   b) DE = EF and the measure of angle E = 90°.
   c) DE<EF<DF.
   d) Angle D is obtuse and triangle DEF is isosceles,
4. Your question:

IV. ON YOUR OWN! The answer is not in the selection. You need to use your own background knowledge and experience to answer the questions.

1. Given that the measure of angle NMO = 20°, prove that triangle LMN is an obtuse triangle.

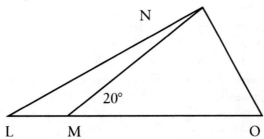

2. Triangle RST is isosceles. Find the perimeter.

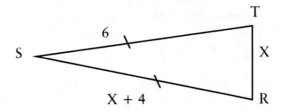

3. PUBLIC WORKS: A fire hydrant is to be located on the highway in such a way that it is as close as possible to two buildings each 1 block from the highway and 1 block apart.
   a) What kind of triangle will be formed using the buildings and the hydrant as vertices?
   b) Why will this triangle satisfy the conditions necessary to locate the fire hydrant?
   c) Your question:

Three-Level Guide

The three-level guide is similar to the QAR activity, please refer to Table 1 for a description of the instructional characteristics that match the three-level guide as well. However, unlike the QAR that uses questions to guide students through the levels of thinking, the three-level guide uses statements that help students to recognize information at the literal level, to interpret the reading, and, finally, to apply the author's ideas to their own ideas and experiences.

Why statements instead of questions? As Herber (1978) writes, "Questions are assumptive." Students need to be able to recognize the relationship between the question and the content. In many of our observations of students working with question study guides a student will tell us, "I can't find the answer to the question." Frequently, they are looking for the answer "Right There" in the text. They cannot identify a paraphrase, an interpretive element, or any content that would provide evidence to higher levels of questions. The statements help students recognize information. They don't have to interpret the question before they can find evidence to respond to it. The statements simulate the process of interacting with text at a designated level of thinking and help students focus on getting the evidence accurately.

What is the advantage of using statements in study guides?

Teachers tell us that as a result of the practice of using these level guides, either the QAR or the Three-Level guide, their skilled students become less sloppy in their thinking. Rather than simply using their intuition to respond to questions regarding their reading, they more carefully check the nature of the question. While taking tests, they appear as focused on the "how" of what they are doing as well as the "what" of the content. And for learners with problems who understand little about how to process text, these guides provide a language and a system for making meaning.

Let's examine a three-level guide to develop a sense of this instructional activity. To begin, read the biology text provided on the history of the banana. Then note how the directions guide students' thinking about their reading on it and how they are led systematically through the material. We encourage you to work in a small group on this activity to experience how these guides, if used in discussion, promote comprehension at a number of levels.

Three-Level Guide: "The Banana"

A. Right There! Check those statements that can be found directly in your reading "The Banana." The statements may or may not be in the exact words of the author. Come to consensus in your group.

_____ 1. The banana probably originated in Asia in ancient times.

_____ 2. Thousands of years ago, the fruits of the banana plant were tasteless, with black and bitter seeds.

_____ 3. Through cultivation and genetic change, the banana has developed to the fruit it is today.

_____ 4. A single bunch of bananas consists of hands, and each hand contains 12 to 20 fingers or bananas.

_____ 5. The banana plant flowers many times, producing several crops.

B. Think and Search! Check the statements which are reasonable inferences and conclusions based on what the author wrote. Discuss your choices with members of your group.

_____ 6. Bananas are ancient and worldwide travelers.

_____ 7. Sex has been eliminated in cultivated bananas.

_____ 8. A "tree" is always made of wood.

_____ 9. Fruits such as bananas, grapes, and tomatoes are really berries.

_____ 10. The lifetime of a banana is a long one.

C. On your own! Check those statements that you agree with based on your reading and your own background experience. Come to consensus with members of your group.

_____ 11. The cultivated banana and the mule share a secret.

_____ 12. Living things are not static.

_____ 13. A banana today; a banagerine tomorrow.

_____ 14. Your turn:

For the sake of understanding this activity, we will discuss each level. Of course, skilled readers move among these levels naturally. Depending on the nature of the reading, they move back and forth many times, oblivious to their thinking processes. However, the three-level guide is a way of systematically help-

---

FIGURE 4.2.   THE BANANA

There is a Hindu legend that the banana was the forbidden fruit in the earthly paradise, and that it was the leaves of this plant with which the first man and woman covered their nakedness. Let's see if this could be true.

The banana tree and its fruits, bananas, have been known since ancient times, even before the cultivation of rice. The banana is probably native to tropical Asia, where it has long been domesticated. Alexander the Great encountered it there on his expedition to India. Polynesians spread it through most of the Pacific, as did the Arabian merchants across Africa, where the name "Banana" originated. The Portuguese and Spanish colonizers carried the banana to the rest of the warm regions of the world, especially America.

The banana has not always been the flavorful and fragrant fruit we know today. Thousands of years ago, prior to man's tinkering with the banana's sex life, the fruits of the banana plant were tasteless with black and bitter seeds. Through cultivation and genetic changes, we now enjoy the common yet sterile banana with its aborted ovules and abundant endosperm. This berry, yes, berry just as the grape and tomato are botanically known as berries, is a dieter's dream at 280 calories per large banana. It can be eaten raw, fried or baked and is as rich in vitamins B and C as oranges and tomatoes, higher in sugars and starches than potatoes and rich in iron, phosphorus, potassium, and calcium. The banana tree is actually a very tall herb arising from a fleshy rhizome, with a trunk of overlapping, sheathlike leaf stalks leading to gigantic leaves (8-12 feet long) which fray in the warm tropical breezes. The flower starts as a bud from the underground corm, travels through the center of the leaf stalks, and exits as a pendulous hanging cluster of flowers below the crown of leaves. The staminate flowers are sterile and form the tip of the large bud, while the unfertilized pistils at the base of the bud develop into bananas. A single bunch of bananas consists of the hands (flower clusters of about 6 to 15 per plant) and each hand contains 12 or 20 fingers or bananas. The banana plant lives to flower only once, as it is cut down after harvest. New plants are grown from bits of rhizome or suckers from this perennial plant and therefore are clones. During its short life span above ground of about two years, the banana plant, nonetheless, produces larger yields of food mass per acre than any other agricultural crop.

From the *Sex Life of Plants* by A. Bristow. Copyright 1978. Reprinted by permission of Shelley Power Literary Agency Ltd.

---

ing students study and articulate these gymnastics. Good readers learn a language for the thinking they bring to reading and become more conscious of the process they use.

Literal Level

When students comprehend at the **literal level they can recognize the information which is explicitly stated in the text.** In the example on "The Banana," students are directed to examine the statements of the guide and determine if the author states this information or not. The reader simply searches the text, "reading the lines" to confirm or refute the statements. Researchers agree that if the

Define the literal level.

Raphael (1982)

*Pearson &
Johnson (1972)*

information is "right there" or "textually explicit," it is literal. This level allows for little ambiguity; the facts, concepts or ideas are stated or paraphrased in the text.

After the students have examined the facts and come to some consensus, they move to the Interpretive Level.

Interpretive Level

Students comprehend at the interpretive level when they can construct ideas or opinions that are based on the material read but not stated explicitly in the text.

*Define the
interpretive level.*

At this level, students are "reading between the lines." Herber (1978) characterizes this level as one in which "readers perceive the relationships that exist in that information, conceptualizing the ideas formulated by these relationships, and expressing these relationships in either written or oral form. The result is the development of an idea that is not explicitly expressed by the authors" (p. 45). Raphael refers to the mental process students use to function at this level as "Think and Search." Students look for the bits and pieces of information that support the ideas communicated in the text.

Raphael (1982)

A second grader had one of the best methods for defining this level of thinking. While conducting a research study, one of the authors met Angel, who quickly became her precocious collaborator. The college professor had a difficult time explaining to second graders how to find support for the interpretive statements they were discussing. Intuitively most students seemed to know which statements were interpretations of the reading. They could agree or disagree with the statements. However, they seemed to be stymied in explaining why they agreed or disagreed with the statements.

Angel, however, seemed to have a handle on the process and was doing a good job of explaining it to her small group of peers. She was invited to explain to the class what she did when she thought about why she agreed or disagreed with an interpretive-level statement.

Drawing herself up to her fullest second grade stature in front of the class, she began, "The interpretive level is really like a puzzle. You look back at your story and take a fact from here and a fact from there. These are your pieces and you put them all together. If they are the right pieces, they fit and make a picture, and you have the interpretive level." This explanation appears to work—even with graduate students today.

Applied Level

Students comprehend at the **applied level when they connect and integrate the information, ideas and values from their reading with their own experience or apply these in other contexts.** Pearson & Johnson (1972) call this process "reading beyond the lines." Herber explains that "...prior knowledge and experience relate to what you read: that is when you see a relationship between the ideas acquired from other sources and the ideas derived from the reading selection. Out of that perceived relationship, you evolve broad generalizations or principles which embrace both sets of ideas, but which represent something more than just the sum of the two" (p. 47).

*Define the
applied level.*

Herber (1978)

Modeling Discussion of a Three-Level Guide

Teachers should spend some time modeling how students approach the guide. By writing examples from the three levels of the guide on the board or a transparency, teachers can discuss the process of locating support for the items at each level. How students arrive at the choices they make is critical to the discussion. This introductory lesson to guides in general helps students develop a feel for how a discussion of the guide develops.

Donlan (1978)

For example, in discussing the applied level, teachers could focus initially on generalizations. What are they? Have students cite some they are familiar with, e.g., "The grass is always greener on the other side of the fence." Select an example from your study guide and work through the relationships involved. Copy a statement on the board such as "Life is not static." Ask students to examine how the concepts involved in this generalization interact.

You might begin with definitions. What does "static" mean? Once the students determine that "static" probably refers to "not changing," they are guided to see the connection between, "life" and "static." From their background, they draw on examples of changes they have seen, e.g., medical advances. Or they may draw upon examples of situations where change did not occur and what the results were, for example, the failure of industries such as logging to attend to the increasing influence of the environmental movement.

Students should be encouraged to come up with several examples. Write these on the board. Then have students examine their reading on "The Banana" and see how the information supports the statement "Life is not static." For example, students may talk about how the banana evolved from a wild, bland berry to a cultivated, profitable cash crop. If the examples from both their background experience and their reading support the statement that life indeed is not static, they then come to consensus and agree with it.

How do generalizations promote relevance in learning?

Kauchak & Eggen (1989)

What do generalizations do for students? These generalizations describe patterns or trends. They summarize a large amount of information into a comprehensible pattern. Many of these facts in isolation are unimportant, e.g., "The banana probably originated in Asia in ancient times." However, this fact, when coupled with traveling and genetic manipulation, takes on greater significance over time. Students are able to explain and predict change in general. They are able to apply what they have learned about the banana to myriad examples from life.

This kind of reasoning helps students see the relevance of their studies to the world at large. Students are making generalizations and connections. They are going beyond the words and connecting their newly associated ideas to their present world. This process of thinking helps in retaining the essential information. It also ensures long-term retention because of the hard evidence and analysis the students have provided and developed while discussing applied statements.

Science teachers may use laws or principles in this section. Laws and principles are generalizations with no exceptions. They are accepted as true, e.g., the Law of Conservation of Energy—energy cannot be created or destroyed but may be changed from one form to another. This principle describes a relationship among such concepts as energy and change. We can use it to explain and predict. Note these principles are not facts. They do not describe a single event, but rather summarize all cases involving their integral concepts.

In the discussion at this level, it is critical to let students know they are to use their own ideas in conjunction with ideas from the text. We observed one student who remarked to the teacher, "You mean I can use the stuff in my head to answer!" It was obvious that this student thought that in classroom discussions only text-bound content had merit. His own thoughts and experiences were typically set aside. How relieved a number of students will be in your classroom to find their own individual experiences and knowledge about classroom subjects are respected and accepted in the course of discussion.

However, a word of caution. When students are discussing the applied level of their study guide, it is critical to monitor their responses. Their support of the statements must be the result of both their learning and their background knowledge. Frequently, students get sidetracked by the vividness and application of their experience and fail to correlate that experience with the content they are learning. Their argument needs to stand the test of supporting the statement both from relevant experiences as well as from what they have read and studied.

Adapting the Three-Level Guide
As you adapt this guide to your subject areas, you may change the format depending on your content. However, check to see that your design reflects the various levels of thinking. The following example highlights a mathematical version of the three level-guide.

Example: **Mathematics**

The Pythagorean Theorem

I.   What did the author say? Discuss your choices with members of your group. Check each statement below that you think is right there in the section you just read.
   _____ 1.   The right triangle shown here is called the Pythagorean Theorem.
   _____ 2.   In the illustrations the square on a side represents the square of the length of that side.
   _____ 3.   Since $9+16 = 25$, $a^2 + b^2 + c^2 = $ ____.
   _____ 4.   To form a right angle, the Egyptian "rope stretchers" divided a rope into 15 equal parts with 14 knots.
   _____ 5.   In the second example, each square is divided into triangular tiles.
   _____ 6.   In a right triangle, the square of the length of the hypotenuse is equal to the sum of the squares of the lengths of the legs.

II.   What did the author mean? Think and search for the support for these statements. Discuss your reasoning with the members of your group. Check the statements below that state what the author meant in the section you just read.
   _____ 1.   If the lengths of 2 sides of a triangle are known, the length of the 3rd side can be computed.

_____ 2. The sum of the area of the squares on the legs of a right triangle is equal to the area of the square on the hypotenuse.

_____ 3. The Egyptian rope stretchers were the first to show the right-triangle relation.

_____ 4. The converse of the Pythagorean Theorem is necessary to prove a triangle is a right triangle.

_____ 5. The proof of the Pythagorean Theorem given in the reading section is the only way to prove this theorem.

III. On Your Own. Now that you've read the section, apply what you've learned to the following problems. Discuss which problem(s) could be solved by using what you've learned about the Pythagorean Theorem. Discuss your choices with your group members and be able to defend your group choice during class discussion.

_____ 1. In a baseball game the runner on first base attempts to steal second base. He travels 90 ft. from first to second base. The catcher throws the ball from home plate to second base to make the out. How many feet (in a straight line) does the ball travel?

_____ 2. Some builders are moving a piece of glass for a picture window through a doorway of a house. The glass is 2.3m wide and the doorway is 0.9 m wide and 2.2m high. Will the glass fit through the doorway?

_____ 3. The minute hand of Big Ben is 14 ft. long and the hour hand is 9 ft. long. What is the distance between their tips at 4:00 p.m.?

Expository Text Structure Guides

TABLE 3

INSTRUCTIONAL SUMMARY OF EXPOSITORY TEXT STRUCTURE GUIDES

Literacy Strategy	Expository Test Structure Guides
Primary Focus	Comprehension ❑ Cause/ Effect ❑ Description/Enumeration ❑ Sequence ❑ Comparison/Contrast ❑ Problem/Solution
Learning Principles	❑ Active Involvement ❑ Talk Time ❑ Organizing Information

When to Use	After reading
Goals: National or State Literacy Standards	❑ Promote comprehension ❑ Increase awareness of question types ❑ Recognize a variety of text structures
Materials	❑ Expository text definitions ❑ Study Guides
Time	30 Minutes

Why is it critical to understand organizational patterns in text?

Textbooks are meant to explain something. As such their authors use frequent doses of cause and effect; description/enumeration; sequence; comparison and contrast, and problem and solution text structures in order to illustrate content. Once students know how to look for these structures, they can grasp the meaning of text more easily. These patterns are the connecting blocks that good readers use all the time (Meyer, Brandt, & Bluth, 1980; Taylor, 1980). Frequently, how well students comprehend these patterns determines how well they learn.

Poor readers consistently are not aware of text structures and do not use them in recall. When asked to write about their learning, unskilled readers make random lists of information rather than structure it to demonstrate patterns or relationships connecting facts or ideas they've learned.

TEACHER TALK

Understanding organizational patterns is like understanding chess. Students need to have 1) an understanding about the true purpose of the opening strategies, 2) a knowledge of the planning skills and the thinking processes that will make this happen, and 3) an understanding of the most elementary ending strategies.

Teach compare/ contrast, cause/ effect, and enumeration patterns.

The good news is that given some guidance and a lot of practice, developing readers, like emergent chess players, can cultivate an awareness of these patterns and learn to use them in reading and writing. Before we present strategies simulating these patterns, it is important for students to understand what is meant by these terms. In countless content area classes, we have watched such words as cause and effect, comparison and contrast fly by students who can't or don't make the connection with their meaning. What is a cause? What is an effect? How does one compare and contrast? In the following summary of these patterns, we will use some examples from textbooks or supplemental readings that teachers use in a classroom.

Common Patterns Used in Text Material

Define cause and effect.

Cause and Effect. One would define this pattern as a process in which one situation occurs because of the action of another. Cause answers the question "Why did this happen?" Effect answers the question "What will this do?"

Example: **Social Studies**

An Iron Curtain across Europe

Americans watched with concern while the Soviet Union crushed all freedom and all opposition in the nations of Eastern Europe in the years after 1945. Former British Prime Minister Winston Churchill dramatically described the "iron curtain" that now divided Europe. In a speech in March, 1946 at Fulton, Missouri, with President Truman on the platform, Churchill declared that "from Stettin on the Baltic to Trieste on the Adriatic, an Iron Curtain has descended across the continent" of Europe. The West, said Churchill, must meet this grave challenge. It must use force, if needed, because the Communists had no respect for weakness. Truman and his advisors came to agree that a "get tough" policy was their only choice.

Churchill's warning won widespread support in the United States. Many Republicans in both houses of Congress who bitterly opposed Truman on domestic issues backed him in his dealings with other nations. Foreign policy became bipartisan, that is, it was supported by both parties. Both parties opposed the expansionist policies of the Soviet Union. Senator Arthur Vandenberg, ranking Republican member of the Senate Foreign Relations Committee, was a leader of this bipartisan movement. Vandenberg worked closely with Truman in forming policies and winning support for them. Truman in turn publicly thanked the Republicans for their support.

Source: Ritchie, D. (1985). *Heritage of freedom.* NY. Macmillan.

If we were to examine the cause/effect patterns in this selection, the following would emerge:

CAUSE	EFFECT
Iron Curtain	"Get tough" policy
Churchill's warning	US bipartisan support

Enumeration. A definition of this pattern would include a listing of facts, characteristics, or features. The listing usually follows given criteria such as kind, size or importance and serves to connect ideas through description.

Define enumeration.

Example: **Language Arts—Descriptive Writing**

Astoria may very well have the highest concentration of bakeries per block in Queens, in New York, or even in North America. In the five blocks from my house to the elevated station at Ditmars Boulevard, for instance, I pass Island Bakery (semolina rolls and anisette toast); the Victory Sweet Shop (Greek cookies in shallow bins with hinged glass lids, and Greek men crowded around two little tables, drinking coffee and arguing—they're really just talking, but they always sound like they're arguing); the Lefkos Pirgos Zacharoplasteion (rich, honey-soaked Greek pastries and more Greek men arguing); and Rose & Joe's Italian Bakery (Sicilian pizza). Rose & Joe's happens to be between two non-aligned doughnut shops, Olympic and Twin, which cater to the people who work for the Transit Authority (Ditmars is the end of the line), and around the corner there's a Dunkin' Donuts.

Source: Mary Norris, *Wigwag* (1989), p. 54.

If we were to track a series of details that the author has listed, our chart might look like the following:

Island Bakery	Victory Sweet Shop	Lefkos Pirgos Zacharoplasteion	Rose & Joe's
semolina rolls	Greek cookies	honey-soaked pastries	Sicilian pizza
anisette toast	Greek men arguing	More Greek men arguing	

Define sequence.

Sequence. In this text structure, ideas are ordered or sequenced.

Example: Mathematics

On Which Day of the Week Were You Born?

Birthdays are special occasions for sharing with family and friends. Follow the formula to find the day of the week you were born. If you already know the day, find out the day for a friend or a relative.

First, write the last two digits of the year in which you were born. Call this number A. Second, divide that number (A) by 4, and drop the remainder if there is one. This answer, without the remainder, is called B. Third, find the number for the month in which you were born in the Table of Months. Call this number C. Fourth, on which date of the month were you born? Call this number D. Fifth, add the numbers from the first four steps: A+B+C+D. Sixth, divide the sum you got in step 5 by the number 7.

What is the remainder from that division? (It should be a number from 0 to 6.) Find this remainder in the Table of Days. That table tells you on which day of the week you were born.

This method works for any date in the twentieth century. You can't use it to find out days before 1900. It will help you to find out on which day of the week a certain holiday or your next birthday will fall. In many almanacs there is a perpetual calendar. That calendar will confirm your work.

Table of Months		Table of Days	
JANUARY	1 (0 in Leap Year)	SUNDAY	1
FEBRUARY	4 (3 in Leap Year)	MONDAY	2
MARCH	4	TUESDAY	3
APRIL	0	WEDNESDAY	4
MAY	2	THURSDAY	5
JUNE	5	FRIDAY	6
JULY	0	SATURDAY	0
AUGUST	3		
SEPTEMBER	6		
OCTOBER	1		
NOVEMBER	4		
DECEMBER	6		

From Distant View, by R. Allington, 1997, page 44.

Comparison and Contrast. In text, this pattern illustrates similarities and differences between two or more things, persons or events.

Example: Spanish *(Text in Appendix A & B)

COMPARING AND CONTRASTING LITTLE RED RIDING HOOD AND LA HIJA DEL TORRERO

La Caperucita Roja		La Hija del Torrero
La escena - el bosque	Los personajes principales	La escena - la costa
Los cazadores	Las muchachas jovenes	Los marineros
El malo -El Lobo	Alguien esta enferma	Los malos - los piratas
El heroe -El cazador	Los malos avaros	La heroe - Teresa
La accion-usa la pistola para resolver el problema	Las muchachas tienen una problema	La action -usa ingeniosidad para resolver el problema
La caperucita roja esta salvada	El tema de interdependencia	Teresa es la salvadora
Las diferencias	*Las similitudes*	*Las diferencias*

Problem and Solution. Text includes the development of a problem and offers one or more solutions or asks the reader to provide one.

Example: Science

Quality of Water

Water is necessary to all life on the earth. So it is important to maintain the quality of water. Yet many of the earth's sources of fresh water are becoming polluted. Normally water is naturally filtered through soil and sand, which help to remove impurities. But carelessness in dumping sewage, silt, industrial wastes, and pesticides into water has caused serious problems. Since these substances are easily dissolved in water, water is becoming more and more polluted.

Federal laws have been passed to prevent industry from dumping certain chemical wastes into the earth's waters. Wastewater treatment systems are being constructed to remove pollution from rivers and lakes. What other steps might be taken to stop water pollution and save one of the earth's most important natural resources?

Source: Coble, C. et al. (1991). *Earth Science*. Englewood Cliffs, NJ: Prentice Hall. pp. 256-257.

A graphic organizer identifying the problem and solution in the preceding excerpt would include:

Another organizational structure that students find helpful in learning to think about problems in their reading is the Problem-Solution Frame. This serves as a note taking technique as well as a means of thinking critically about the essentials of the reading.

Problem:	Pollution
Result:	Contaminated fresh water
Cause:	Dumping sewage, wastes and pesticides
Solution:	Federal laws and wastewater treatment

What we have presented with these few examples represents only a small offering of text structure study guides. Consistent, systematic practice will help your students gain a clearer understanding of how to make better connections among ideas in their reading and learn and retain their content material efficiently. These guides become easier to design and implement over time. For some alternate visual diagrams for framing these text patterns, check out this site: http//www.sdcoe.k12.ca.us.

Teaching Text Structures

It is our belief that text patterns should be taught in the context of the classroom: a math teacher using a mathematics text, a social studies teacher using a history text, etc. Students thereby experience how readers approach certain disciplines.

Why should text patterns be taught in the classroom?

Horowitz (1985)

Chi et al. (1988)

Text research reports that skilled readers come to any discipline with expectations about the patterns used in that subject area. For example, students come to history texts with expectations for cause-effect. For less skilled and inefficient readers, this is not the case. The following procedure may prove helpful in helping students become competent users of text patterns to implement in studying their subject material.

TEACHER TALK ──────────────────────

Since most of my students need a more structured approach, I've tried using story grammar frames, graphic organizers and Venn Diagrams to help them organize their ideas. This past year I taught a creative writing class for students with learning disabilities. I got all sorts of interesting things—one student wrote a compare/ contrast essay on two types of heavy metal bands and another wrote about the differences between wildland and structural firefighting.

Procedure.

1. Select a representative piece of content prose that illustrates a pattern that you want to demonstrate.
2. Teach students to look for signal words, such as first, second, third, or, but, however, whereas. See our chart in Figure 4.3 for the more common connectives that authors use to call attention to the organizational patterns used in their writing.
3. Duplicate a piece of content area text—secondary students usually can't write in their textbooks. To recognize these patterns, have students underline on the duplicated text, for example, a comparison they have identified, and then highlight the signal word.

Example: Social Studies

I had looked forward to watching contemporary lumberjacks demonstrate their mastery of <u>axes and cross-cut saws</u>, tools that gradually became obsolete in everyday logging after Andreas Stihl invented a <u>crosscutting chain saw</u> in 1926. The throck-throck sounds accompanying the chopping events soothed me. In contrast back at Camp Grisdale, the <u>power saws</u> emitted <u>eardrum-threatening screams</u>. ...At the camp, I regretted the fact that million-dollar <u>cable-bearing machines</u> had replaced <u>horse-drawn skidders.</u>

Hank Nuwer, *fireside Companion*, July/August 1989, p. 20.

FIGURE 4.3.   USEFUL TEXT PATTERN WORD SIGNALS

Cause/Effect	Comparison/Contrast	Sequence	Enumeration
accordingly	although	additionally	also
as a result	by contrast	another	and then
because	different from	first	for example
consequently	finally	last	for instance
leads to	furthermore	later	in addition
since	however	meanwhile	in particular
so	like	next	most importantly
thereby	likewise	now	specifically
therefore	on the other hand	subsequently	
	similarly	then	
	unless		
	unlike		
	whereas		
	yet		

4. Have students make a visual representation of the patterns in the writing. In the above example, the author compares and contrasts the kinds and sounds of contemporary versus obsolete logging tools.

Example: Comparison/Contrast of Logging Tools

❏ axes ❏ cross-cut saws ❏ crosscutting chain saw ❏ horse-drawn skidders	Kinds of Tools	❏ power saws ❏ million-dollar cable-bearing machines	
❏ throck-throck-throck	Sounds	❏ eardrum-threatening screams	

National Education Association 2002

Why is expository text more difficult to read than narrative text?

5. Have students write paragraphs that follow a specific text structure.

An Organizational Pattern Guide Lesson

Recognizing organizational patterns in expository text is hard work. Expository text is more difficult to read than the narrative text found in stories. Vocabulary tends to be more abstract and the sentence structure is often more difficult to follow. As a result, students need to chisel out the details carefully for meaning to occur. However, the teacher, by designing activities which capitalize on organizational patterns, simulates for the students the process of selecting the critical material and draws attention to the role the pattern plays in connecting ideas. Students, on the other hand, have the opportunity to use the activities as a guide for their own thinking about the content. They can agree or disagree, elaborate, and clarify their thinking as they discuss the guides.

May (1989)

One thing we should point out in talking about rhetorical patterns is that writers, like speakers, do not always signal the reader to the text patterns they are using. Our students need to know how to distinguish these patterns without cues as well. In the following piece of text, "Tell Your Children," the pattern of comparison and contrast is clearly established, but the author does not use transitions to set up these comparisons. See Figure 4.4. Yet with a determined focus on the contrasting pattern developed, students can detect the meaning without these indicators.

We would like to use this reading to demonstrate how a teacher can design an instructional activity that directs students' attention to the use of patterns by writers and leads them quite easily through the information. This organizational pattern guide facilitates a comprehensive discussion when completed in small groups.

First, have the students read, or you can read aloud, the poignant speech "Tell Your Children."

After the students complete their reading, ask them to use the following guide to discuss the ideas they think the Indian Chief was attempting to convey to his listeners. By discussing the guide (see Figure 4.5) students experience how these patterns are used to connect ideas in the reading.

Use discussion in small groups to maximize understanding.

FIGURE 4.4.   SPEECH, "TELL YOUR CHILDREN"

Tell Your Children

You tell all white men, "America First." We believe in that. We are the only ones, truly, that are one hundred percent. We, therefore, ask you while you are teaching school children about America First, teach them the truth about the First Americans. We do not know if school histories are pro-British, but we do know that they are unjust to the life of our people—the American Indian. They call all white victories, battles, and all Indian victories, massacres. The battle with Custer has been taught to school children as a fearful massacre on our part. We ask that this, as well as other incidents, be told fairly. If the Custer battle was a massacre, what was Wounded Knee?

History books teach that Indians were murderers—is it murder to fight in self-defense? Indians killed white men because white men took their lands, ruined their hunting grounds, burned their forest, destroyed their buffalo. White men penned our people on reservations, then took away the reservations. White men who rise to protect their property are called patriots—Indians who do the same are called murderers.

White men call Indians treacherous—but no mention is made of broken treaties on the part of the white man...

White men called Indians thieves—and yet we lived in frail skin lodges and needed no locks or iron bars. White men call Indians savages. What is civilization? Its marks are a noble religion and philosophy, original arts, stirring music, rich story and legend. We had these...

We sang songs that carried in their melodies all the sounds of nature—the running of waters, the sighing of winds, and the calls of the animals. Teach these to your children that they may come to love nature as we love it.

We had our statesmen—and their oratory has never been equaled. Teach the children some of these speeches of our people, remarkable for their brilliant oratory.

We played games—games that brought good health and sound bodies. Why not put these in your schools? We told stories. Why not teach school children more of the wholesome proverbs and legends of our people? Tell them how we loved all that was beautiful. That we killed game only for food, not for fun. Indians think white men who kill for fun are murderers.

Tell your children of the friendly acts of Indians to the white people who first settled here. Tell them of our leaders and heroes and their deeds ... Put in your history books the Indian's part in the World War. Tell how the Indian fought for a country of which he was not a citizen, for a flag to which he had no claim, and for a people that have treated him unjustly.

Source: 1927 Speech to the mayor of Chicago by representatives of the Grand Council Fire of American Indians.

FIGURE 4.5. COMPARISON AND CONTRAST ORGANIZATIONAL PATTERN GUIDE:

Directions: Read the attached copy of the speech entitled "Tell Your Children." It is a speech which was written by representatives of the Grand Council Fire of American Indians. It was presented to the mayor of Chicago in 1927. As you read, notice how the authors of the speech demonstrate that the white man and the Indian hold many similar beliefs and attitudes, even perform many similar actions for the same reasons, but through the eyes of the white man they are viewed as one thing when applied to the white man and viewed as something quite different when applied to the Indian. After reading the speech, proceed with the following exercise.

Part I. Directions: Consider the Indians' and white men's attitudes regarding the following terms. Fill in the blanks with the word or phrase you believe the speaker has said or implied. Be sure to discuss your choices with members of your group.

1. White victories were considered _____.

2. Indian victories were seen as _____ by the whites.

3. Treaties were broken by the _____.

4. The Indians' _____ was marked by a noble religion, original arts, rich story and legend.

Part II. Directions: Check the items you believe convey what the authors of this speech wished to express. Check your response with members of your group.

_____ 5. The labels the white man has imposed upon the Indians are unjust and unwarranted.

_____ 6. The First Americans loved America.

_____ 7. The melodies and songs of the Indian more accurately reflect the sound of nature than those of the white man.

Part III. Directions: Even though it was presented more than 50 years ago, many of the issues addressed in this speech are still major concerns among Native Americans today. Check the items below which you feel are supported by the speech and by your experience. Discuss your selections with your group members.

_____ 8. Real history exists in peoples' nerves and emotions, not on paper.

_____ 9. Heroes are heroes only if their side wins.

_____ 10. History accurately records events.

Reciprocal Teaching

TABLE 4

INSTRUCTIONAL SUMMARY OF RECIPROCAL TEACHING

Literacy Strategy	Reciprocal Teaching
Primary Focus	❑ Prediction ❑ Summarization ❑ Clarification ❑ Questioning
Learning Principles	❑ Active Involvement ❑ Talk Time ❑ Thought Demanding Activity
When to Use	During reading
Goals: National or State Literacy Standards	❑ Information ❑ Apply a wide range of strategies to interpret text.
Materials	❑ Reciprocal Teaching Guide Cards ❑ Reading
Time	30 minutes

Classroom Application: Mathematics Model

Example 1: Reciprocal Teaching

Reciprocal Teaching Guide—All questions are placed on individual cards or slips of paper. Sets are made for the number of small groups in the classroom.

Procedure.
1. After the cards have been distributed, the students are asked to read silently the title, margin notes, or any information that may give them a clue to the reading content. In the case of a math problem, students would read it once silently. The first student then asks her question, "Does anyone have a prediction about this reading?" Or in the case of a math problem, "Does anyone have a prediction about this problem?" See below for the full complement of questions for a math activity or a generic model that can be applied to most text material.
2. Students are directed to read a certain amount of text, usually a paragraph or two. The rest of the questions are then asked by members of the group.
3. After this segment of text is read or the problem is solved, students rotate the questions. Math students move on to another math problem and other subject areas continue with assigned segments of text. The rotation of questions continues until the reading is completed.

Why is the Reciprocal Teaching Guide popular?

Card # 1 (Encourage students to skim the question before reading through carefully) What is the problem about? What is the main question of the problem? Does anyone have a prediction about the solution?	Card # 2: What information is given? How do you represent the information given with variables and/or equations? Is there any information that you think you might need that you don't already have to solve this problem and why?
Card # 3: What is the relationship between the problem and the information given? What mathematical operations are needed and why? What steps or strategies are needed to solve this problem? How can you represent the problem in an equation with the information given?	Card # 4: Can you solve the problem? If not, what additional information would you need to solve the problem? What part of the equation represents the additional information needed?
Card # 5: What isn't clear about this problem?	

In designing this reciprocal teaching activity, the teacher can use these cards or adapt them to specific content area. For example a science teacher in a lesson on environmental adaptations might substitute the #4 question in the generic guide with "What is being compared in this science reading?"

Hoyt (1999)

According to the feedback from teachers, they like the reciprocal teaching guide because it engages all the students and is non-threatening at the same time. In each small group, the student is only responsible for asking the question. The response for the question depends on the synergy of the group. In addition, it simulates a number of powerful reading processes: predicting, summarizing, clarifying and raising personal questions. Through this activity, students develop strategies for gaining meaning from the printed page.

Encourage students to raise questions.

Reciprocal teaching concentrates on teaching students how to work out meaning. As Palincsar (1984) writes "reciprocal teaching is a dialogue between teachers and students for the purpose of jointly constructing the meaning of the text" (p. 119). Initially, teachers may lead the questions, then students assume the role of leader. At this point, teachers provide feedback and coach the small groups.

*Why should
students
generate their
own questions?*

Depending on the reading ability of students, teachers may need some up front time to teach specifically how to make predictions, to summarize material, to clarify and to practice raising "How," Why," or other appropriate questions. Frequently, students become more involved when they generate the questions than when they merely respond to teacher questions. Many times these questions become the enrichment part of the lesson because students need to go elsewhere to find the answers.

The following are activities for guiding students' understanding of the four reading processes involved in reciprocal teaching:

❏ Prediction. Ask students to hypothesize about the next event in the text, describe what the reading may be about, or which details, they predict, are important in solving a math problem.
❏ Summarization. Ask students to identify and paraphrase the main ideas in the assigned reading, either a short passage, a section or a problem.
❏ Clarification. Ask students if there is anything in their reading of the paragraph or short reading that they want cleared up.
❏ Questioning. Ask students to develop their own questions on the text. Encourage the use of "Why", "How," "Who," and "When" questions. As students become more comfortable with developing their own questions move into questions that demonstrate comparisons and contrasts, and cause and effect.

For the instructor who would like to conduct a structured instructional lesson using reciprocal teaching strategies to create a whole class discussion, simply (a) share a brief review of the reading processes noted above, (b) read the title or direct students' attention to critical elements of text format for student predictions, (c) read a small section of the text, (d) ask questions, (e) ask students to summarize and, finally (f) add clarifications. The following Your Turn illustrates a generic version that would fit most subject area content.

Your Turn

Name _____ Date _____ Subject Area _____

Reciprocal Teaching Guide Questions (Generic)

Directions: After selecting an informational or fictional reading for students, distribute a set of cards to each group. The cards within the set are then distributed to each member of the group. Each student is responsible for one question or more depending on the size of the group. Each group selects a leader to moderate the discussion. The teacher can serve as a member of the group or rotate from group to group. After one rotation of the questions, pass the cards to a new leader and redistribute the cards for the next part of the reading.

Card # 1 (Encourage students to skim and scan before reading the selection.) Does anyone have a prediction about this reading?	**Card # 2:** (After reading) Are there any ideas for us to clarify? Write a question(s) you have.
Card # 3: Would someone please share an interesting or puzzling WORD they found and tell why it interests you? Record each word on a piece of paper or file card.	**Card # 4:** How does this reading relate to a film, story or real life experience you have had?
Card # 5: This reading was about...	**Card # 6:** What do you predict is going to happen next?

Directed Reading-Thinking Activity

Another comprehension activity that teaches students how to use a multiple of reading skills for exploring text is the Directed Reading-Thinking Activity.

TABLE 5

INSTRUCTIONAL SUMMARY OF DRTA	
Literacy Strategy	**Directed Reading-Thinking Activity**
Primary Focus	❏ Activating Prior Knowledge ❏ Comprehension Development ❏ Extension of Thought
Learning Principles	❏ Active Involvement ❏ Metacognitive Experience ❏ Thought Demanding Activity
When to Use	Pre, During, Post Reading
Goals: National or State Literacy Standards	❏ Use relevant and specific information ❏ Apply a wide range of strategies to interpret text.
Materials	❏ Reading Material, Lecture Notes ❏ Teacher–prepared Questions
Time	30 minutes

Using the DR-TA, the teacher choreographs the students' reading. This activity models how good readers address text and provides students with insights on how to approach independently their reading of text. The DR-TA includes activities for prereading, guiding reading, post-reading, and extending reading.

1. Prereading Activities
   ❏ Build students' background to help them make connections between what they know and the concepts they will be learning. Introduce critical vocabulary.
   ❏ Preview whole text by examining title, subtitles, charts, and maps. Ask students to make predictions based on these cues.
2. Guided Reading
   ❏ Read first section of the reading together or in small groups.
   ❏ Ask students questions using such models as:
   "What do you think..."
   "Why do you think so?"
   "Can you prove it?"
   ❏ Continue with the rest of the reading. Encourage students, however, to read these sections silently, stopping and asking students questions along the way. Guide students in noticing stated and implied relationships and textual conventions. Check learning of content.
3. Post-Reading—Use text to support ideas, to review learning, to synthesize material and draw conclusions.

4. Extended Reading and Follow-Up Activities—Provide students with student inquiry projects or writing activities that encourage further connections, or explore textual implications.

A good way to get started is to duplicate a short section from a student textbook or trade book and have students interact with it as you guide them through the steps.

Planning Steps with Examples for DR-TA

As a lead in to a social studies lesson on The First Americans, guide students through a Barry Lopez reading, "The Blue Mound People" In *Desert Notes, River Notes*. (New York: Avon, 1979)

1. Select the text segment for the first modeling. Read aloud to the students:

   > Once there was a people here who numbered, at their greatest concentration, perhaps two hundred. It has been determined by a close examination of their bones and careful reconstruction of muscle tissues that although they looked as we do they lacked vocal cords. They lived in caves ranged in tiers in the bluffs to the east on the far edge of the desert and because of this some of their more fragile belongings, even clothing, can still be examined intact. The scraps of cloth that have been found are most frequently linen, some of them woven of over a thousand threads to the inch, cloth the thickness of human hair. As nearly as can be determined, there were no distinctions in clothing between the sexes; everyone apparently wore similar linen robes of varying coarseness and sandals made of woven sage.

   > …A number of glass and crystal shards have been found in the dirt on the floors of the caves, along with bits of bone china and porcelain. A pair of heavily worked pewter candlesticks together with scraps of beeswax were also located. (p. 33)

2. Generate predictions on the basis of the topic of the unit, The First Americans, and what the students have just learned about the Blue Mound people. E.g., "What seems strange in this reading selection?"

   "Why do you think the text may indicate a fictional account of early Americans?"

3. Once students have a sense of the narrative, encourage them to read the next section silently, raise questions then proceed through the rest of the text in similar fashion.

4. Post-Reading—Discuss with students the incongruities in this account. E.g. , How could the Blue Mound People possibly have linen, crystal or pewter at so early a period of time? Draw some conclusions.

5. Extension and follow-up activities—Compose a RAFT (See Ch. 5-Writing).

Role: Man with beaded cloth
Audience: Traders
Format: Sales Script
Topic: Dialogue with traders convincing them that the Blue Mound People need to sell their bead-work quickly. (Remember the Blue Mound people have no vocal chords.)

Critical Thinking Map

TABLE 6

INSTRUCTIONAL SUMMARY OF A CRITICAL THINKING MAP	
Literacy Strategy	**Critical Thinking Map**
Primary Focus	Comprehension
Learning Principles	❑ Active Involvement ❑ Talk Time ❑ Variety in Organizing Information
When to Use	After reading
Goals: National or State Literacy Standards	❑ Identify main ideas ❑ Evaluate information ❑ Form conclusions ❑ Extend and deepen comprehension
Materials	❑ Reading ❑ Critical Thinking Map Visual
Time	40 Minutes

At this particular time in our history, critical thinking skills are essential. As the Internet bombards us with information, we need the ability to distinguish credible information from the improbable. The Association of Supervision and Curriculum Development (2000) describes a student who wrote in his term paper that the Jews were sent to wellness centers rather than concentration camps during the Holocaust. His source—one Web site report. Did this student demonstrate that he could use technology to locate information? Yes. Did this student demonstrate that he was selective in choosing a piece that was supported by credible sources? No.

As we teach students how to access Web information, we also need to demonstrate that they need to explore sources that reflect varied opinions. From these several sources, students can sort the credibility and worth of the evidence provided and, ultimately, draw well-supported conclusions.

One method is to work with a powerful cross-referencing strategy called the "link" command on the Web. While collecting resource material, students copy the address of the Web site they are on. Then they go to a search engine like Alta Vista. Students then type "link:" in the search box, and paste the Web address

Describe the World Wide Web "link" process.

after the colon and click on Search. The search engine will provide the student with a list of Web sites that link to the topic they are investigating.

As secondary teachers provide the help for students to develop skills in handling their textbook reading, they also need to encourage students to think critically about this material. Skills needed to begin to think critically about issues and problems do not suddenly appear in our students. Teachers who have attempted to incorporate any kind of higher-level questioning in their class discussions or tests are frequently dismayed at the preliminary results. Unless the students have been prepared for the change in expectations, frustration occurs for the student and the teacher.

What is needed to cultivate a critical mindset? A number of researchers claim that the classroom must nurture an environment providing modeling, rehearsal, and coaching for students and teachers alike to develop a capacity for informed judgments. For example, Central Park East Secondary in East Harlem encourages critical thinking by designing all its courses at the high school around the following questions:

❑ Whose voice am I hearing? From where is the statement or image coming? What is the point of view?
❑ What is the evidence? How do we or they know? How credible is the evidence?
❑ How do things fit together? What else do I know that fits this?
❑ What if? Could it be otherwise?
❑ What difference does it make? Who cares? Why should I care?

Questions like those used at Central Park East can be posted on large bulletin boards in every classroom. The teacher can tuck them into her plan book and refer to them frequently. One biology teacher we know keeps a list of critical questions under her glass cover on the desk and refers to it at opportune moments. We would like to stress "opportune" moments. We don't suggest that any of these strategies become rigid and mechanistic devices to use in every lesson. They should serve as guides to foster the kind of classroom you want and your students will enjoy. Your classroom should be one where students need not preface every comment or question that challenges what is being discussed with "This may sound stupid, but ... ?"

Every student should feel that their question, not necessarily their answer, is what is valued.

Tama (1989)

Brown (1984); Hayes & Alvermann (1986); Hynd (1999)

Anrig & LaPointe (1989)

Commend students for their questions.

Design a higher-level question guide for quick reference.

Teacher Talk

I really value the Critical Reading-Thinking Map. It gives me an eye into the students' reasoning abilities, as I read their conclusions and lists of main ideas. Most were very thoughtful on the conclusion section and would have written more if time and space allowed. This guide focused our discussion and led us on a few paths that initially I had not foreseen. The students did not see it as a mere "worksheet," they saw that their writing had value and was a vehicle for communication.

Critical Thinking Map

Developing a critical view in your students can be fostered using the following strategy, which also provides practice in getting the main idea. Modeling, rehearsing, and coaching are all prevalent in the following exercise.

Procedure.

Step 1. Have the students look at the Critical Thinking Map and explain each of the components.   *Donlan (1978)*

A. **MAIN IDEA.** This is the most important message conveyed by the author and can be found "Right There" (explicit) in the text, or the reader needs to "Think and Search" (implied), or the reader needs to use his or her own thinking in deriving the main idea. Like the other phrases mentioned, "On Your Own" is a good mnemonic for students to use in determining the main idea when the reader needs to come up with it.

B. **VIEWPOINTS/OPINIONS.** Readers respond with their own viewpoints and opinions about what they have read. In addition to their own opinions, students should be asked what other information or other opinions would apply to the reading which the author hadn't mentioned. Finally, the readers could be asked what else they know about the topics which hasn't been mentioned.

C. **READER'S CONCLUSION.** The readers respond by integrating what they have read with what they know. They must decide whether the author's conclusions are valid or invalid. Students need to provide support for their thinking by stating the final conclusion about the passage.

D. **RELEVANCE TO TODAY.** The readers are asked to draw a comparison between present and past events so that they gain an understanding of how the past influences or can influence our choices today. Students fill in the map with an original and synthesized response to the question of relevancy.

Step 2. Show students how to use the Critical Thinking Map. Teachers can facilitate the activity by

a. Reading the piece of text aloud or have the students read it silently.
b. Filling in the map components after discussing the items with the students.

Step 3. Let students work in small groups and fill in the Critical Thinking Map with their partners. Check for consensus and discrepancies. Discuss discrepancies.

Step 4. Provide a significant amount of lessons which use this tool so that students become accustomed to thinking about an issue in this manner. When discussion questions alone elicit this kind of thinking, discontinue the map.

Step 5. To provide extended practice and skill in the areas suggested by the Critical Thinking Map, have students write paragraphs which pertain to each of the components of the map.

Adapted from Idol-Maestas, L. (1985). A critical thinking map to improve content area comprehension of poor readers. *Remedial Reading and Special Education, 8(4), 28-40.*

FIGURE 4.6.   A MAP FOR CRITICAL THINKING

Name: _____ Date: _____ Period: _____

Article: _____ Author: _____ Date: _____

Main Idea

Records about eugenic practices in Oregon have vanished from the Oregon State Archives.

Supporting Ideas and Key Points

Unauthorized shredding of the documents—misdemeanor offense. No other records of what happened, other than people's hazy memories. Want Governor Kitzhaber to apologize for the state's eugenics law, which wasn't repealed until 1983!

New Vocabulary Words and Definitions

Eugenics - Social and "scientific" movement in early 1900's to purify the human race by encouraging people with "good" genes to reproduce, and discouraging people with "bad" genes (minorities, "idiots," "cretins") from reproducing (often by forced sterilization).

Other Viewpoints, Opinions or Questions

What happened to the scientific method during the Eugenics Movement? How could rational people have believed this stuff? And how could these records of what happened here in Oregon have been destroyed? In my opinion, we acted no better than the Nazis.

Reader's Conclusions

This article left me wanting to know more about the American Eugenics Movement. What I read is both sad and disturbing. Because we as a society need to remember things like this so that we can educate others and prevent such atrocities from happening again.

Relevance to Society and to Me

As a citizen who can vote in the near future, I need to be knowledgeable about potential legislation like that dealing with immigration today. Minority children born in the States potentially may not be given citizenship, isn't this a form of Eugenics? I will vote in the future; I can e-mail my congress representative now.

Your Turn

Directions: Locate a text selection that lends itself to critical thinking. Fill out each section of the graphic. Use this completed graphic as a guide to write a critique of this reading.

Name: _____ Date: _____ Period: _____

Main Idea   Text: _____

_____

Supporting Ideas and Key Points

_____

New Vocabulary Words and Definitions

_____

Other Viewpoints, Opinions or Questions

_____

Reader's Conclusions

_____

Relevance to Society and to Me

_____

Finally, we would like to share the following Bill of Rights and Responsibilities of Critical Readers. Please share it with your students.

The Bill of Rights and Responsibilities of Critical Readers

Responsibilities

1. You have the responsibility of getting all of the facts and getting them straight.
2. You are responsible for separating verifiable facts from opinion when you read.
3. You are responsible for resisting fallacious lines of reasoning and propaganda.
4. You are responsible for deciding what is relevant and irrelevant when you read.
5. You have the responsibility to entertain the author's point of views objectively Negativism and criticism are not the same thing.
6. For better or worse, you are responsible for the conclusions you draw when reading, even if the author provides you with false or misleading information.

Rights

1. You have a right to all the facts, though you may have to root them out for yourself.
2. You have the right to be exposed to contrasting points of views.
3. You have the right to ask questions, even though it annoys the teacher.
4. You have the right to your opinion, even if it contradicts recognized authority.

Source: J. Mangieri & R.S. Baldwin. In R. Baldwin & J. Readance (1979). Critical reading and perceived authority. *Journal of Reading*, 617- 622.

In conclusion, critical thinking is a part of the human condition. It is no accident that the movers and shakers behind the dramatic political events in eastern Europe in the closing months of the 1980s were poets, playwrights, lawyers, and scientists. These are people who take risks with their thoughts and words every time they put pen to paper, study problems, or represent clients. Although this critical spirit is part and parcel of these occupations, it should not be limited to them alone. This spirit enables any individual to think critically about all aspects of life, to think about one's own thinking, and ultimately to act on the basis of this thinking. We provide our students with an invaluable life skill if we provide the opportunity to think critically in our classrooms.

V. I. P. (Very Important Point)

One of the most popular comprehension strategies we have found both for teachers to guide students in understanding their reading and for students to construct meaning for themselves is the V. I. P. (Very Important Point).

TABLE 7

INSTRUCTIONAL SUMMARY OF THE V.I.P.

Literacy Strategy	V.I.P. (Very Important Point)
Primary Focus	Comprehension
Learning Principles	❑ Background Knowledge ❑ Active Involvement ❑ Talk Time ❑ Thought Demanding Activity
When to Use	During, Post-reading
Goals: National or State Literacy Standards	❑ Use relevant and specific information ❑ Make personal connections with reading ❑ Note literary style/author's craft ❑ Use to problem-solve
Materials	❑ Sticky notes ❑ Reading material ❑ Pen/pencil
Time	20-30 minutes

Hoyt (1999)

As we work with preservice and inservice teachers, we are always assessing which literacy strategies seem to find their way readily into lesson and unit plans. Over the years, we have found that teachers select strategies that are effortless to design, are economical in terms of teacher and student time, and meet the specific curriculum objectives set by local and/or state guidelines.

Although a little hard on a school's allotment of sticky notes, the V. I. P. meets the above criteria. Teachers find it useful in teaching:

❑ Locating the main idea of a reading selection
❑ Marking sections that are confusing and need clarification
❑ Marking personal connections to reading
❑ Noting a writer's literary style
❑ Locating specific information to support an argument
❑ Locating supportive details for additional information.

Mathematics teachers also find this literacy strategy useful in teaching problem-solving. Using this strategy, students demonstrate that they are knowledgeable about:

❑ Identifying the mathematical problem and selecting information to solve it
❑ Demonstrating the steps they are using to solve the problem
❑ Identifying the answer
❑ Verifying their findings

Procedure.

1. Select a piece of reading material. It is best to start with a shorter segment of text that most members of the class can read. A math teacher would choose a math problem.

2. Have students take a sticky note and cut it into strips. Demonstrate how to cut or tear them to keep the sticky strip intact. In this instance, modeling helps improve efficiency, and lessens waste.

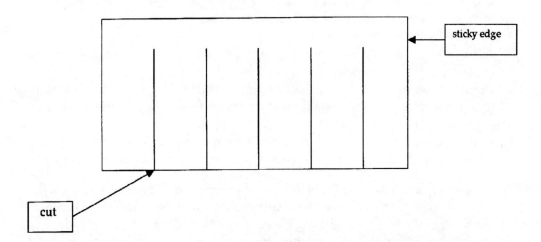

3. Depending on what purpose you have established for reading, have students mark the strips accordingly. For example, strips may be labeled "main idea", "needs clarification", "figure of speech", "personal connection," etc. The math students would label their strips accordingly: "identification of problem", "problem-solving process", "answer", and "verification of findings."

4. As students read, they then tear off these strips and post them, thereby, connecting the place in the text with the literacy activity assigned.

5. Finally, as a post-reading activity, students compare their findings and justify their choices. For the math students, this is an opportunity to check whether they have completed each step of the problem-solving process. In addition, they can see how their peers have chosen to solve the problem. Their observations may affirm their own decision-making, or provide insights into how others solved the problem differently, but still arrived at the same answer.

Further opportunities for evaluative thinking and discussion can be promoted by asking students in their small groups, for example, to evaluate the multiple main ideas they had selected individually. Based on their discussion and support of their thinking, ask them to come to consensus on the one main idea that best represents the topic or theme of the text. We have watched students, who initially pasted their strips anywhere they identified a key term, thoughtfully change its placement when a classmate pointed out a better choice. In addition, we've observed how students learn from their peers to use the entire text: margin notes, pictures, or an italicized notation to make connections.

Inclusion Techniques

Do teachers comprehend the heavy load of content material that students with special needs experience in the secondary classroom?

Schmidt et al. (1989)

Students with special needs find lengthy content area assignments difficult.

The research demonstrates that these learners find it difficult to complete lengthy reading assignments in their subject areas. Most of the inclusive students have this difficulty because of their nonsystematic approach to class reading assignments, their poor reading ability in general, and their poor attitude toward these reading tasks. However, the good news is that the special needs student learns significantly when certain activities are in place.

Students with special needs:

Tama & Martinez (1986)

1. Learn when taught. When the instructor demonstrates, models, defines, and explains, these students learn.
2. Learn when they are taught to focus on the task. These learners can attend to group instruction, particularly if they are taught to monitor their own on-task behavior.
3. Learn when given sufficient practice. Students need to learn to perform quickly, accurately and automatically. Increased practice provides this opportunity.

Classroom teachers need a portfolio of intervention strategies that incorporate these activities. In addition, these strategies need to be sufficiently practical for the average student as well as the special needs student. With daily loads of 120 to 150 students, secondary teachers have quite a job catering to the needs of talented, average, and special needs students.

Comprehension strategies help all students.

McConnell et al. (1990)

Fortunately, the learning characteristics described for the special needs student also correlate highly with learning for every child. Therefore, if we were to look back on the instructional activities presented in this chapter, we would find that they all incorporate the behaviors previously outlined. The study guides are designed to provide all students with modeling, rehearsal and practice, and involve students in active on-task behavior.

However, we would like to caution you to the time and specificity involved. Gaskins and Baron (1985), in a study to improve the thinking habits of students having trouble reading, found that three key phrases could be taught to these students and significantly improve the way they handled thinking tasks:

❏ Take time to think. (REFLECTIVITY)
❏ Stick with it. (PERSISTENCE)
❏ Consider the alternatives. (FLEXIBILITY)

These were posted in the classroom. At the beginning of each class, the students were directed to explain the meaning behind these statements. They were asked to attempt to work on at least one of the qualities each class session and describe how they would do it. Many students are impulsive, overdependent, nonpersistent, and inflexible in their approach to classroom tasks. Incorporating a healthy dose of the above seems a practical place to begin.

The following activities are designed specifically with the student with special needs in mind.

TELSQA

TABLE 8

INSTRUCTIONAL SUMMARY OF TELSQA

Literacy Strategy	TELSQA
Primary Focus	Comprehension/Vocabulary
Learning Principles	❑ Background Knowledge ❑ Active Involvement ❑ Talk Time ❑ Thought Demanding Activity
When to Use	During , Post-reading
Goals: National or State Literacy Standards	❑ Use relevant and specific information ❑ Locate information ❑ Analyze information ❑ Form conclusions
Materials	❑ TELSQA Study Guide ❑ Reading material ❑ Pen/pencil
Time	20-30 minutes

Describe the TELSQA activity.

In a program directed by Martinez (1988), TELSQA was found to be helpful in promoting reading comprehension of narrative and expository materials among learners with special needs. The first part of the acronym, TELS, is an adaptation of an advanced organizer designed by Idol-Maestas (1985). She found that not only average readers but also learning-disabled students could benefit from advanced organizers. Teachers working in the pilot program with Martinez found that adding a self-questioning component to the Idol-Maestas strategy further strengthened the students' comprehension.

Procedure. In the acronym TELSQA, each letter stands for a step in the reading process. The reader is asked to identify the (T) title; to (E) examine the materials to see what it is about; to (L) look for important or difficult words; to (SQ) self-question, raising questions at designated stops to check for meaning, and to (A) answer comprehension questions.

Step 1. Prepare students for the reading. Help students tap into their background knowledge about the subject to be discussed or broaden their thinking about it.

Step 2. Describe what the acronym stands for and describe the specific learning behaviors the students should demonstrate. A rationale for using the strategy should be presented, helping students understand that this strategy will help in learning and recalling the reading material more easily Post a chart for easy recall. Model TELSQA. Demonstrate each activity designated by the acronym.

Step 3. Provide practice sessions where the students work in small groups to complete the activity.

Step 4. Talk about TELSQA periodically. Ongoing dialogue with the students serves to direct their attention to the strategy and determine if modifications are necessary. Students will begin to adapt and take short cuts. This is to be encouraged. Again let's see how this works with a piece of text. See Figure 4.7 for the reading material and Figure 4.8 for the TELSQA procedure.

FIGURE 4.7. FIRST EUROPEANS IN THE OREGON COUNTRY

(Para. 1) Will Rogers enjoyed reminding people who boasted of their descent from the Pilgrim Fathers that his ancestors had met them at Plymouth Rock. He also had plenty of relatives in the Oregon Country, where they too greeted the first outsiders arriving there since the native peoples had themselves come sometime in the remote and barely remembered past. At the mouth of the Columbia River, the Clatsop Indians are said to have called such strangers and interlopers "Tlohonnipts," or "those who drift ashore." Who were they? When and how had they reached these shores?

(Para. 2) Among the candidates for this distinction are the ships, the famous Manila galleons. These vessels left the Philippines each year in June or early July, sailing northward past Japan to the vicinity of 40° N. latitude, whereupon they turned eastward under the influence of the Kuroshio or Japan current and the summer westerlies. If all went well, they made landfall on the California coast somewhere from Cape Medocino, to the Channel Islands (off Santa Barbara) in September or October; and then, scudding before brisk northwesters, they sailed southward along the coast to Mexico, reaching Acapulco before the winter storms set in.

(Para. 3) There are indications that at least one of these ships came to grief on the Oregon coast. In 1705, the galleon, San Francisco Xavier, under the command of one Santiago Zabalburu, departed Manila for New Spain, never to be heard from again. Were survivors of the shipwrecked Xavier, as forlorn castaways on a remote and alien shore, the first Europeans to set foot in Oregon? Is a tangled skein of Indian legends and pioneer tales of such an incident a reflection of some real event, recorded otherwise only by cakes of beeswax and the remains of shattered porcelain luxuries? No one can say with certainty. But if so, the desperate plight of those unwilling pilgrims would have equaled or exceeded the sufferings experienced by their counterparts across the continent at Plymouth.

Used with permission of the author, Herb Beals (1982).

Figure 4.8.   TELSQA

Directions: Transfer Figure 4.8 onto a transparency. Using this transparency, guide the students through the following steps with paragraphs one, two, and three of "First Europeans in the Oregon Country. In the classroom, post a chart that briefly explains the behavior and activities each letter of the acronym represents.

T—Title	What is the title? (First Europeans in the Oregon Country) What do you think this story is about? (First people who arrived in the Oregon Country)
E—Examine	Examine each paragraph and skim the paragraphs for clues as to what the passages are about. What do you think the author is writing about in paragraph 1? (Strangers, outsiders, native peoples, Indians) In paragraph 2? (Ships, galleons, vessels) In paragraph 3? (Shipwrecks, survivors)

The teacher then invites the students to suggest additional topics discussed in each paragraph. The teacher is not only modeling the procedure but is also encouraging students to exercise their own initiative.

L—Look   Look at each paragraph for important or difficult words. List them, pronounce them, and determine what they mean. The teacher now prepares a list of these for paragraph one. Then the teacher and students may prepare lists for paragraphs two and three.

Paragraph 1	Paragraph 2	Paragraph 3
Will Rogers	_____	_____
ancestors	_____	_____
Oregon Country	_____	_____
Columbia River	_____	_____

SQ—Self-Question   Lightly circle the last period of each paragraph. Ask a question after each of these signal markers and record a question mark in the margin. These circles are intended to serve students. They should be told that signals are used to help them monitor their understanding and enhance their recall of the material. If the paragraphs are very long or quite complex in conceptual information or ideas, more signals could be used. Eventually, these signal markers would be phased out as students gained proficiency in self-questioning.

FIGURE 4.8   TELSQA (CONT.)

Recording a question mark in the margin after the circled period ensures that the student has indeed emphasized the self-questioning procedure.

The teacher may further verify that self-questioning has occurred by asking the students to state or write the question that has been generated. If the students are working in pairs, they may ask each other questions about the paragraphs just read. Students should be encouraged to answer their own questions.

Examples:

Paragraph 1: What did the Clatsop Indians call those who drift ashore? (Ilohonnipts) Where is the Columbia River? (Between Oregon and Washington)

Paragraph 2: What is another name for ship or vessel? (Galleon) Where did the galleons sail from? (Manila) Where is Manila? (In the Philippines) Why did the galleons sail from Manila to Acapulco? (Infer) Trade, transportation. [Invite students to generate other questions about paragraph 2.]

Paragraph 3: When did the San Francisco Xaxier depart from Manila? (1705) What happened to the San Francisco Xavier? (Not sure, but believed to be shipwrecked) How could the San Francisco Xavier be shipwrecked in Oregon? (Strayed off course, perhaps due to a storm.)

A—Answer question   These may be teacher-made questions or questions traditionally found at the end of textbook chapters. These questions could be answered orally or in writing. As the students become more proficient in generating self-questions, they may, in fact anticipate questions posed at the end of the selection or chapter.

Examples:

What Indian tribe lived at the mouth of the Columbia River? When did the Manila galleons generally depart for Acapulco? At what latitude is the mouth of the Columbia River? Who might have been the first Europeans in the Oregon Country?

From *Social Studies*, 79, pp. 274-277. Reprinted with permission of The Helen Dwight Reid Educational Foundation. Published by Heldref Publications, 1319 18th St, N.W., Washington, DC 20036-1802. Copyright 1988.

PLAN-Predict / Locate / Add / Note

TABLE 9

INSTRUCTIONAL SUMMARY OF PREDICT LOCATE ADD NOTE

Literacy Strategy	PLAN-Predict / Locate / Add / Note
Primary Focus	❏ Comprehension
Learning Principles	❏ Background Knowledge ❏ Active Involvement ❏ Thought Demanding Activity
When to Use	❏ Before, during, post-reading
Goals: National or State Literacy Standards	❏ Identifying main ideas, details ❏ Locating information ❏ Extending meaning ❏ Application of information
Materials	❏ PLAN reading guide ❏ Reading material ❏ Pen/pencil
Time	❏ 30 minutes

PLAN Strategy

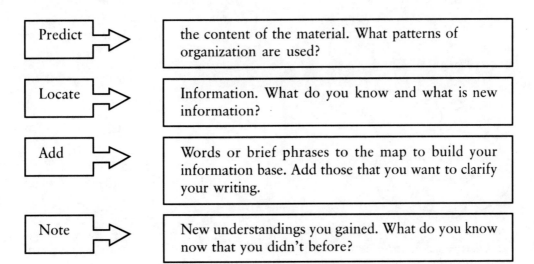

Predict ⇨	the content of the material. What patterns of organization are used?
Locate ⇨	Information. What do you know and what is new information?
Add ⇨	Words or brief phrases to the map to build your information base. Add those that you want to clarify your writing.
Note ⇨	New understandings you gained. What do you know now that you didn't before?

Example 1: Science Sample

Name: _____ Date: _____ Period: _____

Text: <u>*Cultivating Oysters*</u> Author: <u>*Brandan Borrell*</u> Date: <u>*Wednesday, August 2, 2006*</u>

Directions: Use your PLAN strategy, fill in your graphic organizer from your text reading. Then write a summary using your notes.

❏ Will involve researchers and conservationists
❏ Problems causing disappearance
❏ Advantages of Oyster Project
❏ Pattern of Organization: Problem/ Solution

❏ Netarts mudflats - ideal setting-salt water influenced by tidewaters
❏ Whiskey Creek Shellfish Hatchery-Nursery process
❏ Captive-reared oysters attached to discarded shells
❏ Oysters distributed from mesh bags on ecological acre plots
❏ Native oysters glue themselves together and form reefs several feet tall

LOCATE

Store of Olympic Oysters in Netarts Bay

NOTE

2005–2006 Oyster Conservation Project

❏ Died out a century ago
❏ 130,000 bushels a year harvested; remaining "Olys" drowned in wood pulp over a century ago

❏ Small Chinook salmon will benefit. Oysters keep algae in check
❏ Estuary creatures keep oysters in check
❏ Process improves water quality

Summary

Since I saw oysters on every menu as well as huge banners advertising them in this coastal town of Netarts the times we visited the coast, I always thought they were abundant. Apparently not, overharvesting a century ago as well as pollution especially from the logging industry caused their demise.

Borrell writes about the conservation project to restore the particular Northwest Olympic oyster. Researchers and conservationists have identified Netarts Bay as an ideal mudflat with sufficient salt water to cultivate the "Olys."

In a few ecological acres in the Bay, the researchers are distributing native oysters raised in the nearby Whiskey Creek Shellfish Hatchery to the Netarts mudflats. The oysters will form reefs that attract and hide the small Chinook salmon and pump the seawater through their gills eating the algae and improving the water quality.

Comprehension Strategies for Second Language Learners

In many of the classrooms of the preservice teachers we supervise, we have found the numbers of language minority students growing steadily. In many instances little thought has been given to their level of proficiency or their readiness for classes in English language arts, mathematics, science or social studies. For teachers with limited or no preparation in working with English Language Learners (ELL), several strategies have been found to be helpful. We have selected those that exemplify the learning principles outlined in the Preface of this text. Before cognitive strategies are introduced, certain interactive social activities should be in place:

Richard-Amato (1992)

Shanton (1999)

- ❏ Collaborate. Ask colleagues who are successful with ELLs to attend your classroom and debrief with them on their observations and suggestions. Frequently, talk to them about strategies they have used to communicate with their minority language students.
- ❏ Communicate directly with ELLs. Use their names and pronounce them correctly. If we do not know them well, we cannot teach students well.
- ❏ Avoid calling on students who are not ready to speak.
- ❏ Reassure students that their first language is important and acceptable. If several students in your class speak the same language, encourage them to help each other using their own language when necessary. In fact, this is a critical International Reading Association and National Council of Teachers of English standard. <http://www.ncte.org/standards/thelist.html>

What do interactive social activities accomplish for the ELLs?

Cognitive/Academic Activities

- ❏ Emphasize key words. Use gestures and facial expressions to get these vocabulary terms across to students.
- ❏ Use visuals to clarify key ideas and concepts. Objects, maps, illustrations, transparencies, and videos help students attach meaning to your lectures or their reading.

❏ Use direct definitions, simplifications or analogies that help students comprehend their lessons.

❏ Prepare students for your lessons and their reading assignments.

❏ Summarize and review frequently.

❏ Request that appropriate content-area books that are in their native languages be ordered for your school media center. When planning units include these trade books in your classroom materials.

❏ Encourage students to use their bilingual dictionaries when necessary or to ask questions when they don't understand important concepts.

Which ELL academic activities can you implement immediately?

Framed Outline

The framed outline is an advanced organizer that teachers find extremely useful for providing students with a contextual overview of the content to aid them in understanding ideas in their content area text or in the teacher's lecture. By providing students with a framed outline, the students receive a number of cues. For example, in designing this activity, teachers indicate how many main ideas and details will be identified; which concepts are critical and finally, how to organize information. Ausubel (1968) maintained that learners subsume new material under general, more inclusive concepts and principles. In order to learn, students need to see the big picture. A framed outline helps in presenting a global picture of the content they need to study. Yet the content is presented in a simplified, manageable format—easy to access and to review.

TABLE 10

INSTRUCTIONAL SUMMARY OF A FRAMED OUTLINE

Literacy Strategy	Framed Outline
Primary Focus	❏ Comprehension Development ❏ Listening Comprehension ❏ Main Ideas & Details
Learning Principles	❏ Active Involvement ❏ Talk Time ❏ Organizing Information
When to Use	During, Post Reading
Goals: National or State Literacy Standards	❏ Use relevant and specific information ❏ Identify main ideas and details
Materials	❏ Reading material, lecture notes ❏ Teacher-prepared Framed Outline
Time	30 minutes

Classroom Application:

Example 1: Science Model

Directions: Using your Framed Outline fill in the blanks of the **Stages in Mitosis** or **Cell Division**. The teacher will model the key terms on the master transparency on the overhead. Use the transparency to check for spelling. We will review these after the mini-lecture. Don't worry if you missed some items. There will be class time to check these with members of your team.

STAGES IN MITOSIS OR CELL DIVISION

STAGE 1: _____	1. No _____ takes place. 2. The _____ in the nucleus copies itself. 3. The _____ also copies itself.
STAGE 2: _____	1. The doubled _____ shortens and _____. 2. The _____ make long fibers called _____. 3. The _____ _____ disappears.
STAGE 3: _____	1. The DNA threads _____ _____ in the _____ of the _____. 2. It looks like a game of _____ - __ - _____.
STAGE 4: _____	1. The double _____ threads separate into _____ groups and _____ to opposite ends of the _____.
STAGE 5: _____	1. A nuclear _____ forms around each group of _____. 2. The cell _____ pinches in the middle.
STAGE 6: _____	1. The _____ cell divides into two identical _____ cells. 2. Each _____ cell has a complete set of _____ and a _____ outside its _____.

Response Key: STAGES IN MITOSIS OR CELL DIVISION

STAGE 1: Interphase	1. No <u>division</u> takes place. 2. The <u>DNA</u> in the nucleus copies itself. 3. The <u>centriole</u> also copies itself.
STAGE 2: Prophase	1. The doubled <u>DNA</u> shortens and <u>thickens</u>. 2. The <u>centrioles</u> make long fibers called <u>spindles</u>. 3. The <u>nuclear</u> <u>membrane</u> disappears.
STAGE 3: Metaphase	1. The DNA threads <u>line up</u> in the <u>middle</u> of the <u>spindle</u>. 2. It looks like a game of <u>Tug-of-War</u>.
STAGE 4: Anaphase	1. The double <u>DNA</u> threads separate into <u>two</u> groups and <u>move</u> to opposite ends of the <u>spindle</u>.
STAGE 5: Telophase	1. A nuclear <u>membrane</u> forms around each group of <u>chromosomes</u>. 2. The cell <u>membrane</u> pinches in the middle.
STAGE 6: Daughter Cells	1. The <u>parent</u> cell divides into two identical <u>daughter</u> cells. 2. Each <u>new</u> cell has a complete set of <u>chromosomes</u> and a <u>centriole</u> outside its <u>nucleus</u>.

The benefits of this structure are clear. Teachers can adjust the format to the proficiency level of their students. Students can practice transferring what they hear into writing. The content of the text is reduced to the most salient points they need to learn. Finally, students have a set of notes that they can use to study for exams or to write an extended paragraph summarizing this information.

MULTIPASS

TABLE 11

INSTRUCTIONAL SUMMARY OF MULTIPASS

Literacy Strategy	MULTIPASS
Primary Focus	❏ Comprehension
Learning Principles	❏ Background Knowledge ❏ Active Involvement
When to Use	❏ Before, During, Post Reading
Goals: National or State Literacy Standards	❏ Identifying main ideas, details ❏ Locating information ❏ Summarizing information
Materials	❏ MULTIPASS reading guide ❏ Reading Material ❏ Pen/Pencil
Time	❏ 30 minutes

LD & ELL students require much support

Both students with learning disabilities and those learning English as a second language need more guidance to be successful with expository text. In addition, the research has shown that teachers must play a substantial role in providing step-by-step instructional strategies (Williams, 2000). The MULTIPASS strategy has proven a useful strategy for many of our preservice as well as in-service teachers.

TEACHER TALK

My students use the MULTIPASS strategy to read an article from either the Time for Kids website or the Science News for Kids website. They go on their laptop computers, find the article and use the strategy. I like MULTIPASS, because I think it is really comprehension-oriented and it helps them pick up the big "chunks" from a nonfiction article. I created a worksheet that goes with the article. It works in class. Do they use it on their own? I want it to become a habit, but I haven't seen that yet.

MULTIPASS Strategy

The teacher needs to walk the students initially through the parts of the MULTIPASS strategy. Depending on the skill level of the students, each section can be taught individually or the guide sections can be taught as a whole.

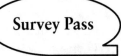

1. Student looks for the main ideas and details using: the title, captions under the headings and pictures.

2. Student looks for specific information in the reading without reading it from beginning to end.

Looking for vocabulary words in bold or italic; skimming the text; looking at the questions at the end of the reading or guide questions made up by the teacher.

3. Student reads and answers the questions at the end of the chapter or those on the MULTIPASS reading guide.

Source: Adapted from Schumaker, J.B., Deshler, D.D., Alley, G.R. Warner, M.M., Denton, P.H.(1982). Multipass: A learning Strategy for improving reading comprehension. *Learning Disability Quarterly*, 5, 295-304

Example 1: Current Events: Social Studies

Math Moves Speed Skating Star

Name: _____ Date: _____ Period: _____

1. What does the title mean?

   _____

2. What is the caption under the heading about?

   _____

3. What do the pictures show?

   _____

Vocabulary

4. What do you think "promote" means?

   _____

5. What do you think "calculating angles" means?

   _____

6. What do you think "relays" are?

   _____

Preview Questions

Read the questions below so you know what information to pay close attention to when you read the article. Make a mark next to any questions you can already answer. Read the article to answer the questions.

7. Why was Apolo Ohno in Washington, D.C.?

_____

8. Is Apolo good at math?

_____

9. How is math used in speed skating?

_____

10. What does a medal at the Olympics mean to Apolo?

_____

Sort-Out Pass

Summarize - Now that you've read the article answer the above questions and summarize the article's main idea.

11. What was the main idea of this article?

_____

Source: Adapted from Comprehension Guide by Jill Sawyer, May 8, 2006. Text found @ http://www.timeforkids.com/TFK/kidscoops/printout7 0,19787,1192528,00.html

Endings: A Summary

Comprehension is a constructive process of exploring and making meaning. As teachers we can provide students with learning strategies that empower them to assume the responsibility to explore and discover meaning on their own. Various literacy activities which enable students to "be there" and to "do something with their reading" (Wilhelm, 1997) were presented.

If we are to prepare students for their future, an indispensable part of their learning experience must include critical thinking activities. Both teachers and students need a "comfort zone" in working with conceptual conflict. Ways of creating a comfortable environment to cultivate a critical view among our students are illustrated.

Finally, in this chapter we dealt with strategies which the content area teacher can use with students with special needs and English language learners.

Expanding Understanding through Discussion

Directions: In small groups, use the following chapter overview designed as a reading road map to review your understanding of this chapter.

In the Field Applications

A. Create a comprehension study guide. Use a lesson from a content area text or supplementary reading for this exercise. Implement it in your classroom. Finally, write up your reflection on the exercise, including what went well and what could be improved.

B. Develop a lesson that promotes critical thinking. Use current material from the newspaper or a magazine that is related to a controversial topic in your classroom.

C. Check several textbooks in your specialty area. List several questions from these sources that require the students to provide the main idea. Design a lesson helping students respond meaningfully to a range of main idea questions.

D. Design and implement a comprehension strategy that takes into consideration the special needs of your students. In addition, design a self-evaluation activity that requires your students to provide you with specific feedback about this strategy. Summarize this feedback for a report.

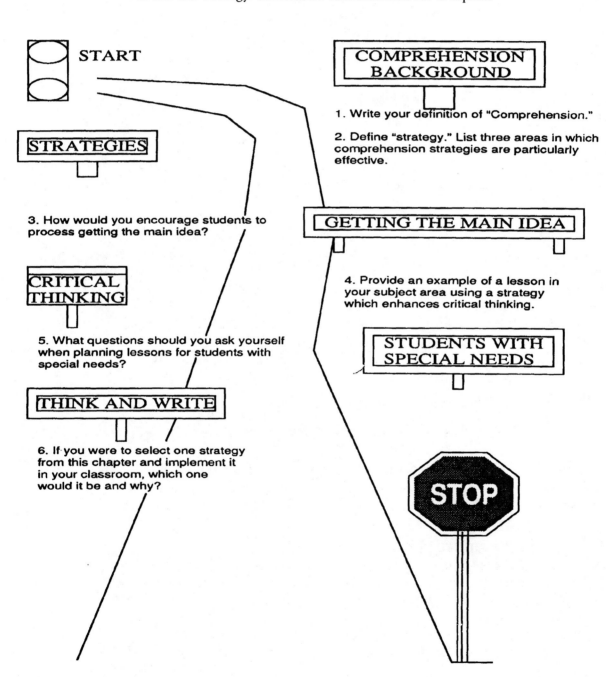

START

COMPREHENSION BACKGROUND

1. Write your definition of "Comprehension."

2. Define "strategy." List three areas in which comprehension strategies are particularly effective.

STRATEGIES

3. How would you encourage students to process getting the main idea?

GETTING THE MAIN IDEA

CRITICAL THINKING

4. Provide an example of a lesson in your subject area using a strategy which enhances critical thinking.

5. What questions should you ask yourself when planning lessons for students with special needs?

STUDENTS WITH SPECIAL NEEDS

THINK AND WRITE

6. If you were to select one strategy from this chapter and implement it in your classroom, which one would it be and why?

STOP

References ❏ ❏ ❏

Adair-Houck, B. (1996). Practical whole language strategies for secondary and university-level FL students. *Foreign Language Annals*, 29(2), 253–270.

Allende, I. (1986). *The house of the spirits*. NY: Bantam.

Anderson, R., Hiebert, E., Scott, J., & Wilkinson, I. (1985). *Becoming a nation of readers*. Urbana: University of Illinois, Center for the Study of Reading.

Anrig, G., & Lapointe, A. (1989). What we know about what students don't know. *Educational Leadership, 47,* 4–9.

Ausubel, D. (1968). *Educational psychology*. NY: Holt, Rinehart & Winston.

Beck, I. (1986). Using research on reading. *Educational Leadership, 43,*13–15.

Beck, I. (1989). Improving practice through understanding reading. In L. Resnick & L. Klopfer (Eds.), *Toward the thinking curriculum: Current cognitive research*. Association for Supervision and Curriculum Development, 40–58.

Borrell, B. (2006, Wednesday, August 2, 2006). Cultivating Oysters. *The Oregonian*, pp. BIO, B19.

Bristow, A. (1978). Sex life of plants. NY: Shelley Power Literary Agency Ltd.

Brown, A. (1984). *Teaching students to think as they read: Implications for curriculum reform*. Paper commissioned by the American Educational Research Association Task Force on Excellence in Education. ERIC Document Reproduction Service No. ED 273 567.

Chi, M., Bassok, M., Lewis, M., Reimann, P., & Glaser, R. (1988). *Self-explanations: How students study and use examples in learning to solve problems*. Pittsburgh, PA: Learning Research and Development Center.

Coble, C. R., Rice, D. R., et al. (1991). *Earth Science*. Englewood Cliffs, NJ: Prentice Hall.

Donlan, D. (1978). How to play 29 questions. *Journal of Reading , 21* (6), 535–541.

Erichsen, G. (2006). 'Little Red Riding Hood' in Spanish. Retrieved August 4, 2006, from http://Spanish.about.com/cs/vocabulary/a/caperucita_roja.htm

Gaskins, I., & Baron, J. (1985). Teaching poor readers to cope with maladaptive cognitive styles: A training program. *Journal of Learning Disabilities, 18,* 390–394.

Harris, T., & Hodges, R. (1995). (Eds.). *The literacy dictionary: The vocabulary of reading and writing*. Newark, DE: International Reading Association.

Harrison, S. (1991). Tools for Learning Science. In (Eds.), *Science learning: Processes and applications*. Newark, DE: International Reading Association: 114–121.

Hayes, D., & Alvermann, D. (1986). *Video assisted coaching of textbook discussion skills: Its impact on critical reading behavior*. Paper presented at the annual meeting of the American Research Association. San Francisco: ERIC Document Reproduction Service No. ED 272 734.

Herber, H. L. (1978). *Teaching reading in content areas* (2nd ed.). Englewood Cliffs, NJ: Prentice-Hall.

Horowitz, R. (1985). Text patterns: Part II. *Journal of Reading, 28,* 584–542.

Hoyt, L. (1999). *Revisit, reflect, retell: Strategies for improving reading comprehension*. Portsmouth, NH: Heinemann.

Hynd, C. R. (1999). Teaching students to think critically using multiple texts in history, *Journal of Adolescent & Adult Literacy 42*(6): 428–436.

Idol, L. (1987). A critical thinking map to improve content area comprehension reading of poor reader. *Remedial Reading and Special Education, 8*(4), 28–40.

Idol-Maestas, L. (1985). Getting ready to read: Guided probing for poor comprehenders. *Learning Disability Quarterly, 8* (Fall), 243–254.

Kauchak, D., & Eggen, P. (1989). *Learning and teaching*. Boston: Allyn & Bacon.

Martinez, D., & Tama, C. (1988). *Compendium: A resource guide for students-at-risk: Comprehension strategies.* Portland, OR: Portland State University. Unpublished manuscript.

May, F. (1989). *Reading as communication: An interactive process (3rd ed.).* Columbus, OH: Merrill.

McConnell, J., Brown, S., Eddins, S., Hackworth, M., & Usiskin, A. (1990). *Algebra.* The University of Chicago School Mathematics Project, Glenview, IL: Scott, Foresman.

Meyer, B. J. F., Brandt, D. M., et al. (1980). Use of top-level structure in text: Key for reading comprehension of ninth-grade students. *Reading Research Quarterly 16:* 72–103.

NEA Association (2002). Using Text Structure. Retrieved July 26, 2006, from http://www.nea.org/reading/usingtextstructure.html

Palincsar, A. S., & Brown, A. L. (1984). Reciprocal teaching of comprehension-fostering and comprehension-monitoring activities. *Cognition and Instruction* 1: 117–175.

Pasluk, I. (2006). Math Moves Speed Skating Star. *Time for Kids.* Retrieved August 4, 2006, from http://www.timeforkids.com/TFK/kidscoops/printout/0,19787,1192528,00.html

Pearson, P. D., & Johnson, D. (1972). *Teaching reading comprehension.* NY: Holt, Rinehart & Winston.

Raphael, T. (1982). Question-answering strategies for children. *The Reading Teacher, 36,* 186–191,

Richard-Amato, P., & Snow, M. A (1992*). The multicultural classroom: Readings for content-area teachers.* NY: Addison-Wesley.

Schmidt, C., Barry, A., Maxworthy, A., & Huebsch, W. (1989). But I read the chapter twice. *Journal of Reading, 32,* 428–433.

Schumaker, J., Deshler, D., Alley, G., Warner, M., & Denton, P. (1984). MULTIPASS: A learning strategy for improving reading comprehension. *Learning Disability Quarterly,* 5, 295–304.

Shanton, K.D. (1999). Paradox, politics and bilingual education. *Northwest Reading Journal,* pp. 22–26.

Simpson, M. L., & Nist, S. (1999). An update on strategic learning: It's more than textbook reading strategies. *Journal of Adolescent & Adult Literacy* 43(6), 528–541.

Steinbeck, J. (1988). *Cannery Row.* NY, Viking Penguin Inc.

Tama, C., & Martinez, D. (1986). *Reading comprehension and the learning disabled reader: Generalizations from five years of research (1980–1985).* Vancouver, B.C., ERIC Document Service No. 278 968.

Tama, C. (1989). Critical thinking has a place in every classroom. *Journal of Reading* 33, 64–65.

Taylor, B. M. (1980). Children's memory of expository text after reading. *Reading Research Quarterly 15:* 399–411.

Tovani, C. (2001). *Holding thinking: Teaching readers how to reuse and remember what they read.* Paper presented at the International Reading Conference, Orlando, FL.

Vislocky, E. (2004). PLAN-Predict/Locate/Add/Note. Retrieved August 4, 2006, from http://www.somers.kl2.ny.us/intranet/reading/PLAN.html

Wilhelm, J. (1997). "You gotta BE the book." NY: Teacher's College Press.

Williams, J. (2000). Strategic processing of text: Improving reading comprehension for students with learning disabilities. Retrieved August 3, 2006, from http://ericc.org/digests/e599.html

Discussion Strategies

Ashamed of not understanding and fearful of asking questions, I dropped out of school in the ninth grade.... Most of my life I felt like a target in the crosshairs of a hunter's rifle. When strangers and outsiders questioned me I felt the hangrope tighten around my neck and the trapdoor creak beneath my feet. There was nothing so humiliating as being unable to express myself, and my inarticulateness increased my sense of jeopardy. Behind a mask of humility, I seethed with mute rebellion....

Jimmy Santiago Baca (1999), *Coming into Language*

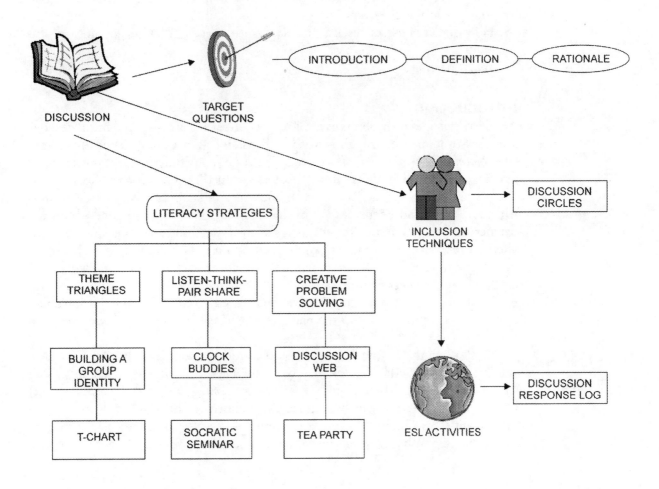

189

Target Questions

Consider the following questions before reading this chapter. Discuss these with a colleague. Continue writing notes and develop specific questions regarding discussion that you want to explore.

Target Questions

1. What are the essential qualities of a class discussion?
2. How does discussion nurture students' ability to communicate in any life situation?
3. What is the pay-off for teaching students both the language and the activities of the varied roles they could play in a discussion?
4. What are the methods of grouping students for discussion?
5. What do students achieve by self-assessing their behaviors during a discussion?
6. What techniques could you suggest to a teacher who is having difficulty with managing a smooth interactive flow of discussion?
7. Describe several discussion strategies that you can implement to improve comprehension.
8. What evidence is there that the use of discussion is an adaptive tool serving all students in the classroom?
9. How does the use of discussion relate to the needs of language-minority students?
10. Your question.

Introduction

A university supervisor observes a third-level Spanish class noting that the teacher and the students are struggling with a discussion concerning *Como Agua Para Chocolate (Like Water, For Chocolate)*. The room colorfully displays posters with irregular verb conjugations; travel posters of bustling Barcelona, Mexico City, and the Prada; book jackets of Hispanic authors such as Cisneros, Marquez, Allende, Anaya and Esquivel. But in the midst of this is a dead zone—both the teacher and the students are struggling with discussion questions that seem to elicit no response. The students know their Spanish—on entering the classroom they speak to each other in animated Spanish, check each others' homework, and catch up on the latest teen news. But as the teacher poses questions on the chapter for the day's conversation, the students seated around the table look blankly at her then glue their eyes on the page. The teacher proceeds to answer her own questions.

Theme Triangles in Gallagher (2004)

In another third/ fourth level class the students are sprawled on the floor, spilling out into the hallway as they work on Theme Triangles posters in which: 1) they discuss what they think the theme of *Como Agua Para Chocolate* is, 2) brainstorm and decide which films may be related to this novel's theme, set up opportunities to watch it on their own time and 3) discuss one more example of the theme in another medium or genre: contemporary songs, art, books, poems.

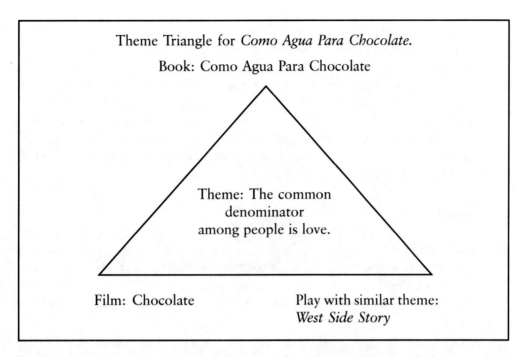

Theme Triangle for *Como Agua Para Chocolate.*

Book: Como Agua Para Chocolate

Theme: The common
denominator
among people is love.

Film: Chocolate

Play with similar theme:
West Side Story

Comparative Summary:
In all three genres the main characters conquer through love. In *Como Agua Para Chocolate*, Tita and Pedro like Tony and Maria are star-crossed lovers who love each other but are stymied in being together for different reasons. In the movie *Chocolate*, an unconventional mother with her daughter use the love of chocolate to win over many of the townspeople. Chocolate like the food in *Como Agua Para Chocolate* mesmerizes all who eat it.

What makes one group silent as dust or as chatty as friends at the local coffee hangout? How teachers structure the discussion; how an environment is established for discussions, and, finally, how students are actively engaged by this structure are key elements in the discussion process.

Townsend & Pace (2006)

In the first scenerio, the teacher was center stage, developing and posing the questions, and completely stymied by the students' lack of response. In the second one, the teacher played "guide on the side." Students were given a theme triangle structure and trusted that what they brought to the discussion personally would guide their talk.

Definition

Dillon (1981) describes a discussion occurring when a teacher plans to have one, the students rated it as such, and the students provided at least 40 percent of the total talk. McKenna and Robinson (1993) portray true discussion as including a sharing of opinions and ideas in an atmosphere of mutual trust and respect. Thouless (1953) writes that "one obvious condition that must be fulfilled before a real discussion can take place is that both parties must have a sufficiently lowly opinion of the finality of their own judgements to be willing to have their opin-

Define discussion

ions changed by what the other person tells them." Finally, Alvermann, Dillon and O'Brien (1987) summarize many of these qualities into three criteria for a discussion:

1. the discussants must present multiple points of view and then be ready to change their minds after hearing convincing counterarguments;
2. the students must interact with one another as well as with the teacher, and
3. a majority of the verbal interactions, especially those resulting from questions that solicit student opinion must be longer than the typical two or three-word phrases found in recitations (p. 3).

Rationale

Although the increasing size of secondary textbooks would convey the impression that content exists in and of itself, and the debate on how much to teach rages professionally, content does not exist in a vacuum. It is married to process (how), and to purpose (why).

Primarily, teachers select discussion as a means of examining content and use it specifically to:

❏ analyze, explore, evaluate, and modify attitudes on issues,
❏ problem-solve, and
❏ promote subject mastery.

We will provide concrete examples later in this chapter of each of these; however, let's examine one purpose, examining issues in the content classroom.

Discussion can provide an antidote to the problematic schooling of our students. Numerous educational writers prescribe the use of discussion in the classroom. Through this approach, students develop a tolerance for the opinions and interpretations of others, recognize that the interpretations of others will vary, learn how to cope with ambiguity, stretch the boundaries of their knowing and participate in problem solving.

What life skills are nurtured through discussion?

Furthermore, it cultivates individuals who have consensus-building skills, a spirit of cooperation, and who know how to dialogue about their concerns regarding the tremendous problems we face as a global community. The development of these skills warrants making time in the classroom for extended discussion. By providing extended time to students, the opportunities for fresh insights and an understanding of the process of negotiation is cultivated.

How often have we said, if not thought, the following about discussion activities in our classrooms?

❏ "Discussion is fine in the English class, but in math, students need drill and practice."
❏ "Students like it better when I give them answers or stress what is important through notetaking activities in class. When we have class discussions and I raise questions for problem solving—they inevitably demand to know what I think is right."
❏ "These kids need to be in a structured environment. I couldn't turn them loose in small groups."
❏ "I tried it (small group discussion) once; it was a disaster."
❏ "I just don't have the energy to get the students into a group. The noise, the commotion, the time are more than I can deal with."

Successful discussions depend on creating a conducive environment. We don't deny that there are problems and dilemmas in this process, but we have learned much about overcoming these.

Preparing students for discussion activities is as critical as preparing them for reading and writing. We frequently assume that as social beings, qualities that make us communicative are innate and can be tapped at will. In the classroom, this is not the case. Students need to be prepared for the interactive roles necessary for discussion. The Ford Teaching Project on Inquiry/ Discovery Learning recommends students learn how to discuss as one form of guidance required if students are to develop "independent reasoning" (Bridges, 1979, p. 84).

Students need to learn skills for conducting a discussion.

Students need to feel that even the most "idiosyncratic, divergent, recalcitrant and alien opinion" (Bridges, 1979) will be encouraged in the classroom. Helen Simons further adds, "The fear of ridicule by other pupils is, in my view and in the view of the great majority of pupils I have interviewed, the single most important factor in pupil silence" (Bridges, p. 84). Helping students move beyond this ridicule and develop a level of tolerance for others' ideas can be accomplished.

Unlike Baca in our opening quote, students needn't fear opportunities to express themselves. Through discussion, they learn how to take a stand and nurture a belief in the power of their own thinking as well as confidence in sharing their thoughts. Baca's threatening "alligators of fear slumber powerless in their lairs" desperse when students discover their own articulateness. If teachers are persistent in cultivating these activities and consistent in their expectations that students can participate, no student should leave school without the ability to communicate in any life situation. When students are artfully prepared for discussion, classrooms become places where students feel emotionally and physically safe, and also places where they share real thoughts and feelings. Teachers create this environment with activities that encourage students to listen, interact, trust, and care for each other.

What is the greatest fear students have about a discussion activity?

Bigelow, et al. (1994)

A great poster to hang up in the classroom or duplicate for students that emphasizes this approach to thinking is the Tug O'War Thinking Creed (Bellanca, 1991, p. 140). See Figure 5.1.

One topic that we would like to discuss before we go on to specific discussion strategies is grouping.

FIGURE 5.1.   TUG O'WAR THINKING CREED

TUG O'WAR THINKING CREED
We pledge to...
Tug at ideas, not people.
Examine all sides of the issue.
Actively listen and clarify.
Modify our position when appropriate.
Seek the best decision, not the winning position.

I must add that the classes are small, only thirteen in each, and it seemed better for us to talk as a group rather than with just one person. The discussion was quite emotional and very good. I must also add that these two classes are very low in skills and in enthusiasm for anything beyond Nintendo and shopping. It was a great topic because for once they were emotionally charged about something of significance.

Grouping

Teachers want to know the ideal number of students for the group process to be efficient and effective.

Is there an ideal group configuration?

Gall & Gall (1976)

Task groups usually are comprised of two to five students of different abilities and motivation. Research shows this type of mixing ability maximizes student achievement and helps develop skillful thinking and increases self-esteem.

Groups can be structured in many ways. Typically, there are three kinds: informal, formal and base groups.

Define informal grouping.

Informal grouping usually involves students working with activities that are quick and random, having few guidelines and roles. It is used for content review activities. A typical activity would be to instruct students to turn to their neighbor and practice a dialogue in a Spanish class.

Define formal grouping.

Formal grouping involves extended classroom activities. It includes the implementation of roles, criteria for achieving success, and a group processing strategy. Students learn the procedures of the group process. Rather than students simply working with their neighbor the teacher selects groups randomly, or based on student interest and ability. For example, a formal group activity would be a jigsaw exercise in which students in groups of three are each given three different words to define and illustrate. Then they are to teach the other members of the group their terms using these illustrations as a focus. In fifteen minutes all students must know all terms. A final check is done through a classroom quiz.

Define a base group.

Unlike informal and formal groups where the groups work together only for the duration of the task, **base groups** work together for extended time periods. They may work together several times a week for at least the duration of a unit or perhaps as much as a year. Typical activities for base groups include reviewing the week's work, setting goals for the week, planning social events, solving problems, and working in situations that require extended support, such as writing groups. To develop strong base groups, have students design their own group logo, develop a motto, and set group goals.

Critical to the formation of base groups are opportunities to practice social skills and group processing. A typical strategy is for students in the base groups to get together for ten minutes at the beginning of the week and set their individual or group goals, such as trying out a new system of notetaking for the rest of the week. A check is done at the end of the week to see how successful they've been in realizing these goals.

Your purpose for grouping determines the make-up of the group. Figure 5.2. illustrates some of the most common types of grouping practice.

Group process has a richly researched base in the classroom. Yet, particularly at the secondary level, student talk is still a rarity. Goodlad (1984) writes:

Students rarely turn things around by asking questions. Nor do teachers often give students a chance to romp with an open-ended question … the intellectual terrain is laid out by the teacher. The paths for walking through it are largely predetermined by the teacher (p. 109).

FIGURE 5.2.   METHODS OF GROUPING STUDENTS

1. **Random grouping.** Direct students to "pair up" or "move their desks in groups of four." This can be used for quick exercises, e.g., to help students clarify difficulties or summarize what they have learned.
2. **Social grouping.** Allow students to work with peers of their own choosing. Sometimes students should have the opportunity to work with their friends.
3. **Tutorial grouping.** Pair students so that both can learn from the experience. Students who have learned the material should be assigned to those who have some difficulty. The interplay of questions and responses should expand each learner's understanding.
4. **Ability grouping.** Group students according to ability to comprehend the specific material. One group might use the textbook; another might use materials adjusted for students reading below grade level.
5. **Interest grouping.** Group students who share a common interest to undertake projects either of their own creation or suggested by the teacher. This allows students to have a voice and exercise their own judgment.
6. **Needs grouping.** Group students according to their strengths and their challenges. This grouping can help eliminate reteaching of materials and provides a vehicle for grouping students who need additional help, e.g., minilessons on writing conventions.

Common types of grouping students.

Why is this the case when there are strong arguments for using talk with peers to learn and to grow developmentally. Psychologists, linguists, philosophers, and educators have contributed much to this research that establishes the relationship between talking and learning. In fact, one is hard pressed to find anyone disproving this connection. Vygotsky (1978), in particular, theorized that a social environment provides learners with the opportunities to observe higher levels of cognitive processing, thereby, enabling learners to achieve more because of the assistance of peers in contrast to learning independently. Discussion does much to create this social environment.

Rogoff (1990); Dillon (1984); Gall & Gall (1976)

Why we aren't seeing this increase in the time students have to speak in the classroom, we believe, is reflected in the teacher remarks in our section on designing an environment for discussion. These indicate that such factors as the perceived constraints of the content area curriculum, a need for control, stamina,

Suppose these constraints did not exist. What would the effect be on classroom discussion?

previous bad experiences, lack of training—all contribute to the paucity of student talk in the secondary classroom.

TEACHER TALK ——

I teach all the procedures I want to have as a routine. Having procedures and routines—provided in a relaxed manner—allows students to feel secure and comfortable and, therefore, more willing to work together as well as volunteer in front of the classroom. I use a blend of ideas from Harry Wong's *The First Days of School, Time to Teach.* I also use "desk Olympics" having students practice getting into different group configurations (pairs, threes, or fours) and time them on how fast they can do it. They practice a few times. I give them feedback on how quickly and quietly they move their desks. I find giving students,notice about the next activity such as "Finish what you are reading, finding a good place to stop at the end of a paragraph" helps move them along quickly.

In the following section, Literacy Strategies to Promote Dicussion, we have included strategies for role playing as well as dicussion formates per se in order to highlight the necessity for preparing students to be skilled dicussants. The following strategies well help students learn communication skills as well as explore their own thinking and that of others: Bulding a Group Identify, Listen-Think-Pair-Share, Clock Buddies, Socratic Seminar, Creative Problem Solving, Discussion Web, Literature Circles, and a Discussion Response Log.

Literacy Strategies to Promote Discussion

Role Playing Strategy: Building a Group Identity

TABLE 1

INSTRUCTIONAL SUMMARY OF BUILDING A GROUP IDENTITY

Literacy Strategies	Building a Group Identity
Primary Focus	Communication
Learning Principles	❏ Active Involvement ❏ Metacognitive Experience
When to Use	Before, or during lesson
Goals: National or State Literacy Standards	❏ Use a variety of descriptive words appropriate to audience and purpose ❏ Demonstrate effective listening strategies
Materials	Discussion task
Time	25 minutes

Many of the content discussion activities that follow will be more successful if students have some time to practice. We have included a few activities that will provide the students with role playing practice. Although a teacher will change and mingle group membership depending on the task, ability, motivation, social skills, sex, race and ethnic backgrounds, the base groups serve as a place for students to set goals, to review the class's work, to plan and to work out differences and solve problems.

This activity, Building a Group Identity, is designed to give students the opportunity to try different roles and set the tone for building community.

Procedure.
1. Ask students to get in groups of 4-5. Assign students the following roles: Coordinator, Reporter, Go-For, Artist and Time Keeper (See Figure 5.3 for description of group roles).
2. Discuss with the class the purpose of keeping a folder for group activities, e.g., a place for keeping the group's journal entries, admit or exit slips, a chart that tracks the date and different roles tried by members of the group, etc. Then, ask students to design its cover with a group name, and logo. Depending on the class, this can be adapted to include a group flag, or a group song.
3. After the groups are finished with this project, ask the reporter from each group to share with the class the group's creation.
4. Ask students to evaluate their role playing activities by using the following T-Chart. Since the object of this activity is to foster cooperation, the students are asked to identify specific behaviors that fostered this cooperative spirit.

FIGURE 5.3.   COOPERATIVE LEARNING ROLES

Coordinator/Facilitator	Defines the task and keeps the group on task.
Reader	Reads directions, problems, and resource materials to group members.
Checker	Checks for group members' comprehension of material.
Reporter	Conveys actions and findings of group to other groups.
Evaluator	Keeps notes on group processing and social skills.
Go-For	Gets materials and equipment and runs errands for group.
Encourager-Praiser	Makes sure all group members have a turn and provides positive feedback to group.
Timekeeper	Keeps track of time allotted for assignments and keeps group on time.
Artist	Illustrates and displays projects.

T-Chart

COOPERATION	
LOOKS LIKE	SOUNDS LIKE
E.g., Everyone on task.	E.g. "What do you think will work here?"

Over the years while observing classrooms, whether first grade or graduate-level, we have noted that teachers who enable students by providing practice with discussion roles create comfortable environments for it to occur. Having the discussion basics become automatic as in driving a car or using a word processor results in a smoother, and, usually, far more successful conversation.

Listen-Think-Pair-Share

TABLE 2

INSTRUCTIONAL SUMMARY OF LISTEN-THINK-PAIR-SHARE

Literacy Strategies	Listen-Think-Pair-Share
Primary Focus	Listening, Thinking, Socialization Skills
Learning Principles	❑ Active Involvement ❑ Thought-demanding Activity
When to Use	Before, during, after reading
Goals: National or State Literacy Standards	❑ Make connections and transitions among ideas ❑ To practice articulating thoughts to others
Materials	Discussion task
Time	5-7 minutes

This strategy encourages student participation in the classroom. It provides an activity where students can analyze, explore, evaluate, and even modify attitudes about ideas and issues. Through listening, thinking, and sharing, students construct enhanced meaning. This strategy also builds levels of acceptance, peer support, achievement, self-esteem, liking of other students, school, and the teacher.

The students have the time to reflect on the material and rehearse mentally and verbally with other students before sharing publicly. They have an opportunity to practice their listening skills, synthesize their understandings, and practice *consensus* building. All students have a chance to share their ideas. Students appear to spend more time on task and to listen to each other more when engaged in Listen-Think-Pair-Share. Teachers also have more time to concentrate on asking higher-level questions, observing student performance, and listening carefully to students' responses.

Procedure.

1. A purpose is established for listening by the instructor. For example, students *listen* in order to respond to a question, to react to a prose selection the teacher is reading, or to summarize a lecture.
2. Students are given time in which to *think* of a response.
3. Students are *paired* with a neighbor and discuss their responses. Then a pair may be paired with another pair to provide additional discussion.
4. Finally, a reporter from the pair or combined pairs *shares* the responses with the entire classroom.

Example: Listen-Think-Pair-Share

A language arts teacher is about to teach a unit on communication. A creative way of jogging students' divergent thinking is to begin with a story. This story will serve as a stepping-stone to a broader discussion of communication: its elements, sources, the problems, its power (or lack of power) and the role of the media.

A great way to start students thinking about communication is to have them think about its opposite—what if there were no sound? What if there were no way for any creature to communicate in the manner that they do now? A great book by William Stafford, *The Animal That Drank up Sound, is* an excellent starting point for this discussion. From the first lines, "One day across the lake where echoes come now an animal that needed sound came down," students can begin to predict what will happen if the animal begins to consume sound from the planet. After an initial warm-up with the story, teachers can shift into a Listen-Think-Pair-Share activity.

Building themes around trade books enriches students' background and experience and creates powerful images for learning.

LISTEN:	Students are asked to listen to the story *The Animal That Drank up Sound,* read by the teacher or another student.
THINK:	Students are directed to take a few minutes to reflect on one word they think would capture their feelings about this story. (3-5 minutes)
PAIR-SHARE:	Students are then directed to turn to their partner and spend a few minutes talking about the words they have selected and to come to consensus on one word they will agree to share with another pair.
	Students find it fun to pair using the Clock Buddies activity. See the following description. (5 minutes)
	Then, students are instructed to find another pair of students and share their words. They are to choose one word from all those that they discussed and report on it to the class. (5 minutes) They are assured that each word has value but are invited to select a word which most completely describes the feeling they have about this story.
	Finally, a reporter from each group is directed to come to the front of the room and report on their group's selection. Each reporter has three minutes to talk about her group's choice.

How does Listen-Think-Pair-Share foster peer collaboration?

Many of the words we have noted in the workshops we have conducted using this story include disconnectedness, isolation, hope, courage, struggle, and change. These are related superbly to a topic like communication. As the students studied the elements of communication, the teacher referred them back to the story and their word selections to illustrate the connections among communication, their feelings, and situations from the story.

Many other points of departure exist when planning discussion stemming from this story. For example, teachers can segue into the power of communication and talk about the eternal vigilance needed in monitoring communication wherever it occurs, eliciting from students their interpretation of the closing lines (Stafford, 1992):

> But somewhere a cricket waits.
> It listens now, and practices at night.

In classrooms and workshops, both locally and internationally, we have found this strategy to be a natural way to initiate the process of discussion. It simulates the roles of careful listening, thinking through one's own ideas and sharing them, and consensus-building. Teachers adapt the strategy to fit their needs.

TEACHER TALK

By using this method, Listen-Think-Pair-Share-Spokesperson, I was able to get better results and more involvement than by using the oral question-answer discussions I initially tried. It was exciting to see so many students on task.

TABLE 3

INSTRUCTIONAL SUMMARY OF CLOCK BUDDIES

Literacy Strategies	Clock Buddies
Primary Focus	❑ Discussion
Learning Principles	❑ Active Involvement
When to use	❑ Talk Time
Goals: National or State Literacy Standards	❑ Before, During or After reading ❑ Sharing information ❑ Eliciting information ❑ Requesting and sharing ideas ❑ Revising ideas for accuracy
Materials	❑ Clock Buddies Handout
Time	❑ Fifteen minutes

Clock Buddies is a quick and easy way to create pairs for partnered activities while avoiding kids pairing up with the same partners.

Procedure.
1. Give each student a clock handout. See Figure 5.4. Have students place numbers on clock face if needed.
2. Each student then goes to a classmate to find a partner for each hour. If Shawna goes to Max. Shawna signs Mike's clock at_____p.m. and Max signs Shawna's clock at the same time
3. Students cannot use a name twice and all hours must be filled in.
4. Clocks are kept in a notebook or folder for easy access.
5. When you want students to work with a buddy, call out a random time, for example, "It's time to work with your_____o'clock buddy.
6. Students will then move to work with the partner indicated on their clock.

FIGURE 5.4. CLOCK BUDDIES

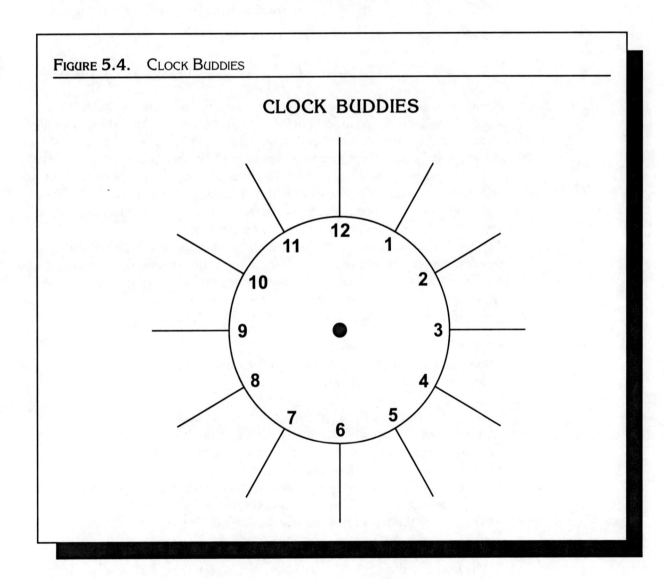

CLOCK BUDDIES

Socratic Seminar

TABLE 4

INSTRUCTIONAL SUMMARY OF A SOCRATIC SEMINAR

Literacy Strategies	Socratic Seminar
Primary Focus	Thinking Skills
Learning Principles	❑ Active Involvement ❑ Thought-demanding Activity
When to Use	After reading
Goals: National or State Literacy Standards	❑ To develop clarity, accuracy and relevance in thinking and speaking ❑ To practice articulating thoughts to others
Materials	Discussion task
Time	15-30 minutes

Vacca (2000)

Seabright (1999)

Paul et al. (1995)

A Socratic discussion gives students the opportunity to develop and test their ideas. It is designed to help students develop higher order thinking skills through discussing and questioning. Through Socratic questioning students explore what they mean, their assumptions, the implications and consequences of their thinking as well as examine their biases, and the concepts they choose or disregard in making their argument. This activity is based on Socrates', the ancient Greek philosopher, notion that people learn more effectively through self-discovery than through being told the answer or correct interpretation.

Couglin & Huhtala (2003)

The teacher's role is to select the curriculum material, to check on students' background knowledge and to assign the reading. Seminar topics usually emerge from primary source documents, which include, myths, poems, stories, plays, novels, historical documents, science features and works of art. Discussion procedures help move this discussion efficently and productively.

Procedure.
1. Arrange students in a circle. Although fifteen students are ideal—believe us, it does work with a large class.
2. Create a seating chart.
3. Review with students the guidelines for a Socratic Discussion.
4. Everyone needs to read the assigned text or hear it read aloud in order to participate. If at all possible, we encourage a second reading.
5. Students can talk only about the material read.
6. Students must be able to support their answers with details from the text or make a connection to another text or experience they've had.
7. As the leader, the teacher or student leader will only be asking questions—not giving answers.

We have found the seating chart to be indispensable to this process. At any given moment you can see who is participating and who isn't. In addition, explain the leader's role as a facilitator. The facilitator will:

❏ Pose questions only. Other members of the circle will be responsible for exploring the answers or responses.
❏ Prepare a set of discussion questions that raise issues and that probe, and synthesize information.
❏ Enable students to collect their thoughts by doing a quick write on the posed question—if needed.

A critical element of the Socratic seminar is the staging of questions: opening questions, core questions, text analysis questions, follow-up questions and closing questions. The following table summarizes these. See examples of these questions in the Socratic Planning Guide.

Opening questions	These questions begin the discussion. They establish the theme and ideas of the discussion as well as the interests of the group members
Core questions	These establish the main issue to be discussed. They are broad questions and should sustain an involved discussion. Other questions hould be able to spin off the main core question.
Text analysis questions	These are designed to bring the reader's discussion back to the text for support or to examine something specific raised in the discussion. They usually focus on a key assage or word.
Follow-up questions	These are not prepared but follow from the group's discussion. They are used to clarify or to establish support of discussion points.
Closing question	These promote personalization of the discussion. They explore how the text can relate to the participants' lives.

Staging questions Couglin/ Huhtala (2003)

For teachers who are beginners at this process, a planning tool for teachers (Couglin & Huhtala, 2003) may prove helpful. See Figure 5.5.

Some other guidelines that provide for a smooth discussion include:

1. Encourage students to enter the conversation naturally.
2. Encourage students to make eye contact with each other or recognize each other's contributions rather than maintain eye contact only with the leader.
3. Summarize what's been said after 7–10 minutes. Ask students to explain terms that may have come up and were ambiguous.

FIGURE **5.5.** SOCRATIC SEMINAR PLAN EXAMPLE

Socratic Seminar Plan

Reading/Art Selection: Etheridge Knight's "The Idea of Ancestry"

Objective (s):
- ❏ Active particpation
- ❏ Informed discussion
- ❏ Concensus building
- ❏ Enhancing listening skills

Core Question: Have you ever been in a situation where you felt invisible to another or others? Describe it.

Key Concepts: Invisibility, Ancestry

Key Skills: reading, discussion, writing, reading for comprehension and clarification

PRE-ACTIVITIES SEMINAR CORE QUESTIONS POST-ACTIVITIES

PRE-ACTIVITIES

1. Seminar overview and expectations

2. Journal writing: Describe an instance in which you felt invisible to others?

3. Play a recording of Etheridge Knight's "The Idea of Ancestry" from the Library of Congress, Watershed Tapes

SEMINAR CORE QUESTIONS

1. How does prison keep inmates invisible to others in prison as well to society in general?

2. How do the metaphors of the "salmon-leaping and bucking up his birthstream" and "grey stone wall damming my stream" capture Knight's story?

3. How does the fact that Knight wrote this poem after being in solitary confinement, called only by a number, affect your understanding of it?

4. Your questions?

POST-ACTIVITIES

1. Use current examples from such prison experiences as political prisoners in Guantanamo Bay to contrast Knight's experience with theirs.

2. Knight writes about his family: "They are farmers, I am a thief." Design a poster showing the work or professions of family members past or present that you can trace.

3. Write a poem connecting your own ancestry with your sense of yourself.

FIGURE 5.5.   SOCRATIC SEMINAR PLAN EXAMPLE (CONT.)

OPENING QUESTIONS:

1. Now that you've heard and read Knight's poem, how does he show that in prison his existence depends on reaching out to the familiar—the family? Why? How does the ability to use language make Knight come alive in your eyes?

TEXT ANALYSIS QUESTIONS

1. Why would the pictures taped on his cell wall be given so much attention in Knight's poem?
2. From this drab opening scene of the prison cell, Knight moves to a richly described nature scene in Mississippi. Yet even in this familial environment, he can't rise above his own overwhelming need for "caps—the monkey on his back." What does this phrase mean?
3. Why does the last line "I have no sons to float in the space between" become so touching in light of the theme of his ancestry?
4. Does anyone have an idea we haven't heard?

CLOSING QUESTIONS

1. Robert Cormier wrote a book, Fade, the story of a nephew and uncle who have the ability to become invisible, to fade at will. This ability proves not to be as much fun as the nephew thought it would be. In this poem, Knight's uncle disappeared, why would this invisibility cause uneasiness generally?
2. Why is this theme of invisibility an important theme in Knight's poem?

After students get used to the process of the Socratic Seminar, they can use the following Figure 5.6 for developing their own questions for discussion. In the process students develop an ability to look for the "second right answer" (Von Oech, 1990). Rather than seek one answer, students look for multiple answers, results, and meanings and realize as Linus Pauling, the Nobel Prize winning chemist, did "The best way to get an idea is to get lots of ideas."

In addition, writers, Keene and Zimmerman (1997) in their review of the research found that many students are inert as they read, never questioning the content, style or intent of the author. Anything that we can do to promote shared inquiry will stir these dormant minds into lively, thoughtful ones. Through questions we learn more deeply as will our students and both of us may change as a result of "risking the blood of our tongues repeatedly" (Williams, 1994).

FIGURE 5.6.   SOCRATIC QUESTIONING SAMPLES

Questions of Clarification

- ❑ What is your main point?
- ❑ Is your basic point _____ or _____?
- ❑ Could you put it another way?
- ❑ Let me see if I understand you: do you mean_____ or _____?
- ❑ How does this relate to our discussion/problem/issue?
- ❑ Beth, would you summarize in your own words what Brea has said? Brea, is that what you meant?

Questions that Probe Reasons and Evidence

- ❑ What would be an example?
- ❑ What other information do we need to know?
- ❑ But is that good evidence to support your thinking? Why or why not?
- ❑ Who is in a position to know if that is the case?
- ❑ Can someone else give evidence to support that response?
- ❑ How could we go about finding out whether that is true?
- ❑ What led you to believe that?
- ❑ What would convince you otherwise?

Questions that Probe Assumptions

- ❑ You seem to be assuming_____. Do I understand you correctly?
- ❑ Is it always the case? Why do you think that assumption holds here?
- ❑ Why have you based your reasoning on_____rather than _____?

Questions about Viewpoints or Perspectives

- ❑ Why have you chosen this rather than that perspective?
- ❑ How would other groups/types of people respond?
- ❑ What would someone who disagrees say?
- ❑ Can/did anyone see this another way? Explain.

Questions that Probe Implications and Consequences

- ❑ When you say_____, are you implying_____?
- ❑ What are you implying by that?
- ❑ But if that happened, what else would also happen as a result? Why?
- ❑ What effect would that have?

Your Questions:

From *Critical Thinking Handbook.*

Your Turn

Name _____ Date _____ Subject Area _____

Socratic Seminar Plan

Directions: (For instructor) Identify a theme or topic for class discussion, select a reading and design questions for the Socratic Seminar using the following guide.

Reading/Art Selection: _____

Objective (s)

_____

_____

_____

Core Question: _____

Key Concepts: _____

Key Skills: _____

PRE-ACTIVITIES	SEMINAR CORE QUESTIONS	POST-ACTIVITIES
OPENING QUESTIONS	TEXT ANALYSIS QUESTIONS	CLOSING QUESTIONS

Elaine Coughlin and Jack Huhtala (2006). "Socratic Seminar Plan" Used with permission.

Creative Problem-Solving

TABLE 5

INSTRUCTIONAL SUMMARY OF CREATIVE PROBLEM-SOLVING

Literacy Strategies	Creative Problem-Solving
Primary Focus	Listening, Thinking, Socialization Skills
Learning Principles	❑ Active Involvement ❑ Thought-demanding Activity
When to Use	Before, during, after reading
Goals: National or State Literacy Standards	❑ Use descriptive and accurate words appropriate to the purpose ❑ Analyze and evaluate verbal and nonverbal messages and their delivery
Materials	Discussion task & artifacts
Time	30 minutes

Linking Stein's (1975) notion that "creativity is a process that results in a novel product or idea which is accepted as useful, tenable, or satisfying by a significant group of others at some point in time," (p. 253) to a problem-solving activity enhances students' ability for divergent and imaginative thinking. In the following example, students practice their thinking and foreign language skills simultaneously. This activity is built around a problem that is clearly defined, allows a number of different solutions, and involves a situation in which reality is manipulated.

Can a creative problem-solving strategy be adapted to content in your subject area? How?

The students are engaged in the problem, and the emphasis becomes one of content and communication rather than linguistic form. This shift seems to encourage students to take risks and enjoy their play with another language. The activity is structured in a way to enable students to be successful even with limited second-language skills.

Directions depend on the proficiency level of the class. A beginning class may answer the questions only and rarely discuss any other dimension of the problem. In contrast, an advanced class would discuss the problem freely and not refer to the questions.

Example: Creative Problem-Solving in the Foreign Language Class

A typical lesson includes preparation, presenting the problem, checking comprehension, presenting vocabulary, reviewing grammar, eliciting a list of questions to be answered, dividing the class into small groups, letting the groups seek solutions, and calling for reports from the group secretaries. Students are frequently asked to role play, which helps in promoting divergence of thought. In the following case they are asked to role play antique dealers.

*Why is role
playing an
effective method
of problem-
solving?*

Sadow (1983)

Procedure.

Select an object that will not be familiar to students. Artifacts from faraway places such as figurines, masks, or musical instruments work well. The stranger they are, the better. Students are likely to come up with richer, varied interpretations if the object is mystifying.

Tell the class: Tengo un problema. Esta mañana caminando a la escuela me encontré con un hombre que llevaba una bolsa grande de papel. El sacó de la bolsa este objeto y me aseguró que tenía muchísimo valor. Sin embargo, como a él le hacía falta dinero, ofreció venderme el objeto por cien dólares solamente. Bueno, yo nunca puedo resistir una ganga, asi que se lo compré en seguida.

Ahora bien, no tengo ninguna seguridad de haber hecho una buena compra, puesto que no tengo ni la más mínima idea de lo que puede ser este objeto. No obstante, como sé que todos Uds. son expertos en antigüedades, por favor, díganme qué es este objeto y si engañó o no.

(I'm very puzzled. This morning on the way to school, I was stopped by a man carrying a large paper bag. He took this object from the bag. He assured me that it was of great value but, since he needed the money, he would sell it to me for only $100. I can never pass up a bargain, so I bought it immediately. Now I'm not so sure I did well since I have no idea what this thing is. I know all of you are experts in antiques, so I'm asking you to explain this thing to me and tell me whether I have been cheated.)

Check comprehension:

1. ¿Qué tenía el hombre?
   (What did the man have with him?)
2. ¿Por qué compré yo el objeto?
   (Why did I buy the object?)
3. ¿Qué necesito saber?
   (What do I need to know?)

Present vocabulary:

antiguo, artificial, blando, costoso, cuadrado
(old, artificial, soft, costly)

Ask the class: What questions will you need to answer? Write questions on the blackboard.

Possibilities:
1. ¿Qué es?
   (What is it?)
2. ¿Cuántos años tiene?
   (How old is it?)
3. ¿Qué hace?
   (What does it do?)
4. ¿De qué color es? ¿De qué forma?
   (What color is it? What shape?)
5. ¿A qué se parece?
   (What does it resemble?)

6. ¿Tiene una historia?
   (Is there a story behind it?)
7. ¿Tiene valor? ¿Mucho valor?
   (Is it valuable? Very valuable?)
8. ¿Fue engañado el maestro?
   (Was the teacher cheated?)
9. ¿Si fuera mío, ¿qué haría con él?
   (If it were mine, what would I do with it?)

Divide the class: Form groups of 3-5 students. Have each group choose a secretary. Remind them of the questions on the board.

Do the activity.

Call for reports: The reporters read the conclusions. Encourage other students to ask questions and make comments.

From *Foreign Language Annals* by S. Sadow. Reprinted by permission of American Council on the Teaching of Foreign Language.

Although this activity is designed for the foreign language class, it can be adapted to any curriculum to teach problem-solving. By shifting roles to those of an anthropologist, a geologist, or a mathematician, the same problem under discussion could take on a completely different dimension.

Discussion Web

TABLE 6

INSTRUCTIONAL SUMMARY OF A DISCUSSION WEB	
Literacy Strategies	**Discussion Web**
Primary Focus	❑ Listening, Speaking, Pro-Con Argument ❑ Consensus-Building
Learning Principles	❑ Talk Time ❑ Thought-demanding Activity
When to Use	Before, during, after reading
Goals: National or State Literacy Standards	❑ Understand relationships among issues and events ❑ Use of persuasive mode
Materials	❑ Discussion Web handout ❑ Reading materials
Time	30 minutes

The discussion web encourages students to examine both sides of an issue before making a decision. It thereby encourages students to choose based on the most convincing argument possible. This adaptation of Duthie (1986) enables

How are a discussion and a web alike?

students to think through an issue, determine their position, and attempt to convince others. In the process they hear multiple points of view, stretch the boundaries of their thinking, and carry on a dialogue about their beliefs.

Example: Discussion Web

Duthie (1986); Alvermann et al. (1987)

The following model is from an eighth grade inclusion class in English. A visual discussion guide is used by the students to facilitate their interaction. See Figure 5.7.

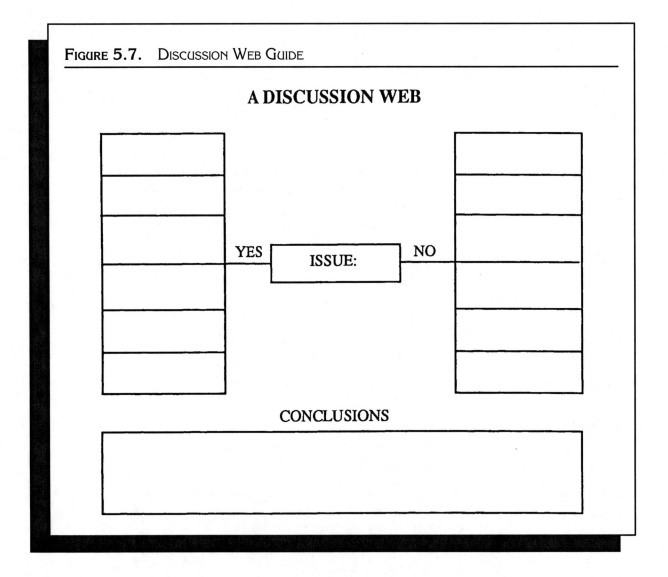

FIGURE 5.7.   DISCUSSION WEB GUIDE

A DISCUSSION WEB

YES   ISSUE: NO

CONCLUSIONS

Procedure.

1. The students read in class "The Summer of the Beautiful White Horse" by William Saroyan. After discussing the plot, setting, and the characters, the teacher distributed the Discussion Web Guide.
2. Students were assigned to partners. Their task was to agree or disagree with the value system of one of the characters as they understood it from the following quote:

> Well, it seemed to me stealing a horse for a ride was not the same thing as stealing something such as money.

3. A reporter was directed to copy the quotation in the center of the visual guide. Then students discussed the quotation in terms of the evidence found in their short story finding support for both the Yes/No columns.
4. Students were advised to use key words and phrases. They were also told they
did not have to fill all the lines.
5. Students drew their own conclusion at this point, favoring a YES or NO position.
6. Then students were advised to seek out another pair and come to consensus in terms of a conclusion. If the other pair argued a dissenting view, the group as a whole was asked to come to consensus.
7. Finally, the group representative reported its finding to the entire class. If the group didn't reach consensus, the minority conclusion was also shared.

A student pair's example:

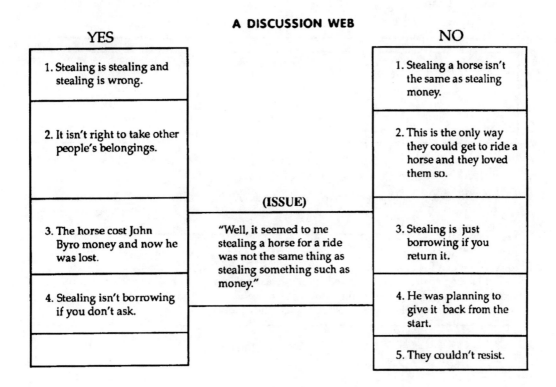

A DISCUSSION WEB

YES

1. Stealing is stealing and stealing is wrong.
2. It isn't right to take other people's belongings.

(ISSUE)

"Well, it seemed to me stealing a horse for a ride was not the same thing as stealing something such as money."

3. The horse cost John Byro money and now he was lost.
4. Stealing isn't borrowing if you don't ask.

NO

1. Stealing a horse isn't the same as stealing money.
2. This is the only way they could get to ride a horse and they loved them so.
3. Stealing is just borrowing if you return it.
4. He was planning to give it back from the start.
5. They couldn't resist.

Conclusion: "We don't agree that stealing John Byro's horse isn't the same as stealing money even though Mourad and Aram returned it. If Mourad considered stealing the horse for a month to be borrowing without asking, he could have asked John Byro if he could borrow the horse. John Byro probably would have let him borrow the horse for a while.

One other reason we don't agree is that stealing is stealing and stealing is wrong. Taking someone's belongings is stealing if you don't ask. Mourad could have ruined his family's reputation for being honest by stealing the horse. Mourad would have probably felt a lot better if he would have asked to borrow the horse from John Byro."

Example 2: Una Guía de Discusión Basada en, *"La Hija del Torrero"

¿Debería Teresa obedecer su mamá y no encender el faro?

Sí	No
1. Su mamá está correcta. Teresa está muy chica para encenderlo.	1. Teresa es inteligente y puede comprender como encencer el faro.
2. Puede ser que Teresa se caiga tratando de encender la mecha.	2. Puede ser que los barcos se naufraguen y pierdan toda su carga.
3. Puede ser que Teresa se queme.	3. Puede ser que los marineros se mueran sin la luz del faro.
4. Teresa debería cuidar su mamá enferma.	4. Puede ser que los habitantes del pueblo se enojen con su familia.
5. Puede ser que Teresa le prenda fuego al faro.	5. Puede ser que su mama no reciba su mendicamento.

El mejor porqué:

From "Practical Whole Language Strategies for Secondary and University-Level," by Bonnie Adair-Hauck, 1996, *Foreign Language Annals*, 29, p. 267.

* Spanish Reading, "La Hija del Torrero" in Appendix A.

TEACHER TALK

After using the Discussion Web with both mainstream and resource room students, I would like to conclude that it was a useful tool in both settings. Both groups of students were offered a new way of looking at an idea and responding to it in a safe but active way. I think that with continued use in the resource room setting, students will feel more free to share ideas and do more thinking. It will also help develop conversational skills and social skills for these students.

Your Turn

Name _____ Date _____ Subject Area _____

DIRECTIONS: Select a controversial statement from a unit you are teaching in your content area class. Design a lesson using the Discussion Web. Create a Discussion Web model that you would use to demonstrate to students how to complete it.

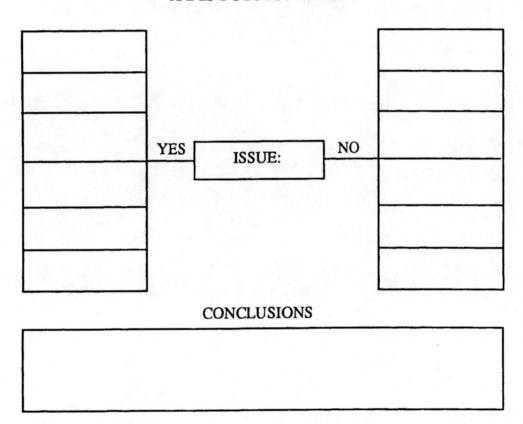

A DISCUSSION WEB

YES   ISSUE: NO

CONCLUSIONS

Tea Party

TABLE 7

INSTRUCTIONAL SUMMARY OF A TEA PARTY

Literacy Strategies	Tea Party
Primary Focus	Listening, Role Playing, Writing Skills
Learning Principles	❑ Active Involvement ❑ Talk Time
When to Use	Before reading
Goals: National or State Literacy Standards	❑ Communicate knowledge of the topic ❑ Recognize and examine how character development contributes to text meaning
Materials	Role cards & activity sheets
Time	40 minutes

Tea Party: A Lesson Plan

Activity: The Double Helix Tea Party Character Roles

Directions. Type up multiple copies of one character's description per sheet of paper. Then cut into individual roles for students. When copying these, color-code the paper to differentiate the characters. Students will gravitate towards the different colors to complete their collection of all characters.

   JAMES (JIM) WATSON: I was a precocious American student who entered the University of Chicago at 15; however, both Harvard and CalTec turned me down for graduate work. Hardly a good start for someone who went on to win the Nobel prize in 1962. Even today, I remain a controversial figure in biology. I have been called the "enfant terrible" because of my lack of consideration of others' work.

   I merged with the Cambridge, England scene by growing my hair wildly and bumming cold-water, dismal rooms to live while working on DNA and talking to Francis Crick even if others hated to listen to him. Did this collaboration pay off smashingly? Loved having sherry with the girls at Pops. Did I like Rosalind Franklin? You'll need to read the book to find out how I felt and what I accomplished.

   FRANCIS CRICK: I loved to question, in fact was driven to ask questions. I could ponder the consequences of my friends' ideas by the time they were out of their mouths. People said I was bright and had novel ideas but would never claim any intellectual awards. Odile, my wife, and I shared food, general gossip and scientific conversation with Jim in a warm, cheerful flat—probably saved his stomach. I know I drove my colleagues crazy at the Cavendish physics laboratory in Cambridge with my unrestrained, loud, boisterous talking and the shattering bang of my laughing, it worked out, didn't it?

FIGURE 5.8.   PREREADING ACTIVITY FOR *THE DOUBLE HELIX*

Lesson Plan: Humanities Class(Science, English, Social Studies)

Grade: 10

Topic: DNA and *The Double Helix* by James D. Watson

Purpose: To help students gain knowledge of the discovery of the structure of DNA and analyze this accomplishment by examining the relationships among the scientists that led to this discovery.

State Content/Literacy Standards:
1. To understand science as a human endeavor;
2. To understand that scientific knowledge is subject to change based on new findings and results of scientific observation and experimentation;
3. Identify relationships in a literary selection and draw conclusions about their meaning.

Student Objectives:
1. Students will be able to identify, compare and contrast the scientists who contributed to the discovery of the structure of DNA by completing a role play assuming their identify and introducing themselves to other students.
2. Students will make predictions on what might happen in *The Double Helix* based on what they found out about the scientists involved in the project.
3. Students will be able to demonstrate their understanding of the relationships among these scientists by completing a diagram, graph or picture that represents how these characters fit together and writing an explanation of that visual.

Introduction:
Tell students that in preparation for reading their next book *The Double Helix*, they are going to participate in a tea party and their job is to find out as much as they can about the other characters attending the party. Since scientists are the main characters in this book, let them know they will be assuming an identity of one of the scientists that are featured in the book at the party. (2 minutes)

Learning Activity: (35 minutes for learning activity)
1. Give each student a color-coded character description and an index card.
2. Encourage students to read their role and answer Questions 2 & 3 on their handout. See Figure 7.11 *Double Helix* Tea Party Student Handout below.
3. Once students are comfortable with their roles ask them to move about the room and learn who the other people are attending the party. Encourage them to internalize their characters and act as if they are truly James Watson or Rosalind Franklin, or any other designated character. They should gather sufficient information so that they can complete their "Other character notes." Serving treats is an added incentive. Students can eat as they go. In addition, ask them to take their index card with them and take some notes on the characters they meet.
4. After students have met all the characters ask them to return to their seats and complete questions 4-7 of the handout.
5. Choose several students to share their answers with the class for each section.

Closure:
Students illustrate pictures, diagrams or graphs to demonstrate how characters fit together. They also write an explanation of their visual.

Evaluation:
Students' handouts and drawings are assessed for: a) accurate understanding of characters' interrelationships, b) reasonableness of their predictions, and c) connectedness of visual to the topic of the structure of DNA.

ROSALIND (ROSY) FRANKLIN: Watson and Crick thought I was more trouble than I was worth. With my acid smile, I let them know to keep their opinions to themselves about a subject for which they weren't trained. I almost assaulted Jim and Maurice over the stupidity of their ideas especially the helix model a few times. I had a temper. You wouldn't find any warmth or frivolity in anything I did.

Others referred to me as a genius who, unfortunately, died at 37 from cancer. However, without my renowned work on X-ray crystallography, it would have taken much longer for this discovery. My pretty X-ray pictures had Jim drooling, but I never really gave them my experimental data. But Jim and Francis got it anyway. Jim was particularly wrong about my behavior as a flaming feminist; I was a scientist on equal footing with all of them. I was thrilled with the Double Helix discovery because our data supported its DNA structure.

LINUS PAULING: Born in Oregon in 1901, I was motivated by my curiosity and imagination. I am generally considered among the greatest chemists of the twentieth century. I was also a two-time Nobel laureate. The State Department or CalTec's governing board—my employer at the time did not appreciate my celebrity status and position on peaceful co-existence as well as my pernicious charm. My success with the helix structure was due to my reliance on the simple laws of structural chemistry. My prodigious mind and infectious grin, if not my dazzling presentation of my polypeptide chain model, led to Jim's tinkering with his DNA models. However, in a major paper on DNA, I forgot elementary college chemistry. This blooper was critical in determining whether the Americans or the Brits won the race to the gate for the discovery of the structure of DNA. Who won?

MAURICE: The molecular work on DNA was my personal property. I had duplicated Rosy and Gosling's X-ray work and given it to Jim and Francis. Through my own X-ray diffraction work, I demonstrated the well-defined patterns within DNA. I continually frustrated Francis because I had a habit of understating his arguments. Yet, I turned Jim Watson on by my photographs on DNA and hooked him on the importance of chemistry. My photographs saved them 6-months to a year's worth of work.

My troubles with Rosalind Franklin were legendary. To think I handed over to her my best crystalline DNA data. And then she wouldn't share the results of her work—not very British-like! Linus Pauling and Francis Crick were always breathing down my neck for copies of my crystalline DNA X-rays photographs. Who won the glory as well as making the ultimate discovery? Read and find out.

FIGURE 5.9. TEA PARTY STUDENT HANDOUT

1. Read your role.

2. Write the key points about your character in the space below.

3. Write some questions or thoughts about your character after reading the description.

4. Write about each of the other characters you meet at the tea party. Write notes on your index card as the person introduces him or herself to you.

   1st character name: _____

   Description:

   2nd character name: _____

   Description:

   3rd character name: _____

   Description:

   4th character name: _____

   Description:

5. Now that you've met a few of the characters, you probably have some questions about them or the book. In the space below, write at least three questions you have about the book or the characters.

6. What predictions do you have about what happens in this book? Who will be successful? Who won't? Make at least three predictions.

7. In the space below, draw a diagram, graph, web, picture, or some kind of visual representation that shows the connections between the characters. Feel free to add other words into your creation.

Adapted from "The Tea Party: Enticing Reluctant Readers to Read," in *Reading, Writing, and Rising Up: Teaching About Social Injustice and the Power of the Written Word*, by Linda Christensen (pp. 115-120). Copyright 2000 by Rethinking Schools, Ltd.

Inclusion Techniques

A poignant poem about growing up black by Thomas (1993), "Brown Honey in Broomwheat Tea," speaks well to children growing up with special needs:

> There are those who
> Have brewed a
> Bitter potion for
> Children kissed long by the sun.

Children with special needs are frequently served a bitter reminder of their lack of communication ability in discussion-oriented classes. Groups of students carry on lively conversations among themselves, while their less communicative peers struggle to participate or tune out in despair. On the other hand, when all students are recognized as individuals who belong to the larger community of the classroom, and whose needs are understood, and whose rights are respected, all students' wellbeing and self-esteem are cultivated.

A powerful story, "Voice of Inclusion: Everything about Bob was cool, including the cookies," (Villa, 1995) shows the way a class and a school can welcome a student with special needs and create a community where all are welcome. By preparing the students and asking them to volunteer in helping create a school where Bob's social and academic needs would be met through their help, his inclusion in the life of the school became everyone's responsibility. Because of this community planning, his arrival and acceptance into the school were relatively smooth processes.

What intrigued us about this story was how concrete the steps were in creating this environment. Teams of teachers sat down and identified Bob's individual educational goals and objectives to be emphasized during general education activities, and articulated these to the students so that they could help. For example, in a biology class, students were working on dissecting a frog. Bob's lab group was working on a lap tray connected to his wheelchair. Amid wiggling frog parts in front of each other's faces, the students would ask Bob if he wanted something to drink, or if he had looked at the blue cup. The students were mindful of his educational objectives regarding object discrimination and making choices. The students helped Bob realize his objectives while going about the business of realizing their own.

Many studies demonstrate that when students are allowed to work together, their social skills are enhanced, and they are better able to take the role of the other. Talking is the medium of cooperative learning and discussion; students are engaged in making meaning about the subject area through speaking to each other. Talking in itself is an adaptive tool that leads to content and language acquisition.

Developing discussion sessions that take advantage of all students' strengths is a crucial step in building a classroom community.

Cohen (1990)

TABLE 8

INSTRUCTIONAL SUMMARY OF DISCUSSION CIRCLES

Literacy Strategies	Discussion Circles
Primary Focus	❏ Discussion/Comprehension
Learning Principles	❏ Variety of ways to organize information ❏ Talk time a ❏ Thought-demanding activity
When to use	❏ After reading
Goals: National or State	❏ Promote comprehension
Literacy Standards	❏ Increase awareness of discussion roles ❏ Draw connections between reading and other experiences ❏ Revising ideas for accuracy
Materials	❏ Role cards ❏ Reading
Time	❏ 1 class period

For many years, students have been using Literature Circles (Daniels, 1994) in regular classes. Because of the structure inherent in this strategy, we believe that these could function well for students with special needs.

For more about the traditional use of Literature Circle Discussion please see Daniels (2001), *Literature Circles: Voice and Choice in Book Clubs & Reading Groups*. In this text, forms are designed in English and Spanish. Several well-designed adaptations for literature circles both for fiction and nonfiction can be obtained from the website "Teaching Resources from the classroom of Laura Candler," http://home.att.net/%7Eteaching/litcircleblacklines.htm.

For our inclusive students' purpose we have changed the activity from "Literature" to "Discussion" Circles to demonstrate that these can be used in other content areas.

Student roles that work for students with special needs include: a Director, Summarizer, Word Finder, Question Writer, Connector and Illustrator.

Each of these roles needs to be modeled with students. Books should be selected with these students in mind, usually shorter and easier texts. A good source for such books as *Abraham Lincoln: From Log Cabin to the White Rouse, Sally Ride, Volcanoes*, etc. is http://www.readinga-z.com. Books about characters with disabilities are effective at evoking discussion like Haddon's (2003) *The Curious Incident of the Dog in the Night-Time*, a story told by Christopher, an adolescent with autism, or Tashjian's (1997) *Tru Confessions*. A journal format is used in this book where Trudy questions why her twin brother is affected with a disability and she isn't. Books like Lipp's (2001) *The Caged Birds of PhnomPenh*, and Filipovic's (1995) *Zalta's Diary* appeal to English language learners. Multiple copies of the same title are needed to conduct these circles. Instructional assistants or parent aids can read selections with small groups, and guide the role-playing.

In addition, teachers should elicit from students what make discussions work and the kinds of questions that enable good discussions to occur. Post these questions in the classroom for those moments when discussions lag. Students can use these as a reference.

Depending on the students, a Director can be chosen from the group which is the ideal situation. The instructor or instructional assistant can also model this role until students become comfortable with assuming it themselves. The roles can be handed out to individual group members, or all students in the group can practice with one role at a time.

The following Description Cards will get you started.

FIGURE 5.10.   DESCRIPTION FOR DISCUSSION CIRCLE ROLES

CARD 1   Director

Use the following steps to guide the discussion, help everyone participate.

1. Ask someone to summarize the reading for today.
2. Discuss words that students have selected.
3. Ask everyone to select their best question and have students present their questions and recognize anyone who wants to answer.
4. Present someone's drawing and ask others to relate it to something in the reading. Then ask the illustrator to talk about the drawing.
5. Close by asking students to make predictions of what might happen next. Check if they know what to read for the next discussion.

CARD 2   Summarizer

1. Summarize your reading. You need to select only the important details. You may want to start with one of the following questions:
   a. Who did What to Whom?
   b. What happened? And Why?
2. You may want to draw a story map or a graphic organizer first showing the relationship among characters or incidents, then write your summary from it.
3. Be prepared to read your summary to the group.

FIGURE **5.10.** DESCRIPTION FOR DISCUSSION CIRCLE ROLES (CONT.)

CARD 3   Word Finder

1. Choose two new words from your reading.
2. Write each word, the page you found it on, and its definition in your journal.
3. Be prepared to share these words with your group.
4. Ask others what words they found interesting.

CARD 4   Question Writer

1. Create 3-5 interesting questions.
2. General questions work best:
   a. What stood out in the reading for you?
   b. What was an important idea in this reading?
   c. What surprised you in this reading?
   d. How could you use this information in your life?
3. Ask your group members to support their answers to your questions by reading the section that shows this support.

CARD 5   Connector

1. Select something from the reading that reminds you of something you did, or that happened to you, or connected with something you read about.
2. Make sure to write the page number down so you can find it, if needed.
3. Ask others if there was something they connected with in the story.

CARD 6   Illustrator

1. Draw a picture related to the reading. It can be a cartoon, a diagram or stick figure scene.
2. Be prepared to show it to your group.
3. Ask them what the picture means to them, or how it relates to their reading.
4. When they are finished with their ideas, explain why you drew what you did.

A Variation on Discussion Circle Roles

Once students are used to this process, it is helpful to guide them in guiding their own discussion without formal roles. In a real world conversation, individuals jump in with ideas and naturally follow up their colleagues' speech with their own ideas, challenges or information. Using students' own response simulates this process. This variation places the responsibility for bringing something to the discussion on the students themselves.

As students read, they can use sticky notes to mark important points that they want to bring to the discussion circle. One teacher shared with us her booklets that students keep (personal communication, Maren Black, October 19, 2006). Each student receives a booklet that they title with their reading and their name. They can decorate the cover page as well. While reading they raise questions on sticky notes, such as making a connection, or writing in puzzling or interesting words. They are guided in their note-taking by referring to a list of possibilities that the teacher has included in the booklet. They may use the sticky notes to label an important passage they want to share with the group. After reading the part of the text to be discussed, and making notes, they transfer these to their booklet.

Sticky Note Possibilities	Sticky Notes Posting
1. Ask a QUESTION of the text or author.	
2. CHALLENGE the text ("I don't think this is true because...").	
3. AFFIRM the text (Yes, this is true because...").	
4. IDENTIFY A key word, phrase, sentence or image.	
5. Make a CONNECTION to another reading.	
6. CONNECT the reading to your own experience or a movie you've seen, a song you've heard.	
7. Make a PREDICTION about what will follow next in the reading	
8. SUMMARIZE a small portion of text	
9. Make an INFERENCE or draw a	
10. IDENTIFY a word you do not know.	
11. LABEL the most important passage.	

Students use the notes for their discussion and are given credit for them.

For students with special needs, it is often helpful to include an evaluation component to this activity. The following provides a weekly assessment of the student's work.

FIGURE 5.11. DISCUSSION CIRCLE STUDENT HANDOUT

Name_____Week_____

Book/Chapter Title_____

	Monday	Tuesday	Wednesday	Thursday	Friday
Pages Read					
Role task completed					
Contributed to Discussion					
Stayed on Task					

Ex = Excellent   S = Satisfactory   N = Needs Improvement   U = Unsatisfactory

Weekly Discussion Circle Rating

STUDENT TALK

I like playing these roles in the Discussion Circle. Depending on the role, I need to focus on one thing in particular. I don't seem to get as confused when I know what I need to pay attention to.

Discussion Strategies for English Language Learners

Krashan (1982) has argued that language competence is acquired through use rather than learned by direct teaching. Language minority students, in particular, seem to benefit from working in small groups (Kagan, 1992). In this arrangement, students teach and are taught by their peers, who sometimes speak different languages, and have different social and academic abilities. In the process, English language skills are fostered, racial and ethnic barriers are overcome, and students' enjoyment of subject matter is enhanced.

Faltis (2001)

Providing students with roles and responsibilities as well as having them try out repeatedly ways of asking questions, talking about the assignment, turn-taking, responding to ideas, and respectfully disagreeing when they need to, enable students to work together comfortably and productively. Small group conversation can be sustained easily through the use of scaffolding, a process of providing functional support for activities that might prove too difficult otherwise. Dialogue strategies can be considered scaffolding, the structure that invites students into the discussion easily and meaningfully.

Define scaffolding

TABLE 9

INSTRUCTIONAL SUMMARY OF DISCUSSION RESPONSE LOG

Literacy Strategies	Discussion Response Log
Primary Focus	❑ Discussion
Learning Principles	❑ Active Involvement ❑ Talk Time
When to use	❑ After reading
Goals: National or State Literacy Standards	❑ Sharing information ❑ Eliciting information ❑ Requesting and sharing ideas ❑ Revising ideas for accuracy
Materials	❑ Response Log Guide ❑ DVD or reading
Time	❑ 2 class periods

Chris Tovani (2004) asked her students what they didn't like about groups. Many felt that they'd rather work with their friends rather than the teacher selecting the groups. Others didn't like that some students slacked off, while a few did all the work; others stated they didn't know what to do in the group, and no one would help them (p. 92). Tovani suggests that students be allowed to work with their friends occasionally and that the teacher ask those who haven't done the work to move to a quiet place, do their work and then join the goup. Finally, regarding students who do not know what to do, she suggests the use of learning guides to structure group discussion. With a concrete guide to follow, students have a template which provides the direction they require. No more cries of "Teacher, I don't know what to do."

For second language learners, we can't overlook the use of media in the classroom. Through the use of videos or DVDs, students see, and hear the subject matter develop.

How can media enhance an ELL class?

Through film, the imagery can be powerful enough to almost evoke smell, taste, and touch as well. For conceptual development, it is a powerful medium. For example in teaching a science or geography lesson, teachers can prepare ELL students for a unit on habitat by showing segments of "March of the Penguins".

Through the viewing and discussion of the first six minutes of the film, students learn something about the location, the methods of travel, and the motivation for the penguins to come to the pitiless ice desert, Antartica.

We have adapted a reading response guide that Tovani uses (p. 130) for the use of discussing film in the classroom (Figure 5.12). It can be used as a model for students to follow and respond in their learning logs, or they could be distributed as a guide to be completed.

Before showing the segment, teachers need to set up the film, connect it to the students' experience, and weave in the connection to the subject matter they're teaching. Students then should be directed to complete these guides individually after viewing the DVD segment. When finished they bring their guides to their small group for discussion.

FIGURE 5.12.   DISCUSSION RESPONSE GUIDE

Discussion Response Guide

Name _____ Date _____

Title of Video or DVD _____

Producer or Director _____

1. Summary (2–3 sentences). Retell what you remember from seeing this DVD segment.

2. Write your response to what you've seen (3-5 sentences). You will discuss this with your group members. Remember to use any one or some of our discussion starters:
    I wonder.....
    I noticed.....
    My favorite part was.....
    I felt.....
    What if.....

3. Go back to your written response and underline the "golden line/ that special sentence, that you want especially to share with your discussion group.

4. Write one thing you didn't know or think about before seeing this DVD.

Endings: A Summary

A video shot of a discussion in the classroom would capture the exchange of students with their peers and teacher through extended dialogue. The careful listener would hear multiple points of view about a topic and the openness to change.

We believe through the medium of discussion students stretch the boundaries of their knowing, cultivate consensus-building skills, and address the concerns regarding the problems we face as a global community. Teachers design discussion activities to analyze, explore, evaluate and even modify attitudes on issues, to problem-solve, and to promote subject mastery. In planning and preparing these activities, teachers hope to expand their students' understanding of their content areas. We have presented decision factors to help the teacher develop content topics that lend themselves to discussion and expand students' ability to explain, draw analogies and generalize specific characteristics to form a conceptual framework, gaining crucial insights about their content material in the process.

We have suggested that building a conducive classroom environment for discussion involves providing adequate time, preparing students for their roles, and adopting various grouping practices.

Furthermore, we have addressed the difficulties of facilitating the discussion process. If difficulties arise—and they will—many well-established classroom management practices have been outlined to improve students' interactions with each other.

Finally, we have included many cooperative learning strategies that teachers have found helpful in structuring discussion. We have found that very few open-ended or spontaneous discussions work well in our classrooms. In contrast, students appear to find the structure provided by these strategies helpful in thinking through the content and organizing it in a meaningful way for their discussion and learning. The structure enables them to bring their particular "gifts"—as one of our classroom teachers says—to the task and weave their individual understandings into a rich fabric of meaning.

Expanding Understanding through Discussion

After reading this chapter on discussion, complete the discussion web posted in this section. Brainstorm an issue you wish to explore. Discuss the issue and record your thinking both pro and con. Come to consensus and be prepared to present your group's argument to the class.

In the Field Applications

A. Use the following Three-Question Format to design a discussion around a topic of interest in your subject area. Identify the topic, include the source material, and develop procedures that you would use in conducting this lesson.

1. What did you think, or what do you suppose, influenced the writer?
2. What did the author say.
3. What might one learn from this?

B. Locate a trade book like *The Animal That Drank up Sound* that can be used to broaden students' understanding of a topic in your curriculum area. Then design a cooperative learning lesson using one strategy from this chapter or one of your own creation.

A DISCUSSION WEB

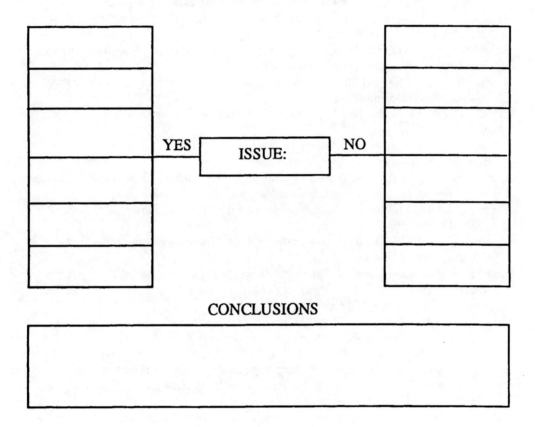

YES   ISSUE: NO

CONCLUSIONS

C. Videotape a discussion in your classroom. Evaluate it using the following criteria. Discuss what instructional decisions you will make as a result of your findings.

1. Describe the pacing. Were students given sufficient time to answer?
2. Who controls the discussion? Is there a back-and-forth, natural tempo to the discussion?
3. Is the discussion sustained? Are students' and teacher's remarks probed, clarified or reinforced?
4. How sensitive are the speakers to their audience? Particularly note how the regular education students include those with special needs or vice versa.
5. Is there evidence of risk-taking among the speakers?

References ❑ ❑ ❑

Activities for ESL Students (2006). *The Internet TESL Journal.* Retrieved October 23, 2006, from http://www.a4esl.org

Adair-Hauck, B. (1996). Practical whole language strategies for secondary and university level. *Foreign Language'Annals, 29*(2), 267.

Alvermann, D., Dillon, D., & O'Brien, D. (Eds.). (1987). *Using discussion to promote reading comprehension.* Newark, DE: International Reading Association.

Baca, J. S. (1999). Coming into language. In B. G. Chevigny (Ed.), *Doing time: 25 years of prison writing.* NY: Arcade.

Bellanca, J., & Fogerty, R. (1991). *Blueprints for thinking in the cooperative classroom.* Palantine, IL: Skylight Publishing , Inc.

Bigelow, B., et al. (1994). Rethinking our classrooms: Teaching for equity and justice. Milwaukee, WI: Rethinking Schools: 4–5.

Bridges, D. (1979). *Education, democracy and discussion.* Windsor: NFER Publishing Company Ltd.

Candler, L. Teaching resources: Literary lessons. Retrieved October 19, 2006, from http://home.att.net/~teaching/litcircles.htm

Christensen, L. (2000). *Reading, writing, and rising up: Teaching about social justice and the power of the written word.* Milwaukee, WI: Rethinking Schools.

Ciamarra, J. G. (2002). Internet resources for special children. Retrieved October 23, 2006, from http://www.irsc.org

Cohen, E. (1990). Continuing to cooperate: Prerequisites for persistence. *Phi Delta Kappan, 72*(2), 134–138.

Conversation questions for the ESL/EFL classroom (2006). *The Internet TESL Journal.* Retrieved October 23, 2006 from http://iteslj.org/questions

Cormier, R. (1991). *Fade.* NY: Laurel Leaf.

Couglin, E.β, & Huhtala, J.(2003). *Coaching the brain: Socratic seminars* (pp. 1–9): Unpublished paper, Pacific University, Forest Grove, OR.

Cugino, C. Luedtke, P., & Ponder, T. (2006). Eureka:Teaching and learning strategies. Retrieved October 23, 2006, from http://literacy.kent.edu/ eureka/ strategies

Daniels, H. (2001). *Literature circles: Voice and choice in book clubs & reading groups (2nd ed.).* Portland, ME: Stenhouse.

Dillon, J. (1981). Duration of response to teacher questions and statements. *Contemporary Educational Psychology, 6,* 1–11.

Dillon, J. (1984). Research on questioning and discussion. *Educational Leadership, 42,* 50–56.

Duthie, J. (1986). The web: A powerful tool for the teaching and evaluation of the expository essay. *The History and Social Science Teacher, 21,* 232–236.

ESL/EFL Teaching/learning Resources:Reading. (2006). Retrieved October 23, 2006, from http://academics.smcvt.edu

Esquivel, L. (1994). Like water for chocolate. NY: Anchor.

Faltis, C. J. (2001). *Join fostering: Teaching and learning in multilingual classrooms.* Columbus, OH: Merrill Prentice Hall.

Filipovic, Z. (1995). Zlata's diary. London: Penguin.

Gallagher, K. (2004). *Deeper reading: Comprehending challenging texts,* 4–12. Portland, ME: Stenhouse Publishers.

Gall, M., & Gall, J. (1976). The discussion method. In N. L. Gage (Ed.), *Psychology of teaching methods* (pp. 166–216). Chicago: University of Chicago Press.

Goodlad, J. (1984). *A place called school.* NY: McGraw-Hill.

Haddon, M. (2003). *The curious incident of the dog in the night-time.* NY: Doubleday.

Kagan, S. (1992). *Cooperative learning.* San Juan Capistrano, CA: Cooperative Learning.

Keene, E. O., & Zimmermann, S. (1997). *Mosaic of Thought: Teaching comprehension in a reader's workshop*. Portsmouth, NH: Heinemann.

Knight, E. (1986), *The essential Etheridge Knight*. Pittsbugh, PA: University of Pittsburgh Press.

Krashen, S. (1982). *Principles and practices of second language acquisition*. Oxford: Pergamon Press.

Lipp, F. (2001). *The caged birds of Phnom Penh*. NY: Holiday House

McKenna, M., & Robinson, R. (1993). *Teaching through text: A content literacy approach to content area reading*. NY: Longman.

Paul, R., Binker, A., et al. (1995). *Critical thinking handbook: A guide for redesigning instruction*. Santa Rosa, CA: Foundation for Critical Thinking.

Rogoff, B. (1990). Apprenticeship in thinking: Cognitive development in social context. NY: Oxford University Press.

Sadow, S. (1983). Creative problem-solving for the foreign language class. *Foreign Language Annals, 16*(2), 115–119.

Saroyan, W. (1966). The summer of the beautiful white horse. In W. Saroyan, *My name is Aram* (Rev. ed., pp. 1–10). NY: Dell.

Schlick Noe, K. L., & Johnson, N. J. (1999). Preparing for discussion. Retrieved October 19, 2006, from http://www.litcircles.org/Discussion/prep.html

Seabright, W. (1999). *Getting started with Junior Great Books: Mini-units for beginning your program*. Chicago, IL: The Great Books Foundation.

Stafford, W. (1992). *The animal that drank up sound*. San Diego, CA: Harcourt, Brace, Jovanovich.

Stein, M. (1975). *Simulating creativity*. NY: Academic Press.

Tashjian, J. (1997). *Tru confessions*. NY: Holt.

Thomas, J. (1993). *Brown honey in broomwheat tea*. Illus. by F. Cooper, NY: HarperCollins.

Thouless, R. (1953). *Straight and crooked thinking*. London: Pan Books.

Tovani, C. (2004). Do I really have to teach reading? Portland, ME: Stenhouse Publishers.

Townsend, J. S., & Pace, B. G. (2005). The many faces of Gertrude: Opening and closing possibilities in classroom talk. *Journal of Adolescent & Adult Literacy, 48*(7), 594–805.

Vacca, R. T. (2000). Taking the mystery out of content area literacy. In M. McLaughlin & M. Vogt (Eds.) Creativity *and innovation in content area teaching*. Norwood, MA: 13–27.

Verdaguer, A. (2005). Early intervention school-based family literacy programs: The key to reduced dropout rate of Hispanic ESL students.   Retrieved May 18, 2006, from http://nces.ed.gov/

Villa, R. (1995). Voice of inclusion: Everything about Bob was cool, including the cookies. In R. Villa & J. Thousand (Eds.*), Creating an inclusive school* (pp. 125–135). Alexandria, VA: Association for Supervision and Curriculum Development.

Von Oech, R. (1990). *A whack on the side of the head: How you can be more creative*. Stamford, CT: U.S. Games Systems, Inc.

Vygotsky, L. (1978). *Mind in society*. Cambridge: Harvard University Press.

Watson, J. D. (1968). *The Double Helix: A personal account of the discovery of the structure of DNA*. NY: New American Library.

Williams, T. T. (1994). *An unspoken hunger: Stories from the field*. NY: Pantheon.

Writing Strategies

6

Dear Vietnam Wall,
You are so covered in sorrow that anyone can feel it by a mere glimpse of you.
When I saw you I felt so much misery for those who died or are missing, ... that
I sat down by your side, and wept quietly for those who cannot. I could not take
a single picture of you, because nothing imaginable can capture the incredible
emotional experience one experiences at your side...

ETCETERA letter *in Ask Me If I Care, p. 147*

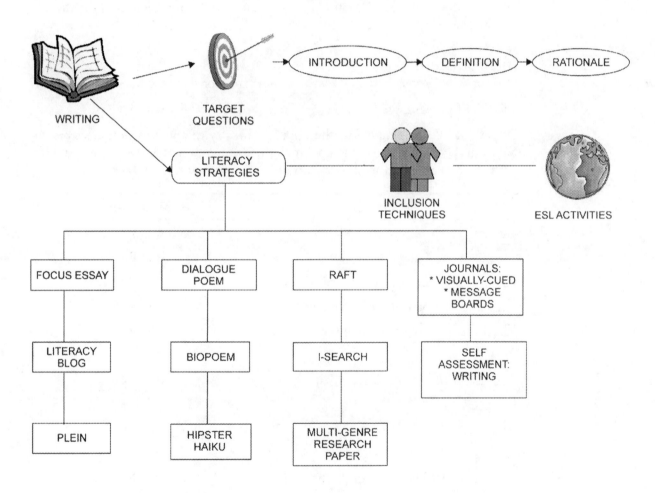

WRITING

TARGET QUESTIONS

INTRODUCTION → DEFINITION → RATIONALE

LITERACY STRATEGIES

INCLUSION TECHNIQUES

ESL ACTIVITIES

FOCUS ESSAY

DIALOGUE POEM

RAFT

JOURNALS:
* VISUALLY-CUED
* MESSAGE BOARDS

LITERACY BLOG

BIOPOEM

I-SEARCH

SELF ASSESSMENT: WRITING

PLEIN

HIPSTER HAIKU

MULTI-GENRE RESEARCH PAPER

Target Questions

Target Questions

Consider the following questions before reading this chapter. Discuss these with a colleague. Continue writing notes and develop specific questions regarding writing that you want to explore.

1. Describe writing across the curriculum.
2. What are the principles that inform quality writing?
3. What role can poetry play in the content area curriculum?
4. Why are purposeful writing exercises critical to students?
5. Compare and contrast the multi-genre and I-Search research papers.
6. How do Questions in 4-Learning Styles provide diverse avenues for learning and success?
7. Describe the benefits of using journals across the curriculum.
8. How can the tension between best writing practices and the demands of state writing standards and assessment be alleviated?
9. Discuss the role of the teacher in evaluating assigned writing.
10. How does the use of writing activities enhance content learning for the second-language learner?

Introduction

How knowledgeable are you on writing shorthand for your text messsaging, or IM?

Take the following quiz to check your electronic literacy with-it-ness.

Directions: Before matching the abbreviations with their meaning, cover the MEANING column and come up with your own, then match the following terms with their meaning. How did you do on your own? With matching?

Meaning	Abbreviations
	A. ☹
_____ 1. Laughing out loud	B. B/F
_____ 2. Let's meet in real life	C. LMIRL
_____ 3. Sad or frown smiley	D. L8R
_____ 4. Happy or laughter	E. PMFT
_____ 5. Super sad	F. B4
_____ 6. Name, address, zip	G. F2F
_____ 7. Before	H. :-<
_____ 8. Parent over shoulder	I. LOL
_____ 9. Later	J. POS
_____ 10. Thanks a lot	K. NAZ
	L. TA
	M. :-D
	N. :-@ q.

From NetLingo.com. Dictionary of Internet Terms. Answers at end of chapter.

Written expression today is found in many different formats such as email, blogs, text messages and IM (Instant Messaging) adding other dimensions to the traditional standard fictional, nonfictional or poetic writing.

Students are writing copiously today.   Besides writing emails and blogs, our own children or grandchildren are punching out text messages, or calling their friends on cell phones to see if they are ready to IM on their computers in realtime chatting with each other about homework, school events, mall shopping or whatever is of a "right now" concern. Their very existence appears to depend on their making an electronic connection.

What is the secret to this writing? Aren't these the same individuals who appear to be in a coma when asked to write in class—a veritable flatline of no ideas, no writing materials, no ideas how to start, and little compunction about any of this!

Street (2005)

It all comes down to choice. Electronic writing is about something students are vitally interested in or need to talk about in the "now." How can we transfer this immediacy into writing that emanates in the classroom?

For those of us who—look forward rather than dread—assessing students' writing projects like the I-Search or Multigenre research paper that are developed around students' choice of topic, we have experienced the care and attention to detail that student-initiated writing nurtures. And it is good!

Definition

Annie Dillard in *The Writing Life* (1989) writes about the effort it takes for a finished writing piece to emerge:

> This night I was concentrating on the chapter. The horizon of my consciousness was the contracted circle of yellow light inside my study— the lone lamp in the enormous, dark library. I leaned over the desk. I worked by hand. I doodled deliriously in the legal pad margins. I fiddled with the index cards. I reread a sentence, maybe a hundred times, and if I kept it I changed it seven or eight times, often substantially (p. 30).

Of the many definitions for writing given by *The Literacy Dictionary* (Harris & Hodges, 1995), two exemplify what Dillard describes. First, "writing is the use of a writing system or orthography by people in the conduct of their daily lives and in the transmission of their culture to other generations." Second, it is also "a process of arranging ideas to form a clear and unified impression in order to create an effective message."

Writing is physical and mental. How we approach it depends on whether we are a Dillard-type who perfected her work sentence by sentence or a Frank O'Connor, the Irish writer, who dashed through an entire piece as if riding a roller coaster, then went back over the piece as if he were riding the local train, interrupting the ride by getting off where he wished to take a closer look and adding or deleting according to his vision. Or your writing approach may be some variation of these types. The purpose no matter how we approach it, however, remains the same, writing begins with the need to say something.

Lane (1999)

Rationale

How has writing changed in the content area classroom?

Rubin (1994)

Opportunities to write in the content area class have increased in recent years. Previously, the most writing students did outside the language arts classroom was limited to filling in blanks, writing short essay responses to tests, and occasionally writing a required term paper. Today, most teachers believe that students increase their thinking, analysis and problem solving abilities through writing.

In the opening quote of this chapter an ETCETERA letter is used for discovering meaning and also exploring it. Students are asked in this assignment to write to anyone or anything, etcetera. Whether writing to a wall, to their aching back, to their hormones, to lacrosse, or to Juliet, students are talking about something relevant to them, discovering their thinking and their feelings in the process.

Writing promotes thoughtful exploration of content.

Writing is a focusing activity. While we write we are intensely engaged with words as they appear for the first time on paper. The specifics come into play as we closely attend to what we construct. By promoting writing activities across the curriculum, teachers and students are developing this art of focusing attention on the facts and ideas of the content in order to thoughtfully explore complicated issues.

Literacy Strategies to Promote Writing Across the Curriculum

The literacy strategies presented in this chapter illustrate general writing principles defined by numerous writers. Writing learning activities such as the focus essay, blog, dialogue poem, biopoem, I-Search and Multigenre paper, RAFT, Journals, Peer Editing Guide, as well as Inclusion Techniques, and ESL Strategies incorporate the following writing principles:

Atwell (1987)

Routman (1991)

Reif (1992)

Fox (1993)

1. Students learn to write by writing.
2. Writing activities ought to be integrated with curricula.
3. Teachers need to write with their students.
4. Students need to have opportunities to share their writing.
5. Writers need feedback.
6. Students learn to write by reading excellent and varied writing.
7. Repeated successful encounters with writing help unmotivated learners.
8. Imagination guides and grows out of what we see, experience and render.

We have incorporated these into our Instructional Summaries as well as our guiding principles described in the Preface.

TABLE 1

INSTRUCTIONAL SUMMARY OF A FOCUS ESSAY

Literacy Strategy	Focus Essay
Primary Focus	❏ Writing
Learning Principles	❏ Active involvement ❏ Intrinsic motivation
When to Use	❏ Before a writing lesson
Goals: National or State Literacy Standards	❏ Subject focused ❏ Voice appropriate for topic, purpose and audience ❏ Word choice is natural
Materials	❏ Notebook, pen or laptop
Time	❏ Fifteen minutes

One of the more illustrative suggestions we found that maximizes students' "communication in present time" is inviting them to present a focus essay they wrote on their own concerning something they were motivated to write. Time is set aside at the opening of writing class for students to present their piece. A writing community grows as topics like mall profiling, the negativity of political election-time ads, obesity, and weekend curfews find their way into rich writing that has immediacy, passion, and detail. Generally, a question and answer period follows for students to pursue the topic offering their own insights or reactions. Or the writer simply presents it as a way of making her thoughts public. As a member of this community, the teacher periodically reads one of his focus essays as well. Teacher as author is an important part of this activity. Many of us like Yorkshire (2006) have had students come back to visit after some absence and talk about our writing and its influence, she writes "And it hits home to me just how powerful it is—to be a teacher as well as an author."

TEACHER TALK ─────────────────────────────

Your book has been an influence and has impacted the way I teach. What's even better is that the way I teach is influencing a lot of students—and that is influencing my district to get me talking to other teachers about the way I teach. So, there is a lot of influence there!

Teacher Blogs

Teachers are the new versatile blogerati—people sophisticated in operating blogs (Safire, 2006). These Web-based tools arranged like a writing journal provide students with an opportunity for an extended conversation with the teacher about classroom issues. They also give parents and guardians information such as teacher bios, news about classroom happenings, announcements, literacy activities they can do with their children and RSS feeds (Rich Simple Syndication, other meanings as well).

Principle 3: Teachers need to write with their students

Watson & Lacina (2004)

Examples of RSS Feeds such as *Subscribe to Book Recommendations* and *Subscribe to Structural Analysis* provide students and parents with a wealth of literacy resources as well as other academic information. Parents, in turn, scour the blogs for news about the school day or to post their comments. Teachers also can contribute to more specific blogs such as "For Writing Essays," a blog with multiple teacher entries at http://teach-essay.blogspot.com. The following Figure 6.1 is a typical teacher blog written for her high school students.

In addition to teachers finding a rich outlet for communication in the use of blogs, students are becoming writers who get attention not only from their teacher but also from other students who seek out, for example, their critiques of books they've read and blogged.

All kinds of writing can be done in a blog. Wells (2006) found students assessed using the 6-trait rubric on their blog made fewer mistakes and took pride in the ownership of their writing. High-risk to high performance students find a learner-friendly medium in their blogs. No matter the literacy level of students in your class, we urge you to foster student writing in this medium.

Observation: A Critical Key

A key to developing voice is a developed sense of observation. Students need to read to see how writers incorporate their observations in their fiction, nonfiction or poetry. Once they've read about the "HOW," they need to practice.

Fletcher (1996) writes that "writers are like other people, except for at least one important difference. Other people have daily thoughts and feelings, notice this sky or that smell, but they don't do much about it. All these thoughts, feelings, sensations, and opinions pass through them like the air they breathe. Not writers. Writers react. And writers need a place to record these reactions."

A good start to awakening these powers of observation is a technique called Plein Air writing that has its roots in "en plein-aire painting" (on location, in open air). Like the plein artists who put their observations on canvas, the plein air writers record their observations in a personal note book.

TABLE 2

INSTRUCTIONAL SUMMARY OF PLEIN AIR WRITING

Literacy Strategy	Dialogue Poem
Primary Focus	Writing
Learning Principle	❏ Active Involvement ❏ Experience fuels imagination
When to Use	❏ Before, During or After reading
Goals: National or State Literacy Standards	❏ Ideas and content clear, and focused ❏ Voice appropriate for topic, purpose and audience ❏ Word choice is precise and natural
Materials	❏ Notebook, pen or laptop
Time	❏ Class period

FIGURE 6.1. A HIGH SCHOOL TEACHER'S LITERACY BLOG

Canby High School Homepage Blog

Undivided Attention By Taylor Mali

A grand piano wrapped in quilted pads by movers, birthday gift to the insane - tied up with canvas straps - like classical music's is gently nudged without its legs out an eighth-floor window on 62nd street.

It dangles in April air from the neck of the movers' crane, Chopin-shiny black lacquer squares and dirty white crisscross patterns hanging like the second-to-last note of a concerto played on the edge of the seat, the edge of tears, the edge of eight stories up going over, and I'm trying to teach math in the building across the street.

Who can teach when there are such lessons to be learned? All the greatest common factors are delivered by long-necked cranes and flatbed trucks or come through everything, even air.

Like snow...

Profile
I'm very pleased to be part of the Canby High School staff as a reading specialist, and I look forward to working with students to encourage and nurture their reading skills and interests.

Please visit my homepage often—I'll post helpful strategies that can boost readers' comprehension and enable them to retain more of that they read.

Joan

Joan Flora's Calendar

Joan Flora's Calendar

Announcements

❏ **November 30, 2006 13:52** Reading Skills Flora Journal #5——-Due Friday, 12/1/06 1. This list in your journal 2. Spelling Sort #4—-with rules pasted into your journal 3. Words of the day: Clique, Ante Bellum, Carte Bla ... Read More »

❏ **November 16, 2006 13:38** I gave students their fifth progress report of the term this week, and I highlighted any missing assignments. They can earn 5 pts. extra credit by showing parents / guardians the reports, having parents ... Read More »

❏ **November 07, 2006 08:57** Journal #4 is Due Thursday, Nov. 9th 1. Daily Agenda and fact of the Day—10/31-11/9/06 2. Word of the day: Risque, deja vu, carpe diem, passe 3. Free Write—1/2 writing on any topic of you ... Read More »

❏ **November 06, 2006 18:10** EOU's fabulous Dr. Ruth Davenport visited our classroom last Wednesday. She will return later in November to work with me and our students on miscue analysis. I'm sending this permission letter ... Read More »

Figure 6.1. A High School Teacher's Literacy Blog (cont.)

School Calendar

RSS Feeds

❏ Subscribe to Reading

❏ Subscribe to Scope and Sequences

❏ Subscribe to Book Recommendations

❏ Subscribe to Literacy Team News

❏ Subscribe to English Skills 1

❏ Subscribe to English Skills 2

❏ Subscribe to
Structural Analysis Word Study

Permission floraj@canbyk12.or.us

If we want to spark an avid use of detail, we need to prepare students who can see clearly and translate what they see into words. Through plein air writing we nurture this education of our powers of observation. As one writer wrote "This is what it is to be a writer; to be the carrier of details that make up history, to care about the orange booths in the coffee shop in Owatonna (Goldberg, 1986, p. 44)."

Ideally, teachers and students armed with their notebooks and pens or laptops should prowl the outdoors to find the spot that has a story to tell them, a place that stops them in their tracks and beckons them to provide the words sketching the image just as the painter does with canvas, brush and paint. For those who are locked into class schedules that limit or don't permit time spent outdoors—colorful artwork, and photographs can also kindle hypnotic moments that continue to haunt the writer long after viewing them. As Goldberg writes "Writers live twice... The one (life) that lives everything a second time. That sits down and sees their life again and goes over it. Looks at texture and detail" (p. 48).

Procedure.

1. As a writer you need to observe closely, seeing what's going on around you or in a picture. Chose words that create the same impression that an artist would. All your senses need to be working like the most sensitive antennae; what do you see? smell? hear? feel? taste? Describe your observation in detail. Note the effect of the wind, sun, rain on the world around you.

2. Work quickly. If working outside, there is no opportunity to revisit. You capture this moment in time. With an art piece or picture as the focus, you can capture additional impressions.

Case (2006); LaLumia (2006)

3. This is a challenging style of writing and skill grows with practice. The right word, the right emphasis captures the setting ideally. For example when looking at the sky note what it reminds you of? What it makes you think about, the mood it creates, associations

4. Writing done in this style is usually short because the scene needs to be captured in moments.

The following plein aire writing sketch is based on a picture as well as the experience of having been in this Mexican village, Ajijic.

Fifteen-foot tangerine walls that reach out to skies so blue—they stun my mist-filled Oregon eyes—surround the blazing orange, and alternating melon-painted stucco home. Purple bougainvilla spill over the walls modeling for the aspiring artist sitting on the corner stoop, capturing the scene in water-color.

Raw fish and camerones, chorizo and tortillas sizzling on makeshift grills, ripening cantaloupes, stunted bananas scent the air in the Wednesday tianguis around the corner. Blind straw-hatted companeros greet each of the regulars by name, begging for pesos. Offerings drop into their outstretched hands. In her recognizable red and blue native dress, Huichol artisan, Balbi, and her bubbly two-year-old, Yamina, invite me to view their beaded bracelets sparkling with golds, greens, and reds woven into intricate patterns that I can't resist. We haggle,

"¿Cuánto sale?"
"¡Diez pesos!"
"¡No, seis!"
"¿No, ocho?"
"OK!"

Life flows over the cobble-stoned streets. We wrap ourselves in the warmth of people, the laughter of the running children, the real Mexico so different from the northern-walled border intent on stopping hope.

Poetry in the Content Areas

There is nothing like poetry to foster a love of words, to cultivate the art of selecting the exact phrase the "writer wants to use. Poetry flows from mundane topics to the abstract. One of our mundane favorites is the poem "Oatmeal" by Galway Kinnell (1990). Examine the language in the excerpt:

... "Nevertheless, yesterday morning, I ate my oatmeal—porridge, as he called it—with John Keats. Keats said I was absolutely right to invite him; due to its glutinous texture, gluey lumpishness, hint of slime and unusal willingness to disintegrate, oatmeal must never be eaten alone. He said that in his opinion, however, it is perfectly OK to eat it with an imaginary companion" (p. 37).

In this section, we present a variety of poetic strategies that can be used in the content area:

a) the **Dialogue Poem** enables students to work collaboratively and view topics from different viewpoints.

b) in the **Biopoem**, students synthesize characteristics of a character, thing, place, event or concept.

c) the **Hipster Haiku** shouts to the "the savvy young adult to observe the exotic herds of latte-slurping, vintage-clothing-wearing, indie-rock downloading hipsters" or anything else writing these observations up in haiku form (Adcock, 2006).

Dialogue Poem

TABLE 3

INSTRUCTIONAL SUMMARY OF A DIALOGUE POEM

Literacy Strategy	Dialogue Poem
Primary Focus	Writing
Learning Principle	❏ Active Involvement ❏ Learning to write by writing
When to Use	During lesson
Goals: National or State Literacy Standards	❏ Identify dialogue ❏ Identify author's purpose; recognize how structure and word choice contribute.
Materials	Dialogue Poem models
Time	30 Minutes

One of the most popular writing activities that teachers report that works without fail is the Dialogue Poem. In this poem, students illustrate in two voices a situation viewed from two different perspectives. It teaches students to examine an issue from multiple viewpoints and to use their own creativity through writing to explore their personal thinking.

In humanities classes, we have seen students take on a socially conscious role in a historical situation and develop evocative voices in the process. In one class we visited, students had been exposed to poetry in two voices and particularly the poem, "Two Women," written by a working-class Chilean woman in 1973 shortly after the overthrow of Chile's president, Salvador Allende. After this experience, a student wrote a moving poem using the same style. See Figure 6.2.

TEACHER TALK

Through the use of the dialog poem I intended for my students to explore at a much deeper level what life might have been like for those who were at the top of the class pyramid and those who were at the bottom. In so doing, my students could explore why there is so much suffering and economic injustice in Latin America. Truly, it is my contention that in order to understand Latin America; students must understand the historical roots of colonialism and how that rigid class system has continued to effect the people who live there today....

Creating a sense of empathy during this lesson was something that I considered to be essential to the whole process of teaching this literacy strategy.

FIGURE 6.2.   POEM IN TWO VOICES

Two Mothers—Two Voices

I am a mother.
I am a mother.

I am 33.
I am 16.

I have a husband.
I had a boyfriend.

We share our child.
We shared our bodies.

Our son was born healthy.
My son was born sick.

My husband stands beside me.
My boyfriend walked away from me.

The doctor says I am healthy.
I never went to the doctor.

My labor was easy.
My labor was horrible.

When we go home, there's a
beautiful nursery waiting.
If he goes home, there's nothing
waiting.

As I nurse, his grandmother and
great-grandmother cry.
As I nurse, his grandmother cries.

My mother shares her joys of motherhood
with me.
My mother shares her anger with me.

Finally, we go home, mother, father and
child.
Finally, we go, mother and child.

We stand together.
I stand alone.

My husband brings flowers and toys.
My boyfriend brought nothing.

My mother visits every day.
My mother disowned me.

My baby is first in my life.
My baby means more than my life.

He goes on to prep schools.
He goes on to junior college.

He's our future.
He's my link to the future.

I love my son.
I love my son.

I am a mother.
I am a mother.

FIGURE 6.3.   POEM IN TWO VOICES - ROMEO AND JULIET

Juliet: She is in love with Romeo but her parents want her to marry someone else. They hate Romeo's family	**Lindsay:** She is in love with Chad but her parents don't approve.

My parents will never accept my love.	My parents think my boyfriend is a loser.
My family and his are enemies.	My family doesn't even know his family.
My parents think they can tell me who to marry.	My parents think they can tell me what to do.
I feel trapped.	I feel angry.
I will do anything to be with him.	I'm going to with him no matter what anyone says.
He will do anything to be with me.	He feels the same way.
We will run away so that we can be together.	We will see each other even if my parents give me grief.
I'm willing to let my parents think that I am dead to be with him.	I'm willing to live with my parents being mad me. They will get over it.
Oh No! He thinks I am dead and he has poisoned himself?	Oh Yes! My parents are getting to know him and they like him!
I've stabbed myself. I am dying.	If I behave myself and show them that we are good together, they will accept him.
We will be together in heaven.	We can finally be together.

By Laura Cummings, 2006

These exercises promote students' learning to write by providing them with a reason for writing. Most students seem to have a perspective on issues. Mem Fox (1993) tells a story of examining her own feeling about writing. She had an interest in why writers write, and she caught herself answering the question in a comment she made while talking about her own writing: "I like doing this (writing) because it matters. I heard myself say 'it matters,' and my mind leapt to its feet in a single bound. So that's why I wrote: because it matters" (p. 2). Such writers tell us that classroom writing activities need to be meaningful and purposeful to students.

Biopoem

TABLE 4

INSTRUCTIONAL SUMMARY OF THE BIOPOEM

Literacy Strategy	Biopoem
Primary Focus	Writing
Learning Principles	❑ Thought demanding activity ❑ Integrate writing with curriculum
When to Use	During unit
Goals: National or State Literacy Standards	❑ Write for varied purposes in a variety of modes and forms. ❑ Make connections among ideas
Materials	Biopoem Outline
Time	20 minutes

Many writing activities can be initiated quickly in the content area because of their formula design. In the process of following the structure, students' experience with their content is enriched and extended. These poems engage students in synthesizing what they know about a character, thing, place, event, or concept they have studied. They need to go beyond the facts to weave their understandings. The following model includes:

Line 1.   First name
Line 2.   Four traits that describe character
Line 3.   Relative of ("brother," "sister," etc.)
Line 4.   Lover of (list three things or people)
Line 5.   Who feels (three items)
Line 6.   Who needs (three items)
Line 7.   Who fears (three items)
Line 8.   Who gives (three items)
Line 9.   Who would like to see (three items)
Line 10. Resident of
Line 11. Last name

Biopoem : A Lesson Plan

What does a biopoem look like in the context of a lesson? The following lesson illustrates how to incorporate this literacy strategy. In addition, we have added a scoring guide to demonstrate how the writing activity designed in this lesson can be evaluated. We will talk about the usefulness of scoring guides in writing later in the chapter.

FIGURE 6.4.   BIOPOEM LESSON PLAN

Lesson Plan: Women's Rights Movement

Grade: 8

Topic: Contributions of Susan B. Anthony

Purpose: To analyze information about the contribution of Susan B. Anthony to the Women's Rights Movement through a cooperative learning jigsaw.

State Content/Literacy Standards: 1) To communicate knowledge of the topic, including relevant examples, facts, anecdotes and details, 2) To select functional, precise and descriptive words appropriate for audience and purpose.

Student Objectives:
1. Students will be able to analyze the contribution of Susan B. Anthony to the Women's Rights Movement.
2. Students will be able to synthesize this information as a group through the creation of a biopoem.
3. Students will be able to evaluate the biopoem through guided discussion.

Introduction:
1. Show students a brief segment from the PBS video series on the Women's Rights Movement in the U.S. Brainstorm students' understanding of Susan B. Anthony's activities. (10 minutes)
2. Divide students into 4 groups. Give each group one of the following roles: Susan B. Anthony as a suffragist, an abolitionist, a women's rights campaigner, and labor activist. Distribute markers and poster paper for group biopoems. (3 minutes)

Learning Activity:
Monitor reading and demonstrate design of biopoem. Assign each group a biopoem on their particular Susan B. Anthony role. (20 minutes)
Reporters present their biopoems. (10 minutes)
Class evaluates biopoems as they are presented using scoring guide rubric.

Closure:
Students write a one-sentence summary of what they have learned about Susan B. Anthony and their reaction to how well the biopoem allowed them to express their ideas on an exit slip. (3 minutes)

Evaluation:
Students' biopoems exhibit characteristics illustrated in the following Scoring Guide. See Figure 6.5 below for model.

Example: Social Studies
Susan B.
Independent, persistent, pioneer activist.
Relative of Daniel and Lucy.
Lover of equal rights, education, freedom
Who feels passionate about women's rights.
Who needs to promote women's right to vote.
She fears – nothing.
Who gives her whole life to her cause.
Who would like to see women held with the same regard as men.
Resident of Rochester, NY
Anthony

FIGURE **6.5.**   BIOPOEM SCORING GUIDE: SUSAN B. ANTHONY

6
The poem is accurate.
Strong specific words are used with fresh and original expressions.
A clear and vivid picture of the character is created.
Poem format is complete with all lines filled in with the required information.

5
The poem is factual.
Strong words are used.
A clear picture of the character is created.
Poem is complete with all lines filled in with the required information.

4
The poem is correct.
Words work, but do not energize the poem.
A picture of the character is created.
Poem is complete with all lines filled in with the information.

3
The poem is accurate.
Words are quite ordinary and tend to lose the reader's interest.
A picture is created.
Poem is mostly complete with lines filled in with information.

2
The poem is mostly correct.
Words are monotonous.
Picture of the character is fuzzy.
Poem is incomplete with all lines filled in.

1
The poem is inaccurate.
Words are misused and vague.
Reader is left wondering who or what the poem was about.
Poem is incomplete with blank lines.

Our work with teachers is always an adventure. Typically, they employ their creative and unique styles and adapt these strategies in marvelous and useful ways. The following is an example of science teachers adapting this writing strategy to their unit on the Planets. In this activity, students in small groups were assigned different planets to research and to create an Astro poem to synthesize their findings.

ASTRO POEM

Line 1:	Planet Name	**Pluto**
Line 2:	Nickname	Planet X—God of the Underworld
Line 3:	Neighbor to...	Past Neptune, another 873 million miles, I'm the farthest one out.
Line 4:	Who looks like... (list three traits)	I am a small, moon-like, collection of methane and silicate.
Line 5:	Who feels like... (three items)	It is lonely out here; I feel inadequate, icy cold, and quite unloved.
Line 6:	Parent of... (moons?)	Charon, my moon, is half my size but she won't admit it.
Line 7:	Whose day is...	There is time for 51 straight baseball games in one Pluto day (6.38 earth days).
Line 8:	Whose year is...	Get cozy, it takes 247.7 earth years for me to go around the sun.
Line 9:	From here the sun looks like...	Leave the sunscreen at home; the sun blends in with the other stars.
Line 10:	Over the years, I have seen...	I've seen other sides of Neptune, check my scrapbook if you want.
Line 11:	Humans would exploit me for...	Earthlings would use as a base-port for further galactic explorations.
Line 12:	Whose future is...	I'm just waiting for the day when enough solar radiation melts Halley so she'll quit swinging by here all the time!

created by—Julie M., Tadd R., Michael M., Rob M., 1999

Material adapted from W.K. Hartmann. *The Cosmic Voyage.* Wadsworth Publishing, 2nd ed.

The second example is an adaptation of the biopoem format guiding students' reading about humans' part of the earth's ecosystem and how they deliberately or inadvertently alter the equilibrium in ecosystems, e.g., logging. Students are divided into groups: environmentalists, loggers, politicians, consumers and endangered species. After reading their respective articles, they complete the biopoem from the viewpoint of their assigned role.

FIGURE 6.6.   ENVIRONMENTAL SCIENCE: LOGGING

Line 1 My position in logging is…	Logger
Line 2 The main idea of my article is.	Work as a logger is unpredictable.
Line 3–6 Each other role of this issue affects me by…	**Environmentalists** - legal challenges to timber industry, thereby stopping my work
	Politicians - NW Senators seek resolution of old-growth logging and for road decommissioning on federal lands, again halting my work until resolved.
	Consumers - Seek lowest cost of lumber and oppose new and onerous taxes on foreign wood; potentially lowering cost of US lumber and my wages.
	Endangered species - Spotted Owl and the Pacific fisher halt logging its habitats and prevent our jobs.
Line 7 My main fear in logging is…	No resolution to loggers like me. Would rather have no logging available than this eternal waiting around to see if I have a job, the frequent lay-offs and call-backs.
Line 8 My side is responsible for the current condition of logging by…	Going along with the industry's decisions: e.g., "grade setting", targeting high quality wood for cutting, but writing it off as poorer quality thus avoiding govenment stumpage fees—the fee paid for removing logs.
Line 9 I resolve this issue by…	I stay busy working on my own five acres, renovating our home, playing hockey and ski patrolling when I'm not on the job.
Line 10 My own personal viewpoint of logging is…	I love it. Being outside and using my skills to ensure the safety of myself and others give me a lot of satisfaction.
Line 11 A local example of this issue is…	NW logging near standstill. Mount Hood National Forest east of Portland, officials have even stopped issuing permits to local residents who want to cut firewood.

By David Burmester, 2003

TEACHER TALK

Last year, I had a group of tough 5th grade boys, who audibly groaned when I mentioned poetry. I convinced them that it was easier than regular writing (punctuation rules can be creative; it's shorter and more to the point). I brought in lots of examples (humor, teens, etc.). They especially liked writing "Poems for Two Voices," and the books, *Joyful Noise* and *I am Phoenix* by Paul Fleischman because they could work together on their poems. The unit culminated with a "Poet's Corner." The students built a stage and invited their parents to sip mochas and lattes while they performed. The principal couldn't believe that the same boys who regularly visited him were the same ones performing and serving!

S. Johnson, 2006

TABLE 5

INSTRUCTIONAL SUMMARY OF HIPSTER HAIKU

Literacy Strategy	Hipster Haiku
Primary Focus	Writing
Learning Principles	❏ Active involvement ❏ Successful writing experiences motivate more writing
When to Use	❏ Before, during or after reading
Goals: National or State Literacy Standards	❏ Voice appropriate for topic, purpose and audiene ❏ Word choice is precise and natural
Materials	❏ Notebook, pen or laptop
Time	❏ Class period

Language captures our life. Every content area has its unique vocabulary. Writing poetry such as hipster haiku helps students capture our times and shows us how we see ourselves and the world today. It is closely allied with contemporary lyrics young adults memorize effortlessly and is an easy way to invite students into the writing process.

Your Turn

Name _____ Date _____ Subject Area _____

Directions: Write your own biopoem. Use content that you are teaching or studying to create your poem.

Line 1. First Name

Line 2. Four traits that describe character _____.

Line 3. Relative (brother, sister, etc...) of _____.

Line 4. Lover of _____. (list three things or people)

Line 5. Who feels _____. (three items)

Line 6. Who needs _____. (three items)

Line 7. Who fears _____. (three items)

Line 8. Who gives _____. (three items)

Line 9. Who would like to see _____. (three items)

Line 10. Resident of _____.

Line 11. Last name

Annie Dilliard (1998) writes

"Who will teach me to write?...

The page, the page, that eternal blankness, the blankness of eternity which you cover slowly, affirming time's scrawl as a right and your daring as a necessity; the page, which you cover woodenly, ruining it, but assuming your freedom and power to act, acknowledging that you ruin everything you touch but touching it nevertheless..." p. 59.

Figure 6.7.

Example 1:   Craigslist, ultimate
Buying, selling receptacle
Recycling at large.

Example 2:   Can you meet me at
The WIFl cafe on Holt
To munch on manga?

With a twist, students can seek out topics in their content areas to write a haiku: politics, global warming, literature, weaving and the quadratic formula—the topics are endless. Yet the form remains simple enough.

Example 3:   Science /Social Studies
Melting ice floes and
Drowning polar bears signal
Warming on the way.

Procedure.

1. Have students compare classical haikus with hipster haikus.
    A classical haiku usually refers to the season it describes, or it may refer to something in the natural world. On the other hand, hipster haiku refers to something contemporary: vintage Air Jordans, anime, gamers, footless leg warmers.
2. Review the Haiku form:
    5 syllables
    7 syllables
    5 syllables
3. Demonstrate how classical haiku usually contains one phrase that shows a shift in thought. Hipster Haiku is informal and non-conforming, often pursuing one thought to its conclusion.
4. If students are into the hipster vocabulary, a teacher might explore alternate forms of hipster sonnets, sestinas, limericks and the villanelle (Adcock, 2006).
5. For students who really become addicts to writing haiku see the following site Writing Ideas for Poets. A Haiku Every Day at the website
    http://www.writingfix.com/forpoets/haiku.htm

I-Search

TABLE 6

INSTRUCTIONAL SUMMARY OF THE I-SEARCH

Literacy Strategy	I-Search
Primary Focus	Writing
Learning Principles	❏ Organize information ❏ Integrate writing with curriculum
When to Use	During unit
Goals: National or State Literacy Standards	❏ Use research to express ideas appropriate to audience and purpose ❏ Structure information
Materials	I-Search Outline
Time	Unit Timeline

All process skills like reading, writing, speaking and listening should grow out of the content students are studying. Students need to know that these activities develop supportive communication skills that enable them to learn more efficiently. The I-Search is an ideal writing activity that demonstrates writing integrated with content. The purpose of the I-Search is to discover information about a topic, to inform readers about the information discovered, and how the writer discovered that information.

This strategy appears to take the onerousness out of report writing. In this era of fostering student independence and responsibility for their own learning, teachers often have students make choices among several related topics, but these topics typically are not defined by the students.

In contrast, the I-Search paper (Macrorie, 1988) begins with a question raised by the student. Typically, this question emerges from an interest the student has in a topic. It works best when the topic is open-ended, demonstrating the specific interest of the student. However, in a class where the students are studying a specific topic, e.g., the Civil War, they are directed to raise questions about interests they have concerning this period in history. The search that follows is a journey to find the answers to their question. Students are held accountable for the story of the search. What sources did they use? What were the twists and turns of the journey that moved them forward or stymied their search? In this technological age of electronic mail, the web, CD-ROMS, newsgroups, etc., students have the world at their fingertips. The I-Search paper ties into these resources. This process develops a sense of how information gathering works as students seek out the most valuable resources to them.

Emphasize the journey and the sources students use to complete their I-Search.

Procedure.

1. Students are introduced to a topic or theme that is on the roster for the content area class. In a language arts class, the topic may be open-ended; the student can choose whatever topic she wants to write about. Universal themes like exploring frontiers, caring for planet Earth, people who make a difference, change, cultural differences, conflict, and so forth cross all subject areas and provide students with a wide range of choices. After students have had a chance to develop some understanding of the topic or theme through discussion, viewing videos, or listening to guest speakers, they brainstorm questions that they may be interested in exploring. In providing this introduction, teachers model the many resources that students can use. For example, a student who is interested in recycling as a way of demonstrating caring for the planet may develop a question like the following: How is the recycling process changing to enhance my community?

    Teachers should give a seal of approval to students' questions before they begin their search. If a question is too limiting, the student will quickly become bored with the search; if the question is too broad, she will probably grow frustrated with the tremendous amount of material she will have to wade through.

    Help students develop a question worthy of investigation.

    Some students can handle refocusing the questions themselves. However, the initial question should be provocative enough to engage the writer for the duration of the writing process.

2. Students develop their own search plan. Brainstorming areas where students may look helps them design their plan. Books, newspapers, and magazines are starting points. CD-ROM references, interviews, experiments, videos, and the World Wide Web offer students rich resources.

    School districts that routinely use this process have developed I-Search guide packets to help students walk through it. Moreover, the media specialist should be a major consultant in this project. The teacher who has invested time in cultivating the media specialist's support will expedite the process immeasurably for her students. Students' plans will change over time. But being prepared with an initial travel plan to negotiate the task makes for a healthy start.

    Enlist the help of the school media person.

    If interviews are going to be part of the search, it is helpful for teachers to spend some time preparing students for interactions with the community. What students say, how they look, and their body language will be critical factors in obtaining the information they need. Opportunities for mock interviews in the classroom before students conduct the actual one serve the students immediately as well as foster life skills.

3. Students draft their papers. Over the years we have learned that this part of the process needs to be nurtured and celebrated. It is helpful to form student writing groups that meet on a regular basis to share their progress and drafts of their papers. In this manner, students have an opportunity to see the resources others are using to explore their topic, how they are synthesizing materials, and the , difficulties that they face. They also help each other over hurdles by providing resource suggestions and general support.

These meetings also help students move from their typical ways of doing reports. We overhear students saying to one another "How did you find that out? You need to put how you discovered that in your paper." The "how" is stressed rather than the "what." Sometimes it takes quite a bit of work for students to realize that you are interested in their journey as well as their discoveries.

Regularly schedule student editing or response groups to discuss I-Search papers in progress.

4. Students write their final paper and conclude it with a section on what they have learned as a result of the process. They use this section to talk about the successes they had in doing the search as well as the agonies. Zorfass and Copel (1995) suggest adding another section to the report, "What This Means to Me." They quote one student with learning disabilities writing: "In this project I learned a lot about myself because I did this project all by myself but sometimes I needed help. I feel that I did very good" (p. 51).

See Figure 6.8 for a sample guide that helps student writers plan an I-Search paper as well as check the quality and thoroughness of their work.

FIGURE 6.8. PLANNING I-SEARCH GUIDE

Sections	Your Notes
I. Rationale	
1. Rationale for topic research	What do I know about the subject?
2. Questions used to guide I-Search	What do I want to know about the topic?
II. Process	
1. What I know	What sources have I used?
2. Story of my search:	With whom have I talked?
sources—library, interviews,	What other strategies have I used to locate
electronic networks	information?
3. Successes and difficulties	What are my frustrations?
	What do I feel good about?
III. Research Results	
What have I learned?	What information have I found?
	What surprises emerged from the search?
IV. Opinion	
Was the search worthwhile?	Was what I learned about my topic from
	writing the I-Search worth the effort?
References.	
Use an appropriate style:	What books, magazines, people, websites
MLA, APA, etc.	and other sources did I use in my search?
	Are they in the proper style?

I-Search Example:

Industrial Arts: Woodwork

Wood Chippers

Why wood chippers? I own a little forest land that needs maintenance to clean up the fallen branches and slash. My question is : What wood chipper would be the most appropriate to suit my needs? How much would it cost? To answer these questions, I wonder:

How much wood would a wood chipper chip
If a wood chipper could chip wood?
It would chip, it would, as much as it could,
and chip as much wood as a wood chipper would
If a wood chipper could chip wood.
(Adaptation from The Tongue Twister Database, 2006)

The beginning of my quest began at Lowe's Home Improvement Store with some questions about their wood chippers.

For the last couple of months, I looked but never pursued any real information except for the prices. So, when I noticed that two identical chippers had two different prices, I needed to find out why one was cheaper than the other.

Armed with some questions and a curiosity, I hunted up and down several aisles for one of those elusive creaures most commonly called "the salesman". Where was the "Welcome to our store" host found in every Wal-Mart-like store? When I finally saw one, I swiftly made my way down one aisle, around the corner, and down another until I cornered him. Then I proceeded to pommel him with questions about the price difference.

The salesman was a young 30ish man standing six feet, two inches. I was envious. Have I hit my full growth yet? What started off with a vengeance, turned out to be quite a pleasant conversation filled with more information than I had anticipated.

He explained that the price difference was because some had already been purchased and returned. He also explained that the used machines had been checked and were as good as new, and they carried the same warranty as the new ones.

This is when I'm starting to think that I might save a couple of hundred dollers by purchasing a used one.

I'm psyched. My search is over. If I buy one today, next weekend—I could be chipping. But, this is where the salesman told me that he thought that these chippers would be too small for my intended use, and I watched my thoughts go through one of those chippers. I needed at least one with ten horsepower or more.

260   Chapter 6

On the bright side, I really appreciate the fact that this guy saved me from a big costly purchase (Lowe's Improvement, personal communication, October 2003).

I continued my search to see what the internet had to offer. 67,000 sites showed up when I googled "wood chipper" and I began to wonder how I was going to chip my way through this forest of information. I decided to stick primarily with the first 20 sites to concentrate on the information I needed.

The "DR® Chipper" caught my eye. This is the same company that advertises "DR® Mower" and other products. The web page displayed a place to register for free information including a free video of their product. When my video arrived, I learned that DR® Chipper had four different models to choose from. The cheapest and the smallest that they offered was a ten horsepower. Their largest and most powerful was an 18-horsepower model, top discharging, towable behind a truck and devouring up to 4.5-inch diameter branch. "Huh, huh, huh," as Tim Allen would say, but the price tag stopped me cold—$4000.00.

A used chipper seemed the only option left. Web sites of used chippers reminded me that I should use another readily available source searching the classifed ads in both *The Oregonian* newspaper and in the *Nickel Ads*. Each weekend, I looked for chippers—only to find this a total bust, no ads surfaced.

My breakthrough came in talking to a fellow industrial arts teacher. I happened to be showing him some pictures taken on my property north of Spokane. The pictures showed some of the piles of logs ready for the saw mill. During this conversation, he informed me that he had an eight or so horsepower chipper that he would be willing to part with, for only $300.00 (Zig Coneybear, personal communication, October, 2006).

Yes, I know it is too small, but for the price, it is worth looking at. Besides I could always sell it somebody else—of course, for a profit.

My quest continues. I have a pretty good idea that the chipper that I purchase will be an older industrial model. It needs a minimum of 25-hosepower and consumes a five-inch diameter piece of wood.

Next on my list is the Vermeer Oregon., Inc. A local Vermeer equipment dealer, Rich, is going to meet with me and show me what they have on the lot.

I now know the appropriate size of chipper to meet our needs. I've discovered the answer to my question:

How much wood would a wood chipper chip
If a wood chipper would chip wood?

The answer is in direct proportion to how much money ($$$) is spent.

References

Bandit Industries (2006). Remus, Ml. Retrieved 11/27/2006 from http://www.banditchippers.com.

DR.® Chipper (2006). Retrieved 11/27/2006 from http://www.drpower.com.

Nickel Ads (2006, Nickel Publications, Portland, OR. Retrieved 11/18/2006 from http://www.nickelads.com.

The Oregonian (2006). The Oregonian Publishing Company, Portland, OR. Retrieved 11/18/2006 from http://www.oregonian.com.

The Tongue Twister Database (2006). Retrieved 10/21/2006 from http://www.geocities.com/Athens/8136/tonguetwisters.html.

Vermeer Midwest, Inc. Aurora, IL (2006) Retrieved 11/30/2006 from http://www.usedwoodgrinders.com

James V. Fox, 2006

This question spoke to this teacher's need. In addition to serving a practical need, he used this paper as a model in assigning an I-Search paper in his course. Most students found it the most meaningful writing they had done in school so far, even going so far as to show it to their parents, not throwing the graded paper in the class circular file. As Ken Macrorie wrote in The I-Search Paper (1988): "curiosity, need, rigor in judging one's findings" are a critical goal in inquiry.

The I-Search paper establishes "a context for students, encouraging them to enjoy inquiry, not fear it" (Luther, 2006). The I-search paper helps students identify problems, raise questions, search and test findings for their veracity and draw conclusions. Dewey argues that the "origin of thinking is some perplexity, confusion, or doubt" (1910). The I-Search paper requires thought.

Finally, this paper avoids poorly written, even plagiarized versions of internet or encyclopedia content. Also, we can assure you these will be papers that you really "enjoy" reading.

Lyman (2006)

FIGURE **6.9.**   SCORING GUIDE: I-SEARCH PAPER

Level	Rationale	Search Process	Source Information: References
5	❑ in-depth questions raised ❑ I-connection ❑ purposeful/meaningful	❑ authentic network apparent ❑ sense of fascination the topic ❑ clearly stated sequence of process	❑ appropriate to the topic ❑ shows creativity in search and thoroughness in use of style
3	❑ developing questions ❑ limited connection to writer ❑ cloudy intent	❑ some networking ❑ some interest apparent ❑ search process generally developed	❑ randomly related to topic ❑ some exertion evident ❑ reference style occasionally consistent
1	❑ no question posed yet ❑ working on developing an I position ❑ purpose/intent not clear now	❑ working on networking ❑ personal interest faintly emerging ❑ search process not evident at this time	❑ infrequently related to topic ❑ limited exertion ❑ reference style unclear

Multi-Genre Paper

TABLE 7

INSTRUCTIONAL SUMMARY OF MULTI-GENRE RESEARCH PAPER	
Literacy Strategy	**Multi-Genre Research Paper**
Primary Focus	Writing
Learning Principles	❑ Active involvement ❑ Experience fuels imagination
When to Use	❑ Before, during or after reading
Goals: National or State	❑ Knowledge of language structure, conventions, media techniques, figurative language and genre applied ❑ Wide variety of technological and information resources used to gather and synthesize information ❑ Spoken, written and visual language used to accomplish purpose of writing.
Materials	❑ Computer internet access; project materials: paper, colored pens, etc.
Time	❑ Teaching-unit time span

Books like Avi's (1993) *Nothing But the Truth: A Documentary Novel*, Draper's (1994) *Tears of a Tiger*, Klise's (1999) *Regarding a Fountain: A Tale, in Letters, Of Liars and Leaks and Myers'* (1999) *Monster* tell one story in a mix of letters, memos, pictures, journal entries, newpaper articles and even through passports like Kumar's *Passport Photos* (2000). These formats have motivated teachers to incorporate this use of various genres in research papers—the multi-genre paper.

Gardner (2006)

Typical genres include:

Advice columns	Travel poster	Post card
Book jacket	Personal commentary	Grocery list
Campaign speech	Informative essays	Recipe
Map w/legend	Photos with description	Biopoem
Diary	Advertisements	Poem in two voices
Interview	CD cover	Collage
Menus	Greeting card	Play

See Gardner (2006b) for more extensive descriptive lists of genre.

What is a multi-genre research paper? Tom Romano (1995) defines it as a collection of self-contained pieces illustrating a central theme or topic. These mini-compositions are of varying length and form: poems, narratives, scripts, sketches, maps, games, videos, etc. that reveal a slice of the theme or topic unconnected to any of the other creative pieces.

Davis (1999)

In light of the ever-present state standards, teachers wonder how they can incorporate such a student-centered, creative activity. We found that teachers examine the state curriculum goals, their students' needs and their own instructional interests to determine how to teach what is required and what is desired. Rich, integrative learning does not have to be the antithesis of standards. In fact, students discover how to meet them in their own self-directed and self-assessing learning activities. Standard reading and writing proficiencies abound in multi-genre writing.

In this kind of research writing, teachers see their job as guides, helping students to conceive, draft and complete their projects, while taking into account the complicated interconnectedness of the standards, and students' own interests and needs.

Principle 1: Students learn to write by writing.

For example, for a unit she was teaching, Africa: One Continent, Many Worlds, a teacher, Melinda Lapore, wrote a multi-genre paper as a model for her students. She had visited Tanzania and wanted students to share her experience and also demonstrate how they could translate their readings and information exploration about a topic on Africa of their own chosing. Her Table of Contents included:

TANZANIAN CHARMS

Melinda Lapore, 2006

Her multi-genre power-point project included amazing pictures she had taken of her climb up Kilimanjaro, the porters and what they carried. In addition, she included pictures of her reaching the summit as well as her safari. Tucked in between she placed maps to identify Africa's place in the world; and specific maps of Tanzania. Unfortunately, we can't do justice to this project by including it in this chapter. But the following excerpts will give you a taste of the various genres.

Letter to the Reader (Excerpt)

"Tanzania Charms" is inspired by this foundation of travel dreams. Think of it as a vivid "charm bracelet"/a collage of writings created to share great joys and tales of this grand adventure. These stories began as seeds of wonder and discovery, I am thrilled to share them with anyone interestd in reliving this journey through the wide eyes of a passionate traveler.

In 2005, Chris and I, together with our friends Julia, Blake and Eleanor, embarked upon an adventure that could encompass an entire charm bracelet in itself—we traveled for six weeks throughout Tanzania, Africa...

RAFT from Kili (Excerpt)

Role: Mountain
Audience: Future Climbers
Format: Letter Topic:
An Introduction Dear Climber,

I understand you are eager to explore my terrain, Yon, already know that I am Africa's highest mountain and that my peak reaches 19,327 feet into the Tanzanian heavens. If you make it to my highest peak, Uhru Peak, you will see with your own eyes that I am an ice-capped, dormant volcano. You will join a cast of thousands who have had the honor of standing on the rooftop of Africa!...

Kilimanjaro Porter - Poem (Excerpt)

Twenty-two of you to carry our load—
Cajole us up this magnificent mountain.
You stand so proud, walk so strong
Your muscles strain under the weight of our load.
Words you share—Sounds of Africa,
"Jambo", "Asante", "Missouri sana",
"Hakuna matata rafiki..."

Journal Entry - Climbing Kili, Day (Excerpt)

We began, "Pole, Pole, Step, Pause, Step" using our poles trying to get some kind of a breathing pattern. It was just so hard to get oxygen. The mountain, boulders and the skree, all a dark grayish coler were all that we saw—for hours. Every once in a while I would look up. The sky was magnificent. All the bright beautiful starts glimmered, but the mountain ahead looked ominous. I decided it would be best to just focus, focus on the step-pause-step. Try to get some oxygen...

Narrative Introduction: Looking for Life at the Watering Hole (Excerpt)

...The sun was setting and the shadowy darkness was slowly blanketing the forest. I was determined; I wholeheartedly believed that if I sat still and focused long enough, I would spot something spectacular. I guess I was secretly hoping that if I believed deep enough and concentrated hard enough, my eyes would morph into some kind of night vision goggles that could see everything taking place. I hadn't experienced this kind of anticipation since I was a child looking out of grandmother's window up at the December sky trying to spot Santa flying by with his reindeer. Africa has a way of casting this sort of spell...

Tanzania Post Card (Excerpt)

Dear Mom,

Yes, we are so close to the elephants that we can see the baby and how these elephants watch over it! Oh how I wanted to hug him. I have to say when we came upon the lions, I almost ended up in Eleanor's lap in fear. Will write more in the next card.   Melinda

Poem in Two Voices

Two Women: Two Different Continents, Same World

Directions: Divide class in two parts. Each part is assigned one role; lines are read aloud depending on role. Lines in bold, all students read aloud.

I am an American woman	I am a Maasai woman
We live on different continents, but share the same world	**We live on different continents, but share the same world**
I live in Oregon, North America near the Pacific Ocean. More than 40 degrees north of the Equator	I live in Tanzania, Africa, near the Indian Ocean. Just south of the Equator.
Where flowers bloom bright and it doesn't rain much during the summer...	Where the grass is sinewy and brown and there is little water during the dry season...

Adjustments continue to enhance this activity. Teachers have found the more reading the students do, the better the project. In addition, a month-long project usually produces better quality work. If the students have an opportunity to study models—the easier it becomes for them to understand the nature and scope of the multi-genre project as well as replicate one.

Endnotes used after each presentation provide an explanation and include the source of the material and how the genre has been selected. They also serve to assure the instructor of the scope of the research that supported this item, often providing much more information than the product itself renders. For example, a poster is fairly limited in its presentation of information, but the endnote serves to connect the information and the student's thinking in designing it. Finally, teaching types of genre during the course of the project helps students in developing different discourse forms.

FIGURE 6.10.   SCORING GUIDE MULTI-GENRE RESEARCH PROJECT

The project is scored and assessed on a scale of 1 – lowest score, through 6 – highest score, on the following categories:

Ideas and Content
Research reflects thorough exploration of the topic or subject.   _____

Multi-Genre Application
5 Multi-genre categories are included.   _____

MLA Format
Citations and a Works Cited Page are present in the project.   _____

Command of the language
Word usage, conventions, and spelling are correct.   _____

Presentation
Writing is typed, and genres creatively completed.   _____

Punctuality
Project was turned in on _____.   _____

Total Points: /36   _____ X 5 =   /180
                                        A - 180-162
                                        B - 161-144
                                        C - 143-126
                                        D - 125-108

—Alex G., 2000
11th-12th Grade Language Arts

RAFT

TABLE 8

INSTRUCTIONAL SUMMARY OF THE RAFT

Literacy Strategy	RAFT
Primary Focus	Writing
Learning Principles	❏ Thought demanding activity ❏ Integrate writing with curriculum
When to Use	During unit
Goals: National or State Literacy Standards	❏ Communicate knowledge of the topic ❏ Make connections among ideas
Materials	RAFT Outline
Time	20 minutes

What are the essential features of RAFT?

This popular writing activity helps writers develop a sense of their role as a writer, their audience, the format of their work, and the content. In every RAFT activity these elements are included. Almost every content area teacher can find use for this writing activity. Students enjoy it because the activity enables them to be creative in the context of any subject. The RAFT is an acronym for:

Santa (1988)

R: Role. Who do you represent? You may want to personalize a whole note, a soldier, a mathematical operation. The sky is the limit on roles students can play.
A: Audience. Who might you be writing to or presenting this to? A mother, parliament, or polluters?
F: Format. What form will your written piece take? Listed below are some possibilities:
T: Topic. What are you trying to convey? What emotions? What information? Do it concisely and decisively (e.g., acting as a note, persuade a composer to include you in a movie score). Use strong verbs.

Other Formats:

Advice Column	Complaint	Dialogues and
Blog	E-mail	Conversations
Editorial	Farewell	Human Interest Story
Inquiry	Interview	Letter to the Editor
Letter	Radio Script	News Story
Memos	TV Script	Skits

Procedure.
1. Explain the meaning of the RAFT acronym. Guide students through the elements making sure that they understand that this activity requires focusing on all four parts.
2. Brainstorm topics for writing.
3. Select a topic and brainstorm possible roles, audiences, formats, and strong verbs that are appropriate for each topic.
4. Have students write on one of the generated topics.
5. After students develop an understanding of the process, have them come up with their own RAFT exercises at the beginning of a unit to determine students' background knowledge or at the end of the unit to summarize key ideas and content.

RAFT Examples:

In a unit on earthquakes, a science teacher showed students a segment from the video "The Big One." This helped set the mood for the writing activity. Then she assigned groups of students roles of those people most likely to be involved in an earthquake and asked them to assume these roles: a Media team, a "victims" group, a team from the scientific community, and an emergency response team. Each group was given an explanation sheet that told them what group they would portray and what would be expected of them. After explaining the RAFT activity, she asked the students in their groups to respond to the situation given their assigned roles. After they wrote these they made an oral presentation.

What would students learn from a RAFT activity that they may not from a lecture on earthquakes?

The "victims" group wrote:
R: Victims
A: Governor of the state
F: Petition
T: Plea for immediate help

To: Governor of Oregon
From: Earthquake victims

> We are holed up in this elementary school. We have warm clothes, good, hot food, and medicine if we need it, but no privacy. When are we going to be allowed to go home? Our children are getting out of control with nothing to do. We are worried about our homes, our dogs and cats. Now that the soldiers have secured the area, can't we go back to our homes if they are still standing?.

Your constituents:

Mr & Mrs. Joe Fault, Multnomah County
Ms. Mary Plate, Washington County
Mr. Peter Seismic, Clackamas County

Mr. Allen Shake, Yamhill County
Sasha Aftershock, Marion County

The emergency personnel team wrote a radio info spot.

R: Members of a emergency personnel team
A: Community hit by earthquake
F: Radio information spot
T: Directions for emergency services

> For all of those who have nowhere to go, please report to the nearest school. A large Red Cross sign will mark the entrance if the school is safe to enter. For all those who need medical care, ambulances, police, soldiers, and firemen are canvassing the neighborhoods looking for earthquake victims.

> Please stay put if you are in a safe area. If you have a member of the family or a neighbor who can go to the nearest shelter have them report your injuries. Emergency services like food, clothing, medicine, and disaster relief teams from the insurance companies are available at the shelters.

> Please call this number, 231-8032, your KBOO, 90.7 radio station for further information. Continue to listen to your radio for emergency relief updates.

The media group wrote a skit interviewing the victims as well as cutting back to the main desk for updates on the disaster and relief efforts. Finally, the scientific community featured a panel that would be televised on the evening news.

What did students learn from this exercise? As we examine their writing, the disaster takes on a human face. The earthquake is not just a geological phenomenon that they study, but it becomes multidimensional involving an entire community who must face this disaster. Students put themselves in the shoes of some of the groups who will be affected, examining the problems surfaced during such a catastrophe, and seeking solutions. It is a comprehensive, relevant extension of the unit study.

RAFT writing that grows out of lessons can be content specific also.

Example: A chemistry RAFT assignment

R: An electron involved in covalent bonding
A: Young chemistry students who will vote for you
F: Campaign speech
T: Describe your extraordinary role, talents and versatility in forming covalent chemical bonds. Use Chapter 14 for assistance.

Topics to include in your campaign speech:

- ❑ Bond Dissociation Energies
- ❑ Covalent Bond Definition
- ❑ Exceptions to the Octet Rule
- ❑ Molecular Orbitals
- ❑ Polar Bonds
- ❑ Single Covalent Bonds
- ❑ VSEPR Theory
- ❑ Coordinate Covalent Bonds
- ❑ Double Covalent Bonds
- ❑ Hybrid Orbitals
- ❑ Intermolecular Attractions
- ❑ Properties of Molecular Substances
- ❑ Resonance
- ❑ Triple Covalent Bonds

The teacher adapted this assignment in awarding grades depending on the number of pertinent topics that were included in the campaign speech.

Graduated Difficulty Grading Criteria
For an "A" include 14 of the assigned topics.
For a "B" include 12 of the topics.
For a "C" include 10 of the topics.
Less than 10 topics will win you no votes and no grade.

Mr. M., 1995

More RAFT suggestions:

Content Area	Role	Audience	Format	Topic
Science	Citizen	Dem., Rep., Ind.	Letter	Vote for recycling
	Chemist	Chemical company	Instructions	Warn about combinations to avoid
	Pretzel	Other pretzels	Travel guide	Journey through the digestive system
	Plant	Sun	Thank you note	Explain sun's role in plant's growth
	Newswriter	Public	News release	Explain how ozone layer was formed
	Scientist	Charles Darwin	Letter	Refute a point in evolution theory
	Trout	Self	Diary	Describe effects of acid rain on lake
Math	Square root	Whole number	Love letter	Explain the relationship
	Acute angle	Obstuse triangle	Article /ketter	Convince obtuse triangle to shape up and lose weight. Explain differences

Social Studies	Columnist	Public	News column	Demand more/less gun control: Choose one position
	Constituent	U.S. Senator	letter	Plead to abolish capital punishment
	Criminal	Judge	Plea	Explain why you should be paroled
	Supreme Court Justice Candidate	Senate confirmation committee	Resume	Explain why she /he is the best candidate for the position
	Bolsheviks	Peasants	Advertisment	Convince peasants of better situations

By Nick Fenger, 2002

Journals

TABLE 9

INSTRUCTIONAL SUMMARY FOR JOURNALS

Literacy Strategy	**Journals**
Primary Focus	Writing
Learning Principles	❏ Uses writing to learn ❏ Builds metacognitive awareness
When to Use	❏ Before, during or after unit
Goals: National or State Literacy Standards	❏ Uses writing to communicate knowledge of topic ❏ Uses writing to reflect on learning
Materials	Journal format
Time	5-10 minutes

One can't read *The Adrian Mole Diaries* (Townsend, 1986) without thinking, "How can I translate this delight with writing into a comparable classroom activity?" Adrian, the main character, is 13 3/4 years old. He mixes his adolescent worries with his perceived intellectual development in such entries as:

Joined the library. Got *Care of the Skin, Origin of Species*, and a book by a woman my mother is always going on about. It is called *Pride and Prejudice* by a woman called Jane Austin. I could tell the librarian was impressed. Perhaps she is an intellectual like me. She didn't look at my spot, so perhaps it is getting small (p.18).

Writing in journals enables students to personalize their learning. Their voice, their concerns come peeking through about their learning. By processing information and ideas through writing, students have the opportunity to connect concretely with their own thoughts, rehearse their ideas for future use, and relate to the subject under consideration. The goal is not to produce a perfect piece of writing, but rather to explore meaning about the topic for themselves.

Journals are a medium for students' voices.

In addition, there is the social component of the journal. In journals where students are asked to dialogue with others, students have the opportunity to raise questions, share opinions, follow through with a peer on ideas presented in their reading, or class lectures. These journal entries tend to be a rich combination of critical thinking and relationship building that serve to bring the class together as a community.

Student Talk

I have never been a fan of journals. Moreover, I got off to a shaky start in this class. For the first three classes, I arrived late, after the journaling swap had occurred. I had to share my journal entries not in class, but with other friends in my classes. I wrote up their reactions, but I missed the feedback process in class. "Missed" it in the temporal sense, and missed it in the sense that I found the in-class feedback I got on later entries very helpful. Both because their comments were insightful, and because sharing with classmates helped break down the isolation and intimidation I felt both because I'm not a journaler and because I hardly knew anyone in the class.

Journals take many forms. Teachers implement dialogue journals, diaries, learning logs, writer's notebooks, art sketchbooks, electronic dialogue journals, etc., with the same purpose in mind—to cultivate a student's individual interaction with the material under study. The journal lies somewhere between the diary and the notebook. It is personal, yet academically oriented.

Procedure.

1. We have found that classrooms that celebrate journals are more successful at promoting their use. In these classes, teachers provide students with their own journals, usually a bound collection of looseleaf sheets and a durable cover. Students are encouraged to decorate the cover, thereby fostering ownership and a sense of pride in their own work. Students can hand their entries in individually. These can be quickly read by the teacher and returned to the student. There is nothing like boxes of journal notebooks to discourage even the most enthusiastic teacher.

Encourage students to personalize their journals.

2. Once students have designed their personal journal, they then move on to the writing. After reading class material, observing a class demonstration or art slide, or listening to a lecture, students are encouraged to respond in their journals. Some teachers encourage students by beginning with probes such as "Today I learned. ..."; "I would like to know more about...

3. Students write in their journals a few times a week. Consistency seems to be the measure of success. If students know that journal writing is a part of the curriculum, they are more inclined to follow through. Most teachers give points for producing the writing. They do not grade journal writing. When teachers talk about the value of journals to show what students are learning and what students are feeling, they frequently conclude that this genre is not the place for red ink and critical comments.

Build connections from past experiences to new ideas through first thoughts.

Other quick journal entries that content area teachers can use are "First Thoughts" and "Stop-n-Write" (Zemelmann, 1993). First Thoughts is an exercise that can be used at the beginning of a unit. Before students begin the topic under consideration, they spend one or two moments doing a free- write making predictions about the subject. They may also write about personal connections or understandings they recall about the upcoming topic.

Stop-n-Write exercises are interjected within lessons. At opportune times during a discussion or lecture, the teacher instructs students to write a few things down related to the topic at hand. In addition, students can use this method while they are doing independent reading to check their understandings.

TEACHER TALK

I wasn't pleased with my students' journal entries. They were selecting haphazardly quotes from their reading and writing lackadaisical responses. On the other hand, I was having success in having students' talk about their own thinking while reading. So rather than have students select quotes from their reading to respond to in their journals, they would write about their thinking while reading. I called it "Avoiding 'Homering'."

Homering" something is a reference to "The Simpsons" when Homer is saying and doing things while truly thinking about one thing—eating ham. I show the scene in class at the beginning of the term, and because students think it's funny, they remember it and started using the phrase, "Homering"— as in "I don't 'Homer' much anymore in my reading and writing. This clears up my thinking." Flora, 2006

Journals can be used in many ways. Some that teachers find most valuable include:

Santa (1988); Alverman & Phelps (1994)

- ❏ to write about what was just learned in a particular class.
- ❏ to problem-solve.
- ❏ to predict.
- ❏ to make preliminary sketches.
- ❏ to answer questions posed by the teacher.

- ❏ to respond to a piece of reading.
- ❏ to let off steam.
- ❏ to brainstorm ideas.
- ❏ to practice writing.

Visually-Cued Journals

A variation on journal writing has been adapted by Megan Owens (personal communication, August 5, 2000) who has used visually-cued journals with her middle school language arts students. Adapting Knight's (1990) coded journal entries, she designed students' journals using three column entries. The first column consists of text passages that students want to write about. The middle column includes responses students make to visual cues that are matched with the reading skills required by the state assessment. Students are asked to demonstrate their recall of their reading, and to extend their understanding by showing its relationship to other texts, experiences, issues or events that they have experienced. In addition, students are asked to identify text structures like cause and effect and analyze and evaluate an author's ideas and craft. In the last column, students pass their journal entry to a partner who provides them with feedback. As a result of using these entries, her students understand the expectations of their classroom tasks as well as their state assessment.

Principle 6:
Students learn to write by reading excellent writing.

Principle 4:
Students need opportunities to share their writing.

TEACHER TALK

Although I'm not thrilled about the amount of testing our students face in this state, I am excited about the way they approach their reading. As a result of the practice they get in working on assessment tasks, they are not just looking for the right answer anymore. Their ability to raise questions, to make connections to real life and to evaluate a writer's message as well as their style in creating their ideas has improved. Consequently, although this practice was directed at helping students with the state assessment, it has enhanced their ability to discuss their reading in the classroom and, I hope, it has modeled what readers do whether for class, tests, or for leisure.

FIGURE 6.11. VISUALLY-CUED JOURNALS

Recall	Connections	Prediction	Evaluation	Questioning
R	◯—◯	↻	△丁△	?
Facts Main Idea Plot Summary	Relationship to other texts Experiences Issues Events	Consequence Hypothesis Cause Effect	Value Evaluation Judgment Rating	Questions about: reading plot character setting, or style

Example: Language Arts

TEXT—2 passages with page #s	R, ◯—◯ , ↻ , △丁△ , ? **Your thoughts about text — Use cues.**	**A partner's response to your writing.**
p. 65 "He was standing near the wall, bowed down, his shoulders sagging as though beneath a heavy burden. I went up to him, took his hand and kissed it. A tear fell upon it. Whose was that tear? Mine? His? I said nothing. Nor did he. We had never understood one another so clearly.	This passage is very similar to the ending of "The return of the Jedi" where Luke Skywalker lifts off his father's mask and discovers a beaten man. In both cases, the strong son feels very sad about the condition of the father he once resented. Unlike Elie, however, Luke talks to his father. The author uses vivid descriptions of characters, a moving point of view and little dialog to create a loving yet sad mood. I predict Elie's father will not pass the next selection because of his condition. Why do the Nazis beat Elie's father so much?	I like how you compared *Night* with "Stars Wars." I agree with your prediction because it seems true from Elie's dad's weakened state. Because he is weak and they have no use for him anymore.
p. 77 "I've got more faith in Hitler than anyone else. He's the only one who's kept his promises, all his promises, to the Jewish people." Wiesel, E. *Night*	This passage can relate to the part in "Jingle all the Way" where the boy finds more faith in his friend's father with bad intentions than his own father simply because he never keeps his promises. Both situations have a person losing trust in the good guy and finding trust in the bad guy because the bad guy is more reliable. This passage uses indifferent characters and bold dialog to create a shocking effect. I predict the person will die.	I again like your comparison with the book and a movie. They have faith in their oppressors because they are becoming delirious from their ill treatment.

TABLE 10

INSTRUCTIONAL SUMMARY OF MESSAGE BOARDS

Literacy Strategy	Message Boards
Primary Focus	Writing
Learning Principles	❏ Active involvement ❏ Varied writing promotes better writing
When to Use	❏ Before, during or after reading
Goals: National or State Literacy Standards	❏ Use technological and informational resources to gather and synthesize information and to create and communicate knowledge. ❏ Apply knowledge of language structure, language conventions, figurative language, and genre to critique and discuss print.
Materials	❏ Reading material: novels, nonfiction, textbook ❏ Computer, internet access
Time	❏ Study time at home or school

Message Board Dialogue

Message boards enable students to post topics and reply to others' topics. Discussion builds up without all users having to be online at the same time. Also, students have the time to think about what their peers are writing and respond thoughtfully.

Students are comfortable with text messaging and IM. The message board is an extension of this form of communication. As a result, frequently, they write more on the message board than they do in their reader response journals. Many of them return to the same message board to continue their writing—an option seldom available in a response journal.

In addition, the teacher has a chance to step in and clear up misunderstandings like some in the following dialogue where students confused the period of time and historical events that provide the context of the story. This can be done on the message board or become part of a mini-lesson the following day in class. Another positive result is that students not only interact with students in their own class but also can message to students in other periods who are reading the same text, thereby receiving the opinions and thoughts of a hundred peers rather than one or more in a response journal or in a literature circle.

Procedure.

1. The teacher sets up a link to the Message Board on their own homepage, in this case, a *To Kill a Mockingbird* Message Board.
2. Each class can have a new topic for each discussion, for example, a chapter in the book they are reading.

3. Students register according to class period, first name and last initial (ICamiM).

   This registration helps teachers greatly in managing these discussions.

4. After students read each chapter in class, students will reply to a prompt that the teacher sets up, or respond to anything in the text that interests them, confuses them, makes them wonder, etc. This is done at home for homework or after class on a computer at school.

5. After reading the topic, students log in and post their responses in the forum for their class.

6. In class the next day, students read others' work and post a reply to any student in the other classes.

7. A forum administrator typically has the ability to edit, delete, or otherwise modify any topic on the forum. The writer of the response should be told why the message is altered.

8. Forum software packages are widely available on the Internet, and are written in a variety of programming languages, such as PHP, Perl and Java. Most Internet Service Providers (ISP) offer forum software free of charge. Installing the software is as easy as logging into the control panel of your website and pressing the install button. The company hosting the teacher's website can be contacted regarding the forum options available.

Supplementary Activities

1. For example, while reading *To Kill a Mockingbird*, the teacher sets up topics such as "Boo's Journal," where students retell any two chapters from Boo's perspective. And students respond from the same point of view.

2. Students can post their own topics, especially if they have a question they want others to consider, and sometimes the teacher posts a question where students can choose from multiple choice responses.

From M. Carrol Tama & Anita McClain (2006). "Writing to Respond" in *Write More! Learn More! Writing across the Curriculum*, Kendall/Hunt, p. 48.

Example

http://www.grammarface.com

8th grade English

Posted 22 May 2006 Chapter 20, *To Kill a Mockingbird*

Predictions? Questions? Thoughts? **Mrs. O**

Posted 22 May 2006 05:20 PM

Wow! Atticus is a really great lawyer! His closing argument was awesome. It made me totally believe Tom's story. I was kind of on the fence but now I'm on the Ground! The only question I have is will he win? I feel bad for Scout that she missed a lot of the testimony because she seemed really interested but Dill had to ruin it. I find it weird that, the guy feels that pretending to be drunk is better than letting people make up their own excuses of why he lives the way he does. I would just let them think what they want and live my life the way I like. I mean, it is my life. I can't wait to see if Tom wins the case but I think he will and Mayella is just making things up because she did something wrong. **CIKallieN**

Posted 22 May 2006 05:34 PM

Atticus is a good lawyer, but unfortunately, I think that the prejudice against the African Americans overide the facts, even though that Tom is most likely innocent. I think that Tom will lose and be killed. I'm not sure why the jury would trust someone as foul as Mr. Ewell, even though he's white. If there was no medical evidence that Tom raped Mayella, then Mr. Ewell would've beat his own daughter for "evidence" that Tom attacked her. Atticus's closing statements were powerful, but the people of Maycomb might think differently. **Ben Au**

Posted 22 May 2006 05:42 PM

This is Jordan. Yes, you're right. Atticus is a great lawyer, he persuaded me. But in such a town as they live in, and with such a serious case, and all of the circumstances, that it is a black man raping a white woman, the jury might not be too persuaded. And even though there are no cold facts against Tom, Bob and Mayella still are sticking to what they said, and even though they know they are wrong, they cannot turn back now. Atticus has played it so calmly and neat, but I don't think the citizens would stand up for a black man, even after Atticus's strong ending. Good luck, Atticus! **Jordan B**

Posted 22 May 2006 05:43 PM

Mr. Au already read the whole book I bet. The odds are that this one will not have a happy ending. The jury will probably have too much prejudice and give a guilty verdict.

I did not know you could get the death penalty for sexual abuse. In the modern world you would just serve some time. **Kevin J**

Posted 22 May 2006 06:06 PM

I wouldn't be surprised if Tom was indicted. If the jury absolutely hates the defendant like a white man despised a black man back then, the defendant is doomed. If you really think about it, no word, speech, or act will convince a person with hate of such a caliber. If you really hated someone for doing something horrible to you would you be nice to him just because someone on HIS side stated logical facts that almost evidently proves him guilty? You might swallow their cold hard facts but chances are that raging fire that is your hate for him would probably not be put out. Even though the African Americans did nothing that would annoy the Caucasians they hated them. Why? Probably because the mere fact of them existing in the United States almost ripped the country in half, or maybe because they think they are inferior to them, but all we know was that they had a hate that could only disappear after years and years of their fighting for real freedom and civil rights. That's how hard they hate and I don't think Atticus himself would convince the jury that Tom Robinson was not guilty. **Spider Man, aka Kevin J.**

Posted 22 May 2006   07:54 PM

I enjoyed this chapter very much. Not only because of Atticus's closing statement, but because I was able to make predictions. First off, Atticus's closing
statement was amazing. It was longer than I think actual closing staements are,
but brought up the right points. And made Tom's story even more believeable. I
think that Tom is DEFINITELY telling the truth and I am not positive why Mayella
lied and said that Tom raped her. It could be because Mr. Ewall forced her to say
that Tom raped her or that she said it on her own to try to get her father to believe
she didn't approach him and he saw wrong. I think it is most likely my first
thought. The jury, I believe, knows that Tom is innocent, but because he is black,
they will prove him guilty. I don't think this is right at all and the jury should start
to think about things. About Mr. Raymond, I don't think he should pretend to be
drunk just to give people a reason for the way he lives. This just makes it seem
like he wants to cover up the fact that he has different views from other people
and think that they are wrong about things. I think that Mr. Raymond should
stand up for his beliefs and try to change other peoples' minds, make a difference. Well, I can't wait to hear what the jury comes up with. I hope that they will
prove Tom innocent. **CI SarahD**

Posted 22 May 2006   08:27 PM

OK, it seems like Atticus is quite the attorney! I really hope that he wins the case,
because all of his evidence and his long, long statement make so much more sense
than the stuff Mayelle and Bob Ewell were making up. I just hope that the jury
realizes that, even if Tom Robinson is "just a negro." It's really sad to think that
times were actually like that, where a small child would say that about someone
and feel no guilt or regret about it whatsoever. Anyway, I think Atticus should
win, even if he doesn't. And if he doesn't win that's stupid because it's obvious
that Tom did nothing wrong, let alone rape a white woman. Atticus's statement
was wonderful and I eagerly soaked up every bit during class. I really liked his use
of words, and how he was so put togther and knew exactly what he wanted to say,
and subtly trying to clue in the audience on what he meant. If I were a part of the
jury, I would be completely convinced by Atticus, and not at all by that ridiculous
Gilmer fellow. After this, I just love Atticus! He's an awesome dad, and he's great
at what he does. Also, I agree with him 100% on everything he said about this
case. I think that when someone is in a courtroom, they are, and should be made
equal to everyone else there. But I also believe that the judge, jury, and the audience already have a set opinion in their mind about the case, and sometimes, that
can't be changed, no matter what either attorney says to them. It's sad that there
is even a CHANCE that the Ewells could win this case, because they are no-good
liars, and Bob should be the one going to prison, not innocent, crippled Tom
Robinson. Hopefully everything turns out right in the end, and the jury really
does get convinced by what Atticus said. **CI MadisonP**

Self-Assessment

Writing Assessment

In this section, we'll highlight writing assessment practices such as individual and peer critique activities that help students draft, and revise their writing through collaboration and conferencing. These activities put the "I" in the editing process. The student not the teacher becomes the critic and monitor of the student's writing. In this process, students develop a clear understanding of what criteria is important for successful writing. They develop the skills they need to be discriminating and independent writers, confident of their own abilities to self-assess, and, ultimately, responsible for their own revising and editing.

Student-managed assesssment of their writing can only help students if it is used consistently. We have watched students who can articulate the strengths and limitations of their writing in one grade, and the next year, act as if they don't have a clue about this analysis. The difference is in teacher expectation. One year, the teacher made clear that student editing was going to be an important part of the writing process. Furthermore, students used peer critique guides in discussing their writing with respective audiences: parents, peers and their teacher. The following year these expectations were not evident.

Principle 5: Writers need feedback.

Peer Editing Guide

TABLE 11

INSTRUCTIONAL SUMMARY OF A PEER EDITING GUIDE	
Literacy Strategy	**Peer Editing Guide**
Primary Focus	Writing
Learning Principles	❏ Active involvement in assessment ❏ Talk Time
When to Use	During or after writing
Goals: National or State Literacy Standards	❏ Reflect upon and evaluate writing ❏ Use multi-step writing process
Materials	Critique guide format
Time	30 minutes

This exercise enables students to dive right into the heart of the paper. If they can identify the topic for the writer, the author is on the way to communicating his ideas. Students learn how to look for positive aspects of the paper as well as develop critical evaluative skills.

Procedure. Students are assigned to four member groups. Each member of the group has a piece of writing that she wants some feedback on. The teacher distributes the following response and editing handout. The students select roles by choosing one of the directions from the response sheet. Then they change these roles after the discussion of each paper is completed. Each role is determined by

At what point does a teacher critique best serve a student's writing?

Elbow (1998)

the number of the item on the response and editing handout. By the end of the exercise an students will have had the opportunity to gain feedback and to practice responding to someone else's paper.

Peer Editing Guide

Procedure.

How does the use of roles enhance a peer editing activity?

Begin the editing process with handing out the following Peer Editing Guide. Explain to students that they can use this process to improve their writing before handing it in. If students wish to pass rather than read their writing to the group, they may. However, it may prove helpful to talk to students about this if they persist in passing over time.

For the teacher implementing these activities we can attest that the payoff is well worth the effort. However, the way is not without tribulations. There will be the student who wants to hear only from the expert—you. There will be students who are crushed by their peers' evaluations. There will be students, no matter how well YOU structure the task, who seem to be stuck with responses like "It's good", "It's nice." How well you cultivate an environment for positive, focused feedback will lessen this occurrence.

When we talk to high school teachers about writing across the curriculum, we can almost see the thoughts spring from their heads: "You must be joking, I have 150 students a day. How can I possibly evaluate that many on a regular basis and still take care of my other professional responsibilities?" No high school content teacher will jump on the writing wagon if it means trucking home 150 papers, or worse yet, class sets of journals.

Teachers wrestling with this dilemma have come up with evaluation techniques that enable students to assume much of the responsibility for their own evaluation. A list of strategies (White, 1996) follows that may help you protect your time while still encouraging and nurturing writing across the curriculum.

❑ Correct a portion of the paper only. Then, have students rework that section only. Note if the student has understood and clarified the problem area. Give points (1-5) for the quality of revision with no comments. Students will clamor for these bonus points and argue the worth of their rewrites. Through their arguments they learn increasingly more about the writing process than by any teacher-red-inked paper—no matter how conscientiously done.

❑ Have students underline their favorite line in their writing. Some teachers refer to this as "the golden line." In class discuss students' choices and what makes this sentence work: e.g., a strong verb, parallel structure or a great metaphor. Focus on *how* the student wrote, not *what* they wrote. Exercises like this help students focus on parts of the writing process that can improve writing.

❑ Allot ten minutes for free-writing short, ungraded pieces. These can be related to what they are studying in class. There is no particular prompt. Students simply write. Don't make corrections or comments on these. Use a highlighter to indicate sentences, passages or words that appear especially effective. Students will take risks for that highlighted feature.

❏ Encourage students to use looseleaf binders instead of bound journals and hand in individual journal entries when requested. Dated entries make your record-keeping easier. Read quickly and highlight critical or creative ideas, or comment on one thing that struck your fancy.

All of these strategies do not mean that you never evaluate a major paper in your class, or respond to journals in full measure. You do. However, only after a series of revisions guided by student response activities and students' personal critiques do you assess the final paper.

For a comprehensive student critique see Figure 6.12 Writing Group Critique.

FIGURE 6.12.   **PEER EDITING GUIDE**

Peer Editing Guide

Checklist:

_____ 1. Get in groups of 3-4 members.

_____ 2. Keep your group small.

_____ 3. Let the reading flow, don't work hard at listening.

_____ 4. React to what sticks in your mind.

_____ 5. Decide if a member of your group will take notes for the reader, or will the reader take his own notes.

_____ 6. Rotate through the following roles.

A. **Reader**   - Reads her or his writing.

B. **Listener 1** - Tells the reader the MESSAGE or MAIN IDEA that you heard.

C. **Listener 2** - Tells the reader what you think is the best part—the writer's "Center of Gravity" (parts that seem memorable, phrases that caught your ear).

D. **Listener 3** - Lets the writer know which part, you would like to hear more about (e.g., needs more information, would like to hear what the writer was thinking about when writing this section, asks where the writer is going with a particular section).

Note: As the reader you make the final decision to take the suggestions made or decide that your experience rings true in your writing. Remember that the group has their unique perceptions which may or may not enrich your writing.

FIGURE 6.13. WRITING GROUP CRITIQUE SHEET

Peers' Compliments:
I like the way your paper began...
I like the part where...
I like the way you explained...
I like the order you used in your paper because...
I liked the details you used to describe...
I think your dialogue was realistic, the way characters said...
I liked the words you used in your writing, such as...
I liked the simile or metaphor you used for...
You used repetition effectively in this part...
I like the way the paper ended because...
Your paper is effective because it reminded me of...
Your paper has effective sentence variety in the part where...
I like the tone or mood of your writing because it made me feel...

Author's Clarifying Questions:
What do you want to know more about?
Was there a part that confused you?
Was there a part that didn't make sense?
Are my sentences easy and clear to understand?
Is my vocabulary too difficult or too elementary?
Did I use the best order in my writing?
Is there a part I should take out?
Can I tighten my writing by eliminating words, phrases, sentences? Which ones?
What details should I add?
Do I use tired words or clichés?
Are there sentences I could combine?
Could I add some similes or metaphors? Where?
Did I indent in the right places?
Should I add dialogue?
Do I have any misspelled words?
Do I have any sentence fragments?
Do I have any punctuation mistakes?

Peers' Clarifying Questions and Suggestions for Improvement
Could you write a lead sentence to "grab" your readers?
I got confused in this part...
Could you add an example to this part about...
Do you think you could leave this part out because...
Could you use a different word for _____ because...
Could you eliminate words in this section?
Could you add some direct dialogue in this section?
Is this paragraph on one topic?
Could you combine some of these short sentences?
Your punctuation caused some confusion here...

1. Writer _____

2. Title _____

Peers' Compliments

Name _____

Compliment _____

_____

_____

Name _____

Compliment _____

_____

_____

Name _____

Compliment _____

_____

_____

Writer's Questions

1. _____

_____

2. _____

_____

3. _____

Suggestions for Improvements

Name _____

Suggestion _____

_____

_____

Name _____

Suggestion _____

_____

_____

Adapted checklist. Make it! Take it! Session, NW NCTE Conference by Janis Cramer. Seattle, WA, 1985.

When students believe that their writing is ready for a final edit. Have students check their draft for conventions. Working in pairs usually is more productive than checking one's own paper. The following chart is a handy reference.

Editing Marks	Meanings	*Sentences
	Delete	Mr. See owned a a saw.
	Spell out word	Thank the other 3 brothers of their father's mother's brother.
=	**Change to capital letter**	Friendly fred flips flapjacks.
lc /	**Change to lowercase letter**	I cannot bear to see a Bear bear down upon a hare.
∿	**Transpose letters or words**	Fat frogs flying past fast.
∧	**Insert (letter, word, phrase or punctuation)**	Cows graze in goves on grass which grows in grooves in groves.
	Close space	They have left the thrift shop.
/	**Add space**	They both, though, have thirty-three thick thimbles.
	Start new paragraph	Is that Theophiles Thistle, the successful thistle-sifter? he asked. "Yes," I replied.

Inclusion Techniques

For most students, writing is a difficult task. For students with special needs, writing is frequently a personal challenge. Teachers tell us that these students often will not write, even if it is only to answer a question with a brief written response. However, when students are given choices in choosing topics as well as time and encouragement, writing can become an acceptable form of communication.

Students with special needs may start slowly. They may write slowly and neatly. They may not complete written work and they may be unwilling to share their work. Often they misunderstand what writing is. Researchers have found that they think of writing as "spelling words correctly, writing 'correct sentences,' and having good handwriting. ...writing was not perceived by them as a means of conveying a message, which is considered by experts to be the most important element in writing" (Bos & Vaughn, 1994, p. 215).

Develop with students a definition of writing.

In group read-arounds, students cannot understand frequently the message of a learning-disabled writer's work. It is typical to find that these students have a difficult time planning and organizing their writing. By spending a major part of the class time helping students preplan their writing using organizational strategies, a teacher can help these students succeed.

Address students' difficulties with writing in meaningful contexts.

Teachers have found that by using writing folders that house all of a student's writing, they can most effectively monitor a student's progress. Using these folders as a diagnostic measure, both teachers and students can observe the progress the students are making. A typical folder might include all pieces of unfinished writing, a list of future writing topics, a list of writing skills the student is working on, as well as spelling words the student wants to master.

As the teacher observes students writing and listens to their requests for help she can design appropriate functional lessons (5–10 minutes long) to help students address their writing problems.

All the writing activities we have described in this chapter can be used in the inclusive classroom. We are including a few samples to show what some students with special needs wrote in response to journal, short essay and writing assignments.

Analyzing these pieces, one notes that students have learned something about the role of background knowledge. They can identify main ideas, craft paragraphs and write conclusions. Granted a lot of hard work went into this effort on the part of the teacher and the students, but it is effort that pays human dividends.

Journal Item: Scientific reading and writing

"I am reading an article entitled 'Cell Duplication! I thought it was very confusing. I thought it was confusing because I don't know any background information on this. In conclusion, I really don't understand everything said in this article."

Essay on grade received

"This is an analysis of my grade this quarter. I will tell you how I got the grade I have. Then, how I can do better to bring my grade up in this class. I got a 'C' this quarter in school. I got a 'C' this quarter because I was not here one week of school and that was the week we went elk hunting. I could not make up the work because it was when we listened to the speeches on our oral essay. So next quarter I can bring my grade up by not missing school or by planning ahead so that I can make up the work.

So, I will do better this quarter, and I will get an 'A' in this class."

Writing Prompts

"How do you feel about Wednesday?", or "You are hosting a brunch for historical, literary, or other disreputable persons. What is your menu? Who are your guests?... "—prompts such as these are the stimulus for writing assessments whether for the student entering the University of Chicago or the middle school student with special neeeds.

For the student with special needs, when faced with writing to a prompt on the annual statewide test, the experience can prove daunting. Teachers, however, have found successful methods for providing the practice that students need. As one teacher responded to what she did to help students with special needs learn how to work with state assessment:

> I prepare students for standardized testing by giving them a quick-write once a week, where they have to write on their choice of assigned state assessment sample prompts in a forty-five minute period of time. I use Oregon's prompts so students get used to the phrasing.
>
> Before giving the prompt, I review the rubric. We also brainstorm ideas we associate with the topics by mapping or using a pertinent graphic organizer. This also gives students a strategy for approaching the writing. Students also have the opportunity to self-check or work in small goups to assess their work.   After this time spent practicing, students are far less likely to freeze up and not know what to do when faced with the annual assessment. I equate standardized testing with getting a driver's license. Students understand this analogy. They know they have to study the manual and don't find it difficult to put the time into studying the material. When they get something incorrect in their responses, they reread and check the material to correct it (Stephanie Hall-Zurek, personal communication, August 8, 2006).

Example 1: Expository Prompts

Select one of the following and write your response to it.

1. A rainy day doesn't have to be bad. Some people like rainy days.
   EXPLAIN how to turn a rainy day into a good day.
2. Think of one thing you know how to make. EXPLAIN very clearly how you make it.
3. Think of something you have done. Maybe it was playing an instrument, having a family outing, baby-sitting, riding a bike or a horse for the first time, growing some vegetables or flowers, going for a long hike, taking a bus across town, learning to skateboard or anything else.
   EXPLAIN what you did so that the reader can understand exactly how you did it.
4. EXPLAIN how you celebrate a favorite holiday, event or custom. Be sure to use details so that your reader can picture what your favorite time is like.

from Oregon Department of Education, 2006

Student Sample Writing

Prompt 3: Think of something you have done. Maybe it was playing an instrument, having a family outing, baby-sitting, riding a bike or a horse for the first time, growing some vegetables or flowers, going for a long hike, taking a bus across town, learning to skateboard or anything else. EXPLAIN what you did so that the reader can understand exactly how you did it.

Grand Theft Auto 3

I have been playing grand theft auto III and I just got done beating It. So I'm going to tell how I beat it. I'm going start on Level 27. What I had to do was. Steel a Cartel Crooser and I have to drive to the other Liberty city on a big hill and get into the cartel mansion and kill the cartel leader and kill as many of them as I can. Then the second leader is flying away in a helicopter and you half to follow her in the crosser than you get to a cartel ambush and you half to kill them all. And you destroy the hellicopter with a bazzooka and game over. I thank you for reading my writing prompt.

(No corrections have been made to student's draft.)

Does this writing have voice? Does it have detail? Does it have problems particularly with conventions? Yes, however, this student is writing and has a well-developed sense of story. Not only is this student writing, but he also has the skills to critique his writing. In a six-trait review, the student with his peer group evaluated his writing:

FIGURE **6.14.** SIX-TRAIT ASSESSMENT

TRAITS	Needs Work	Developing	Strong
IDEAS Topic is narrow and manageable. Ideas make sense.			X X
ORGANIZATION Writing has a beginning and end. Details make sense.		X	X
VOICE Writer cares about the writing. Writing matches the purpose.			X X
WORD CHOICE Specific and descriptive words are used. The writing describes a picture in words.			X X
SENTENCE FLUENCY "Sentences have different beginnings. The piece is easy to read aloud.		X X	
CONVENTIONS Spelling is correct. Punctuation is present and accurate. Capitalization is correct.	X	X	X
PRESENTATION The writing is hand-written or word-processed neatly. Overall, this writing is acceptable.		X	X

*Our thanks to Vickie Sorenson for sharing students' structured writing examples and peer review exercises, 2006.

In assessing this student's understanding of his own writing, he has a sense of what still needs to be done. He also has the satisfaction of knowing that some of his writing meets the standard and he needn't start from scratch. In terms of accuracy, this writing indicates to the teacher of students with special needs that this student can write a fully independent response to a prompt.

What role does talk play in the ELL class?

In addition, Flaherty (2004) in studying an Oregon rural area where local public schools have seen a 250 percent increase in the last ten year in students with limited English proficiency examined the research to determine what writing activities effect stronger writing skills in this population. One such researcher, he quotes, is Gebhard (2004) who asserts "that talk in particular can be beneficial to the development of writing skills. Reading and writing lessons are more productive when ELL students can talk to each other as well as their more proficient classmates."

Students who spend time thinking about their writing produce better writing.

However, these activities need to be done regularly. Researchers Graves, Valles, and Rueda (2004) write that consistency is the key in teaching ELL students or students with special needs. These authors further direct teachers to create the "Optimal Learning Environment" (OLE) approach for these students which includes four principles:
1. Purposeful activities
2. Responsive instruction
3. Self-regulated learning
4. Building communities of learners.
   We also believe that these principles work for every student.

More on Revision

An alternative revision process that we found that is really awesome and would help students with special needs in particular focus on the 6-traits typically used in assessing standardized writing tests is found on http://writingfix.com/6Traits/Post_It_Note_Instructions.pdf. These directions for printing revision notes minimize writing, yet provide ample opportunity to talk about writing. Teachers have found that students using these can quickly assess their own writing and then seem more than willing to share their thinking about their writing with peers (Cuevas, 2006).

Revision Technique to printing and using sticky-notes

1. Run a copy of the one-page sheet of revision sticky-notes through your computer's printer found on the above website.
2. Take 6 real sticky-notes (the square kind) and completely cover the six sticky-notes that come off the printer. The square sticky-notes should fit perfectly over the six-trait prints on the page.
3. Open the feeder tray on your computer's printer. Some printers will take the sheet face-up... some face-down. You will need to determine what your printer expects. From your feeder, print the document a second time, this time on the page you covered up mostly with your blank sticky-notes.
4. The checklist will print on the sticky-notes
5. Affix these sticky-notes on a student's paper, once the trait(s) for revision have been determined.
   a. The teacher can select which trait(s) he/she wants the individual to improve upon;
   b. The student can select which trait(s) he/she wants to improve upon;
   c. The teacher can select one trait, and the student can select the other,
   See Figure 6.15 for example of the writing trait Organization arranged for printing on sticky-notes.

FIGURE 6.15.   ORGANIZATION STICKY-NOTES

Organization:	Organization:
Rank **each** skill from 1 (low) to 5 (high) in the following: _____ My introduction grabs the reader's attention. _____ My conclusion links back to my introduction. _____ I used transition words to move from idea to idea. _____ My paragraphs show where my subtopics begin & end. _____ My title stands for my entire draft, not just a part of it.	Rank **each** skill from 1 (low) to 5 (high) in the following: _____ My introduction grabs the reader's attention. _____ My conclusion links back to my introduction. _____ I used transition words to move from idea to idea. _____ My paragraphs show where my subtopics begin & end. _____ My title stands for my entire draft, not just a part of it.
Organization:	Organization:
Rank **each** skill from 1 (low) to 5 (high) in the following: _____ My introduction grabs the reader's attention. _____ My conclusion links back to my introduction. _____ I used transition words to move from idea to idea. _____ My paragraphs show where my subtopics begin & end. _____ My title stands for my entire draft, not just a part of it.	Rank **each** skill from 1 (low) to 5 (high) in the following: _____ My introduction grabs the reader's attention. _____ My conclusion links back to my introduction. _____ I used transition words to move from idea to idea. _____ My paragraphs show where my subtopics begin & end. _____ My title stands for my entire draft, not just a part of it.
Organization:	Organization:
Rank **each** skill from 1 (low) to 5 (high) in the following: _____ My introduction grabs the reader's attention. _____ My conclusion links back to my introduction. _____ I used transition words to move from idea to idea. _____ My paragraphs show where my subtopics begin & end. _____ My title stands for my entire draft, not just a part of it.	Rank **each** skill from 1 (low) to 5 (high) in the following: _____ My introduction grabs the reader's attention. _____ My conclusion links back to my introduction. _____ I used transition words to move from idea to idea. _____ My paragraphs show where my subtopics begin & end. _____ My title stands for my entire draft, not just a part of it.

Permission from Northern Nevada Writing Project, 2006.

How do teachers help students with special needs develop their writing?

How are these skills developed? We believe this development occurs in a classroom where the teacher understands that writing is most effective in environments where it accomplishes something the writer wants to accomplish. Second, an environment exists where writing is a social process, where discussion and feedback are structured and practiced. Third, students are given the opportunity to write in many genres, on different occasions, and for many audiences. Finally, writing is seen as a means of improving learning.

Your Turn

Name _____ Date _____ Subject Area _____

METACOGNITIVE JOURNALS

In this journal you will examine your own thinking about writing.

❏ On the left side of the paper, place the acronym, WRITE, written vertically with an explanation of each letter. On the right side of the paper, record—**What I learned about my writing!**, using the acronym as a guide.
  You may want to work on one or two of these writing revision activities at a time.

❏ Develop one journal entry related to a piece of your own writing modeling thinking about revision.

WRITE	**What I learned about my writing!**
W - Work to develop a strong introduction.	
R - Remember to use strong verbs.	
I - Include transitions (Words like: "however", "in contrast", "but", etc.) for connecting ideas.	
T - Try to use a variety of sentences. Check how you begin each sentence.	
E - Excite your reader (and maybe yourself) with the unusual phrase.	
Other:	

Modified from a writing strategy by DeLaPaz, 1999; Jacobson, 1987

Writing Strategies for English Language Learners

In learning foreign languages, both of us have found that writing was a critical element in the process. All the worksheets and the practice drills that we both experienced had little effect on our use of the language either in speaking or writing. Once we had to put pen to paper, however, and apply what we knew about the language by creating our own essays, journal entries or poems, knowledge of the language increased exponentially. In fact, when we were writing about ourselves, our families, our trips, etc., our foreign language ability seemed to improve almost automatically. What made the difference and how does this apply to our ELL students?

Principle 1:
Students learn to write by writing.

Linking personal experience with academic learning is a fundamental tenet of learning. Through writing ELLs can bring their own culture, their values and their voice to the classroom experience. In the process, the writing requires that students bring their thoughts and knowledge of the new language together—not an easy task—but one made possible with support and guidance.

The strategies, a patterned letter, that is a take-off on "Dear Abby," and the "Reading to Writing" exercise build from students' own experience. They provide students with concepts and the vocabulary to draft their own writing.

Letter Writing

TABLE 12

INSTRUCTIONAL SUMMARY FOR A LETTER WRITING EXERCISE

Literacy Strategy	Letter Writing
Primary Focus	Writing
Learning Principles	❑ Builds on background knowledge · ❑ Uses writing to learn
When to Use	After unit
Goals: National or State Literacy Standards	❑ Uses writing to communicate knowledge of topic ❑ Conveys clear ideas and details
Materials	Patterned Letter starter
Time	20 minutes

In order to read or write, students must bring together their knowledge of language, literacy, and concepts. By providing students with opportunities to play with words, they build a feeling of how their own language, rhythm and experience can serve them academically. Books like *Writing across Cultures* and *Luna, Luna: Creative writing ideas from Spanish, Latin American, & Latino literature* are chock full of ideas to provide students with models of writers they can identify with and emulate.

An activity "Openings and Closings" in which Kovacs (1994, pp. 98-99) teaches his bilingual, bicultural students the most familiar openings and closings of stories and then invites them to write their own legends or stories using these, is

Principle 5:
Writers need
feedback.

similar to a lesson using letter starters for ESL students (Emily Gaffney, personal communication, August 5, 1998).

The letter is one of the most basic means of communication. It provides the foundation of all writing: an opening, body and closing. Providing students with a context that they recognize ensures a successful start. In addition, because of the nature of the letter, it assumes an audience, a recipient who will respond. It allows students to communicate with each other and helps strengthen the classroom community.

After formulating a unit, on the novel Como Agua Para Chocolate (Like Water for Chocolate) for 10th-12th graders in an ESL Spanish for Spanish Speakers program, Emily discussed multicultural traditions surrounding marriage, provided guided reading of the novel in Spanish, as well as graphic organizers demonstrating the connections among characters and events. Students engaged in myriad activities to help them understand the plot and much of the motivation behind the characters' actions. As a culminating activity, she designed the following letter writing exercise.

This variety of activities ensured that student had the vocabulary and the conceptual understandings to proceed with their letters.

Procedure

1. Introduce students to the concept and format of letters.
2. Explain to the students that they will take on the identity of a character from a novel they are reading or a historical figure that they have studied and address a special letter to them,
3. Provide the starter for the letter, e.g.,
   "Querida _____,
   Comprendo tu situación y por eso te aconsejo que..."
   (Dear _____,
   I understand your situation and that is why I advise you to...)
   Any starter could be used depending on the purpose of the letter.
4. When completed, ask students to place their letters in a letter box. Distribute these randomly to another student to respond.
5. After the letters are answered, have students return them to the original writer.

After students have read the response to their writing, they can turn them in for a grade or points. Additional points are garnered for their translations of their letters into English. They can also choose to continue their correspondence.

In this foreign language class for ESL Spanish speakers, the teacher wanted to enhance their language skills in their native language. Many of her students had recently arrived in the U.S. and the teacher wanted them to focus on what they could do. Capitalizing on the wealth of images and experiences from their culture, students transition from one language into the other, always beginning with their strong suit—their native language. Their on-the-spot translations win extra points and painless practice. In addition, the very qualities that good writing evokes "clarity, voice, power and control are much more easily developed through letter writing (than through writing stories) because, perhaps, the audience is so clearly defined and will, if all goes well, respond" (Fox, 1993, p. 28).

Although few ESL classes have the luxury of affording students learning in both their native and second language, such strategies as letter writing in almost

Example: ESL: Foreign Language-Spanish

La letra:	Translation
Querida Tita,	Dearest Tita,
Comprendo tu situación y por eso te aconsejo que abandones a tu mamá y te cases, y que hagas tu vida lejos de ella. Despues puedes regresar con ella y explicarle que estás casada y que de todas maneras puedes cuidarla y ayudarle, sin meterla en una casa para ancianos. Hasta luego, Juan	I understand your situation and that is why I advise you to leave your mother and marry and make your life far from her. Later, you can return to her and explain that you are married but can take care of her and help her anyway or you can put her into an old folks home. Until later, Juan
Respuesta...	**Response...**
Juan,	Juan,
No creo que es buena idea que dejes abandonada a tu mamá. Ella es más importante que tu novia. Sólo tienes una mamá en el mundo pero tú puedes encontrar muchas novias. Te aconsejo que si estás en la misma situación de Tita entonces te casas y te quedas a vivir con tu mamá. Adiós, Anna	I don't believe it is a good idea to leave your mother. She is more important than your girl friend. You only have one mother in the world but you can find many girl friends or boy friends. I advise that if you are in the same situation as Tita then you can marry and remain to live with your mother. Goodbye, Anna

any class provide the necessary structure for students to demonstrate their thinking and learning through writing.

Another strategy that provides cues to enable English language learners to make meaning out of print is Reading to Writing.

Reading to Writing

TABLE 13

INSTRUCTIONAL SUMMARY FOR READING TO WRITING

Literacy Strategy	Reading to Writing
Primary Focus	Writing
Learning Principles	❏ Actively involved ❏ Uses writing to learn
When to Use	After reading
Goals: National or State Literacy Standards	❏ Communicates information and expresses ideas in writing ❏ Conveys clear ideas and details
Materials	Text models
Time	40 minutes

Surrounding English language learners with appropriate reading material is crucial to their understanding of text as well as implanting a habit of reading and writing. Richard Rodriguez writes "I have come to understand better why works of literature—while never intimate, never individually addressed to the reader—are so often among the most personal statements we hear in our lives" (p. 189). Furthermore, Rodriguez writes "my teachers gave me a great deal more than I knew when they taught me to write public English" (p. 188).

FIGURE 6.16. SAVE THE LAST WORD FOR ME

Lesson Plan: ELL: Save the Last Word for Me activity

Grade: 6-10

Topic: The Dust Bowl: *Out of the Dust* by Karen Hesse (Any trade book: fiction or nonfiction)

Purpose: To enhance understanding of both content (The Dustbowl) and text (*Out of the Dust*) through writing.

State Content/Literacy Standards: 1) to identify relevant information explicitly or implicitly stated in literary, informative and practical passages, 2) To foster group interaction and problem-solving, 3) to provide scaffolding for challenging text material.

Student Objectives:
1. Students will be able to select passages that provoke writing about the Dust Bowl and the human suffering it caused as well as those that show the human spirit that endures and wills to survive.
2. Students will be able to develop and share opinions of others' ideas.
3. Students will be prepared to summarize important points of their group discussion.

FIGURE 6.16. SAVE THE LAST WORD FOR ME (CONT.)

Introduction: Show students pictures and information of the Dust Bowl. See several websites such as:

http://www.pbs.org/wgbh/pages/amex/dustbowl
http://www.humanitiesinteractive.org/texas/dustbowl/dustbowl_teacher.htm.
http://eduscapes.com/newbery/98a.html

Pictures by Dorothea Lange, Ben Shahn, Walker Evans, Arthur Rothstein, John Vachon, Russell Lee, Marion Post Wolcott, Carl Mydans, Jack Delano, John Collier, and Gordon Parks are particularly telling of the human condition at this time. These photographers produced 80,000 photographs that are now housed in the Library of Congress, and make up a virtual history of the Dust Bowl.

Do a book talk of Out of the Dust to introduce students to a family who faces human tragedy as well as a natural disaster and how they survive. Read a few pages to set the stage and show students how a story can be told in poetic form. Make sure students have time to ask questions and understand key terms used.

Learning Activity - Save the Last Word for Me
1. Students form reading groups of three members.
2. They are asked to read a few poems from Out of the Dust.
3. After reading, each student writes on one side of a note card or a piece of paper a passage they've selected, and on the reverse side they explain why they selected this passage.
4. Then each student reads his or her passage to the group and the group gives feedback on what they think the passage means to them.
5. When the discussion is finished, the student turns over his or her card and reads what he wrote about his understanding of this passage and how it relates to the topic—in this instance, the Dust Bowl.
6. After this discussion and areas of agreement or disagreement are ironed out, this student summarizes the discussion—thus having the "last word.".
7. Another member of the group shares a passage, and the discussion cycle begins again.

Burke (1993)

Closure: Each group conies up with a story of a natural disaster that makes a connection with a theme in *Out of the Dust*, e.g., the December, 2006 snowstorm in the (USA) NW that stranded mountaineers on Mt. Hood, OR.

Evaluation: All students have the "last word" by sharing what they've learned about the Dust Bowl by writing a One-Sentence Summary (WDWWWWHW).

Who?
Did what?
To what or whom?
When?
Where?
How?
Why?

Endings: A Summary

In this chapter we have described the various ways writers approach the writing process. The elements of the writing process were presented, as well as valuable principles of effective writing instruction to use as guidelines in building your own writing program.

Over the years, our graduate students have asked us such questions as "What creative ways are there to integrate reading and writing with my content area?", "To what standard can a teacher of any subject hold students accountable for their writing?", "Should the teacher evaluate the writing, including this evaluation as part of the grade?" We have responded to these questions with a number of strategies like the I-Search paper, writing created from organizational formats, and reflective writing that provide teachers with direction in answering these questions.

All students must have the opportunity to write.

For writing across the curriculum to be successful, assessment needs to focus on features of students' writing that demonstrate understanding and progress. If students are given opportunities to monitor their own work, revise it, and evaluate it, teachers have more time to facilitate and study this activity. They are in a much better position to document and interpret a wide range of student performance with writing rather than that provided by grading students' papers only. The self-assessment and peer response activities presented in this chapter promote this student-directed learning.

Although we maintain that most of the activities presented in this chapter will work with all students, we have highlighted a few specific writing strategies for students with special needs. We are not only emphasizing that these students find expressing themselves in writing a very difficult experience, but also we are suggesting that all students can write if they have a systematic process for interacting with text, peers and teachers, and most importantly have the opportunity to write.

Expanding Understandings through Discussion

Questions in 4-Learning Styles Writing Activity

Select a question from one of the following boxes. Take ten minutes to review pertinent information from the chapter, and take notes that will help craft your answer to the question. Then take about seven minutes to write out your response to the question. Share and discuss your responses.

Join a mixed question group and share and discuss your answers together. Each of you will serve as experts on your self-selected question.

Finally, as a group, discuss if you would still select the same question. Discuss such questions as: What were the most powerful or interesting thoughts that came from your group?, What would you change?, Why? Optional-Final draft as a writing assignment or extra-credit.

Questions in 4-Learning Styles: Activity Sheet

ST—Sensing Thinkers	SF—Sensing Feelers
List the eight principles of effective writing instruction, select one and share why it is important in your subject area.	If you were asked by your supervisor to present a writing lesson, which strategy would you choose? Write a reflection on your choice.
IT—Intuitive Thinkers	IF—Intuitive Feelers
Compare and contrast a subject area unit that promotes an I-Search approach to a term paper and one that assigns the traditional term paper.	A classroom that promotes students as writers is like a _____ because _____ . (Thoughtfully explain your analogy).

In the Field Applications
A. Keep a writing journal with your students. Complete those writing activities you assign to your students. If you use a dialogue journal format, exchange your journal entry with a member of your class. Use your entries as models as well as those of your students. Allow time for sharing.
B. Develop a lesson plan introducing a writing strategy, e.g., RAFT, Biopoem.
C. Come up with a writing activity of your own that illustrates one of the principles of effective writing instruction. Provide a rationale and clear set of procedures.

References ❏ ❏ ❏

Adcock, S. (2006). *Hipster Haiku.* NY: Broadway Books.

Alvermann, D., & Phelps, S. (1994). *Content reading and literacy: Succeeding in today's diverse classrooms.* Boston: Allyn & Bacon.

Anonymous (1973). "Two Women." In B. Bigelow, L. Christensen, S. Karp, B. Miner, & B. Peterson, (Eds.), *Rethinking our classrooms.* Milwaukee: Rethinking Schools.

Atwell, N. (1987). *In the middle: Writing, reading and learning with adolescents,* Portsmouth, NY: Heinemann.

Bos, C., & Vaughn, S. (1994). *Strategies for teaching students with learning and behavior problems.* Boston: Allyn & Bacon.

Case, P. (2006). Plein air painting & writing returns to Hood River. *Columbia Arts Newsletter,* p. 5.

Chipper, D. (2006). Professional power for homeowners. Retrieved November 21, 2006, from http://www.drchipper.com

Cuevas, K. (2006). Revitalizing responses and revision with trait-specific post-its. Retrieved December 16, 2006, from http://writingfix.com/6Traits/Post_It_Note_Instructions.pdf

Davis, R. (1999). Multi-genre writing and reading (self) assessment: Engaged learning in a regulated system. *Oregon English Journal 21*(2): 33–36.

De La Paz, S. (1999). Teaching writing strategies and self-regulation procedures to middle school students with learning disabilities [Electronic Version]. / *Focus on Exceptional Children,* 31, 1–20.

Dewey, J. (1910). *How we think.* Boston: Heath.

Dillard, A. (1989). *The writing life.* NY: HarperCollins.

Dilliard, A. (1998). *The writing life.* NY: Harper Perennial.

Elbow, P. (1998). *Writing without teachers* (2nd ed.). NY: Oxford University Press.

Elbow, P. (1973). *Writing without teachers.* NY: Oxford University Press.

Esquivel, L. (1994). *Like water for chocolate.* NY: Anchor.

Fox, M. (1993). *Radical reflections: Passionate opinions on teaching, learning and living.* NY: Harcourt Brace & Company.

Flaherty, J. (2004). Strategies for teaching writing to LEP students. *Oregon English Journal,* XXV(2), 3–6.

Fletcher, R. (1996). *A writer's notebook: Unlocking the writer within you.* NY: Harper Trophy.

Gardner, T. (2006a). Reading and analyzing multigenre texts. Retrieved November 30, 2006, from http://readwritethink.org/lessons/lesson view.asp?id+293

Gardner, T. (2006b). Reading and analyzing multigenre texts. Retrieved December 1. 2006, from http://www.sheboyganfalls.kl2.wi.us/cyberenglish9/multi genre/ genre types.htm

Goldberg, N. (1986). *Writing down the bones.* Boston: Shambhala.

Graves, A. W., Valles, E. C., & Rueda, R. (2004). Variations in interactive writing instruction: A study in four bilingual special education settings [Electronic Version]. *Learning Disabilities Research and Practice,* 15, 1–9. Retrieved December 16, 2006 from http://80-search.epnet.com.glacier.sou.edu.

Harris, T. L. Hodges, R. E. (Eds.). (1995). *The literacy dictionary: The vocabulary of reading and writing.* Newark, DE: International Reading Association.

Hudelson, S. (1987). The role of native language literacy in the education of language minority children. *Language Arts 64* (827–841).

Jacobson, A., Ed. (1987). Essential learning skills across the curriculum. Retrieved December 12, 2006, from http://www.sdcoe.kl2.ca.us/score/actbank/rjourfact.htm

Kinnell, G. (1990). *When one has lived a long time alone*. NY: Knopf.

Knight, J. E. (1990). Coding journal entries. *Journal of Reading 34*(1): 42–46.

Krashen, S. (1982). *Principles and practices in second language acquisition*. Oxford, UK: Pergamon.

Kovacs, E. (1994). Thoughts on poetry and lyrical prose. In E. Kovac (Ed.), *A handbook on writing poetry and lyrical prose*. Hillsboro, OR: Blue Heron Publishing, Inc.

LaLumia, F. (2006). Plein-aire painters of America. Retrieved November 8, 2006, from http://www.p-a-p-a.com/whatis.asp

Lane, B. (1999). *The reviser's toolbox*. VT: Discover Writing Press.

Luther, J. (2006). I-Searching in context: Thinking critically about the research unit. *English Journal, 95*(4), 68–74.

Lyman, H. (2006). I-Search in the age of information. *English Journal, 95*(4), 62–67

Macrorie, K. (1988). *The I-search paper.* Portsmouth, NH: Heinemann.

O. D. E. (2006). Using sample prompts: Writing. Retrieved December 11, 2006, from http:/ / www.ode.state.or.us /teachlearn/ subjects /el arts/ writing/ assessment/ usingsam pleprompts.pdf

Power thinking, reading and writing. Kalispell, MT: Kalispell Public Schools.

Rief, L. (1992). *Seeking diversity: Language arts with adolescents*. Portsmouth, NH: Heinemann.

Rodriguez, R. (1982). *Hunger of memory: The education of Richard Rodriguez*. NY: Bantam Books.

Romano, T. (1995). *Writing with passion: Life stories, multiple genres*. Portsmouth, NH: Boynton/Cook.

Romano, T. (2000). *Blending genre, altering style: Writing multigenre papers*. Portsmouth, NH: Boynton/Cook.

Routman, R. (1991). *Invitations: Changing as teachers and learners K-12*. Portsmouth, NH: Heinemann.

Rubin, N. (1994). *Ask me if I care: Voices from an American high school*. Berkeley, CA: Ten Speed Press.

Safire, W. (2006, February 19, 2006). On language: Blargon. *The New York Times*, Section 6, 32.

Santa, C. (1988). *Content reading including study systems: Reading, writing and studying across the curriculum*. Dubuque, IA: Kendall/Hunt.

Schlenk, C. The Dust Bowl-A Learning Activity. Retrieved December 13, 2006, from http:/ / www.humanities-interactive.org/texas/ dustbowl/

Staley, C. T. (2003). Tongue Twister Database. Retrieved November 21, 2006, from http://www.geocities.com/Athens/8136/tonguetwisters.html

Stevens, A. (1993). *Learning for life through universal themes*. Portland, OR: Northwest Regional Educational Laboratory.

Street, C. (2005). A reluctant writer's entry into a community of writers. *Journal of Adolescent & Adult Literacy*, 48, 8.

Townsend, S. (1986). *The Adrian Mole diaries*. New York: Grove Press, Inc.

Watson, P. A., & Lacina, J. G. (2004). Lessons learned from integrating technology in a writer's workshop. *Voices from the Middle*, 12(3), 38–44.

Wells, L. (2006). Blog it: An innovative way to improve literacy. *Reading Today*, 24, 40.

White, M. (1996). Several strategies for making the most of student writing. *The Teaching Professor, 10*(7), 6–7.

Winer, D. (2002). RSS (file format). Retrieved December 16, 2006, from http:/ / en.wikipedia.org/ wiki/RSS_(file_format)

Yorkshire, D. R. (2006). The teacher is an author. *Oregon English Journal*, 28 (I), 16.

Zemelman, S., & Daniels, H., & Hyde, A. (1993). *Best practice: New standards for teaching and learning in America's schools.* Portsmouth, NH: Heinemann.

Zorfass, J., & Copel, H. (1995). The I-Search: Guiding students toward relevant research. *Educational Leadership*, 48–51.

Answers to Chapter 6, p. 2, Internet IM:

(1) I	(2) C	(3) A	(4) M	(5) H
(6) K	(7) F	(8) J	(9) D	(10) L

Literature Strategies

7

I have always imagined that paradise will be a kind of library.

Jorge Luís Borges

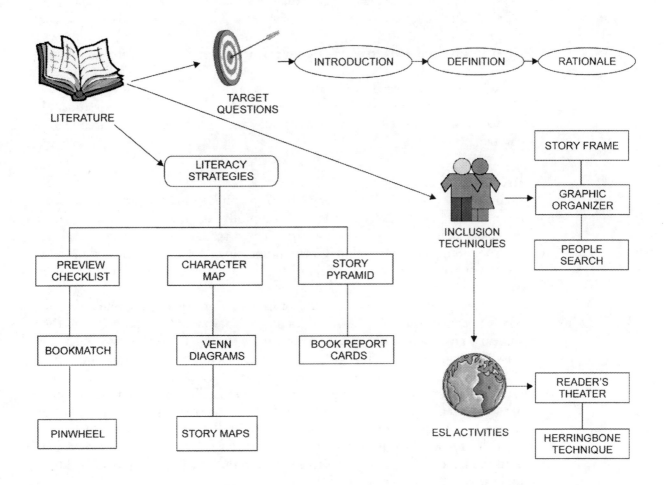

Target Questions

Consider the following questions before reading this chapter. Discuss these with a colleague. Continue writing notes and develop specific questions that you want to explore.

1. What is the importance of using trade books as supplemental readings, or as replacements of textbooks?
2. What is the difference between narrative text and expository text?
3. What are the literary elements of narrative text?
4. What literature strategies are appropriate for you to implement in your content area?
5. Find a poem to supplement or extend a specific facet of your content area.
6. Find a tradebook to supplement or extend a specific facet of your content area.
7. Find a picture book to use as a supplement for a specific topic in your content area.
8. What is the Herringbone strategy?
9. Using literature how could you help an inclusion student or an ESL student to feel more comfortable in your classroom and with your content area materials?

Introduction

In the *Instant Quotation Dictionary* (1987) Joseph Addison reminds us that "reading is to the mind what exercise is to the body." Content area teachers must encourage students to read for pleasure. There is more to the content than the textbook. Supplementary reading may ultimately be what motivates them to enjoy and appreciate a particular field of study—whether it be biographies, historical fiction, poetry or a good, basic novel.

Does reading matter?

Teachers can encourage "outside reading" by giving students bibliographies of titles related to the current topic of study. They can also read books to their students, give book talks, and give students extra credit for reading outside of class. We know that reading for pleasure helps to improve reading competence. We also highly recommend that very little outside reading be disparaged. Booth (2006) writes about his reading experience graphically: "The memory of sitting in the backseat of our old car in the driveway eating apples picked from a tree in the ravine, and reading five new comics books still warms my aging heart" p. 29. This chapter will give teachers a variety of strategies to use with adolescent literature and encourage teachers to make copious stacks of books available to their students.

Definition

Literary works, as opposed to textbooks, are trade books which include fiction and non-fiction information. Teachers include young adult (YA) books in the curriculum in an effort to foster lifelong reading and to provide a rich context for the topic under study. Literature in the classroom:

> ... invites us to participate in the ongoing dialogue of the culture. It presents to us what others have experienced and how they have made sense of that experience, and it invites us to take those perceptions,

combine them with our own, and build out of the mix the conceptions and visions that will govern our lives. Literature provides us not knowledge ready-made but the opportunity to make knowledge (Probst, 1987, p. 28).

Rationale

Reading trade books across all content areas helps students to create vivid understandings of setting, culture and the people involved in the issue under discussion. Regular periods of time scheduled for reading, thinking about reading, discussing a solution with others, and reflecting on what was read provide the opportunity to develop these vivid pictures of time and character. Through such forums as reading logs or small group discussions, students have the opportunity to explore their feelings and thoughts after reading such powerful moving literature as *The Glory Field* (Myers) in a social studies class. What student having read this book would not more clearly understand the effect of slavery on generations of a family and understand the symbol of "shackles" that Myers uses brilliantly throughout the book?

Students need to read both narrative and expository literature across the curriculum. All subject area teachers can supplement their units with appropriate trade books.

In a classroom that nurtures a safe environment, students make their own responses to literature they have read. In order for this to occur, readers need immediate access to reading resources. All content teachers should have a room full of books. Classrooms we visit that honor and cherish books have them on chalk trays, piled on the floor, in makeshift bookcases, etc. These books also become models for good writing. In addition, teachers who model reading and share their reading are likely to become rich resources themselves for supporting good books to read.

We believe that all content classrooms should have supplemental libraries.

TEACHER TALK

To create lifetime readers, students must have time to read and learn skills and strategies for reading. The habit of reading is not a frill—it should be nurtured in all classrooms. This requires that each of us provide time for reading.

Every content area teacher needs to be a teacher of reading. This not only refers to comprehension or vocabulary development but includes the premise that wide reading in all content areas is necessary to better understand each particular subject area. For example, in the biology classroom students can study DNA from a textbook and the biology teacher is responsible for teaching them how to effectively read that textbook. However, the biology teacher enriches her curriculum by supplementing the text in this instance with such trade books as *The Double Helix* by James Watson. In addition to the story of the discussion of DNA, students get a behind the scene look at how scientists work, the vagaries of science, and the role of personal and professional relationships. Through such literature, science is seen as a very human endeavor.

In reading a historical fiction trade book such as *Jip* by Paterson, students have the opportunity to feel what it is like to live in another time and place—the world of the abolitionists and the slaveholders.

The National Council of Teachers of English (1983) stated that students need to 1) realize literature is a mirror of human experience, 2) gain insights from involvement with literature, 3) become aware of writers whose backgrounds are diverse, 4) become aware of past and present classics or masterpieces of literature, 5) learn how to discuss and write about literature, and 6) appreciate the language in literature and become lifelong readers.

Selection Criteria

As a content area teacher do you know what books would interest your students?

When selecting literature a number of criteria need to be considered in order to appropriately match the reader to reading resources. First, one must ask what is the student's developmental level of reading ability? Next, what interests the student? Lastly, how well will this resource supplement the curriculum being taught?

Readability not only includes analysis of reading skills, but also must include an analysis of how the information is presented: Is it "user friendly?" Is it interesting? Does it present the concepts in an understandable format? One can read a chapter about the Civil War in a textbook. It is quite a different experience to read narrative text such as *Steal Away Home* (Ruby), *In My Father's House* (Rinaldi), or *Across Five Aprils* (Hunt).

Narrative Text

Eeds & Peterson (1997)

Narrative literature consists of stories that are fiction and nonfiction. When supplementing textbooks with narrative literature teachers need to consider the reading skills required to understand the selection and how well the selection makes the topic come alive. Teachers will find it helpful in conducting their conversations and those of their students about literature to consider the literary elements of character development, setting, plot, theme, style, and point of view. These elements are meant to serve as means to understanding the text; they are not the goal in the content area classroom. As Eeds and Peterson (1997) assert, we need to be careful in using literature to teach content. They contend that there are those who are using literature to teach facts rather than "to illuminate life" (p. 54).

TEACHER TALK

Additional use of reading materials brings more of the world info the science class. The seventh grade reads **Inherit the Wind.** We have reading groups through the year. We're currently finishing up books with themes related to early human history and I'm reading **Clan of the Cave Bear** to the students. Science fiction will be used when astronomy is the unit in winter. Reading good literature allows students to think and discuss. That in turn, leads to rich discussions about character motivation, subplot, foreshadowing, and the author's goals in presenting plot as she/he does.

Character Development

Characters must be portrayed credibly, must correctly represent the time period or setting in which they live, and should not be stereotyped. Teachers have a wonderful array of choices such as historical books, biographical books or books that deal with current issues and modem problems. In *Until Whatever* (Humphreys), readers will empathize with Connie Tibbs, the main character, who has contracted AIDS and loses all of her friends as a consequence. Readers will further admire Karen who becomes Connie's, only true friend during her final days.

Characters in a book can "assume almost the same potential for influencing the reader as real people" (Weaver, 1994, pp. 33-34). "If this is true, then parents and educators need to beware of the potential influence literary characters can have on today's students" (Leal, 1999, p. 241). It is important to not only discuss character traits, but also relate character traits to their own lives. It is especially meaningful when students view characters as reflections of personal situations. Students should be "free to evaluate and challenge their own understanding while building new individual and group awareness of both character and literature. It also has the potential to encourage more compassion, more respect, and to produce discerning future citizens, more cognizant of their own responses and responsibilities in a society looking for integrity" (Leal, 1999, p. 248). Thus, we recommend that teachers carefully select novels where characters are fully developed, realistic and good role models for students.

Setting
The setting must be believable. It should clearly and correctly reflect the historical period in the genre of historical fiction or cause a make-believe land, such as Narnia in the C.S. Lewis books, to become a possibly real place.

TEACHER TALK

We recently read a piece by Barry Lopez, a fine nature writer. His work described a trip in a river system of Alaska. Filled with clear imagery, simile, metaphor, it modeled the personal voice I was reaching for from my students. Students were then challenged to pick a place they deemed special and write creatively about it. Description was foremost in their work, and some of them went deeper, as Lopez did, and moved into feelings about place and what in a special natural area did for them.

Plot
A well developed plot will have a sequence, a plan of action, and a good conclusion. Students will then become involved and should interact with the author or text. An exciting plot includes an experience where characters overcome conflict. Conflict found in adolescent literature includes person against person, person against nature, person against self, and person against society. In *Cages* (Kehret), the plot revolves around the central character, Kit, who is caught shoplifting and as a consequence selects community service at the Society for the Prevention of Cruelty to Animals. The resolution of the plot finds Kit developing his own inner strength and readers can relate to his feelings of helplessness.

Content teachers need to reinforce the literary elements of books.

Point of View
Authors must decide from what viewpoint the story will be told. One choice is through the use of first person. A second technique is the use of third person in which the third person point of view is an all-knowing perspective. Third, characters and actions can simply speak for themselves. Finally, a third person point of view can be used for all characters except one-the one usually speaks for himself or herself. In *Ryan White. My Own Story* (White and Cunningham) Ryan tells his story of contracting AIDS from an infected blood-clotting agent and is then forced out of school. One of the authors uses first person to tell his story.

Style

How the author creates characters, plots and settings through use of words becomes his or her style. Sounds of words, type of vocabulary, descriptions, and symbolism, create an effective style. Kelly, in *Running Before the Wind* (Woolverton), whose father physically abuses her, relieves her frustrations by running as a member of the track team where the coach helps her to deal with her own rages and feelings. The author uses powerful language to portray the extent of Kelly's emotions and the depth of the coach's caring.

Theme

What cements the plot, characters, and setting is known as the theme of the book. Why did the author write this book? What is the message? In *Nothing To Fear* (Koller) Danny Garver's father must leave his family to look for work during the Depression of the 1930s. Danny becomes the man of the house and faces many hardships. The theme becomes that of a child prematurely assuming responsibilities of manhood.

Students could use a semantic map (Figure 7.1) to better understand the literary elements and the relationships among those elements.

Expository Text

Even skilled readers will often have trouble with expository text.

Most students in the elementary grades are exposed to a high frequency of narrative text. It is not until middle school or high school that students are expected to read more expository text than narrative text. In narrative text students can expect characters, settings, plots, themes, styles and points of view. They can predict how a story might develop. However, as expository text is introduced good readers of narrative stories can begin to have reading problems. The structure is different, the concepts are difficult; the vocabulary becomes specialized, and the presentation of the material is not so predictable.

Expository text informs the reader through explanation, compare/contrast, definition/example, and problem/solution. Students need to recognize these patterns, and teachers should be mindful of the guidance students require in order to identify these. Unlike narrative text that has a predictable sequence, or plot in which a problem or conflict is resolved, expository text typically has few cues. There is a real need for study skills, organizational skills, and reference skills in guiding students through expository text. See Chapters 2, 3 and 4.

Difficult text needs to be graphically organized with semantic maps or outlines. The use of study guides will help students to ferret out the most important information.

Many teachers do not use textbooks for a number of reasons. Primarily, they find that textbooks no longer meet the needs of every student. Teachers prefer supplementary materials to textbooks because the latter provide an overview of content and rarely plumb the rich vein of ideas and events that teachers and students like. In addition, high school teachers need to supplement the text for students who read at the level of second and third graders as well as find books to challenge readers whose skills are beyond the level of the textbook. Moreover, funds for new textbooks are difficult to come by in these fiscally hard times. Thus the older textbooks now used are woefully out of date. Finally, there are not enough textbooks to go around. We observe students reading their textbooks in

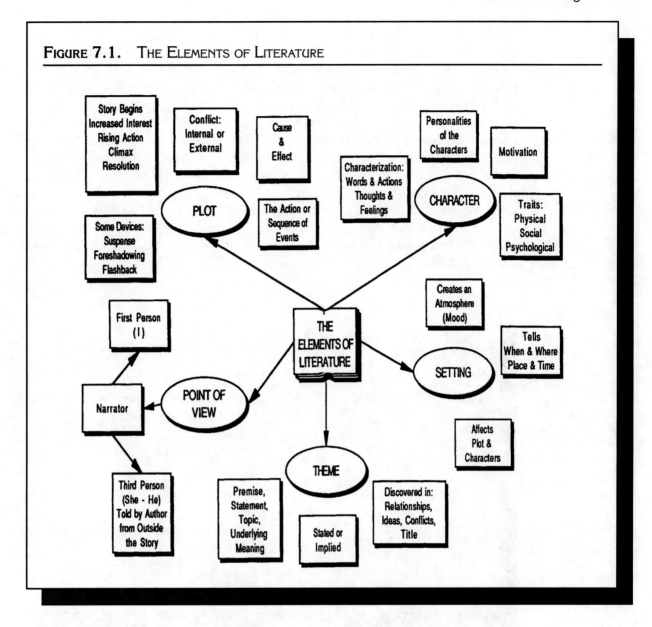

FIGURE 7.1.   THE ELEMENTS OF LITERATURE

class, because they need to share the same text with two other sections of students.

For these reasons, the use of tradebooks becomes a critical part of the curriculum. They are powerful supplements to provide students an understanding of content area topics, as well as an understanding of the human condition as it relates to those topics. Most importantly, students have a personal text to explore, one that is individually selected and read, rather than mandated and endured.

To cause literature to come alive or to engage students, we believe teachers need to familiarize themselves with a variety of trade books. For example, English teachers already teach literature. However, classics such as *To Kill a Mockingbird*

(Lee), *Romeo and Juliet* (Shakespeare), or *The Diary of a Young Girl* (Frank) can easily be supplemented with the use of related young adult novels. See Figure 7.2.

As reported in *Reading Today* (2006), Pappas (2006) suggests that typical information books are designed to give students more content whereas atypical and hybrid information books provide content by telling a story or relating an experience. For example, "the Magic School Bus series is mostly narrative, with elements of typical information text tossed in" (p. 32). Furthermore, Pappas argues "that book selection really matters in science instruction because children move from there-and-now experiences generated by hands-on or inquiry-based curriculum to the abstraction of general concepts and processes that define science as a discipline" (p. 32). It was also reported that Mohr (2006) conducted a study of 190 students in which 159 opted for nonfiction over fiction. This certainly reinforces that teachers should highlight the use of nonfiction books in classrooms.

It is important to plan activities in which students can respond to literature.

FIGURE 7.2.   SUPPLEMENTING CLASSICS

Classic	Supplement
To Kill a Mockingbird (Lee)	*Words by Heart* (Sebestyen) *More Than Meets the Eye* (Betancourt) *The Day that Elvis Came to Town* (Marino)
Romeo and Juliet (Shakespeare)	*The People Therein* (Lee) *When We First Met* (Mazer) *Romeo and Juliet/West Side Story* (Laurents)
Diary of a Young Girl (Frank)	*The Endless Steppe* (Hautzig) *The Upstairs Room* (Reiss)

Another consideration for classroom teachers is the gender gap for boys "when it" comes to language arts. Taylor (2004) states "In the same way that we need to promote success for girls in the areas of math and science, we need to promote literacy success for boys"(p. 291). In addition, he writes "As literacy educators, we believe in the power of literature to help our students understand life and create visions for the future. It is my hope as a parent and as an educator that we will continue to look closely at the unique problems associated with gender and close that gap in literacy so that the lives of all of our students, including the boys will be enriched by the power and beauty of literature" (p. 298). In this chapter's bibliography, we have cited websites and supplemental books particularly dedicated to young adult men's reading.

We believe that all content area teachers are also literacy teachers. Based on that premise, we must all recognize the importance of supplementing our curriculum with expository trade books, consider the needs of all students and send our graduates into the world as literate citizens.

Poetry

Poetry introduces students to a wonderful genre of literature. Too often students go from Mother Goose to Tennyson with little exposure to poetry between the two. No wonder many middle school students dislike poetry! They have not developed an ear for it, let alone a passion to enjoy poetry, read it and write it. We recommend that all content area teachers expose students to poetry. Take the time to find poems that supplement and extend their curriculum.

Kane and Rule (2004) discuss that content area teachers have used poetry for many years. Poetry taps the affective understanding of history, science and math as well as all other content areas of instruction. For example, Danks (1993) used poetry during a unit on the Holocaust to help her students to feel an emotional level of history—not just a cognitive understanding of the facts. Kane and Rule further cite Walders (2000) "who argued for weaving poetry throughout the science curriculum" (p. 660).

In her teacher education literacy classroom, Kane introduced a guest speaker, Audrey Rule, as a geologist/poet. Rule presented an "electronic slide show featuring several of her poems illustrated with striking photographs of gems, mineral specimens, and metaphorical images"(p. 660). "I could see that my students were learning on many levels: increasing their awareness of the motivating effects of connecting beauty with content information, adding new vocabulary while reinforcing prior knowledge of minerals, noticing metaphors in the verses, and thinking about ways they might create or use poetry themselves"(p. 662). Students were then asked to write their own curricular poems. The variety of poems written was astounding, celebrating and describing the lives of famous people, photons, circulatory system, and algorithms. The students used metaphors, similes, rhyme, alliteration and imagery.

Math

At first the students were apprehensive to write a poem about a content area topic. But once they got started and found out it would not be graded the words began to flow! Infusing poetry into the content areas of teaching takes little time, encourages students to read and write poetry and develop a deeper appreciation and understanding of the content topics. Kane and Rule (2004) included an inclusive bibliography of poetry for secondary students in the academic areas of study, which can be found in our reference list at the end of chapter.

Kane and Rule (2004) summarize their research article with suggested instructions for a content area assignment in poetry.

1. Within the curriculum select a topic of personal interest.
2. Find an object such as an idea or event related to the topic.
3. Write what you know about the object and how it reflects the curriculum concepts.
4. Using image-provoking phrases that are colorful to describe the object.

5. Write the moods and emotions related to the object and topic.
6. Consider other events similar to the object, especially comparable moods.
7. What is the message of your poem?
8. Select from the list of ideas those that support the message in the poem.
9. Write the poem.
10. Read the poem out loud and consider changing words and ideas to develop the images you desire.

Metaphor and Comprehension

Poetry depends on metaphor for the fullest extent of meaning. Metaphor is also important to comprehending other genres. Gallagher (2004) states, "We live in a world of metaphor, and those who can appreciate it are richer for it. I want my students to experience this richness. Beyond that, I want them to develop their ability to think metaphorically as a means of reaching deeper levels of comprehension" (p. 125). The OWL (Online Writing Lab) at Purdue University suggests three reasons why students should be taught the importance of metaphorical thinking.

1. Ordinary language is enlivened with metaphors.
2. Higher-level thinking is needed to interpret metaphors.
3. New meanings are created with metaphors.

Thus, as content area teachers we should not only consider poetry infused with metaphor but create instructional activities, particularly expository writing that maximizes the use of metaphor in assignments across the curriculum.

Folk Literature

Folk literature is a genre often overlooked in the content areas. It is important to study the folk literature of a country or a culture so students can better understand the people in terms of who they are, how they got to where they are, how their culture, country and government evolved. This also helps students to understand and accept differences and likenesses in a multicultural world. Please refer to the section, Strategies for Second Language Readers.

Many of the strategies presented in the next section can be used with narrative text, expository text, poetry and/or folktales. We encourage you to be creative and to think about how each strategy could be applied to the various types of text.

Literacy Strategies to Promote Literature Use

Activities that encourage students to respond to literature should be real communication exercises that stimulate their reactions and feelings. They should help guide students in making judgments and relate the reading to their own lives. Such strategies as: Preview Checklist, Pinwheels, and Venn Diagrams encourage students to share their own opinions and develop tolerance for others' ideas as well.

Preview Checklist

TABLE 1

_____

INSTRUCTIONAL SUMMARY OF PREVIEW CHECKLIST
_____

Literacy Strategy	**Preview Checklist**
Primary Focus	Establish prior knowledge
Learning Principles	❑ Talk Time ❑ Metacognitive Experiences
When to Use	Before reading
Goals: National or State Literacy Standards	❑ Use a variety of reading strategies to increase comprehension and learning ❑ Read for enjoyment and information ❑ Establish a purpose for reading a selection
Materials	Preview checklist
Time	30 minutes

Students need to establish prior knowledge and to arouse a curiosity and interest about the reading selection. When we go to a bookstore, we usually preview a book to decide if we want to spend our money to purchase it. We may have heard about it from a friend, read a review about it, or noted that it was written by an author whose style and topics interest us. We read the book jacket, peruse the chapter titles or study graphics, charts and pictures. If we purchase the book, we usually have a plan for reading it. If it is fiction, we delve right in. If it is non-fiction, we proceed more slowly, clarify vocabulary and use the graphs and charts for further clarification. If it is poetry, we look for symbolism, metaphors, etc. As teachers we need to teach our students to go through this type of process. One strategy that might help is the Preview Checklist which follows:

❑ Is the book fiction or non-fiction?
❑ How will I adjust my reading rate?
❑ Are there visual aids such as graphs, charts or pictures to clarify information?
❑ Have I read other books by this author?
❑ What is the author's style?
❑ What do I know about this topic?
❑ Why am I going to read this selection?
❑ What do I want to learn?

Students should apply the use of the above checklist in establishing a preview of the reading selection. This will also help most readers to overcome their inability to select appropriate text. Good, strategic readers think about what they already know about the subject, set a purpose for reading and focus their attention on the reading selection. Next, they monitor their comprehension automatically. They use a "fix-up strategy" when they do not understand what they are reading. See Chapter 3 for "fix-up" strategies such as the SQ3R.

Wedwick and Wutz (2006) suggest that "Independent book selection is of particular significance for adolescent readers as they continue to define who they are as readers" (p. 28). They found that adolescent students' ability to select books was very limited. Their students were not finishing books that they had self-selected, obviously their selections were not a good match. They developed a tool to help students to self-select books at their independent reading level without the help of having the books leveled. The tool, called BOOKMATCH (Wutz & Wedwick, 2005), is an acronym for the following:

> Book length
> Ordinary language
> Organization,
> Knowledge prior to the book
> Manageable text
> Appeal to genre
> Topic appropriateness
> Connection

High interest
When Wedwick and Wutz (2006) interviewed their students they found that what students used as criteria to select a just right book was very different from the criteria used in BOOKMATCH. They adopted procedures to facilitate this process.

Procedures.
1. They introduced students to the new criteria using small groups to discuss the application of BOOKMATCH and the individual selections.
2. They modeled the application of BOOKMATCH through a think-aloud process.
3. After the students used BOOKMATCH for the first time, the researchers met with each student to discuss the book selection process and final book choice.

The students did agree that using BOOKMATCH helped them to be more aware of their "preferences and processes as independent readers" (p. 22). The following form was developed to help students to properly seleet a book (p. 23):

Criteria for Choosing Books	Student Comments
Book Length ❏ Is this a good length for me? Is it too little, just right or too much? ❏ Do I feel like committing to this book?	
Ordinary Language ❏ Turn to any page and read aloud. ❏ Does it sound natural?	

- Does it flow? Does it make sense?

Organization
- How is the book structured?
- Am I comfortable with the print size and number of words on a page?
- Are chapters short or long?

Knowledge Prior to Book
- Read the title, view the cover page, or read the summary on the back of the book.
- What do I already know about this topic, author, or illustrator?

Manageable Text
- Begin reading the book.
- Are the words in the book easy, just right or hard?
- Do I understand what I read?

Appeal to Genre
- What is the genre?
- Have I read this genre before?
- Do I like or expect to like this genre?

Topic Appropriateness
- Am I comfortable with the topic of this book?
- Do I feel like I am ready to read about this topic?

Connection
- Can I relate to this book?
- Does this book remind me of anything or anyone?

High-Interest
- Am I interested in the topic of this book?
- Am I interested in the author/ illustrator?
- Do others recommend this book?

Wedwick & Wutz (2006, p. 29)

It becomes apparent that individual book selection is critical and we suggest that content area teachers use the preview checklist, BOOKMATCH, or their variation of this process. We need to provide the scaffolding that will help the students to independently select a book and know when to remove it once they have become self-reliant.

Character Map

Beck, McKeown, McCaslin & Burkett (1979)

Content area teachers using supplementary trade books to enhance their curriculum may find this character map activity helpful. The character map helps students to better remember and understand narrative text. They can be used to organize vocabulary presented in narrative form. The character map encourage students to analyze the structure of a story: setting, plot, theme and character development. Students begin to realize how stories are organized and what to expect. Incidents from social studies also lend themselves to this activity.

Further, knowledge of structure encourages students to predict or interact with the text. Specific vocabulary unique to the setting, plot, theme and character development can be used in the prediction or analysis of the story. See Figure 7.3 for an example of a story map.

FIGURE 7.3. CHARACTER MAP FOR *ANIMAL FARM (1946)* BY GEORGE ORWELL, NEW AMERICAN LIBRARY

Character 1	Character 2	Character 3
Name: Old Major	**Name:** Comrade Snowball	**Name:** Napoleon
Adjectives that describe: highly regarded, short-lived	**Adjectives that describe:** boorish, vivacious pig	**Adjectives that describe:** fierce-looking, Berkshire boar
Setting: a place beyond good and evil	**Problem:** suffering or prosperity are unconnected to ethical merit	**Resolution:** accountability
Descriptors: symbolized as a farm	**Descriptors:** "rebelliousness against the truth revealed"	**Descriptors:** equality, peace, democracy

THEME(S) *Devastation of Totalitarianism*

Your Turn

Name _____ Date _____ Subject Area _____

DIRECTIONS: Select a story or an incident and complete the chart.

Character 1	Character 2	Character 3
Name:	Name:	Name:
Adjectives that describe:	Adjectives that describe:	Adjectives that describe:
Setting:	Problem:	Resolution:
Descriptors:	Descriptors:	Descriptors:
THEME(S):		

Pinwheels

TABLE 2

INSTRUCTIONAL SUMMARY OF PINWHEELS

Literacy Strategy	Pinwheels
Primary Focus	Individual discussion strategy
Learning Principles	❑ Active Involvement in Searching for Meaning ❑ Talk Time
When to Use	After reading
Goals: National or State Literacy Standards	❑ Increase evaluative comprehension ❑ Demonstrate how the reader is influenced by what is read ❑ Communicate knowledge of the topic
Materials	Game sheet
Time	30 minutes

This strategy is useful for the teacher who wants 100% participation from students. It encourages students to form educated opinions, and to develop their listening to what others have to contribute to a discussion based on a reading selection.

All students in a pinwheel must participate and usually learn that more ideas are generated from a group than from any one individual. Group problem solving is powerful.

After the teacher has read a story or an article to the students she then assigns them to form pinwheels.

Procedure.
1. Students are put into groups of preferably six. This can be adapted to meet odd numbers.
2. Three students sit in the middle of the group with their backs to the center. Each of the additional students sits facing one of the students in the middle.
3. Each of the three students in the middle is assigned a different discussion question. The questions can be formulated by the teacher or students.
4. Students on the outside proceed clockwise to each member of the center to discuss that member's question.
5. A recorder summarizes on butcher paper the various solutions for each question.
6. Summaries are posted and the various groups of six circulate to read what other groups have suggested.

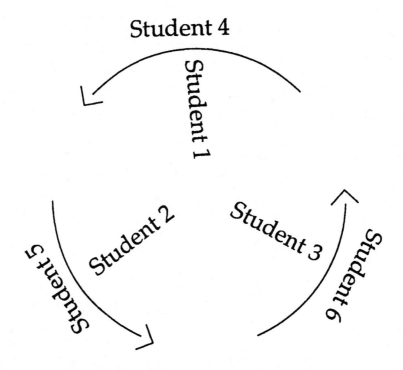

Example of Pinwheel: Biology

A biology teacher wants students to begin a discussion of environmental cleanup. The book selected to make an impact is a children's picture book. This choice should not offend secondary teachers or their students. Many picture books have strong messages that older students can find stimulating as well as enjoyable when read for a more mature purpose. After reading *The Last Free Bird* by Stone, or *The Lorax* by Dr. Seuss to the class, a pinwheel discussion would begin. Students would form pinwheels and the assigned questions to be discussed might be:

1. Why is it important to save the environment?
2. What can students do immediately to help save the environment?
3. What is the government doing to support these efforts?

TEACHER TALK

The pinwheel is a marvelous strategy. It requires that every single student participate in a discussion.

Graphic Question-Answer Relationship

TABLE 3

INSTRUCTIONAL SUMMARY OF GRAPHIC QUESTION-ANSWER RELATIONSHIP

Literacy Strategy	Graphic Question-Answer Relationship
Primary Focus	❏ Discussions ❏ Comprehension
Learning Principles	❏ Active Involvement in Searching for Meaning ❏ Thought-demanding Activity
When to Use	After analyzing a picture, graph, table, etc.
Goals: National or State Literacy Standards	❏ Promote comprehension ❏ Increase awareness of question types ❏ Draw connections between reading and other experiences
Materials	Role sheets
Time	40 minutes

Picture books are a wonderful resource for content area teachers. They have become sophisticated and appeal to students. Language arts teachers can use them as models for the development of the literary elements of setting, character development, plot, style and theme.

Picture books can serve as a catalyst for discussions in content area classrooms (Cassady, 1998; Miller, 1998). Content area teachers can find picture books on their topics and use what we believe is an excellent strategy for better understanding Question-Answer Relationships. In the workshops we conduct for content area teachers, the Question-Answer Relationship (QAR) Graphic Organizer has been popular with the middle school and high school teachers. We have selected the picture book, *The Last Free Bird* (Stone), to demonstrate the use of illustrations for extending literal, interpretive and evaluative levels of thinking. We are using the same title as we used in the Pinwheel strategy to show how a particular title for a content area, in this case, biology, can be used a number of ways. Teachers do not have to find a huge number of picture books to support their curriculum. However, do remember that variety is the spice of life! The following Figure 7.4 demonstrates a lesson plan for the Graphic QAR:

FIGURE 7.4. GRAPHIC QAR LESSON PLAN:

Lesson Plan: Environmental Science

Grade: 10

Topic: Pollution

Purpose: To help students gain knowledge of environmental pollution through the analysis of an illustration from the picture book, *The Last Free Bird.*

State Content/Literacy Standards:
1. Promote comprehension and question strategies for the literal, interpretive and evaluative levels of thinking;
2. Increase awareness of question types;
3. Draw connections between reading and other experiences;
4. Increase discussion abilities.

Student Objectives:
- ❑ Students will be able to analyze a picture from the perspective of **literal**—what they see right there, **interpretive**—how they think and search for the meaning the artist communicates, and **evaluative**—their opinion of what they think is the message conveyed.
- ❑ Students will be able to better understand the term environmental pollution.
- ❑ Students will come to a conclusion regarding how to save the environment.

Introduction:
- ❑ Ask students to review the meaning of literal, interpretive and evaluative levels.
- ❑ Ask students to brainstorm how they might apply these levels to pictures as opposed to a reading.
- ❑ Show students a picture from *The Last Free Bird* (Stone).

Learning Activity:
1. Distribute and explain the Graphic QAR Organizer:

    Directions:
    - ❑ Write the objects that you see in the picture (literal).
    - ❑ Write what the artist/illustrator means by using the objects in the picture (interpretive).
    - ❑ Write the message you think the artist or illustrator is conveying (evaluative).
    - ❑ Model the application of the Graphic QAR Organizer using the guide and a picture for students to discuss, as a class, and to give you information to complete the guide. Record the information on large chart paper.

GRAPHIC QAR Organizer

Literal	Interpretive	Evaluative
What do you see **Right There** in the picture, graph or chart?	**Think & Search** for the meaning the artist/illustrator is communicating.	In **Your Own Opinion**, what is the message of this visual?

FIGURE 7.4.   GRAPHIC QAR LESSON PLAN (CONT.)

1. Select groups of five students. Appoint a facilitator and a recorder/reporter.
2. Direct students to respond to the three levels of questions using the Graphic QAR Organizer.
3. As a class complete the Graphic QAR Organizer on a chart or transparency as information is given from the reporter.

Closure. Students discuss the application of the three levels of question/answer relationships (See QAR in Chapter 4) to pictures and the importance of using pictures, graphs, tables, charts or any other resources when one is reading for content information. Students complete a Graphic QAR Organizer for an assigned illustration.

Evaluation. Students' Graphic QAR Organizer is assessed for understanding of the three levels of question/answer relationships as applied to an illustration.

Venn Diagram

TABLE 4

INSTRUCTIONAL SUMMARY OF VENN DIAGRAM

Literacy Strategy	Venn Diagram
Primary Focus	Comprehension
Learning Principles	❏ Talk Time ❏ Variety of Ways to Organize Information
When to Use	After reading a narrative text, expository text, poetry or folktales
Goals: National or State Literacy Standards	❏ Promote comprehension ❏ Structure information to make connections ❏ Read for enjoyment
Materials	Venn Diagram template
Time	40 minutes

This activity enables students to work through the process of comparing and contrasting events, characters, conflicts, or ideas in two different works. In the overlapping portion of the circles common characteristics are listed. In the outer portions of each circle are recorded those characteristics that are unique to it.

Procedure.
1. Draw a Venn Diagram.

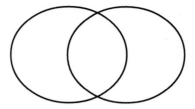

2. Decide the two pieces of writing to be compared and contrasted.
3. Along the outside section of each circle, write characteristics that are unique to that work.
4. In the center—the overlapping section—place those characteristics that each book shares.

Example of Venn Diagram: Social Studies/Language Arts
Using *Across Five Aprils* (Hunt) and *Steal Away Home* (Ruby) compare and contrast information about the Civil War that each book contains.

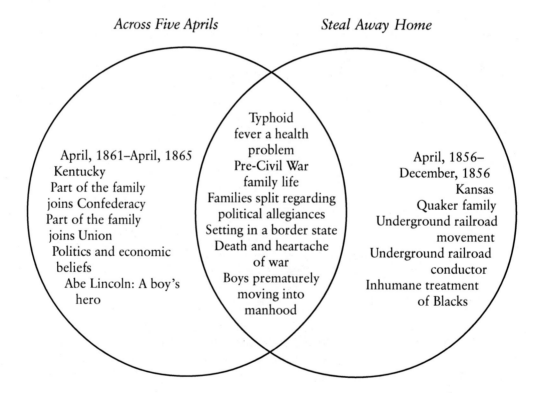

Across Five Aprils

April, 1861–April, 1865
Kentucky
Part of the family
joins Confederacy
Part of the family
joins Union
Politics and economic
beliefs
Abe Lincoln: A boy's
hero

Typhoid
fever a health
problem
Pre-Civil War
family life
Families split regarding
political allegiances
Setting in a border state
Death and heartache
of war
Boys prematurely
moving into
manhood

Steal Away Home

April, 1856–
December, 1856
Kansas
Quaker family
Underground railroad
movement
Underground railroad
conductor
Inhumane treatment
of Blacks

Your Turn

Name _____ Date _____ Content Area _____

Trade books compared and contrasted _____

DIRECTIONS: Complete the Venn Diagram with characteristics from two books in your specialty area that you could use to model the process of comparing and contrasting two pieces of literature.

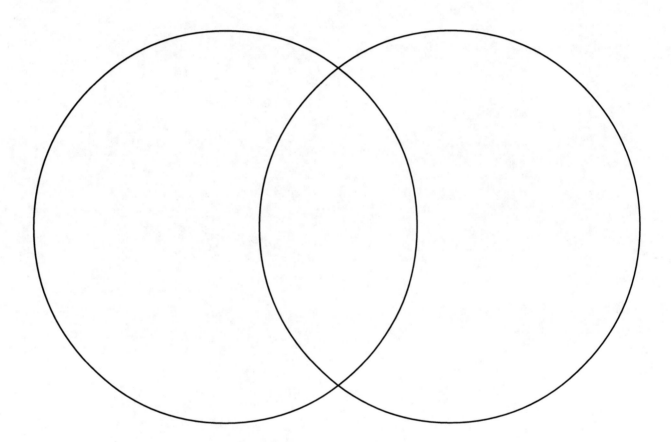

Writing Activities

Reading and writing are interrelated and it is natural for students to respond to literature using a variety of writing activities such as: Story Maps, Shape Story Maps, Story Pyramids and Book Report Cards. Many other extended writing activities can be found in Chapter 6, Writing Strategies. All of these activities provide a structure that captures essential information about the book a student is reading. Using these structures, students then organize their thoughts to create longer writing pieces.

Balance literature discussions and writing activities.

Story Maps

TABLE 5

INSTRUCTIONAL SUMMARY OF STORY MAPS

Literacy Strategy	Story Maps
Primary Focus	Literary Elements
Learning Principles	❑ Way to Organize Information ❑ Active Involvement in Searching for Meaning
When to Use	After reading
Goals: National or State Literacy Standards	Promote comprehension
Materials	Story map template
Time	40 minutes

The skeletal structure in this map provides a summary of the parts of the story. Using this guide students walk through a story's integral sections. In reconstructing the story students' thinking is guided, and information about the story is grounded. By the time they reach the "Story Theme" section, most students will have a concrete knowledge base to draw on and can express their own idea about the theme of the story. In addition, they can make some predictions or draw conclusions about the important message the author conveyed in this story.

Story maps help students to focus on integral elements.

Procedure. Students complete a story map organizer such as that in Figure 7.5. Again teachers should model this activity by working with the students on an overhead. As students gain practice using this structure, they learn how to think about narrative text and can move later to an independent general discussion activity in small groups or as a member of the larger class.

The story map can also take on a shape that represents the book. For example using the book *Stone Fox* (Gardiner) students might design an organizer such as that in Figure 7.6.

FIGURE 7.5.   STORY MAP

The setting/main characters

Statement of the problem

> Event 1

> Event 2

> Event 3

> Event 4

Statement of the solution

Story theme (What is this story really about?)

Important messages

FIGURE 7.6.   SHAPE STORY MAP

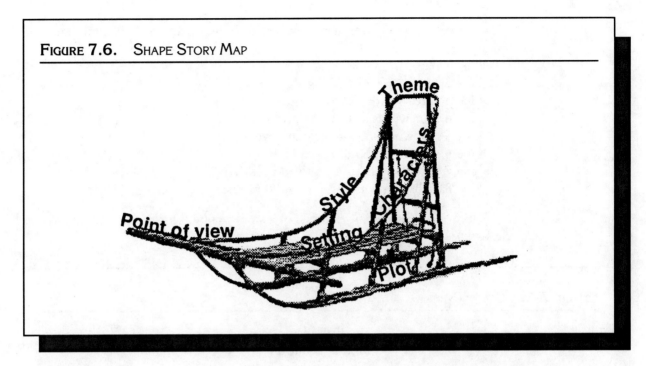

Story Pyramid

TABLE 6

INSTRUCTIONAL SUMMARY OF STORY PYRAMID

Literacy Strategy	Story Pyramid
Primary Focus	Poetic summary
Learning Principles	❑ Active Involvement in Searching for Meaning ❑ Variety of Ways to Organize Information
When to Use	After reading
Goals: National or State Literacy Standards	Promote comprehension and writing
Materials	Pyramid template
Time	40 minutes

This is an organizer in which students summarize the literary elements of a book. Teachers usually use this as an example of a structured poem. This particular exercise demands that students use the most appropriate vocabulary in a succinct manner.

Procedure. Students complete a pyramid-shaped organizer that includes the following:

Line 1 name of main character
Line 2 two words describing the character
Line 3 three words describing the setting
Line 4 four words stating the problem
Line 5 five words about the main event
Line 6 six words about a second event
Line 7 seven words about a third event
Line 8 eight words that refer to the problem solution

We have found that story pyramids are especially popular with students.

Figure 7.7 illustrates an example of a story pyramid for the story, *Priscilla and the Wimps*, by Richard Peck.

FIGURE 7.7. STORY PYRAMID

Priscilla
Bionic, beautiful
Lockers, cafeteria, halls
Overcomes the gang leader
Gang sells passes for eating
Priscilla catches gang leader off-guard
Priscilla holds gang leader in a hammerlock
Leader shoved in locker; school closes for week!

Anita M. 1997

Book Report Cards

TABLE 7

INSTRUCTIONAL SUMMARY OF BOOK REPORT CARDS

Literacy Strategy	Book Report Cards
Primary Focus	Book, poetry or folktale summary
Learning Principles	❑ Thought-demanding Activity ❑ Active Involvement in Searching for Meaning
When to Use	After reading
Goals: National or State Literacy Standards	Promote comprehension and writing
Materials	Report card template
Time	40 minutes

Students evaluate a literary element of literature using a "report card form." This report card would vary in that the descriptors would be selected by the students as they respond to the piece of literature. In the following example we have provided a model that explores the main character in *The Double Helix,* the scientist, James Watson. Characterization particularly lends itself to this strategy.

Procedure. An area of evaluation is determined by the students or teacher or both working together. Students can come up with the descriptors for the area of evaluation or the teacher can predetermine these. Students complete the report card with grades and their comments supporting the grade they gave. See Figure 7.8.

FIGURE 7.8.   BOOK REPORT CARD

Title: *The Double Helix*
Author: James Watson
Story Element: Characterization of James

Area of Evaluation	Grade	Comments
Perseverance	B+	Connected ideas from prominent thinkers
Materialistic	D	Not interested in comfortable living
Divergent thinking	A	Went outside "the box"
Problem-solving	A	Hammered out solutions
Confidence	B+	Assured of his mission
Conventional	D	Followed his own drummer

Inclusion Techniques

Students with special needs can be introduced to literature that supplements the core literature. In addition, English as a Second Language (ESL) students can be introduced to a variety of books, including picture books that are written in the student's native language, and easy-to-read books that would be appropriate to the student's reading level of ability in English. In Chapter 3 we discussed the research findings regarding how to meet the needs of inclusive students. The same principles apply with regard to the use of literature with learners with special needs.

There are many high interest/ low readability supplemental books available for learners with special needs.

Books have the power of taking every reader to other worlds. They mirror the human condition in numerous and illustrative ways. In addition, books bring readers together. What is more fitting than a curriculum in the inclusive classroom that is thematically oriented, and uses young adult literature as the basis for learning about content as it affects or is affected by life situations.

In thematic learning teachers and students examine one area in depth from complex and multiple perspectives. Typically, teachers at the middle and high school levels teach around a set of issues. Issues like survival of the planet, voices of the underprivileged, change, peace, careers, health, etc. allow teachers to bring a host of outside materials into the classroom. Books on every level can be found to meet most of the needs of the students served.

This in-depth approach is critical for the special needs students. In the past, students with disabilities had a difficult time in relating and learning content when it was offered in brief isolated learning blocks. Thematic orientations demonstrate how universal connections and relationships are constructed from specific content.

Keech (1997)

Imagine the classroom that is studying a unit on the Titanic. Beginning with a class reading of Robert Ballard's *Exploring the Titanic,* the students branch out to find related books in their community libraries as well as their school library. Math facts from the students' reading are turned into story problems; marine life, and the ecology of the sea are studied, and the mores of the Edwardian time are contrasted with the layering of classes aboard the Titanic. A class play, art murals, and authentic costumes are created by the students of this class. Further, imagine today's students learning to dance the waltz in order to fully round out the setting by including the music from 1912 in the student written, directed and produced play. What student wouldn't leave this experience enriched through research, writing, drama, art and music, knowing a lot about the content as well as the process of gaining that knowledge.

Brendtro, Brokenleg & Van Bockern (1990)

In an inclusive school important values support the curriculum. Acceptance, belonging and a sense of community are nurtured along with reading, writing and relationships. Writing from a Native American perspective, Brendtro, Brokenleg, and Van Bockern (1990) suggest that these values create a child's "Circle of Courage. This right to "belong is not only a cultural belonging of Native people, but a cultural birthright for all the world's children" (p. 36).

Schools today are increasingly seen as a haven for reclaiming youth labeled "at risk," disabled, homeless, gay or lesbian, and so forth. Students in a literature laden class see characters like themselves who meet head-on untoward challenges and develop admirably for having done so. Teachers can use several strategies to foster this cultural birthright of belonging as well as teach content.

Story Frames

TABLE 8

INSTRUCTIONAL SUMMARY OF STORY FRAME

Literacy Strategy	Story Frame
Primary Focus	Literary Elements
Learning Principles	Thought-demanding Activity
When to Use	After reading
Goals: National or State Literacy Standards	❏ Promote comprehension ❏ Read for enjoyment
Materials	Story frame template
Time	40 minutes

The reader will focus on the basic literary elements mentioned earlier in this chapter. Teachers use story frames to assess knowledge of a story and reactions to the story elements. Because they are structured notetaking strategies, they enable even poor readers to successfully locate and think about information read. After students use this activity a few times, they eventually can complete questions independently that the teacher or their peers would raise in discussion circles. These frames provide a schematic for story elements like plot, setting, character analysis, or character comparisons.

Procedure. Students are asked to complete a generic story frame. This frame is designed by the teacher and features the elements you want to highlight. Developing a similar story frame on an overhead and completing several with students as well as talking about how information is found to support their responses serve to simulate the thinking process and help students see how readers select responses. The story frame provides an excellent "Think-Aloud" opportunity modeling the reading process used by capable readers. See Figure 7.9.

FIGURE 7.9.   STORY FRAME EXAMPLE

Story summary with one character included:

Our story is about _____.

_____ is an important character in our story. _____ tried to _____. The story ends when _____.

Important idea or plot:

In this story the problem starts when _____.

After that, _____. Next, _____.

Then, _____. The problem is finally solved when _____.

The story ends _____.

Setting:

This story takes place _____.

I know this because the author uses the words "_____."

Other clues that show where and when the story takes place are _____

_____

_____.

Character analysis:

_____ is an important character in our story. _____ is important because _____.

Once she/he _____.

Another time, _____.

I think that _____ (character's name) is _____ (character's trait) because _____

_____.

Character comparison:

_____ and _____ are two characters in our story.

_____ (character's name) is _____ (trait) while _____ (other character) is _____ (trait)

For instance, _____ tries to _____ and _____

learns a lesson when _____

_____

_____

_____.

Adapted from: Fowler, Gerald. Developing comprehension skills in primary students through the use of story frames. *The Reading Teacher*, November, 1982.

Graphic Organizer

TABLE 9

INSTRUCTIONAL SUMMARY OF A GRAPHIC ORGANIZER

Literacy Strategy	Graphic Organizer
Primary Focus	Comprehension
Learning Principles	❏ Way to Organize Information ❏ Thought-demanding Activity
When to Use	After reading
Goals: National or State Literacy Standards	❏ Promote comprehension ❏ Draw connections of story elements
Materials	Graphic organizer for story elements
Time	30 minutes

As we described in Chapter 2, a graphic organizer is a comprehensive, hierarchical representation of concepts. Students with learning problems have a tendency to understand and retrieve information in linear fashion. They see facts and ideas as a list of things to study and know. A teacher who uses a graphic organizer or map to demonstrate the critical elements of a book that students are reading helps students see the connections among the elements of the story as well as remember them in a related manner.

TEACHER TALK ———————————————————————————

One of my most severe dyslexics has just gone wild with the mapping technique. She says it helps her keep track of things. For example, when reading a book, she can keep track of characters, their characteristics, and their activities. She has read the Margaret E. Bell Series in the last few weeks, from *Watch for a Tall White Sail* through *Ride Out the Storm*. The mapping she does makes it ideal to discuss the book one-on-one. It makes it easy to show relationships, and I have been able to expand her flow-charting designs. She's excited about reading and making more maps.

LeOra J. in *Tama, et al., 1990, p. 118.*

We have presented procedures for designing a graphic organizer in Chapter 2. The following graphic organizer (Figure 7.10) takes a delightful book, *Just Call Me Stupid* (Birdseye, 1996), about a nonreader grappling with his dilemma. It shows the relationships among integral parts of the story. The student could be given a frame and asked to fill the sections in as she reads or the teacher could guide this process as the conversation proceeds.

*Graphic organizers guide **all** students through the most essential parts of their reading.*

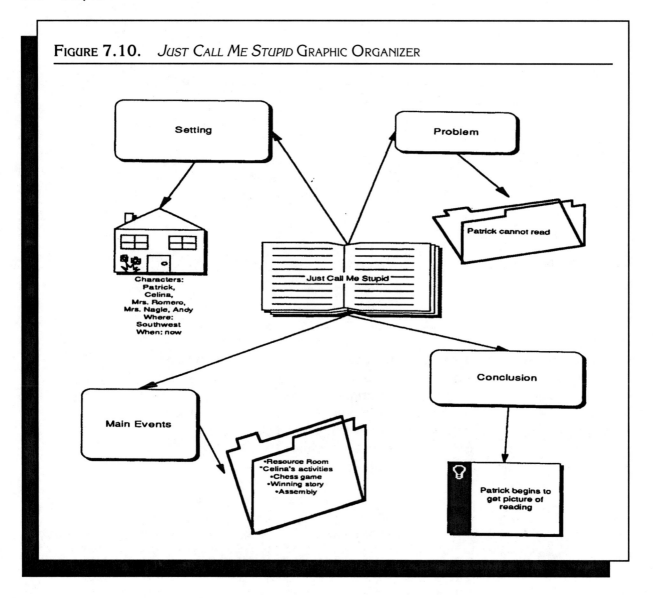

FIGURE 7.10.   *JUST CALL ME STUPID* GRAPHIC ORGANIZER

Your Turn

Name _____ Date _____ Subject Area _____

DIRECTIONS: Design a graphic organizer using a fiction or nonfiction trade book that you would use with your students in your subject area.

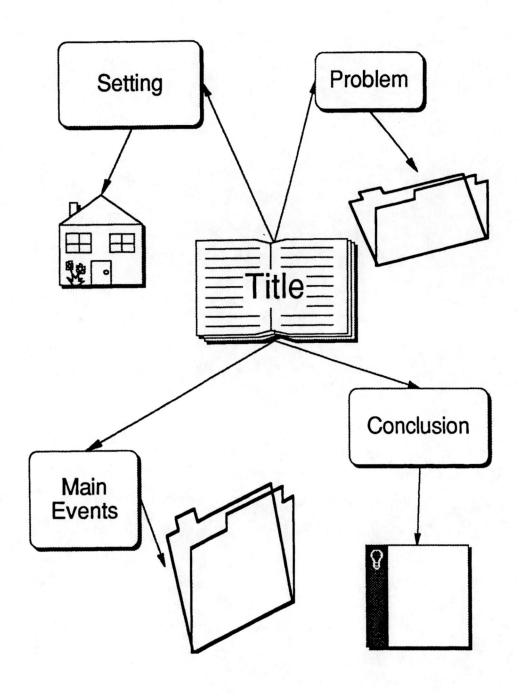

People Search

TABLE 10

INSTRUCTIONAL SUMMARY OF PEOPLE SEARCH

Literacy Strategy	People Search
Primary Focus	Comprehension
Learning Principles	❏ Active Involvement in Searching for Meaning ❏ Talk Time
When to Use	After reading
Goals: National or State Literacy Standards	❏ Promote comprehension ❏ Identify literary elements of a story
Materials	Graphic organizer for story elements
Time	30 minutes

Once students have become familiar with the literature or story elements it might be fun to engage them in a People Search. In a People Search the element of character is emphasized. The task is for students to circulate among themselves and to find someone in the class whose name can be entered in each box. This can also be used at the beginning of the year as a get acquainted activity. The nice thing about this activity is that special students can participate with the rest of the class and feel that they are an integral part of it. See Figure 7.11.

Strategies for Second Language Readers

"We need a range of strategies to cope with the different students and their challenges" (Burke, 1999, p. 235). In this section we will look readers' theater, and the Herringbone Technique as strategies for second language readers. These activities involve oral language development which should support the needs of students whose primary language is not English.

FIGURE 7.11. PEOPLE SEARCH

Has read *Harry Potter and the Sorcerer's Stone* by J.K. Rowling.	Loves fantasy literature, e.g., *Lord of the Rings, The Lion, the Witch and the Wardrobe.*	Knows a busybody like Mrs. Dursley, Potter's aunt.
Has been to a railroad station in London like King's Cross.	Is a Muggle, a nonmagic person.	Knows of someone who was an orphan.
Has gone to a specialized school, e.g., magnet, arts, technical.	Plays, coaches soccer or has a brother or sister who does.	Has seen an owl lately.

Readers' Theater

TABLE 11

INSTRUCTIONAL SUMMARY OF READERS' THEATER

Literacy Strategy	Readers' Theatre
Primary Focus	Comprehension
Learning Principles	❑ Talk Time ❑ Active Involvement in Searching for Meaning
When to Use	After reading
Goals: National or State Literacy Standards	❑ Promote comprehension ❑ Enjoy literature
Materials	Story for adaptation for roles
Time	50 minutes

Readers' Theater is the oral presentation of written material. Unlike most theatrical productions, however, students do not memorize lines, don elaborate costumes, or design settings or props. Instead, students stand or sit and read dialogue that they usually have created from their textbook or trade book readings.

Through this activity students learn how to interpret text and practice oral expression and fluency.

Procedure. There are five basic steps to follow in creating Readers' Theater.

1. Select stories. You may use:
   a. easy to read stories, narrative or expository.
   b. fairly short stories.
   c. stories having not more than six characters.
   d. stories having not more than two narrators.
   e. prepared scripts for all grades, K-12, available from Readers' Theatre Script Service, P.O. Box 178333, San Diego, CA 92177.

2. Write and prepare scripts:
   a. based on books, poetry, music lyrics.
   b. condensed versions of stories.
   c. color code parts so students can easily follow the script.
   d. put scripts in a folder.

3. Assign roles.

4. Read and reread (rehearse).
   a. Know story well.
   b. Read parts as the character would speak.

5. Performance.
   a. Simply stand or sit and deliver lines.
   b. Read lines with expression and fluency.

How do learners with special needs benefit from Readers' Theater?

Readers' Theater is especially appropriate for the learner with special needs. Students have a reason to read their parts a number of times. Rereadings will help students to become more fluent and expressive as a result of increased familiarity of the story and their specific role.

Content area teachers can use Readers' Theater for bringing to life historical characters, musicians, artists, athletes, scientists and other characters who influenced the ideas and times students are studying.

For example, the music teacher might want to consider a script about Mozart, Bach, Debussy or others. A good book, music teachers or their students might script, is *Lives of the Musicians: Good Times, Bad Times and What the Neighbors Thought* (Krull, 1993). This book presents brief stories of twenty notable musicians.

Figure 7.12 demonstrates an example of a reader's theater script that one of our student's wrote. It serves as a summary of the information and is a means for assessing the student's understanding of plant organelles.

Herringbone Technique

TABLE 12

INSTRUCTIONAL SUMMARY OF HERRINGBONE TECHNIQUE

Literacy Strategy	Herringbone Technique
Primary Focus	Comprehension
Learning Principles	❑ Way to Organize Information ❑ Active Involvement in Searching for Meaning
When to Use	After reading
Goals: National or State Literacy Standards	❑ Promote comprehension ❑ Promote notetaking
Materials	Herringbone graphic organizer
Time	40 minutes

The Herringbone is a graphic organizer to record essential elements of fiction and non-fiction.

For second language readers we believe that the inclusion of folk literature that represents the student's specific culture helps students to identify with the topic and to "feel at home" with the instruction. It is also a means for other students to learn about a culture. Folk literature reflects the roots of the people. In social studies we can study the constitution of a country to learn about the people or we can study the folk literature.

FIGURE 7.12.   READER'S THEATER FOR BIOLOGY

Character parts (PLANT ORGANELLES)

Cell wall

Cell membrane

Chloroplast

Cytoplasm

Nucleus

Vacuole

The Story of the Plant Cell

Nucleus:	Hey, we need some more energy in this cell!
Vacuole:	Yes, I am almost out of stored energy.
Chloroplast:	Well… we are going to need some sunlight, carbon dioxide, and water.
Cell membrane:	If the cell wall will help out, I can get the carbon dioxide and water.
Cell wall:	I am busy providing support for the cell, but I will help the cell membrane with transporting necessary substances.
Cytoplasm:	Yeah… and I could help provide a jelly-like substance for some of the chemical reactions.
Nucleus:	Chloroplasts, we will need you to absorb sunlight for the necessary energy to power photosynthesis.
Chloroplast:	No problem, that is why I have these green pigments that make the plant green.
Vacuole:	My, that is some great sugar and water you chloroplasts made!
Chloroplast:	Yes, that is what happens in photosynthesis. The sun helps me turn carbon dioxide and oxygen into sugar and water. Isn't that awesome.!!??
Nucleus:	I appreciate when you all follow my instructions.

Paul Lardy Pacific University

A strategy to use to investigate folk literature is the use of the Herringbone Technique. Using *The Two Mountains: An Aztec Legend* (Retold, Kimmel, 2000) the following application in Figure 7.13 of the Herringbone Technique helps students to build comprehension and appreciate folk literature, as well as deepening their understanding of another culture. The Herringbone Technique is an organizer that uses the who, what, when, where, how and why of a story and culminates with a summary of the main idea of a piece of writing. The following information has been condensed from the text:

Who:

Tonatiuh, the sun god, Ixcocauquil, son of Tonatiuh, Mixtli, goddess of the moon, Coyolxauhqui, daughter of Mixtli, Mictlantecuhtli, lord of death, Tlaloc, the rain god.

What:

Ixcocauquil is tempted to go beyond the garden wall; after marrying Coyolxauhqui, they are tempted to visit the earth; they became mortals; after death they were transformed into two mountains overlooking the Valley of Mexico.

When:

Long ago

Where:

Third Heaven and earth

How:

Through determination Ixcocauquil journeyed across the sky; after meeting Coyolxauhqui, his love, continued meeting secretly; by disobeying his father's wishes, Ixcocauquil and Coyolxauhqui are tempted to see what is so special about earth that they are forbidden to visit there; banished to become mortals on earth; after the death of Coyolxauhqui, Ixcocauquil will not leave her; the gods decide to let them be together as long as the earth endures and transformed them into two mountains.

Why:

Legend of the beginning of men and women and reminiscent of the story of Adam and Eve

Main Idea:

There are similarities around the world regarding cultures and their beginnings. This legend explains the beginning of Aztec men and women as seen through the eyes of the gods of the Third Heaven. Interestingly, it parallels the story of Adam and Eve using temptation as the source of evil.

The next step is for the student to condense the information even further. In the Herringbone Technique organizer the information forms one or more statements. See Figure 7.13.

We believe that strategies such as the Herringbone used with folk literature will help to build acceptance and trust with students who have diverse backgrounds. Jackson (1994) recommends that to build trust with various students requires showing an interest in their ethnic backgrounds. Folk literature will certainly encourage teachers to show their interest in each student's heritage.

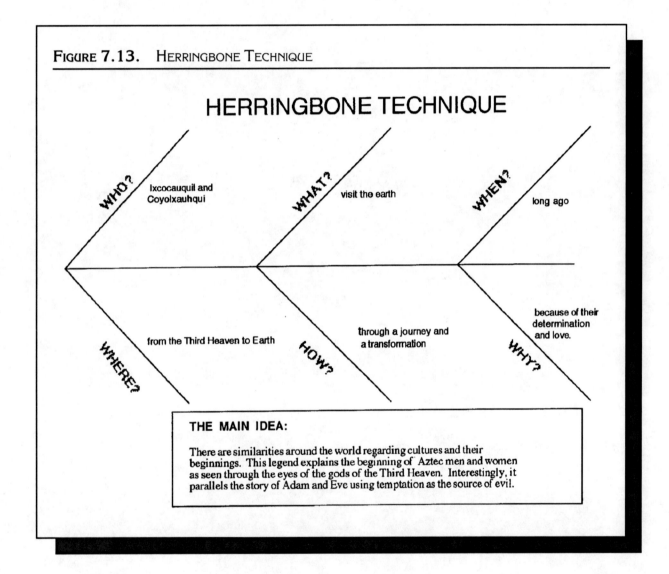

FIGURE 7.13. HERRINGBONE TECHNIQUE

HERRINGBONE TECHNIQUE

WHO? Ixcocauquil and Coyolxauhqui

WHAT? visit the earth

WHEN? long ago

WHERE? from the Third Heaven to Earth

HOW? through a journey and a transformation

WHY? because of their determination and love.

THE MAIN IDEA:

There are similarities around the world regarding cultures and their beginnings. This legend explains the beginning of Aztec men and women as seen through the eyes of the gods of the Third Heaven. Interestingly, it parallels the story of Adam and Eve using temptation as the source of evil.

Notes

Your Turn

Name _____ Date _____ Subject Area _____

DIRECTIONS: After reading a story, poem or folktale complete the Herringbone Technique Organizer.

HERRINGBONE TECHNIQUE

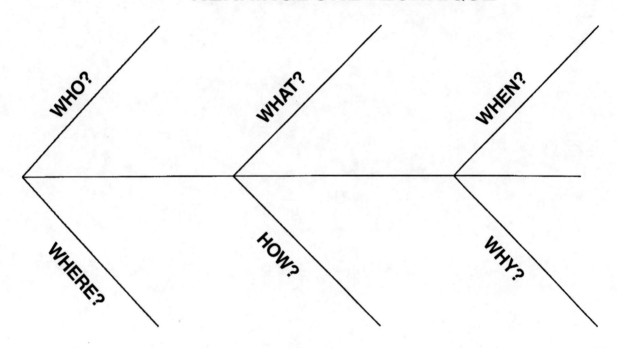

THE MAIN IDEA:

Endings: A Summary

In this chapter we have discussed the exciting use of trade books to supplement the textbook and the core curriculum. Students better understand and relate to a concept when they read and study about it in the context of situations that depict real people and places, or fictional—but nonstereotypical characters and settings.

To engage all students in literature we encourage you to experiment with the various activities we have presented. These activities will empower students to analyze and critique literature, to respect the ideologies of others in both literature and in oral communication and to enjoy and have fun with literature.

Reading across the curriculum will expose students to a wonderful variety of books and stories, expand their vocabularies and give them excellent models for their writing.

Our goal is for students to become lifelong readers. Our ultimate hope is that students will find books a vibrant introduction to life, its challenges, and its successes. As they learn more about how many others lived their lives, many students will be motivated to take risks, embrace the challenges, and realize their own potential, living life to the fullest.

Expanding Understandings through Discussion

Directions: Form as many content area groups as necessary (six per group for a Pinwheel Discussion Strategy) and distribute the following questions:

1. Why is the use of narrative literature in your content area a powerful way of teaching a particular topic or unit of study?
2. How can you encourage students to simply enjoy reading in your content area?
3. Which writing activity best fits the needs of your content area?

❑ Students 1, 2 and 3 take their respective questions.
❑ Students 4, 5 and 6 rotate after 10 minutes of discussion per question.

At the end of the three discussions appoint a recorder to summarize your answers and record this on a piece of butcher paper. Ultimately, the recorders of each pinwheel will post their summaries about the room and each of you will read the various postings.

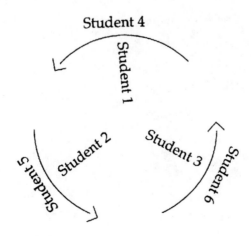

In the Field Applications

A. Select a specific topic in your content area. Visit a high school library and make a list of the trade books that are at an easy-to-read level for your special needs students. Next, visit an elementary or middle-school library and add to your list of books on the same topic.

B. With a class of students develop a graphic QAR. Ask them to bring in authentic items such as bags from chips, candy wrappers, milk cartons, etc. Using the Graphic QAR strategy ask the students to come up with the three levels of questions for their item.

C. Make a report card form for a piece of literature in your content area, read the book to a group of students, and have them complete the form.

References ❑ ❑ ❑

Ballard, R. (1988). *Exploring the Titanic*, NY: Warner.

Beck, L., McKeown, M., McCaslin, E., & Burkett, A. (1979). *Instructional dimensions that may affect reading comprehension: Examples of two commercial reading programs.* Pittsburgh: University of Pittsburgh, Language Research and Development Technical Report.

Birdseye, T. (1993). *Just call me stupid.* NY: Penguin.

Booth, D. (2006). Reading doesn't matter…. Portland, ME: Stenhouse.

Brendtro, L., Brokenleg, & Van Bockern, S. (1990). *Reclaiming youth at risk: Our hope for the future.* Bloomington, IN: National Educational Service.

Burke, J. (1999). *The English teacher's companion: A complete guide to classroom, curriculum, and the profession.* Portsmouth, NH: Heinemann.

Cassady, J. (1998). Wordless books: No-risk tool for inclusive middle-grade classrooms. *Journal of Adolescent & Adult Literacy, 41,* 428–432.

Danks, C. (1995). Using Holocaust short stories and poetry in the social studies classroom. *Social Education, 59,* 358–361.

Eeds, M. & Peterson, R. (1997). Literature studies revisited: Some thoughts on talking with children about books. *The New Advocate* 10(l), 49–59.

Fowler, G. (1982). Developing comprehension skills in primary students through the use of story frames. *The Reading Teacher 36, (2), 176–179.*

Gallagher, K. (2004). *Deeper Reading: Comprehending challenging texts,* 4–12. Portland, ME: Stenhouse Publishers.

Instant quotation dictionary (1987). (D. Bolander, D. Varner, G. Wright & S. Greene, Comp). Mundelein, IL: Career Publishing, Inc.

Jackson, F. (1994). Seven strategies to support culturally responsive pedagogy. *Journal of Adolescent & Adult Literacy, 37,* 298–303.

Kane, S. & Rule, A. (2004). Poetry connections can enhance content area learning. *Journal of Adolescent & Adult Literacy,* 47(8), 658–668.

Keech, A. (1997). Rediscovering the Titanic. *Book Links* 6(4), 34–38.

Kimmel, E.A.(2000). *The two mountains: An Aztec legend.* NY: Holiday House.

Krull, K. (1993*). Lives of the musicians: Good times, bad times and what the neighbors thought.* NY: Harcourt, Brace, Javanovich.

Leal, D. (1999). Engaging students' minds and hearts: Authentic student assessment of character traits in literature. *Journal of Adolescent & Adult Literacy, 43,*3.

Miller, T. (1998). The place of picture books in middle-level classrooms. *Journal of Adolescent & Adult Literacy, 41,* 376–381.

Mohr, K. (2006). Children's choices for recreational reading: A three-part investigation of selection preferences, rationales, and processes. *Journal of Literacy Research* 38,1.

Myers, W. (1994). *The glory field.* NY: Scholastic, Inc.

Pappas, C. (2006, April /May /June). The information book genre: Its role in integrated literacy research and science. *Reading Research Quarterly,* 41(2), 226–250.

Probst, R. (1987). Adolescent literature and the English curriculum. *English Journal 84* (8), 46–50.

Research news to use. *Reading Today* (2006, Aug/Sept). 24(1), 32–33. Newark, DE: International Reading Association.

Tama, M.C., Thomas, M., & McElroy, V. (1990). *A practical guide to student teaching and field experience: Through the looking glass.* Dubuque, Iowa: Kendall/Hunt.

Taylor, D. (2004). "Not just boring stories": Reconsidering the gender gap for boys. *Journal of Adolescent & Adult Literacy,* 48, 4.

Temple, F. (1993). *Grab hands and run.* NY: Orchard.

Watson, J. (1968). *The double helix.* NY: New American Library.

Weaver, C. (1994). *Reading process and practices: From socio-psycholinguistics to whole language.* Portsmouth, NH: Heinemann.

Wedwick, L. & Wutz, J. A. (2006). Thinking outside the book box: Using BOOKMATCH to develop independent book selection. *Voices from the Middle,* 14(1) 20–29.

Wutz, J.A., & Wedwick, L. (2005). BOOKMATCH: Scaffolding book selection for independent reading. *The Reading Teacher,* 59, 16–32.

Suggested Adolescent Literature Content Areas[1] ❏ ❏ ❏

Social Studies

Aaseng, Nathan. *Navajo code talkers.*
> World War II; Native Americans; cryptology

American Federation of Teachers. *Child labor: A selection of materials on children in the workplace.*

Atkins, Jeannine. *How high can we climb? The story of women explorers.*

Bausum, Ann. *Freedom riders: John Lewis and Jim Zwerg on the front lines of the civil rights movement.*

Blackwood, Gary. *Second sight.*

Blumenthal, Karen. *Let Me Play: The story of Title IX: the law that changed the future of girls in America.*

Bolden, Tonya. *Cause: Reconstruction America, 1863–1877.*

Caputo, Philip. *10,000 Days of Thunder: A history of the Vietnam War.*

Chin-Lee, Cynthia. *Amelia to Zorpa: Twenty-six women who changed the world.*

Ching Yoon Louie, Mirriam. *Sweatshop warriors: Immigrant women workers take on the global factory.*

Choi, Sook Nygul. *Year of impossible good byes.*
> Occupation of North Korea; hardship; endurance

Cofer, Judith. *An island like you.*

Corr, Anders. *No trespassing: Squatting, rent strikes, and land struggles worldwide.*

Crew, Linda. *A Heart for any fate: Westward to Oregon - 1845.*

Deem, James M. *Bodies from the ash.*

Delano, M. Ferguson. *American heroes.*

Draper, Sharon M. *Copper sun.*

Fleming, Candace. *Our Eleanor: A scrapbook look at Eleanor Roosevelt's remarkable life.*

Fradin, Judith Bloom and Dennis Brindell Fradin. *5,000 miles to freedom.*

Freedman, Russell. *Children of the Great Depression.*

Grant, K. M. *Blood red horse.*

Harris, John. *Strong stuff: Herakles and his labors.*

Hautzig, Esther. *The endless steppe.*

Hawass, Zahi A. *Tutankhamun: The mystery of the boy king.*

Hill, Kirkpatrick. *Dancing at the Odinochka.*

Hillman, Laura. *I will plant you a lilac tree: A memoir of a Schindler's list survivor.*

Holub, Josef. *An innocent soldier.*

Hopkinson, Deborah. *Up before daybreak: Cotton and people in America.*

Houston, Julian. *New boy.*

Hunt, Irene. *Across five aprils.*

Frank, Anne. *Anne Frank: The diary of a young girl.*

Innocenti, Roberto. *Rose Blanche.*
> Holocaust; Hitler's Germany

Jenness, A. *Come home with me.*

Joseph, Lynn. *Color my words.*

Jurmain, Suzanne. *The forbidden schoolhouse: The true and dramatic story of Prudence Crandall and her students legal precedent of Dred Scott.*

Koller, Jackie French. *Nothing to fear.*
> Depression; immigrants

Levine, Ellen. *Catch a Tiger by the Toe.*

Markandaya, Kamala. *Nectar in a sieve.*

Marx, Trish. *Jeannette Rankin: First Lady of Congress.*

Meyer, Carolyn. *White lilacs.*
> Prejudices; injustices; African Americans

Millman, Isaac. *Hidden child.*

Myers, Walter. *The glory field.*
> History of an African family; psychological slavery

Murphy, Jim. *The boy's war: Confederate and Union soldiers talk about the Civil War.*

Nelson, Marilyn. *A Wreath for Emmett Till.*

Orlev, Uri. *The men from the other side.*
> Nazi oppression; holocaust; heroic efforts

Paulson, Gary. *The rifle.*

Paver, Michelle. *Spirit walker.*

Paver, Michelle. *Wolf brother.*

Reid Banks, Lynne. *Tiger, tiger.*

Reiss, Johanna. *The upstairs room.*

Rinaldi, Ann. *In my father's house.*
> Civil War; morality; southern life

Rochelle, Belinda. *Witnesses to freedom: Young people who fought for civil rights.*
> Fight for freedom; students' contributions to their communities

Ruby, Lois. *Steal away home.*
> Civil War

Shulevitz, Uri. *The travels of Benjamin of Tudela: Through three continents in the twelfth century.*

Spinkla, Renina Keen. *White hare's hares.*
> 16th century; California; Native Americans

Tanaka, Shelley. *Mummies: The newest, coolest & creepiest from around the world.*

Taylor, Theodore. *The bomb.*

Thornton, Lawrence. *Naming the spirits.*

Walker, Sally M. *Secrets of a Civil War submarine: Solving the mysteries of the H.L. Hunley.*

Weir, Alison. *The children of Henry VIII.*

Whiteman, Dorit Bader. *Lonek's journey: The true story of a boy's escape to freedom.*

Winerip, Michael. *Adam Canfield of the Slash.*

Winthrop, Elizabeth. *Counting on Grace.*

Wisler, G. Clifton. *Jericho's journey.*
> Survival; movement west (Tennessee to Texas)

Health

Death

Bode, Janet. *Death Is hard to live with: Teenagers talk about how they cope with loss.*
> Bibliotherapy; real-life accounts; loss of friend or loved one

Humphreys, Martha. *Until whatever.*

McDaniel, Lurlene. *Now I lay me down to sleep.*
> Leukemia

White, Ryan and Cunningham, Ann Marie. *Ryan White: My own story.*

Personal Growth

Campbell, Bebe. *Sweet summer: Growing up with and without my dad.*
> Growing up black and overcoming obstacles

Case, Dianne. *Love, David.*
> Discrimination; apartheid

Conley, Jane. *Crazy lady!*
> Facing death; alcoholism; compassion

Gardiner, John. *Stone fox.*
> Boy coming of age; death of pet

Kehret, Peg, *Cages.*
> Shoplifting; community service; crime; strength

Mori, Kyoko. *One bird.*
> Asian girl coming of age

Rodowsky, Colby. *Lucy Peale.*
> Forced sex; homelessness

Sinclair, April. *Coffee will make you black.*
> Black male/female relationship

Springer, Nancy. *Colt.*
> Spina bifida; overcoming handicaps

Staples, Suzanne. *Shabanu.*
> Pakistani girl's rebellion to tradition

Stoehr, Shelley. *Crosses.*
> Drug and alcohol abuse

Math and Science

Asimov, Isaac. *Words of science and the history behind them.*

Ballard, Robert. *Exploring the Titanic.*

Barnard, Bryn. *Outbreak: Plagues that changed history.*

Barron, T.A. *The ancient one.*
> Logging; redwood trees; environment

Benchley, Peter. *Shark life: True stories about sharks & the sea.*

Brooks, Bruce. *Predator!*
> Food chain; eating and being eaten

Carroll, Lewis. *The annotated Alice: Alice's adventures in Wonderland and through the looking glass.*

Cobb, Vicki. *Junk food.*

Collard, Sneed B. *The prairie builders: Reconstructing America's lost grasslands.*

Cooney, Caroline B. *Code Orange.*

Delano, Marfe Ferguson. *Genius: A photobiography of Albert Einstein.*

Dendy, Leslie A. *Guinea pig scientists: Bold self-experimenters in science and medicine.*

Donovan-O'Meara, Donna. *Into the volcano.*

Farrell, Jeanette. *Invisible allies: Microbes that shape our lives.*

Farrell, Jeanette. *Invisible enemies: Stories of infectious diseases.*

Fradin, Dennis B. *With a little luck: Surprising stories of amazing discoveries.*

Havard, Christian. *Untamed: Animals around the world.*

Hoobler, Dorothy & Hoobler, Thomas. *Lost civilizations.*
> Stonehedge; Atlantis; artifacts

Jackson, Donna M. *ER vets: Life in an animal emergency room.*

Kampion, Drew. *Waves: From surfing to tsunami.*

Lampton, Chistopher. *Endangered species.*
> Extinction; causes

Lasky, Kathryn. *She's wearing a dead bird on her head.*

Lauber, Patricia. *Volcano: The eruption and healing of Mt. St. Helens.*

Myers, Jack. *On top of Mount Everest and other explorations of science in action.*

Roberts, R. *Serendipity: Accidental discoveries in science.*
Ryan, F. *The forgotten plague: How the battle against tuberculosis was won and lost.*
Sayre, A. *Rosalind Franklin & DNA.*
Schlosser, Eric. *Chew on this: Everything you don't want to know about fast food.*
Slavin, Bill. *Transformed: How everyday things are made.*
Turner, Pamela S. *Gorilla doctors: Saving endangered great apes.*
Watson, James. *The Double helix.*
      DNA; genetics
Westerfeld, Scott. *Peeps: A novel.*
Winckler, Suzanne & Rodgers, Mary. *Our endangered planet: Population growth.*
      Global stress; ozone layer; overpopulation

Sports and Physical Education

Aaseng, Nate. *Baseball: It's your turn.*
      Reader involvement; risks; trading
Battista. G. *The runner's literary companion: Great stories and poems about running.*
Dygard, Thomas. *Backfield package.*
      Football; suspense; decision-making
Klass, David. *A different season.*
      Baseball; girls; equality
Mac Lean, John. *When the mountain sings.*
      Snow skiing; state competition
Weidhorn, Manfred. *Jackie Robinson.*
      Biography
Woolverton, Linda. *Running before the wind.*

Business

Gates, William. *The road ahead: Unauthorized biography of Phil Knight.*
Iacocca, Lee. *Iacocca: An autobiography.*
Jennings, Diane. *Self-made women: Twelve of America's leading entrepreneurs talk about success, self-image and the superwoman.*
Nierenberg, Gerald. *The art of negotiating.*
Schlayer, M. *How to be a financially secure woman.*
Smith, Adam. *Super-money.*
Smith, Adam. *Money game.*
Thomas, David. *The money crowd.*

Foreign Language

Spanish

Alberro, Solange. *Estampas de la colonia/ Images of the colony.*
      Mexico; people; customs; 1521–1794
Altman, Linda. *Migrant farm workers: The temporary people.*
Bernier-Grand, Carmen. *Poet and politician of Puerto Rico: Don Luis Muñoz*
Fabra, Jordi. *Noche de viernes/Friday night*
Fernandez Solis, Luis. *La competición de karate:/Entrenamiento de campeónes*
      Karate competition
Galvan. Raul. *Cuban Americans*
Merino, Jose Maria. *Los trenes del verano/Summer trains.*
Swaan, Bram de. *El persequidor de la luz: Albert Einstein/The Pursuer of Light: Albert Einstein.*

Language Arts

Achebe, Chinua. *Things fall apart.*

Andrews, V.C. *Flowers in the attic.*

Angelou, Maya. *Life doesn't frighten me.*

Auel, Jean. *Clan of the cave bear.*

Betancourt, Jeanne. *More than meets the eye.*

Birdseye, Tom. *Just call me stupid.*

Borland, H. *When legends die.*

Bradbury, Ray. *Farenheit 451.*

Camus, A. *The stranger.*

Casagrande, June. *Grammar snobs are great big meanies: A guide to language for fun and spite.*

Crutcher, Chris. *Staying fat for Sarah Byrnes.*

Cushman, Karen. *Catherine called Birdy.*

Golding, William. *Lord of the flies.*

Grimes, Nikki. *Dark sons.*

Kehret, Peg. *Cages.*

King, Stephen. *Firestarter.*

Laurents, Arthur. *Romeo and Juliet/West side story.*

Lawrence, Jerome & Lee, Robert. *Inherit the wind.*

Lee, Harper. *To kill a mockingbird.*

Lee, Mildred. *The people therein.*

Marcantonio, Patricia Santos. *Red ridin' in the hood and other cuentos.*

Marino, G. *The day Elvis came to town.*

Mazer, Norma, *When we first met.*

Orr, Tamra. *Extraordinary essays.*

Orwell, George. *Animal farm.*

Paterson, Katherine. *Jacob have I loved.*

Paulsen, Gary. *The crossing.*

Peck, Richard. *Remembering the good times.*

Peck, Robert. *Priscilla and the wimps.* In *Sixteen,* Donald R. Gallo, Ed.

Pullman, Philip. *The golden compass.*

Sebestyen, Ouida. *Words by heart.*

Seuss, Dr. *The lorax.*

Shakespeare, William. *Romeo and Juliet.*

Soto, Gary. *New and selected poems.*

Stone, Bruce. *Half Nelson, full Nelson.*

Stone, H. *The last free bird.*

Sutton, Caroline. *How did they do that? Wonders of the far and recent past explained.*

Taylor, Mildred. *Roll of thunder hear my cry.*

Taylor, Mildred. *The friendship and the gold cadillac.*

Voigt, Cynthia. *Izzy, willy-nilly.*

Weisel, Elie. *Night.*

Art

Adams, L. *Art cop.*

Clark, Kenneth. *Another part of the wood.*

Esterow, Milton. *The art stealers.*

Hill, Laban Carrick. *Casa azul: An encounter with Frida Kahlo.*

Mill, John. *Treasure keepers.*

National Museum of American Art. *Celebrate America in poetry and art.*

O'Neal, Zibby. *In summer light.*

Raczka, Bob. *Here's looking at me: How artists see themselves.*

Raczka, Bob. *Unlikely pairs: Fun with famous works of art.*
Rees, Douglas. *Smoking mirror: An encounter with Paul Gauguin.*
Resnick, Mike. *Lady with an alien: An encounter with Leonardo da Vinci.*
Scieszka, Jon, and Lane Smith. *Seen Art?*
Sousa, Jean. *A guide to looking at art: Faces, places, and inner spaces.*
Steiger-Rubenstein, C. *American women artists.*

Music

Barber, D. *Bach, Beethoven and the boys.*
Brooks, Bruce. *Midnight hour encores.*
Crofton. O. & Fraser. *Dictionary of musical quotations.*
Haskins, James. *Black music in America: A history through its people.*
Kogan, Judith. *Nothing but the best: The struggle for perfection at the Juilliard School.*
Krull, K. *Lives of the musicians: Good times, bad times and what the neighbors thought.*
Newton, Suzanne. *I will call it Georgie's blues.*
Paterson, Katherine. *Come sing, Jimmy Jo.*
Strasser, Todd. *Rock 'n' roll nights.*

Read-aloud Books

Abdul-Jabbar, Kareem, & Steinberg, Alan. *Black profiles in courage: Legacy of African-American achievement.*
Abner, Allison & Villarosa, Linda. *Finding our way: The teen survival guide.*
Avi. *Beyond the western sea: The escape from home.*
Avi. *Wolf rider.*
Bell, Margaret. *Watch for a tall white sail.*
Bell, Margaret. *Ride out the storm.*
Boller. Paul. *Presidential anecdotes.*
Chambers, Veronica. *Mama's girl.*
Cormier, Robert. *We all fall down.*
Davis, Kenneth. *Don't know much about history: Everything you need to know about American history but never learned.*
Dessen, Sarah. *That summer.*
Earthworks Group. *50 simple things you can do to save the earth.*
Greenberg, Joanne. *I never promised you a rose garden.*
Greene, Bette. *Summer of my German soldier.*
Hazen, Robert. & Trefil, James. *Science matters: Achieving scientific literacy.*
Lee, Harper. *To kill a mockingbird*
Lewis, Sydney. *"A totally alien life-form": Teenagers.*
Paterson, Katherine. *Jip.*
Paterson, Katherine. *Jacob have I loved.*
Paulsen, Gary. *The crossing.*
Peck, Richard. *Remembering the good times.*
Pullman, Philip. *The golden compass.*
Stone, Bruce. *Half Nelson, full Nelson.*
Soto, Gary. *New and selected poems.*
Sutton, Caroline. *How did they do that? Wonders of the far and recent past explained.*
Taylor, Mildred. *The friendship and the gold cadillac.*
Taylor, Mildred. *Roll of thunder hear my cry.*
Weisel, Elie. *Night.*

Bibliotherapy

Friedberg, Joan. *Portraying persons with disabilities: An annotated bibliography of nonfiction for children and teenagers.*

Kaywell, Jane. (Ed.). *Adolescents at risk: A guide to fiction and nonfiction for young adults, parents, and professionals.*
Reidarson, Nina. *Books for disabled young people: An annotated bibliography.*
Zvirin, Stephanie. *The best years of their lives: A resource guide for teenagers in crisis*

Folk Literature
Bettelheim, B. *The uses of enchantment: The meaning and importance of fairy tales.*
Kimmel, E. *The two mountains: An Aztec legend.*
Kimmel, E. *Montezuma and the fall of the aztecs.*
Hamilton, V. *In the beginning: Creation stories from around the world.*
Mayo, G. *Star tales: North American Indian stories about the stars.*
Lomax, J. *Cowboy songs and other frontier ballads.*
Ramsey, J. *Coyote was going there: Indian literature of the Oregon country.*
Jones, S. *Oregon Folklore.*
Yolen, J. *Favorite folktales from around the world.*
Opie, I. & Opie, P. *The classic fairy tales.*
Walker, B. *Feminist fairy tales.*
Auerbach, N. & Knoepflmacher, U. *Forbidden journeys: Fairy tales and fantasies by Victorian women writers.*

Poetry
Angelou, M. *All God's children need traveling shoes.*
Angelou, M. *Now Sheba sings the song.*
Angelou, M. *And still I rise; Shaker, why don't you sing?*
*Brown, K. (1998). *Verse & universe: Poems about science and mathematics.* Minneapolis, MN: Milkweed.
*Bryan, A. (1997). *Ashley Bryan's ABC of African American poetry.* NY: Atheneum Books for Young Readers.
Dunning, S. et al (Eds.) *Reflections on a gift of watermelon pickle and other modern verse.*
*Frost, R., & Young, E. (1988). *Birches.* NY: Henry Holt.
Glenn, M. *Class dismissed: High school poems.*
*Granfield, L., & Wilson, J. (1995). *In Flanders Fields: The story of the poem by John McCrae,* NY: Doubleday.
*Harley, A. (2000). *Fly with poetry: An ABC of poetry.* Honesdale, PA: Wordsong/Boyds Mills Press.
*Hines, A.G. (2001). *Pieces: A year in poems & quilts.* NY: Greenwillow.
*Hopkins, L.B. & Barbour, K. (Eds.). (1997). *Marvelous math: A book of poems.* NY:: Simon & Schuster.
Janeczko. P. *Poetspeak: In their words, about their work.*
*Katz, B. (1998). *American history poems.* NY: Scholastic.
Kovacs, E. *Writing across cultures: A handbook on writing poetry and lyrical prose.*
Janeczko, P. *Preposterous: poems of youth.*
Janeczko, P. *Postcard poems: A collection of poetry for sharing.*
Adoff, Arnold. *All the colors of the race.*
*Lawrence, J. (1993). *Harriet and the promised land.* NY: Simon & Schuster.
Lerner, A. *Dancing on the rim of the world: An anthology of contemporary Northwest Native American writings.*
Larrick, N. *I hear a scream in the street: Poetry by young people in the city.*
*Lewis, J.P., & Thomson, J. (2000). *Freedom like sunlight: Praise songs for black Americans.* Mankato, MN: Creative Editions.
Linwaithe. A. *Ain't I a woman! A book of women's poetry from around the world.*

*Longfellow, H.W. (2001). *The midnight ride of Paul Revere*. Brooklyn, NY: Handprint
    Books.
*Malloy, P. (Ed.) (1968). *Poetry U.S.A*. NY: Scholastic.
*Median, T., & Christie, R.G. (2002). *Love to Langston*. NY: Lee & Low.
*Moss, J., & Leigh, T. (1997). *Bone poems*. NY: Workman.
 *Myers, W.D., & Myers, C. (1997). *Harlem*. NY: Scholastic.
*Nelson, M. (2001). *Carver: A life in poems*. Asheville, NC: Front Street.
*Nordine, K., & Drescher, H. (2000). *Colors*. Orlando, FL: Harcourt.
*Nye, N.S. (1998). *The space between our footsteps: Poems and paintings from the
    Middle East*. NY: Simon & Schuster.
*O'Neill, M., & Wallner, J. (1989). *Hailstones and halibut bones: Adventures in color*.
    NY: Doubleday.
*Philip, N., & McCurdy, M. (Eds.). (1998). *War and pity of war*. NY: Clarion.
*Provenson, A. (1997). *The buck stops here: The presidents of the United States*. NY:
    HarperCollins.
*Rochelle, B. (Ed.) (2001). *Words with wings: A treasury of African-American poetry and
    art*. NY: HarperCollins.
*Rogasky, B., & Tauss, M. (Eds.) (2001). *Leaf by leaf: Autumn poems*. NY: Scholastic.
*Rottmann, L. (1993). *Voices from the Ho Chi Minh Trail: Poetry of America and
    Vietnam, 1965–1993*. Desert Hot Springs, CA: Event Horizon Press.
*Sandburg,. C, & Rand, T. (1993). *Arithmetic*. NY: Harcourt Brace Jovanovich.
*Thayer, E.L. (2000). *Casey at the bat*. NY: Scholastic.
"Weatherford, C.B. (2002). *Remember the bridge: Poems of a people*. NY: Philomel.
*Worth, V. (2002). *Peacock and other poems*. NY: Farrar Straus Giroux.

*Starred items used with permission. Sharon Kane & Audrey C. Rule (2004). Poetry Connections
can enhance content area learning. *Journal of Adolescent and Adult Literacy* 47(8). p. 666–669.

Inclusion

Anderson, R. *The bus people*. Developmental disabilities.
Betancourt. J. *My name is (Brain) Brian*. Learning disabilities.
Christopher, M. *Long shot for Paul*. Developmental disabilities.
Guest, J. *Ordinary people*. At-risk
Hesse, K. *Wish on a unicorn*. Mental retardation.
Kaye, M. *Real heroes*. AIDS
Metzger, L. *Barry's sister*. Cerebal palsy.
Wood, J. *The man who loved clowns*.. Down's Syndrome.
Covington, D. *Lizard*. Physical deformities.
Janover, C. *The worst speller in jr. high*. Self-esteem.
Voigt. C. *Izzy, willy-nilly*. Depression.
Wood, J. *When pigs fly*. Family issues.

Multicultural Literature

Acuna, R. *Occupied America: A history of Chicanos*.
Ancona, G. *The pinata maker/el pinatero*.
Bennett, L. *Before the Mayflower: A history of Black America*.
Braided lives: An anthology of multicultural American writing. Minnesota Humanities
    Commission.
Bruchac, Joseph. *Geronimo*.
Budhos, Marina Tamar. *Ask me no questions*.
Buller, Laura. *A faith like mine: A celebration of the world's religions...seen through the
    eyes of children*.
Canales, Viola. *The tequila worm*.
Carvell, Marlene. *Sweetgrass basket*.

Cheaney, J. B. *My friend the enemy.*

D'Amico, Joan. *The coming to America cookbook: Delicious recipes and fascinating stories from America's many cultures.*

Delisle, Guy. *Pyongyang: A journey in North Korea.*

Ellis, Deborah. *Our stories, our songs: African children talk about AIDS.*

Espada, M. (Ed.), *Poetry like bread: Poetry of the political imagination.*
    Starting with I: Personal essays by teenagers. Youth Communications/Persea Books.

Hobbs, Will. *Crossing the wire.*

Howard, Helen. *Living as a refugee in America: Mohammed's story.*

Jaramillo, Ann. *La Linea.*

Kadohata, Cynthia. *Weedflower.*

King, L. (Ed.), *Hear my voice: A multicultural anthology of literature from the United States.*

Marston, Elsa. *Figs and fate: Stories about growing up in the Arab world today.*

Menchœ, Rigoberta. *The girl from Chimel.*

Mwangi, Meja. *The Mzungu boy.*

Oppenheim, Joanne. *Dear Miss Breed.*

Pearsall, Shelley. *Crooked river.*

Staples, Suzanne Fisher. *Under the Persimmon Tree.*

Tatum, B. *"Why are all the black kids sitting together in the cafeteria?" and other conversations about race.*

Wyss, Thelma Hatch. *Bear dancer: The story of a Ute girl.*

Zenatti, Valerie. *When I was a soldier: A memoir immigrant experience.*

Young Adult Men[2] ❏ ❏ ❏

Alexander, Lloyd. *The book of three.*

Anderson, M. T. *Burger wuss: Feed.*

Bowen, Kimberly. *Reading is for the boys (and girls)!A WebQuest for teachers about boys and reading.* Retrieved November 1, 2006 from http://wwvv.learnnc.org/articles/boysread0602-l.

Bradbury, Ray. *The illustrated man.*

Card, Orson Scott. *Ender's game.*

Heinlein, Robert. *Starship Troopers.*

Hinton, S.E. *The Outsiders.*

Jacques, Brian. *Redwall books.*

London, Jack. *White Fang: The Sea Wolf.*

Lubar, David. *Hidden talents.*

Lynch, Chris. *Extreme elvin: Slot machine.*

Pullman, Phillip. *The golden compass.*

Schwartz, Wendy (2004). *Helping underachieving boys read well and often.* ERIC Digest. Retrieved November 1, 2006 from http://www.ericdigests.org/2003-2/boys.html

Scieszka, Jon (2005). *Guys read.* Retrieved November 1, 2006 from http://www.guysread.com

Sleator, Willian. *Oddballs.*

Tolkien, J.R.R. *The hobbit: Lord of the rings.*

Vandergrift, K. E. (1995). *Coming-of-age stories: Bibliography of male coming of age stories.* Retrieved November 1, 2006 from http://www.scils.rutgers.edu/%7Ekvander/YoungAdult/male.html

Wilhelm, J.D. (2002 October). Getting boys to read: It's the Context! *Scholastic Instructor,* 16–18.

Note 1. We would like to thank the Multnomah County Library School Corps for their help in updating our literature titles by drawing our attention to their Curriculum Booklist Workshops. See Multnomah County Library School Corps "Gotta read this: New books to connect with your curriculum booklist for 6th–12th grade educators. Retrieved August 9, 2006 from http://www.multcolib.org/schoolcorps/2006GRTSecondary.pdf.

Note 2. We are not intentionally overlooking young adult females. In light of current national assessment findings of young men's reading scores falling below young women's, we believe this is a timely addition. For a list of strictly young women coming-of-age stories see Vandergrift, K. E. (1995). *Bibliography of female coming of age stories*. Retrieved November 1, 2006 from http://www.scils.rutgers.edu/~kvander/YoungAdult/age.html. This list is continuously revised.

Assessment Strategies

Anybody who judges intelligence on a single number is a class enemy. The human mind is so great and diverse. My students know all kinds of wonderful things they've had to learn in order to survive. But those things aren't on tests. It's good to know Mozart, but they're never asked about B.B. King. You're supposed to know only a certain kind of grammar, a certain kind of vocabulary.

Chicago public high school teacher in *Race*
by Studs Terkle

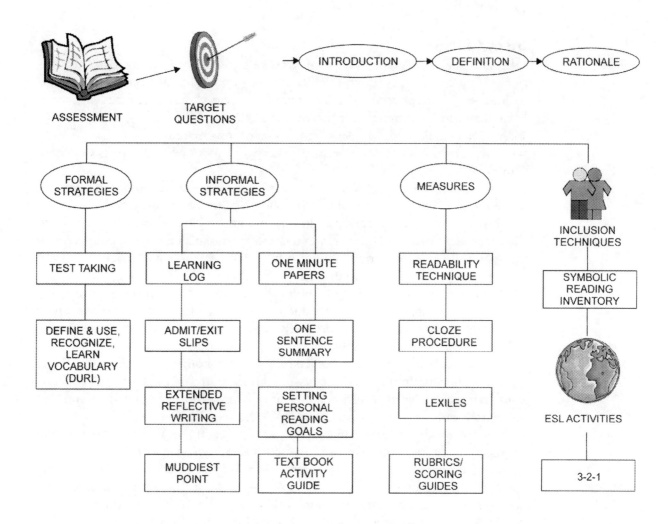

Target Questions

Target Questions

Consider the following questions before reading this chapter. Discuss these with a colleague. Continue writing notes and develop specific questions regarding assessment that you want to explore.

1. What is assessment?
2. Support and refute the importance of high-stakes testing.
3. Compare formal and informal assessment.
4. What is the role of student self-evaluation in the curriculum?
5. Describe self-evaluation techniques that are best suited to your content area.
6. What can you learn about your students by administering a content area reading inventory and a cloze procedure?
7. Why is performance assessment important in evaluating students with special needs?
8. The literacy assessment activities that you would find in a classroom where student differences are valued.
9. Your question.

Introduction

Like most medical doctors who profess to help people and do no harm, the National Council of Teachers of English (NCTE) establishes as their first standard for the assessment of reading and writing: to serve each and every student, not to harm them. In the rationale for this standard, the NCTE further states "that each individual's intellectual, social and emotional well-being must be considered, even when the decision to be made affects other students or an entire class or school (2006)."

As teachers we all realize the effect of assessment on students some postive; some negative. Students' results make the way for their entrance or not into schools of their or their parents' choice, in some instances—from preschool to the university. Assessment results can increase or diminish motivation, affect feelings about learning and most importantly "influence students' understanding of what it means to be literate, educated or successful" (NCTE, 2006).

How many of us have friends who claim they cannot write if their lives depend on it? Yet, they write colorful and engaging emails. But in situations where they need to write on behalf of family interests or for their jobs, they bale—delegating rather than attempting it.

As teachers of literacy, these objections present moments of reflection—How does this happen? In most instances we would venture that assessment for many who do not consider themselves proficient in writing or reading did not center on students' evaluating their own progress or teachers' assessing students for the purpose of making instructional decisions. Rather assessment was viewed and exercised as a top-down mandate for the state, school, department or class.

By examining the following definition for assessment, we venture a clear role for evaluating students will emerge. It will provoke affirmations for those who see assessment in this light or nudge others who see it as a necessary but not productive or informative function of school-life to reflect more positively towards its use.

Definition

One of the best definitions we have run across in our studies of assessment is one based on the derivation of the word meaning "a sitting down with." We believe that if teachers imagined themselves sitting down with students when they designed, interpreted or administered assessment instruments, the task and the outcomes would be most beneficial to teachers and students alike. In eye-to-eye communication a unique perspective develops.

Assessment is a matter of perspective. Mem Fox writes delightfully on this characteristic of assessment:

> In a tutorial on assessment in which hot discussion took place over the effectiveness of gold stars or smiley stamps on children's writing, our student leader told us to rewrite the song "Twinkle, Twinkle, Little Star" to explain our philosophical stance on the issue. Debate then continued on a variety of response and evaluation procedures. At the end of the tutorial we were asked to lie on the floor and put our feet high up on the wall. The student in charge of the tutorial held up a large sign that said ASSESSMENT.
> "Can you all see that?" he asked.
> "Yes," we replied, even though we were looking at it upside down.
> "Good," he said. "You've now looked at assessment from a different perspective." (Fox, 1993, p. 30).

Assessment: A sitting down with.

As teachers our feet may not be high up against the wall, but we are avid designers and consumers of assessment measures.

TEACHER TALK

Spent the weekend assessing the efforts, noble and ignoble, of my charges...the assessments for this class were all in order before calculation, which was a relief, as I've been grading make-up work and recent assignments like a fiend for all of my other classes.

Rationale

In this chapter we will provide many assessment activities that will help answer a question teachers frequently ask us, "How can we gain a better understanding of our students' literacy abilities?" Teachers need to become more proficient in determining how to help students by using multiple assessment measures as high-stakes testing in which a single test score is used to make important educational decisions becomes more firmly entrenched in our schools.

In their position statement the Board of Directors (1999) of the International Reading Association state that they oppose high-stakes testing because of its inherent problems: "making bad decisions, narrowing the curriculum, focusing exclusively on certain segments of students, losing instructional time, and moving decision making to central authorities and away from local personnel" (p. 307). By using high-stakes tests to make important decisions the curriculum is often narrowed and the test becomes such an important focus that other activities suffer. We have heard teachers in the targeted grades where the state testing

High-stakes tests are those that affect grades, promotion or retention, teacher salary, or a school district's standing.

takes place say, "I don't have my students do inquiry-based projects until April, I spend most of the year preparing the students for their state assessment."

Does this attitude need to prevail? We think teachers can make more creative curricular decisions and still help students meet the standards set by high-stakes testing.

We suggest that through informal assessment teachers can make instructional decisions that focus on gathering information systematically about student achievement to inform their actions, however, it needs to be varied. Teachers can create an assessment system in their classrooms and schools that uses informal assessment such as self-evaluation techniques, learning logs, quick writes, teacher recommendations as well as standardized testing.

TEACHER TALK

The last semester I taught high school remedial reading I refused to follow the mandates of my test-oriented district in southern Texas. I had fewer discipline problems and believe my students learned more because I listened to them and changed my practice (p. 582).
Kathy Bussert-Webb, 1999

Rather than emphasize the basic skills orientation mandated by the Texas Achievement of Academic Skills (TASS) test, Bussert-Webb decided to look at self-selected reading and activities that promoted linking her students' background knowledge with their reading, raising questions and writing personal connections to their self-selected books. Did the students do better on the TASS test? The author does not say. Were the students reading more and enjoying it? Yes! Students read the most library books and had the most Accelerated Reader points of any class.

How can teachers honor their own beliefs regarding teaching and testing?

We would wager that many of these activities covered: defining vocabulary in context, identifying details, getting the main idea, determining cause/effect, making predictions, drawing inferences, and evaluating as well as understanding an author's point of view and identifying purpose and propaganda—are all objectives of the TASS. This teacher in developing a curriculum that all could enjoy helped students develop indirectly the needed skills for taking the standardized test.

Does standardized testing have to be the sword of Damocles hanging over our professional lives? We would suggest that it doesn't. Teachers can be true to their belief systems and still teach in a manner that guides students in developing the skills they need to be successful with all assessment techniques.

Our perspective is determined by the response to the question "Whose purpose is best served by our choice of assessment: The teacher's? The student's? The school's? The state's?"

For the purpose of this chapter, we will focus on assessment strategies that are most relevant to the teacher in the content area classroom. In addition, we will examine informal assessment processes that include the gathering, interpreting, and synthesizing of information to aid decision making for instruction.

Define formal assessment.

In order to gather information regarding students' reading ability, teachers can use either formal or informal assessment measures. How are formal measures different from informal ones? Formal assessment typically includes standardized tests conducted by the district or state to provide these agencies with judgments about achievement and performance. In addition, these norm-referenced tests permit comparisons of scores of students of the same age and the same grade, usually across national, state or district regions. Typical standardized tests are the Comprehensive Test of Basic Skills (CTBS), and the Psychological Corporation's new Integrated Assessment System. States also like Oregon develop their own standardized tests such as the Oregon Statewide Reading Assessment.

Since much has been written about formal assessment, we have chosen to focus on informal assessment in this third edition. For a glossary of formal assessment terminology please see the NCTE web site at the end of this chapter. Another helpful reference is A *Teacher's Guide to Standardized Reading Tests: Knowledge is Power* (Calkins et al. 1998).

Informal assessment is a process that knowledgeable teachers use when they observe and document students' performance in varied ways and in different contexts. As Wolf (1993) writes, "Many have come to believe that the most valuable and valid information about student learning comes not from an isolated and decontextualized 'snapshot' of student performance, but from those who work closely with students on a daily basis."

Zemelman, Daniels, et al. (1998)

Test Taking Strategies

Table 1

Instructional Summary of Test Taking Strategies	
Literacy Strategies	**Test Taking Strategies**
Primary Focus	Assessment
Learning Principles	❏ Metacognitive Experience ❏ Active Involvement
When to Use	During testing
Goals: National or State Literacy Standards	❏ Work effectively as an individual ❏ Analyze and evaluate evidence
Materials	Appropriate for learning activity
Time	25 minutes

Students deserve to learn how to become as successful as possible at taking tests. They need to understand the various levels of questions and the types of expected answers related to specific types of questions. We suggest that students approach tests with the following activities in mind:

❏ Skim the test and be aware of the points for each answer. Then pace their writing of answers by budgeting more time for those worth the most points. Also, examine some questions to identify potential or partial answers for another question on the test.

Teach students how to be testwise.

Graham &
Robinson (1984)

McCutcheon
(1985)

❏ Skip those questions that they don't know at first, and complete the ones they are sure of, particularly if the test is timed. Then come back to those items they skipped.

❏ Be aware of universal terms—all, never, always, etc. These can usually be eliminated in multiple choice selections and are usually false in a true-false test. Also, look for choices that are in direct opposition. One is likely to be the answer—unlike the possibility of similar choices.

❏ For an essay question, underline specific points to be addressed. Figure out precisely what is being asked. There is a difference between "compare" and "contrast." Be aware of what is expected with verbs such as defend, explain, analyze, etc.

❏ Go back over answers to look for careless errors or errors that are apparent due to possible information given in other test questions.

❏ Be aware of the kinds of questions that are asked, e.g.,
   1. Literal: The answer is usually from memorized details.
   2. Interpretive: The answer depends on your reading between the lines and will not be from explicitly stated materials.
   3. Applied: You are on your own. Give your opinion BUT be able to substantiate your answer.

Strategies to Promote Informal Assessment

Self Evaluation Assessment

One of the target questions we have set for this chapter is for our readers to describe and design assessment techniques that help students see themselves as learners. Assessment to mean anything to our students must lead to the identification of individual learning goals. As Hansen (1994) writes:

> Self-evaluation leads to the establishment of goals. That is what evaluation is for. We evaluate in order to find out what we have learned so we will know what to study next. People who self-evaluate constantly ask themselves, "Where am I going? Am I getting there? Am I getting somewhere? Am I enjoying the trip? Is this worthwhile? Do I approve of the way I'm spending my time?" (p. 37)

Self assessment
strategies build
life-long learning
habits.
Boud (1989);
Rogers (1969)

Self-assessment facilitates learning, and if cultivated in students' early years of schooling, it will nurture lifelong learning skills. Through self-assessment, students learn to establish criteria they can achieve, set goals which are realistic, and, in the process, establish their own responsibility, and ownership for their learning.

Whether students are taking standardized, or informal teacher-created tests, a certain vocabulary is associated with this process. How many times have we seen classes and testing falter because students didn't understand the process vocabulary used. Cruz (2005) recounts how students in a debate who were schooled in the art of using formal language in a formal setting used the standard patterns of logic, expressed their opinions clearly and maintained their arguments. While students who were second language learners and passionate about the issue as well as having lived it found themselves unable to express themselves as strongly despite their experiences. Speaking the language is a critical part of assessment.

The following activity will give you an overview of the vocabulary students have to have in order to function in an assessment situation. This like Maholic's (1984) Metacognitive Reading Awareness Inventory (see Chapter 3 Study Skills) is a good place to start to cultivate student self-assessment.

TABLE 2

INSTRUCTIONAL SUMMARY OF DEFINE & USE, RECOGNIZE, OR LEARN (DURL) ASSESSMENT VOCABULARY

Literacy Strategies	DURL: Asessment Vocabulary
Primary Focus	❏ Test taking
Learning Principles	❏ Active involvement in searching for meaning
	❏ Self-monitoring and regulating of thought processes
When to use	❏ Before taking tests
Goals: National or State Literacy Standards	❏ Increase vocabulary and use this terminology accurately
	❏ Understand and use information in a variety of texts across the subject area to perform a task
Material	❏ Activity sheet and writing instrument
Time	❏ Fifteen minutes

FIGURE 8.1. DEFINE & USE, RECOGNIZE, LEARN (DURL): ASSESSMENT VOCABULARY

Directions: Check off your knowledge of the following terms in the column that indicates your level of understanding.

	D & U-I can define and use term(s)	R- 1 recognize term(s)	L - 1 need to learn term(s)
ACTIONS:			
Classify			
Compare / contrast			
Conclude			
Describe			
Determine			
Draw conclusions			
Identify			
Interpret			
Locate main idea			
Outline			
Predict outcome(s)			
Summarize			
Support			
Other:			
TESTING TEXT TYPES			
Advertisement			
Captions			
Chart			
Diagrams			
Dialogue			
Drama			
Essay			
Fable			
Fiction/ nonfiction			
Glossary			
Graph			
Paragraph			
Passage			

FIGURE 8.1. DEFINE & USE, RECOGNIZE, LEARN (DURL): ASSESSMENT VOCABULARY (CONT.)

	D & U-I can define and use term(s)	R- 1 recognize term(s)	L - 1 need to learn term(s)
Poetry			
Problem			
Table of Contents			
Other:			
STORY VOCABULARY			
Characterization			
Denoument			
Plot			
Point of View			
Rising Action			
Setting			
Theme			
Title			
Other:			
LITERARY DEVICES			
Alliteration			
Allusion			
Foreshadowing			
Hyperbole			
Imagery			
Irony			
Metaphor			
Onamatopeia			
Personification			
Simile			
Other:			

Examine the assessment types you administer, add key assessment terms you use to this chart.

Encouraging students to examine their own thought processes, whether in writing or in reading, is central to my work as a teacher. The very first day of class we begin discussions on metacognition.

I have students place a sticky note with their names on a white board that has "Metacognition" scrawled on it, and I ask them to "vote" on a knowledge rating scale. It's fun and gets them moving right away, but it also focuses our class for the next 12 weeks. Almost everything we do from that point on—reflection circles, journal writing, miscue analysis, think alouds, retelling, reading conversations—all point back to metacognition because I want students to learn how to constantly monitor their reading, their writing, their thinking for meaning.

Joan Flora, 2006

Several literacy strategies help students develop their self-evaluation skills: the learning log, admit and exit slips, extended student reflections, the muddiest point, the one-minute paper, one-sentence summaries, and the reflective evaluation letter. These data collection strategies help the teacher observe the students' learning progress as it occurs.

TABLE 3

INSTRUCTIONAL SUMMARY OF SELF-EVALUATION STRATEGIES

Literacy Strategies	Self-Evaluation Strategies
Primary Focus	Informal Assessment
Learning Principles	❑ Metacognitive Experience ❑ Active Involvement
When to Use	Before/after reading or lesson
Goals: National or State Literacy Standards	❑ Record, summarize perceptions ❑ Explore and extend thinking ❑ Formulate and test beliefs ❑ Establish goals
Materials	Appropriate for learning activity
Time	5-15 minutes

Learning Log. One of the easiest strategies to use is a learning log. Logs are journal items written by students pertaining to the content under study. They may include students' questions, procedural notes, vocabulary definitions, reflections, and applications. Teachers design any prompt that meets their students' needs. Some prompts that teachers use include:

Fulwiler (1980); Alvermann & Phelps (1994)

❑ What did I understand about the work we did in class today?
❑ What difficulties did I have with the text assignment?
❑ What questions do I have about the work we did today?
❑ Draw a picture of a vocabulary term covered in today's lesson.
❑ Write a reflective piece on how I think the class felt about today's lesson.

Procedure. You need a few minutes at the beginning or at the end of class for this activity. Direct students to write their questions about content or situations in the class, or to share reflections on their progress or lack of it. If students are assigned readings, their reflections on these become part of the journal entry. For this to work, students need to write entries a few times a week at home or in class. This consistency enables students to consciously reflect upon their own learning process.

STUDENT TALK

When I decided to do my project I was doing it by myself, so I researched the topics I was covering, and before I had anything written down I changed my mind and decided to do another project with a partner. It was a last-minute decision, and so my partner and I looked in a book and found a lot of information on one part of our project, so we thought it wouldn't take very long to find the rest or more information. So on the last Saturday before the project was due we went to Powell's Books and the downtown library and we didn't find very much information. For the next project I'm managing my time better and working out time to work with my partner.

Admit Slips. Students enter the class with a short piece of writing summarizing their learning from your previous class. As they enter, you collect these signed slips and read a few to help focus on the topic under study. In addition, a quick perusal will identify students who are connected or not connected to the topic/ issue at hand. Over time some patterns should emerge, identifying students' difficulties as well as their successes.

Zemelman & Daniels (1988); Cross & Angelo (1988)

Exit Slips. These are similar to the admit slips, but the activity occurs at the end of class. Students may respond to a teacher's summary question, write a short reflection on their perceived learning, or raise questions about the class. Again, a survey of these short pieces will provide ongoing data analysis concerning students' progress.

Extended Student Reflections. For a midterm or at the end of a unit of study, have students write a short summary of what they felt they learned from the experience. These can be attached to a test or addressed in a letter to the instructor. See Figure 8.2 for an example developed by a business education teacher.

There seems to be a magic about letter writing. Students take it seriously. We are not sure why this occurs, but we believe that the format "Dear Ms. Dunn" keeps the writer specific and personal. In our own classes, we have used this medium and have observed its merit in the sense of community it builds between the instructor and students, and the honesty it cultivates in students' perceptions of their own learning.

Letter writing to the instructor builds community and cultivates honesty in students' perceptions of their learning.

STUDENT TALK

This class probably has been somewhat of a blessing for me. I was almost to the point of giving up that the government (public school) would ever let a class that was good for me into the system. I really love what we're studying and how we're encouraged to give feedback to the teacher about how we're doing and how we're feeling about the course.

Atwell (1990)

The Muddiest Point

This exercise is one of the quickest ways to determine what students find unclear, confusing, or just difficult to understand. This technique is a safe alternative for students who have difficulty raising questions in class. In addition, teach-

How does this strategy develop self-assessment skills?

FIGURE 8.2. REFLECTIVE EVALUATION LETTER

Direction Sheet

MIDTERM CHECK

Write me a personal business letter responding to the following questions. Answer each question in a new paragraph. Do not write the question in your paragraph; write the answer using sentences. I would like to see at least two sentences per paragraph. See my example on the back of this handout.

- ❏ Use the information in your notes and Century 21 book on formatting letters.
- ❏ Use block format and open punctuation.
- ❏ Use your own words.
- ❏ Use correct grammar and punctuation.

My address is:

> Mrs. Dunn
> Hood River High School
> 1220 Indian Creek Rd.
> Hood River, OR 97031

1. What things are going well in this class?
2. What things do you think we should change in this class?
3. What activities are difficult for you in this class?
4. What activities do you enjoy in this class?
5. What activities would help you learn better in this class?
6. What have you learned in this class this quarter?
7. Any other comments/ feedback?

---

ers get a sense of what students find problematic and can adjust their presentations to remedy these problems. For example, a social studies teacher was teaching about the similarities and differences between the North and South during the Civil War. After reading through the students' written responses to the teacher's question, "What was the muddiest point of the discussion?," the teacher realized that the students didn't grasp the concepts, compare and contrast.

In order for the students to understand the content they needed to understand this organizational process. The next day the teacher conducted a mini-lesson on the meaning of "'compare/contrast," drawing on episodes in the Civil War to illustrate the similarities and differences implied in comparing and contrasting events or elements.

Procedure: After a discussion, lecture, reading, video, or CD-ROM presentation ask the students to write on a 3" X 5" card a quick response to the question "What was the muddiest point in _____?"

Time should be sufficient at the end of class for students to have time to reflect. Then collect these cards as students are walking out the door, or have a Muddiest Point Collection Box, where students can deposit their cards. Since these are brief responses-usually phrases- they can be read quickly Respond to students' remarks during the next class period or as soon as possible to maximize the learning.

TEACHER TALK

As a calculus teacher, I've often noticed that my students didn't want to ask for specific help in doing their problems. On the other hand, they frequently lamented that they were totally lost and didn't understand anything. Since implementing the 'muddiest point' exercise, I'm thrilled with how pointed their questions are. It seems the opportunity to write out their confusions and concerns has transferred into the ability to raise particular questions orally and comfortably in class.

One Minute Paper

This is a writing assignment that a teacher can assign either in class or for an out-of-class assignment. Students write for a minute on a reading, a classroom experience, or a question that the teacher or students pose.

Karre (1994); Cross & Angelo (1988)

This activity enables students to capture the main points of the content with minimum effort. Their summarizing, abstracting, and critical thinking abilities are strengthened and celebrated by the class and instructor. In the sharing process students see how their responses compare to peers. They learn to monitor and adapt their writing, or share their strengths depending on capabilities they bring to the task.

Procedure.

Why do you suppose the consistent use of minute papers enhances learning?

1. Demonstrate what a minute writing experience is like. Give students a brief textbook, current event, or supplemental selection to read. After the class has read it, have them write for a minute on what they think the topic is about. While the students are writing, you also write publicly on an overhead projector or computer (if you have a demonstration class room LCD panel). Let students see how you summarize material in a minute. Have students pair up and read their papers to each other. Debrief on the process to make sure that students understand the purpose of the exercise.

2. Assign a reading to be read outside of class or in class. Students are to write for a minute on the most important thing they got from the reading or they can respond to a question you've posed. Limit student response to a half-page. This activity is referred to frequently as the "half-sheet response."

3. Have students share their minute papers in pairs or in small groups. This enables students to make comparisons between their writing and that of their partner(s). The more students do this exercise, the better they get at capturing the essence of the content material. In the process of sharing their papers, they exchange ideas and help reinforce the major points of the reading. Even if each student's paper captures a different aspect of the reading, it all contributes to a synergistic picture of the reading itself.

4. Collect the papers for participation points or daily assessment. It takes a few minutes at the most to record these entries. It also gives you a diagnostic

opportunity to see which students have strengths in capturing the essence of the content and which students are having difficulty. A few mini-lessons on summary writing with students having problems should alleviate the problem.

One Minute Write Variation

This variation provides for student initiative in selecting the reading and sharing the One Minute Paper. It is also a way of broadening students' awareness of the world that surrounds them. This activity is geared as a warm-up exercise to class and should take minimum time.

Procedure.

1. Initially, the teacher can conduct the reading minute exercise selecting a reading from the newspaper, a current book, a magazine—present high interest material as much as possible.

2. Ask students to write for a minute on what they think the most important idea is in the writing. This could be varied. A purpose might be: to select something that resonated with them, the style of the writer that appealed to them or the reading's application to what they are studying. It is helpful if students keep a section of their notebook for these and date these for easy access. To practice summary writing, limit this to one sentence, Students share these with their partners.

3. Have students sign-up to lead a reading minute. Over the course of the term students should be able to sign up for at least three reading minutes. Encourage students to spread these out and choose different genres for reading. At the end of the presentation, students should thank the presenter for their leadership. We have observed that these are impressive moments when students provide this with their"Awesome's". "Cool", "Thanks" or "High-Five" the presenter. There is no doubt that this establishes a warm classroom climate as well.

4. At the end of the term, students should have a wealth of summary writing experiences. Gallagher (2004) suggests they evaluate this experience by writing about this experience. Possible copies, she suggests:
   a. Which Reading Minute was your favorite?
   b. Which Reading Minute taught you something?
   c. Is there value in the Reading Minute Assignment?
   d. Should I require next term's students to continue the Reading Minute?

Cultivate a supportive classroom climate through the One Minute Write.

One-Sentence Summaries (WDWWWWHW)

This is another summarizing technique a teacher can use to find out how thoroughly, coherently, and creatively students can reduce a given topic to one sentence. The pattern WDWWWWHW (Who Does/Did What to Whom, When, Where, How and Why) guides this summary.

Procedure.

1. Select a topic that your students have studied in your course to date and that you want them to summarize.

2. Ask them to work as quickly as possible in answering the questions "Who Does/Did What to Whom, How, When, Where, and Why?" as they pertain to the topic under discussion.

3. Have students turn their responses into a sensible sentence.

Example. Language Arts

QUESTION	RESPONSE
Who?	Tenorio and his drunk friends
Do what?	come to murder
To what or whom?	Ultima La Grande
How?	Burning
When?	at night
Where?	not clear
Why?	Tenorio accuses her of killing his daughter

Anaya (1991). "Bless me, Ultima" in *Braided lives.*

Sentence: In the story "Bless me, Ultima," Tenorio, with the help of his drunken friends, thinks that Ultima is responsible for the killing of his daughter and wishes to bum her alive.

These are only a few samples culled from many strategies that you can use to promote your students' abilities as self-assessors. As their skills improve in this area, the time you spend on assessment should decrease. Students' ownership of their written products or learning, their growing sense of their abilities as a reader or writer, and their skill as evaluators in a social context should provide you with more time to plan and facilitate learning opportunities rather than test them.

After students have had some experience with responding to these quick cognitive asessment exercises, encourage them to set a few reading goals for themselves. They can select these from the following list or create some of their own.

At the end of the term write a Reflective Evaluation Letter to your teacher in which you explain how well you achieved your goals. What were you successes? Your difficulties? What goal will you work on next?

Assessment Activities Linking Materials and Learners in the Content Area

Our preservice teachers often ask, "How do teachers assess the variety of reading, writing, speaking and listening skills prevalent in the content area classroom?"

A Classroom Assessment Program

In our first chapter we suggested a coaching role as a possiblity for content area teachers—one that is currently glacially materializing at this level. For secondary teachers who take on this responsibility other assessments you may be interested in that focus on the general literacy ability of your students or those students you are working with in this capacity follow:

1. Reading Attitude Surveys like the Burke Reading Inventory that determines how students define reading, and how they solve reading problems.
2. Self-Reflection. Students write about their relationship to reading, writing and school. They write about the kind of students they are, their preferences and their learning style.
3. Encourage students to set reading goals for themselves. See Figure 8.3.
4. Statewide assessments. Provide students with practice, examining a few questions each week, talk about test-taking strategies and practice answering the

---

FIGURE 8.3.   SETTING PERSONAL READING GOALS

Name _____ Date _____ Per. _____

Directions: From the following list of reading goals, please select three goals to work on this term. Number the three you choose: 1, 2, 3. Priortize these goals if you wish.

_____ a. Read everyday
_____ b. Expand vocabulary
_____ c. Finish a book this term
_____ d. Work on comprehending what is read
_____ e. Write a short summary of what is read
_____ f. Take notes, ask questions, think critically
_____ g. Experiment with skimming and scanning.
_____ h. Read strategically—predict, configure patterns, explore inferences
_____ i. Acknowledge being lost or confused and apply fix-up strategies
_____ j. Get a library card
_____ k. Experiment with different genres—read non-fiction if fiction is the preferred choice, or newspapers if podcasts are the preferred news source
_____ l. Work on improving reading speed while still understanding content
_____ m. Carry a book to read while commuting or waiting
_____ n. Other: _____

---

sample questions. Build confidence in taking tests. Most statewide testing samples are available at state Department of Education websites.

5. CATS-Classroom assessment techniques to assess content area learning (Minute paper, the muddiest point, magic squares, etc.).

6. Reader's Theater. See Chapter 7 for examples of this. Students work on a student-chosen piece of literature (or non-fiction). They can use a prepared example or rewrite a text selection to include parts for the readers. They perform in groups of 3–4 students in front of the class. This is an excellent activity for fluency building as well as interpretation of text. Some students are terrified of this experience. They can be given options to help coach teams, to do the writing, or to work with an instructional assistant to build up confidence and fluency.

7. Over-the-Shoulder Miscue Analysis (Davenport, 2002). For students who are struggling, this is a non-invasive activity to trace students' specific difficulties with their reading.

   a) The teacher sets up a reading conference with a student. These should be short eight to ten-minute activities at most. While the student reads, the teacher writes down miscues that the student has made and tracks reading strategies that the student has used. It is helpful if the teacher stands behind the student or sits slightly behind the students so the student is not distracted by the teacher's note taking. If needed, see Davenport (2002) for a chart format to record these.

b) The student selects a book he wants to read in his conference. After a few but significant number of minutes reading, the teacher invites the student to talk about the reading.

c) After this discussion, the teacher reviews with the student miscues made while reading—if any, and the reading strategies the student used.

This process allows the teacher to assess students' book choices. Are they challenging? Are the books on the same topic or from a continuing series of a favorite author? It also enables the teacher to determine if students are self-correcting their miscues, fluent, exhibiting a positive or negative attitude towards reading, and using literacy strategies, for example, context clues, selecting main ideas, connecting with their own experiences, summarizing and synthesizing ideas.

One teacher shared with us the letters she writes to students after this activity. Students paste their letters in their journals in order to track their progress and the strategies they used, and practiced.

An excerpt...

As you read aloud to me, I noticed that most of your miscues were self-corrected, which is wonderful. You and I make very similar miscues in our reading, and we both are reading with meaning in mind. That's good news! Retelling what you've read seems hard for you. Currently you reread a whole chapter to make sure you understand it. That's ok, but it's too much work which will make school harder for you as you get into more challenging classes. Here's what I want you to experiment with: try the sketching bookmark idea I shared with you. Make a quick sketch of what you've read every 1–2 pages to be sure you understand it before you move on to the next part of your reading. Be careful to not get caught up in your sketching—you just want to use it enough to support your reading and not let it distract you from your reading. Let me know how this strategy works for you after you've tried it at least a few times.

These assessment activities work because they are designed by teachers or by reading authorities who have studied students in the classroom. This is their strength, a design to assess students by using materials that students come face-to-face with on a regular basis. The following Textbook Activity Guide is popular because of its ease of design and the useful information it provides.

In the following model, "Your Turn," designed to test levels of comprehension and understanding of vocabulary used in this chapter on assessment, we hope that as you complete it, you will develop an understanding of the process and reflect on possible applications with your own content area materials.

Textbook Activity Guide

TABLE 4

INSTRUCTIONAL SUMMARY OF TEXTBOOK ACTIVITY GUIDE

Literacy Strategies	Textbook Activity Guide
Primary Focus	❑ Informal diagnosis of textbook use
Learning Principles	❑ Use talk to share information and interpretations ❑ Self-monitoring and regulating of thought processes
When to use	❑ Before using textbooks or content materials
Goals: National or State Literacy Standards	❑ Locate Information ❑ Understand and use information in a variety of texts across the subject area to perform a task
Materials	❑ Activity sheet and writing instrument
Time	❑ 25 minutes

Wood, Lapp & Flood (1992)

Text-oriented activities like the Textbook Activity Guide if used early in the term also help teachers learn about the students' interests, attitude or skills involved in learning the specialized subject area.

This guide is another informal diagnostic tool that aids the teacher in assessing how students deal with content area texts directly. The guide is designed by teachers in their specific content areas for students to work collaboratively, helping each other experience the reading process using their textbook. See Figure 8.4.

As they answer the questions and proceed through the guide, students will check their understanding by using the self-monitoring codes. Notice how this guide asks students to use various skills such as surveying, skimming, predicting and organizing.

Procedure. In using this guide, model one or at least a few sections from one so that students get a feel for how self-evaluation works to enhance their learning. In designing this guide,

❑ clarify the chapter objectives for the topic under study.
❑ select headings, portions and diagrams that relate to your objective.
❑ select text features you want to focus on in your guide.
❑ match the reading/study strategy task to your objective(s), e.g., compare and contrast chart to demonstrate relationships.
❑ create a self-monitoring system helpful to students. Use page references to help students move through the guide.

Your Turn

Name _____ Date _____ Subject Area _____

General Directions: Read from the section, **DEFINITION**, to the section, **SELF-EVALUATION**. Close your book and answer the first question. You may then refer to the text to answer the remaining questions. Use additional paper for your responses when needed.

I. What is the main idea?
   1. From the few pages you have read, what would you say is the main idea?

     _____

     _____

II. Literal. You may use the reading selection for the following questions. This material is found directly in the text.
   1. Define the following terms:
     a. assessment
     b. formal assessment
     c. informal assessment
     d. standardized test
   2. How can teachers create an informal assessment system in their own classrooms?

     _____

     _____

III. Interpretive. Answers to the following questions are not directly stated by the authors. You must think about and search through the material for the answers.
   1. How has assessment changed from a teacher-directed to a more student-centered process?

     _____

   2. How does being "testwise" affect a student's assessment performance?

     _____

IV. Applied. The answers to the following questions are not found directly in this selection. You need to apply your own thinking to your response.
   1. What is the role of students' standardized test scores in teachers' planning of instruction?

     _____

     _____

   2. In planning your own assessment program, what strategies could you use? Why?

     _____

     _____

FIGURE 8.4.   TEXTBOOK ACTIVITY GUIDE

Name _____ Date _____

Strategy Codes

RR	Read and retell in your own words.
DP	Read and discuss with a partner.
PP	Predict with a partner.
WR	Write a response on your own.
Skim	Read quietly for purpose stated and discuss with a partner.
MOC	Organize information with a map, chart or outline.

Self-monitoring Codes

Use the following to check how you feel about your understanding of the material you are studying.

a. +   I understand this information.
b. ?   I'm not sure if I understand.
c. X   I do not understand; I need to restudy.

1. _____ PP   pp. 221-227.
Survey the title, picture, charts, and headings. What do you expect to learn about this section?

2. _____ WR   pp. 221-227.
As you are reading, jot down three or more new word definitions for your vocabulary collection.

3. _____ DP   pp. 221-227. Read the next three sections.
a. What two things did the Mayans accomplish that demonstrate growth as a civilization?
b. What did the Mayans do to get enough food to survive.

4. _____ MOC   Map p. 223, or make an outline of the info.

5. _____ Skim   p. 224, Section: A New Mayan King.
Purpose: to understand elements described about the installation of a new Mayan Ruler.
a. Glyphs
b. Double Comb
c. stelae

6. _____ DP   pp. 225. Describe:
a. the Mayan numeral system
b. the most important use of the Mayan numerical system
c. the Mayan calendar

7. _____ WR   p. 226. Who was Quetzecoatl? Why was he important to the Mayans?

8. _____ DP   p. 226. Compare the civilizations of the Mayans and Peruvians with the Eurasian civilizations.

Source of reading material: Dunn, Ross E. (1990). *Links across time and place: A world history*. NY: McDougal, Littell & Co.

*Textbooks
continue to be a
major resource
for content
delivery.*

*Shallert & Roser
(1989); Sewall
(1988)*

The debate over the use of textbooks rages on. No matter their sometimes outdated information, bias, formats and lifeless writing, they ride the waves of use and non-use. However, our experience with secondary teachers shows that textbooks continue to be a major resource to guide students' acquisition of subject area information. Furthermore, some district guidelines mandate a certain portion of instructional time using the textbook. A preservice student says to us in light of this observation, "I would like to know when to use the text and when not to." For our students to understand the complexity of this issue, we advise students to begin with the textbook itself.

Readability

TABLE 5

INSTRUCTIONAL SUMMARY OF READABILITY

Literacy Strategy	Readability
Primary Focus	Informal Assessment
When to Use	Before using content materials
Materials	❏ Readability formulas ❏ Text materials
Time	20 minutes

Define Readability.

*Tonjes & Zintz
(1981)*

A widely used method to measure the difficulty level of printed materials is the application of the readability formula. They are controversial and non-exact measurements; however, it is our pragmatic opinion that they are another tool that teachers have to use in order to make instructional decisions.

When teachers are making decisions regarding the selection of a class text among several being reviewed, readability formulas are particularly useful. These formulas rely on two assumptions:
1. Longer sentences are more difficult to read than shorter ones.
2. Unfamiliar words in text make it more difficult to read.

Fry's (1977) readability formula is one of the most popular because of its range and ease of use. It can be used to estimate a wide range from primary to college-level texts. The procedures for its use are given in Figure 8.5.

Expanded Directions for Working Readability Graph
1. Randomly select three (3) sample passages and count out exactly 100 words each, beginning with the beginning of a sentence. Do count proper nouns, initializations and numerals.
2. Count the number of sentences in the hundred words, estimating length of the fraction of the last sentence to the nearest one-tenth.
3. Count the total number of syllables in the 100-word passage. If you don't have a hand counter available, an easy way is to simply put a mark above every syllable over one in each word; then, when you get to the end of the passage, count the number of marks and add 100. Small calculators can also

Figure 8.5.   Fry Graph for Estimating Readability

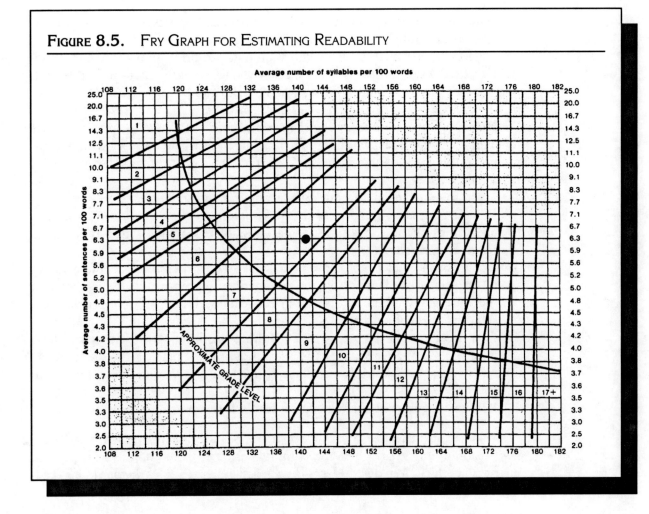

Average number of syllables per 100 words

be used as counters by pushing numeral 1, then pushing the + sign for each word or syllable.

4. Enter graph with *average* sentence length and *average* number of syllables; plot dot where the two lines intersect. Area where dot is plotted will give you the approximate grade level.

5. If a great deal of variability is found in syllable count or sentence count, putting more samples into the average is desirable.

6. A word is defined as a group of symbols with a space on either side; thus 1945 is one word.

7. A syllable is defined as a phonetic syllable. Generally, there are as many syllables as vowel sounds. For example, *stopped is* one syllable and *wanted is* two syllables. When counting syllables for numerals and initializations, count one syllable for each symbol. For example, *1945* is four syllables.

Source: Edward Fry, "Fry's readability graph: clarifications, validity, and extension to level 17." *Journal of Reading.* 21(1977), 242-252. Reproduction permitted—no copyright

*Cullinan &
Fitzgerald
(1985); Fry
(1977)*

Why the controversy about readability formulas? Critics charge that the formulas consider only text characteristics and not other characteristics like student interests, relevance, reading skills required, and prior knowledge in the subject area field. Fry, on the other hand, acknowledges these limitations but defends its utility for teachers, publishing houses, libraries and businesses, who must have some yardstick for estimating the difficulty of texts.

In our response to our students' questions, we encourage them to use these formulas with the understanding that they merely provide the user with an estimate of difficulty. We further suggest that students keep in mind Nelson's (1978) rubber ruler:

1. Learn to use a readability formula as an aid in evaluating text.
2. Whenever possible, provide materials containing the essential facts, concepts, and values of the subject at varying levels of readability within the reading range of your students.
3. Don't assume that matching readability level of material to reading achievement level of students results in automatic comprehension. Remember that there are many other factors that affect reading difficulty besides those measured by readability formulas.
4. Don't assume that rewriting text materials according to readability criteria results in automatic reading ease. Leave rewriting of materials to the linguists, researchers, and editors, who have to analyze and validate their manipulations.
5. Recognize that using a readability formula is no substitute for instruction.

Assigning is not teaching. Subject area textbooks are not designed for independent reading. To enhance reading comprehension in your subject area, provide instruction which prepares students for the assignment, guides them in their reading, and reinforces new ideas through rereading and discussion (pp. 624-625).

Excerpt from Nelson, J. (1978 April). *Journal of Reading.* Copyright 1978 by the International Reading Association. All rights reserved.

Evaluating shorter passages

*What materials
do you use that
could be ana-
lyzed for their
difficulty level
by using the
readability
formula de-
signed by
Forgan and
Mangrum
(1976)?*

A short form of readability that we have found useful is one suggested by Forgan and Mangrum (1976). Much reading material that we use has fewer words than the 100-word limit that many of the standardized readability formulas use, for example, legal forms (used widely in consumer education courses), math problems, directions, and essay questions. How can we estimate their difficulty level?

1. Count the total number of words in the passage. For example, the total is sixty-nine words.
2. Round down to the nearest ten. In this case you would round down the sixty nine words to sixty.
3. Use this number (in this case, sixty) when counting the number of sentences and syllables.

FIGURE 8.6.   EVALUATING READING DIFFICULTY OF SHORT SELECTIONS

Number of words in selection (Less than 100)	Multiply by
30	3.3
40	2.5
50	2.0
60	1.67
70	1.43
80	1.25
90	1.1

4. Multiply the number of sentences and the number of syllables by the corresponding number found in the conversion chart above (see Figure 8.6). With our example of a sixty-nine word passage, rounded down to sixty, you would multiply the number of sentences by 1.67 and then the number of syllables by 1.67.
5. Use these numbers to enter Fry's graph to find your readability estimate.

Teaching students to use a readability formula has some interesting payoffs. Tonjes and Zintz (1981) recount a story an English teacher told them regarding the student use of a readability formula. Her tenth grade students were having difficulty with their writing. After they were taught how to apply a readability formula to their work, many students found they were writing at a third grade level. Suddenly the students were asking for instruction that would help them improve their writing. We can envision some problems with writing to a formula; however, if it provides students with an insight they didn't have before, we say, "Go for it."

Tonjes & Zintz (1981); Vacca & Vacca (1996); Alvermann & Phelps (1994)

To analyze textbooks as thoroughly as you can, we suggest that teachers do a qualitative review of their texts also. There are many checklists available. In addition, it doesn't hurt to check with your district office. Often a district has a checklist for use by its textbook committees. The following checklist examines a textbook's content, format, utility and style.

FIGURE 8.7.   GENERAL TEXTBOOK READABILITY CHECKLIST

Content	Utility
❏ Does the content complement the curriculum? ❏ Is the content current? ❏ Is there balance between depth and breadth of coverage? ❏ How many new or difficult vocabulary terms are included and how are they introduced and defined? ❏ How dense are the new concepts in the text? ❏ Is the content generally appropriate to students' prior knowledge? ❏ Are diverse populations represented? Are varying opinions addressed? Is language nonsexist?	❏ How good are the activities at the end of the chapters? ❏ Do text questions call for interpretation, evaluation, and application as well as literal recall? ❏ Is there a teacher's manual? Would it be helpful? ❏ Does the text or manual suggest additional readings or related tradebooks?
Format	**Style**
❏ Are there good graphic aids and illustrations? ❏ Are they distracting or irrelevant to the content? ❏ How are chapters set up? Are there introductions, summaries, heads and subheads, and marginal notes? ❏ Are layout and print attractive and easy to read?	❏ Is the writing lively and interesting to read? ❏ Is the syntax at a suitable level of complexity? ❏ Is the writing coherent and clear?

From *Content Reading and Literacy* by D. Alvemann and S. Phelps. Copyright (c) 1994 by Allyn and Bacon. Reprinted with permission.

Lexile Measures - Matching Learner to Text Materials

A recent leg to the assessment table is the use of Lexile measures to match students' reading scores with appropriate reading materials. It is an attempt to improve student reading skills and monitor their literacy across the content areas and at home. These Lexile measures determine reading material that challenges students but not to the point of frustration. Secondary teachers are warming up to the use of Lexile measures. They enable them to examine student literacy data and use this in selecting appropriate materials for their classes.

The Lexile measure indicates the difficulty level of a text—a book, magazine or newspaper article. Usually the Lexile Framework® for Reading is linked to a state's reading/literature assessment. Student scores on their state-mandated tests are reported in Lexiles. These can be then matched with textbooks, fiction and nonfiction trade books, newspapers or magazines. Scores range from 200L for materials at the first grade level to 1300L for those at the twelfth grade level. These levels continue upward for materials appropriate for graduate school.

Lexile book databases of thousands of titles are available at such sites as http:// www.ode.state.or.us/ teachlearn/ subjects/ elarts/ reading/ literacy /lexiles/ maps.aspx

READING COACH

The ELL department and I use www.biz3000.com because of the ease of finding Lexiled articles on the same topic, which allows me to have several reading groups, all reading basically the same article with differences in vocabulary and some concepts. It's actually a very useful tool.

Like the Fry Readability Graph, the Lexile measures are based on word frequency and sentence length, they "do not address age-appropriateness, student interest or the quality of the text." As in all assessment matters as well as instructional ones, teachers need to keep a critical evaluative eye on why they choose to use these aids. For reading fiction, the Lexile measures seem appealing. However, to ensure that the "Lexiled" content material is valid, current and has the breadth and depth needed to understand the topic, issue or ideas presented, the content area teacher might test the material suggested with our General Textbook Readability Checklist (Figure 8.7).

Meta-metrics, 2005

Cloze Procedure

TABLE 6

INSTRUCTIONAL SUMMARY OF THE CLOZE PROCEDURE

Literacy Strategy	Cloze Procedure
Primary Focus	Informal Assessment
Learning Principles	❑ Active Involvement ❑ Background Knowledge
When to Use	Before using content materials

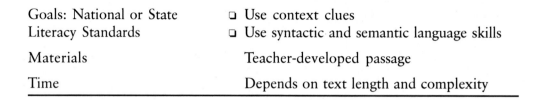

Goals: National or State	❏ Use context clues
Literacy Standards	❏ Use syntactic and semantic language skills
Materials	Teacher-developed passage
Time	Depends on text length and complexity

Describe the Cloze Procedure.

Knowing how successful students are with text materials helps teachers in selecting materials and planning instructional procedures. The cloze technique is another diagnostic tool to use to determine an appropriate fit between the reader and the text. This procedure is a method by which words are deleted systematically from a text passage. After the students supply the missing terms, their ability to accurately determine the words that were deleted is evaluated. This procedure capitalizes on the interplay between the knowledge that the students bring to the reading task and their language competence.

Wilson Taylor (1953) conceived the idea of the cloze technique. Based on the Gestalt psychological term *closure,* it refers to the tendency of a thinking person to anticipate the completion of a not-quite-finished pattern. For example, if someone said to you, "Have a good _____ !", you might automatically fill in the missing word, completing the expression with words like "time" or "day."

In order to complete the cloze exercise, students must have a working knowledge of the meanings of words, their functions as nouns, adjectives, objects, etc., as well as the constructed meaning that comes from the words taken as a whole.

Procedure.
1. Select a representative passage from the text of approximately 275 words that the students have not seen before.
2. Leave the first and last sentences intact.
3. Starting with the second sentence, delete every fifth word, substituting a standard length blank of twelve spaces, until fifty words are deleted.
4. Do not number the blanks or give answer sheets, or you will invalidate the results.

Administering and Scoring the Cloze:
1. Tell the students that this is a procedure to help you make decisions regarding the choice of class materials. It is not a test to be factored into their grade for the class. The knowledge of their ability in reading the textbook will enable you to supplement materials accordingly. Tell them that only one word has been deleted from each blank and that you will not count off for misspellings. They are to try to determine the exact word the writer used in each case.
2. Allow unlimited time for each student to complete the typed passage. You may set up a few practice sessions so that they become familiar with the test-taking technique. Most students are familiar with a multiple-choice format. The cloze procedure may be difficult simply by virtue of its format. Students are used to selecting answers from a list of choices rather than originating their own.

3. When scoring allow only the exact word replacement. Each blank is worth two points. Figure 8.8 shows how to interpret the scores. Scores falling within the instructional level are said to be equivalent to approximately a seventy-five percent score on a multiple-choice test on the same material.

Students typically challenge the nonacceptance of synonyms. Bormuth's (1966) research has shown that overall relative ranking changes very little, regardless of whether synonyms are counted as correct or incorrect. When synonyms are used, the tests are much more subjective and time-consuming to score. Over the years, we have used the interpretation table to explain to students their ranking. When they observe that they are usually on the *instructional level,* even with a score of 44 (22 out of the 50 items correct), their arguments usually fizzle.

We have included a cloze passage for you to try. We'd like you to complete this on your own. After you have completed the cloze activity, score your work. The correct items are given on the next page. What level did you attain? Even with many items not matching the author's, you probably did well, didn't you?

What level would you expect most of your students to score on a given cloze activity?

FIGURE 8.8.   READING LEVEL BASED ON CLOZE SCORES

Score	Level
58–100	Independent
44–57	Instruction
0–43	Frustration

What do these levels indicate to the teacher?

- 58–100%. Students achieving these scores are reading their text material approximately at an *independent level.* They may be able to read the material on their own with very little guidance from the teacher.
- 44–57%. Students scoring at this *instruction level* can read the passage with some competence. However, teacher guidance will greatly enhance the understanding students construct from this passage.
- 0–43%. Students are having a great deal of difficulty with this material. At this *frustration level,* they will probably need other learning material, such as easier reading texts, multimedia presentations of the material, or tutors that will provide one-on-one help.

Notes

Your Turn

Name _____ Date _____ Subject Area _____

Directions: Please complete the following sentences. This is not a test. It is an activity designed to see how well you perform with the materials we use in this class. Do not worry about misspellings.

Cloze Exercise. What is an Old Growth Forest?

Four major components interact to create old growth forests: large live tress, multi-layered canopies, snags, and down woody material. All four are essential _____ the ongoing sustainability of _____ growth forests' ecosystems. Deep _____ the forest, the giant _____ firs form a network _____ layers and branches that _____ moisture and stabilize the _____ floor. Large life trees _____ habitat for wildlife and _____ essential to the cycling _____ air, water and nutrients. _____ , carbon and potassium are _____ and released centuries later _____ the tree returns to _____ forest floor.

A variety _____ smaller, shade-tolerate tree _____ interweave to form a _____- layered canopy. This web _____ branches provides pathways for _____ to travel from the _____ of the tallest fir _____ the forest floor. Over _____ , however, even the mightiest _____ these giants succumb to _____ forces of nature. Fire, _____, disease and decay take _____ toll, transforming some into _____ dead trees or snags. _____ snag soon becomes host _____ a variety of wildlife. _____ , northern flying squirrels, pine _____ and others may use _____ snags for homes or _____ to forage for food.

_____ the giant snag decays _____ , it falls to the _____ floor where it joins _____ downed woody material. The _____ organisms to attack the _____ tree are fungi and _____ . Their activity continues the _____ process of nutrient cycling. _____ downed log also provides _____ nursery for young trees. _____ and trapped nutrients supply _____ for the seeds fortunate _____ to land on the _____ log. Over time, progressively _____ organisms (mites, spiders, frogs, _____ , voles and others enjoy _____ rich organic material and moist environment furnished by the decaying log. The rotting log can remain on the forest floor for centuries.

(308 words, Courtesy of World Forestry Center, Portland, Oregon. No copyright)

Writer's word choice for missing terms:

1. to	11. nitrogen	21. to	31. martens	41. ongoing
2. old	12. stored	22. time	32. the	42. the
3. within	13. when	23. of	33. places	43. a
4. Douglas	14. the	24. the	34. as	44. moisture
5. of	15. of	25. storms	35. further	45. nourishment
6. trap	16. species	26. their	36. forest	46. enough
7. forest	17. multi-	27. standing	37. other	47. fallen
8. provide	18. of	28. the	38. first	48. larger
9. are	19. animals	29. to	39. fallen	49. salamanders
10. of	20. top	30. woodpeckers	40. bacteria	50. the

Questions in 4-Learning Styles

Previously we wrote about "testwiseness," suggesting that students be given ample opportunity to practice and develop test taking skills. This activity Questions in 4-Learning Styles provides students with the time to examine different kinds of questions, assess which they find easier to respond to and develop their abilities in working with those they find less interesting or difficult.

This exercise goes far beyond building skills for assessment purposes only, it also gives students the ability to respond successfully to everyday academic questions, to write essays, develop divergent ways of exploring a topic by writing in different genres, or using artwork and technology to convey their ideas.

TABLE 7

INSTRUCTIONAL SUMMARY OF QUESTIONS IN 4-LEARNING STYLES	
Literacy Strategy	**Questions in 4-Learning Styles**
Primary Focus	Writing and Reading
Learning Principles	❑ Participate actively in seeking meaning ❑ Integrate writing with curriculum
When to Use	During unit
Goals: National or State Literacy Standards	❑ Generate and test interpretations, explanations, predictions and hypotheses ❑ Make reasoned evaluations
Materials	Question Outline
Time	40 minutes

This strategy gives focus to a reading. Students are allowed to select the question they prefer. As they internalize the question, this process motivates them to write using their own methods or abilities. In addition, recording and sharing with others in the class as well as selecting ideas on which to build enhances learning.

Questions are geared to those students who learn by remembering, the Sensing Thinkers (ST); those who learn by making connections, the Sensing Feelers (SF); those who learn by reasoning, the Intuitive Thinkers (IT); and those who

How do Questions in 4-Learning Styles provide diverse avenues for learning and success?

Strong (n.d.)

learn by reorganizing, the Intuitive Feelers (IF). See Figure 8.10 for examples. While this strategy promotes the use and application of factual material, it also provides for the creative retrieval of this information.

Procedure.
1. Explain the task to the students.
2. Have students read the selection.
3. Distribute questions in 4-learning styles; students select one.
4. Encourage students to take notes while looking back over their reading keeping the selected question in mind.
5. Students respond to their question for 5-7 minutes. Writing spontaneously, they can refer to their notes but are to keep writing.
6. Have students read over their writing. Ask them to put lines under the two things they like and circle something that they would change.
7. Share what was written in groups of three or four. Each listener should comment on one or two things that stood out or made an impression. Students having the same questions could be grouped and share their information. Then they could regroup with each student acting as an expert in a mixed question group.
8. Discuss in class. Would you still pick the same question? What would you change? Why? What were the most powerful or interesting thoughts that came from your group?)
9. Optional—Final draft as assignment or extra-credit.

Adapted from Hansen & Silver (1986). Flames. Hansen , Silver & Associates, Inc. Moorestown, NJ 08057.

In designing questions for the student guide, refer to the following Figure. The quadrants highlight thinking skills related to each learning style.

This activity lends itself to many variations. In addition to writing a response to one self-selected question from the pool, students can be encouraged to write in all four styles. This allows students to experience learning from all points of view and stretches their abilities to work comfortably within different learning styles. Another adaptation is a chain write that requires students to respond to a question in the ST style. As soon as the students are finished writing, they are given the next IT question. They continue through the other styles the same way. As a culminating activity, students in small groups compare their writing noting their similarities and differences.

Perkins (1999)

Scherer (1999)

These questions provide powerful entry points to learning for students. This activity allows more students to be reached, particularly by offering them the opportunity to act as an expert representing a topic in their own unique way. Finally, Questions in 4-Learning Styles enable students to discuss, debate, hypothesize, investigate and take viewpoints actively acquiring knowledge and understanding of the topic at hand in dialogue with others.

FIGURE 8.9.   DEVELOPING QUESTIONS IN 4-LEARNING STYLES

ST — Sensing Thinkers
RECALLING

Observing
1. What did you see, hear, note?
2. Describe what you read.

Memorizing
3. Who was the _____?
4. When was the _____?
5. How did they _____?

Sequencing
6. What happened first, second, third?
7. Arrange these objects according to _____.

Categorizing
8. Describe the characteristics of the _____.

SF — Sensing Feelers
RESPONDING

Feeling
1. How would you feel if _____ happened to you?
2. How do you think _____ felt?

Preferring
3. Given a choice, which would you choose?
4. How would you respond if this happened to you?

Valuing
5. Where do you suppose you first got your idea?
6. What else did you consider before you picked this?
7. What would be the consequences of each alternative?
8. Should everyone do it your way?
9. Would you tell the class the way you feel about this?

IT — Intuitive Thinkers
REASONING

Comparing and contrasting
1. List the similarities and differences between _____.
2. Compare and contrast the following _____.
3. Which two are similar?
4. Compare the two in regard to the following _____.

Grouping
5. What belongs together? Based on what criteria?
6. On the basis of some common characteristics, place these items, objects, or ideas into groups.

Analyzing
7. What are the essential factors involved in this?
8. Analyze the data and identify the facts and fallacies.

Summarizing
9. The main idea of the story was _____.
10. Think of a title for the story.
11. Identify the important points.

IF — Intuitive Feelers
REORGANIZING

Associating
1. What do you think of when I say _____?
2. What would happen if _____?
3. Suppose _____. What would be the consequences?

Synthesizing
4. Combine the following unrelated words into a meaningful sentence.
5. Combine the following characters from three books or stories and construct your own story.
6. Given the following purpose and data, develop a plan to achieve this purpose.
7. Given the following arithmetic operations, construct a problem using all of them.

Metaphors/Similes/Analogies
8. A _____ is like a _____ because _____.
9. How would this look to a _____?

FIGURE 8.10. USING QUESTIONS IN 4-LEARNING STYLES EXAMPLES:

Example: Chemistry

ST – Sensing Thinkers. Make a diagram of the periodic table, showing and naming each of the major sections.

IT – Intuitive Thinkers. Compare and contrast the properties of metallic vs. nonmetallic elements. How does the periodic table reflect those differences?

SF – Sensing Feelers. Write a letter to Demitri Mendeleev, the Russian chemist, who first published the periodic table in 1869. Tell him how you feel about his work and how it helped organize the science of chemistry.

IF – Intuitive Feelers. What would the periodic table look like if the transition metal section were missing? What effect would the loss of those elements have in the world?

Example: Language Arts

ST – Sensing Thinkers. Draw a picture of : The most interesting scene in the chapter. Your favorite character. Describe the characteristics of one of the main characters in *The Outsiders.*

IT – Intuitive Thinkers. Compare and contrast: how Johnny, Ponyboy and Dallas deal with this situation or how Johnny reacts with how you expected Johnny to react.

SF – Sensing Feelers. Would you prefer to: Live alone as a fugitive for the rest of your life or go to jail for a defined time? Live honestly outside the law or dishonestly inside the law?

IF – Intuitive Feelers. What would you do if you were Johnny or Ponyboy or Dallas? Write a letter to: Johnny or Ponyboy or Dallas. Explain what you think they should do and why you think they should do it.

Example: Social Studies

ST – Sensing Thinkers. Use a diagram or timeline to show some of the major events of the '60s. Use arrows or lines to demonstrate which events are related.

IT – Intuitive Thinkers. Compare and contrast some of the cultural feelings of the '60s with those of the '50s.

SF – Sensing Feelers. In your opinion, was the Vietnam War or the Civil Rights Movement the most important event of the '60s?

IF – Intuitive Feelers. What if President Kennedy had not been assassinated? How would the '60s have been different?

Your Turn

Name _____ Date _____ Subject Area _____

Directions: Design your own Questions in 4-Learning Styles activity sheet. Use content that you are teaching or planning to teach to create your instructional strategy.

ST — Sensing Thinkers	**SF** — Sensing Feelers
IT — Intuitive Thinkers	**IF** — Intuitive Feelers

Rubrics/Analytical Scoring Guides

Rubrics are under attack! Educators are scrambling to support their use of rubrics/ analytical scoring guides, while others are casting aspersions on their use. Whether used in statewide or classroom assessments, or performance in the arts, rubrics have become an integral part of the evaluation process.

First, what are rubrics/analytical scoring guides? Since districts have different ways of characterizing these guides, we are using these terms interchangeably. Stevens and Levi (2005) define a rubric as "a scoring tool that lays out the specific expectations for an assignment. They divide an assignment into its component parts and provide a detailed descrition of what constitutes acceptable or unacceptable levels of performance for each of those parts" (p. 3).

Second, what is at the crux of the rubrics argument? Alfie Kohn (2006) writes "Rubrics are above all, a tool to promote standardization to turn teachers into grading machines or at least allow them to pretend that what they are doing is exact and objective"(p. 12). On the other hand, Spandel (2006) writes that "rubrics can be the most useful instructional tools we have. They give us direction and a basis for conversation (p.10). " In addition, she writes "a rubric captures the essence of performance at various levels."

Our own experience has forced us to look closely at this issue. A few of our graduate students pursuing teaching licenses have had strong feelings about designing and using these scoring guides. Collectively, they believed like Kohn (2006) and Wilson (2006) that this assessment strips writing in particular of the "complexity that breathes life into good writing." Spandel agrees on this point. Quoting Donald Murray who wrote that "voice is the quality, more than any other, that allows us to recognize writing," she writes that qualties we believe in should be at the center of our rubrics. For example, statewide writing assessments frequently leave out "Voice" as a quality because of the difficulty in defining it. For those of us who are passionate about the role writing plays in the classroom, this decision impacts the writing process tremendously. What message does this give students? Students pay attention to what they are graded on. We venture that they view "Ideas and Organization", "Conventions", and "Sentence Fluency" as the critical elements of writing. "Voice" and "Word Choice" are the stepsisters. Where would a nonfiction writer like John McPhee be without his unique "Voice" and deliberate use of language ("Word Choice")?

We have found rubrics critical in our work on literacy. They provide the language and expectations for an assignment that students on the whole find helpful. Moreover, they level the playing field of the classroom. Our classrooms continue to grow more diverse each year. Students do not have the same academic understandings. Rubrics help introduce them to concepts such as critical thinking, facts versus opinions, and argument versus description. Some students don't have the knowledge of frequently used academic terminology like the meaning of "voice" or "tone." Students who do not bring academic knowledge to their assignments have a chance of performing as well as those privileged to be in the know because of their past learning experiences.

Are rubrics sufficient in themselves? Hardly, assessments using rubrics need to allow for differences, additions or deletions. They develop as you use them. We have found developing these with students or having students design them often improves their understanding of the breadth and depth of the assignment as

McPhee, Annals of the Former World, a tetralogy on geology

Pullitzer Prize, 1999

well as stressing the need for frequently overlooked elements such as citations, spelling and grammar (Stevens & Levi, 2005).

How are rubrics created? This is the hard part. But the pay-off is worth it, in terms of time and quality of feedback available to your students.

Procedure.

*Stevens & Levi
(2005).*

1. Determine what evidence students can provide that would show they were successful in completing the assignment. What are your expectations for the highest level of performance? What would indicate the least exemplary assignment?

2. Determine the criteria for the assignment, such as content knowledge, content skills, competencies and performance quality. In the sample scoring guide (Figure 8.11), Lane expected students to demonstrate the standard elements of good writing: Ideas and Content, Organization, Voice, Word Choice, Sentence Fluency and Conventions.

   Start writing descriptions for the highest level of performance, then write for the lowest level. With these descriptors, it is relatively easy to fill in the mid-level.

3. Design dimensions for the rubric. These typically range from "Excellent", "Competent", to "Developing." The descriptors at each level should be parallel. For example, in Lane's scoring guide under the category "Voice" the same element is described according to proficiency observed:

   Voice

5	Tone and flavor of the piece fit the topic.
3	Tone and flavor of the piece need to be altered slightly to better fit the topic.
1	Tone and flavor are inappropriate for the topic.

4. Work with students in reviewing the rubric before using it. Make sure they understand the criteria of the assignment expected and clarify any confusions or misunderstandings. Providing positive examples can often cement understandings.

   See Figure 8.11 for an example of an analytical scoring guide for writing.

Figure 8.11. Analytical Scoring Guide

IDEAS AND CONTENT

5 Paper. The paper is clear, enhanced by the kind of detail that keeps the reader reading.

Paper is understandable, enlightening and interesting—without bogging down in trivia. Details work together to expand the main topic, giving the piece a strong focus. Writer's background lends the writing a satisfying ring of authenticity.

3 The writer has made a solid beginning in defining the topic, more development is needed.

General information provided; reader longs for specifics. Details blend with repetitive points or trivia. Writer settles for generalities or clichéd thinking.

1 Sketchy, loosely focused information forces the reader to make inferences.

Main topic is out of focus—or not yet known, even to the writer. Missing, limited or unrelated details require the reader to fill in many blanks. Writer reports rather than filters the information through his own background experience.

ORGANIZATION

5 Paper. The order or internal structure of the piece is compelling and guides the reader purposefully through the text.

Piece shows direction and balance. Main ideas stand out. Inviting lead draws the reader in; a satisfying conclusion ends the piece. Transitions are strong and natural.

3 The organizational structure allows the reader to move through the text without undue confusion.

Main ideas are sequenced and appropriate. Introductions and conclusion are recognizable and functional. Transitions are present, but sometimes too obvious or too structured.

1 Ideas, details, or events seem loosely strung together.

No clear sense of direction to carry the reader from point to point. No real lead sets up focus; no conclusion wraps things up. Missing or unclear transitions force the reader to make giant leaps.

VOICE

5 Paper. The writer's energy and passion for the subject drive the writing. The text is lively, and expressive.

Tone and flavor of the piece fit the topic. Writing bears the imprint of the writer. Expository or persuasive text is provocative, lively and designed to hold a reader's attention.

3 The writer seems sincere and willing to communicate with the reader on a functional, if distant, level.

Tone and flavor of the piece need to be altered slightly to better fit the topic. Writer is experimenting with his or her voice—and the result is pleasant, if not unique. Though aware of the audience, the writer only occasionally speaks right to it.

1 The writer seems definitely distanced from topic; as a result, the text lacks life, spirit, or energy.

Tone and flavor are inappropriate for the topic. The writer does not project any personal enthusiasm for the topic. Though writing communicates on a functional level, it takes no risks and does not engage the reader.

Figure 8.11. Analytical Scoring Guide (cont.)

WORD CHOICE

5 Paper. Precise, vivid, natural language paints a strong, and complete picture.

Writer's message is remarkably clear and easy to interpret.
Striking words or phrases linger in the reader's memory, often prompting connections, memories, reflective thoughts, or insights.
Lively verbs lend the writing power.

3 The language is appropriate.

Words are correct and adequate.
Phrases here and there leave the reader wanting more.
Colorful language is full of promise, even when it lacks restraint or control.

1 Writer struggles with a limited vocabulary—or uses language that does not speak to the audience.

Words are used incorrectly.
Vague words and phrases convey only the most general sorts of messages.
Jargonistic language makes the text ponderous to read.

SENTENCE FLUENCY

5 Paper. Easy flow and rhythm combined with sentence sense make this text a delight to read aloud.

Well crafted sentences that invite expressive oral reading.
Purposeful sentence beginnings show how each sentence relates to and builds on the one before.
Sentences vary in both structure and length, making the reading pleasant and natural.
Fragments, if used, add style.

3 The text hums along with a steady beat.

Mostly grammatical and fairly easy to read aloud sentences.
Some purposeful sentence beginnings aid the reader's interpretation of text.
Fragments may be present; some are effective.

1 A fair interpretive oral reading of this text is difficult.

Irregular or unusual word patterns make it hard to tell where sentences begin and end.
Short, choppy sentences bump the reader through the text.
Fragments, if used, do not work.

CONVENTIONS

5 Paper. Writer shows excellent control over standard writing conventions and uses them with accuracy, creativity and style to enhance meaning.

Errors are few and minor, a reader can easily overlook them unless searching for them.
Text appears clean, edited, and polished.
Text is easy to mentally process; there is nothing to distract or confuse a reader.

3 Writer shows reasonable control over the most widely used writing conventions and applies them consistently.

Enough errors to distract an attentive reader; however, errors do not seriously impair reading or obscure meaning.
Writing clearly needs polishing.
Paper reads much like a second rough draft—readable, but lacking close attention to conventions.

1 Writing demonstrates limited control even over widely used writing conventions.

Errors are sufficiently frequent and/or serious enough to be distracting.
Extensive editing is required.
Paper reads like a first rough draft, scribbled hastily without thought for conventions.

Adapted from *The Reviser's Toolbox*, Shoreham, VT: Discover Writing Press, 1999, pp. 177-178. Used with permission

Scoring Guides and Grading

Outside of multiple-choice and T and F tests, assessment in the content area classroom is frequently a dilemma. Is content the focus or should all aspects of a student's written reponse be considered? Grading often implies an arbitrary measuring system that provides little feedback to the student on the specifics of his work. As Lane (1999) writes, a grade signals the end of that instructional experience. No student is going to pick up a paper after a grade has been issued. For this reason, we believe that a grade should be issued only for the final product. Drafts and reviews of the ongoing stages of a written piece should be the work of students and their peer reviewers. While works are in progress, you should be conferencing with students and dialoguing with them in class to discuss their progress, but do not grade these efforts.

A scoring guide is like a lighthouse for the writer because...

TEACHER TALK

After we read selections by R.L. Stine, Beverly Cleary and Charles Dickens, I invited the students to write an imaginative short story. I told the kids what I wanted from them in terms of a grade. I wanted them to focus the paper on three main areas: imaginative writing, conventions and word choice. I wrote along with them, and when we debriefed I focused on these elements in my paper as a model. I also designed a scoring guide illustrating these three traits and we used these in responding to each other's papers.

Finally, we hope that when you begin to use scoring guides regularly you will, like the teachers Routman (1991) studied, "experience less conflict about having to give grades" (p. 336). Your days of defending those "B+" papers without benefit of a rationale are history. You and your students now have a medium to discuss the criteria that guided the grading process. Our graduate students often ask us if rubric scores can be transferred to point percentages and traditional grades. Like most teachers, we would prefer that writing not be graded or that students self-grade along with explanations of strengths, weaknesses, and aspects they think they should work on next time. However, if grades are an issue, we would suggest using the Diederich Scale (Zemelman et al., 1988). After a paper has been revised by the student with input from his peer response group, the following scale can be used to assign grades or point percentages. See Figure 8.12.

How does grading writing discourage students?

Inclusion Techniques

In an ethnography study (Shufton, 1994) on inclusion at the secondary level, the author tracked students with special needs. In this study one of the secondary students, Grace, is learning and enjoying school. In talking to her science teacher, Shufton highlights several factors that are contributing to Grace's successes in school. Shufton writes:

> Ms. D's science class is relaxed and only a little tumultuous, considering that over half of her twenty-some students have been identified as 'special needs' learners.

When Ms. D. is asked what accommodations she makes for her students, she talks about observing all her students first to see what parts of the curriculum seem to be understood and where the problems are. In particular, Grace has a

FIGURE 8.12.   THE DIEDERICH SCALE

1-Poor	2-Weak	3-Average	4-Good	5-Excellent

Reader _____

Quality and development of ideas	1 2 3 4 5	
Organization, relevance, movement	1 2 3 4 5	_____ × 5 = _____
		Subtotal

Style, flavor, individuality	1 2 3 4 5	
Wording and phrasing	1 2 3 4 5	_____ × 3 = _____
		Subtotal

Grammar, sentence structure	1 2 3 4 5	
Punctuation	1 2 3 4 5	
Spelling	1 2 3 4 5	
Manuscript form, legibility	1 2 3 4 5	_____ × 1 = _____
		Subtotal

Total Grade   _____ %

From *Measuring Growth in English* by Paul Diederich. Copyright 1974.

Teacher observations are key to successful curriculum adaptations for students with special needs.

peer tutor so she always has assistance with in-class portions of the course work. Ms. D. feels that her observations have indicated that Grace does well when information is given in small increments and additional time is allotted to process that information. She tells Shufton "that when students with special needs have an experiment that has lots of tasks or lots of ingredients, I pare it down and simplify without sacrificing the content. I ask myself, 'What is the point of this lesson? What is the essential concept or information I want the students to learn? How can I arrange for my students—all of my students—to be successful in their learning? How can I help them to meet the instructional goals and objectives?'"

Students who are treated as successful learners do succeed.

Regarding assessment, Ms. D. comments: "Another modification is that I enlarge her tests for easier reading and give her extra time to complete them-as much time as she needs. In fact, today her tutor was absent, and she took the test all by herself, out in the hallway to avoid distraction ... I use them (tests) to monitor my own success or failure as a teacher." Ms. D. has created an environment characterized by her own extensive, ongoing self-assessment.

Teachers like Mrs. D. provide daily for students with special needs when it comes to their own curriculum. As we look at the standards movement, however, we are concerned about where students with special needs fit.

The Individuals with Disabilities Education Act Amendment of 1997 (Warlick, 2000) mandated that the education of students with special needs is to be based on the same challenging standards as applied to regular students. It is also required that students with special needs be included in state and district-wide assessment.

Researchers and teachers in many states as well as our home state of Oregon are moving expeditiously to find ways to meet this requirement. In the process, they are as Warlick (2000) observed helping students "move from access to the schoolhouse to access to high expectations and access to the general curriculum" (p. 1).

In studying alternate assessment practices for students with special needs, both teachers and researchers are considering performance assessment as a means of evaluating students' progress in meeting state standards. Eisner writes (1999) "Performance assessment is the most important development in evaluation since the invention of the short-answer test and its extensive use during World War I." What is performance assessment? It is a measure that requires students to create evidence through performance that enables those assessing the test to make valid judgments about what students know and what they can do in situations that matter. In the following study we see how performance assessment that uses subject area material in the regular classroom can serve both the content area teacher and the students with special needs.

Academic standards— what students should know and be able to do, typically assessed statewide.

In a two-year study, Arick, Nave and Jackson (1999) found that students on Individualized Education Programs (IEPs) in science and social studies averaged a 3.0 on a scale from 1 to 6 on the state-mandated performance tasks: writing an essay and making an oral presentation. Topics ranged from selecting foreign language offerings to creating inventions with magnetism. Non-IEP students scores averaged near 4.0.

What was particularly significant was the gap between the IEP students and the non-IEP students on performance assessments was much smaller than that between these groups on their standardized achievement tests. What made the difference? Adaptations and modifications—teachers reduced the amount of work, provided extensive explanation of concepts, and assisted with the organization of students' writing or speeches, proofing, and research.

These researchers concluded: "The assessment of students using performance assessment in the regular classroom, at benchmarks for content standards, is an opportunity to better understand students' level of performance in realistic settings and further the development of evaluation tools for assessing student outcomes" (p. 43).

Benchmark standards refer to the determination of students' skill levels at pre-established grades.

Checklist for Performance Assessment

TABLE 8

INSTRUCTIONAL SUMMARY OF A CHECKLIST FOR PERFORMANCE ASSESSMENT

Literacy Strategy	Informal/Formal Assessment
Primary Focus	Informal/Formal Assessment
Learning Principles	❏ Active Involvement ❏ Organizing Information ❏ Thought-demanding Activity
When to Use	During Unit plan
Goals: National or State Literacy Standards	❏ Communicate knowledge of the topic through writing ❏ Structure information ❏ Deliberate on public issues
Materials	Teacher developed project materials
Time	Unit time interval

How did the teachers prepare their students with special needs for these performance tasks in order to realize this degree of success? They turned the responsibility over to the students. Through the use of checklists for content and conventions, students monitored their own work. See Figures 8.13 and 8.14 for examples of checklists that include content and conventions for a persuasive letter writing performance task that IEP students were to complete demonstrating their position on traveling to Oregon on the Oregon Trail.

Twenty years of research and experience demonstrate that the education of children with disabilities can be made more effective by having high expectations for such children and ensuring their access in the general curriculum to the maximum extent possible (Warlick, 2000).

Observational and Anecdotal Records

TABLE 9

INSTRUCTIONAL SUMMARY OF A CHECKLIST FOR OBSERVATIONAL AND ANECDOTAL RECORDS

Literacy Strategy	Checklist for Observational and Anecdotal Records: Teacher-Directed
Primary Focus	Informal/Formal Assessment
Learning Principles	❏ Organizing Information
When to Use	During Unit Plan
Goals: National or State Literacy Standards	❏ Determine students' academic, literacy abilities

FIGURE 8.13. CHECKLIST FOR PERSUASIVE LETTER CONTENT

Paragraph #1	Did you say something friendly?
Paragraph #2	Getting Ready—Did you have at least 3 facts about getting ready to start?_____ 1. 2. 3. Did you add details about what you did to get ready?
Paragraph #3	On the prairie—Did you have at least 3 things that happened on the prairie? _____ List those 3 things: 1. 2. 3. Did you add interesting details about what happened?_____
Paragraph #4	In the mountains and arriving in Oregon—Did you have at least 2 things that happened in the mountains?___ List those 2 things. 1. 2. Did you tell them about Oregon?____ What did you say? _____ _____
Paragraph #5	Did you say good-bye in a friendly manner?_____

FIGURE 8.14. CHECKLIST FOR CONVENTIONS

Directions: Read through your rough draft. Check for the following:

_____ 1. Does each paragraph start on a new line?
_____ 2. Is each paragraph indented?
_____ 3. Move your finger along each line of your paper. Does a capital letter appear after each period?
_____ 4. Read through your paper. Find any words that you are not sure of the spelling and add them to the word bank.
_____ 5. Have one of the "spellers" check your words.

From *Oregon English Journal* by J. Arick and G. Nave et al. Copyright © 1999 by Oregon English Journal. Reprinted by permission.

FIGURE 8.15.   DEVELOPING TO INDEPENDENT STAGES

Name: _____   Dates: _____ 1st| 2nd| 3rd| 4th|

Indicators of Developing Control and Comprehension:

Code: M=Most of the time   S=Sometimes   N=Not yet

Talking and Listening	CODE	COMMENTS
Expects what is heard to made sense		
Monitors understanding of spoken language by asking questions, seeking clarification, etc.		
Uses a variety of speaking patterns to adjust to audience		
Speaks confidently before a group and within the community		

Reading	CODE	COMMENTS
Selects reading material with confidence		
Reads for literary experience		
Reads to be informed		
Reads to perform task		
Constructs meaning, develops interpretation, and makes judgments		
Compares and contrasts, makes applications		
Uses a variety of strategies—prediction, rate, background, information, etc.		
Rereads for different purpose		
Displays an expanding vocabulary		

Writing	CODE	COMMENTS
Initiates writing for specific and personal purposes		
Incorporates models from literature		
Participates in writing conferences by asking questions and giving comments		
Is aware of voice, sense of audience, sense of purpose		

Source: Reprinted by permission of Christopher-Gordon Publishers, Inc. from *Assessment and Evaluation in Whole Language Programs*, edited by Bill Harp. Copyright 1991 by Christopher-Gordon Publishers, Inc., Norwood, MA.

TABLE 9 (CONT.)

Materials	Teacher checklist
Time	Unit time interval

Concerned teachers cultivate an observational assessment system that guides their professional decision making. By systematically watching students engaged in natural learning tasks, teachers obtain a richly detailed, authentic picture of what students can do.

Sui-Runyan (1991); Rhodes & Nathenson-Mejia (1992)

Anecdotes stemming from your observations can be written in a notebook or on post-it notes. These notes can be attached to students' folders or placed in designated sections in the teacher's three-ring binder. If made over time, they provide teachers with opportunities to look for inferences, patterns, strengths and weaknesses in learning content.

Observational notes and checklists become most useful when teachers design them. However, we've included a highly structured observational checklist in Figure 8.15 to demonstrate the variety of reading, writing, speaking and listening activities that content area teachers may want to examine. We suggest that in designing your own version of this model, you include observation items germane to your content.

Johnston (1992)

Symbolic Reading Inventory

TABLE 10

INSTRUCTIONAL SUMMARY OF SYMBOLIC READING INVENTORY

Literacy Strategy	Symbolic Reading Inventory
Primary Focus	❑ Informal diagnosis of text
Learning Principles	❑ Self-monitoring and regulating of thought processes ❑ Active involvement in searching for meaning
When to use	❑ Before using content materials
Goals: National or State Literacy Standards	❑ Use imagery to retell story or convey informational ideas ❑ Understand and interpret imagery that author uses to comunicate
Materials	❑ Drawing, writing instruments and materials
Time	❑ Class period

Research shows that students who learned how to develop visual images while they read improved from a 35 percent comprehension and recall rate to a 86 percent comprehension and recall rate after learning how to use imagery. Kajder, (2006) writes about the student who was asked to take digital pictures represent-

Center for Research on Learning, 2006

ing what he knew and believed about reading. Not only did he return to class animated and ready to talk about reading—something rarely experienced up to this point, he also showed his teacher a sketchbook depicting the entire school year in pictures that he had kept. When asked why he never shared this in his journals or in class he retorted, "This isn't English stuff, Ms. Kajder. It doesn't count. It's just play" (p. 4).

For students who have a narrow view of school as being a place for information-gathering and tests, the Symbolic Reading Inventory (SRI) is a technique that can "open the window into the hidden processes of readers" (Wilhelm, 2004, p. 147). Students are able to describe their understandings and strategies while reading text. It forces them to use their imagination to get inside the reading and pull out particular understandings, they typically never explored without this visual instruction.

For example, Edmiston (1990) had students create a series of cutouts that represented characters in a story, as well as something that represents themselves as a reader. As the students retell the story, they manipulate these cutouts to show relationships, feelings, memories, and predictions (p. 19), cognitive processes little evidenced with a straightforward writing or retelling assignment.

Baer (2005) capitalizing on the visual/spatial intelligence many students exhibit took this same idea and had students create a "snapshot" scene from a book they were currently reading representing themselves as a reader. The students then wrote about their scene and why they had drawn themselves and their placement in the story as they did.

For example, students could read the 2006 Honors Book *A Wreath for Emmet Till* by Marilyn Nelson and illustrated by Phillip Lardy. Among the sonnets that constitute this horrific true story, students could take one of their chosing e.g., "The memory of monsters: That bleak thought." They can draw the scene portrayed in this poem as well as where they see themselves in this scene: an observer, or a personified object such as the ax, the doorknob, or one of the characters—the blind girl, the mob.

For students with special needs, students retell orally the story using their artwork. Specific questions a teacher or instructional assistant could ask to explore students' understanding are found in Figure 8.16. It is helpful when the teacher also does the drawing with the student. Avoid questions that don't fit the student's scene. Or you can use these to extend student's discussion of their reading.

As Baer concludes "Allowing our students to respond to a text through a means other than writing will surely bring about amazing connections" (p. 224). As an adaptive technique the SRI seems made to order in permitting students to use a medium they may be more comfortable in using. And for struggling readers who may be capable but do not exhibit these literacy capabilities, this is an assessment that registers students' understandings not evident in the usual assessment activities.

FIGURE 8.16.   INTERVIEW QUESTIONS FOR THE SYMBOLIC READING INVENTORY

Interview Questions for the Symbolic Reading Inventory

1. Tell me about the snapshot you created from the story that you read?
2. Why did you choose to create this picture? What was it about that particular scene that made you want to take your time to work on it?
3. When you were creating the picture, what was going through your mind?
4. Why did you make yourself look like this? (The graphic representing self as reader).
5. When we were doing the SRI what was going through your mind? What thoughts were you having?
6. Tell me about what you did, where you placed yourself.
7. What did you see?
8. What did you feel?
9. What did you hear?
10. What did you smell?
11. What did you taste?
12. Anything else you want to tell me about this?

International Reading Association. Baer, Allison (2005) Do you hear voices? A study of the Symbolic Reading Inventory, *Journal of Adolescent and Adult Literacy* 48 (3), p. 218.

Assessment for Second Language Learners

As Delpit (1995) writes, "Educators need to find out about and build on the intellectual legacy of the children we teach." In ESL classes that we observe, students are actively engaged in similar activities that we see in the regular classroom. Students take tests, do read alouds, retellings, provide writing samples, do experiments and demonstrations, projects and exhibitions, response journals, learning logs and student conferences. Yet when we see these ESL students transplanted into the regular classroom, we perceive a prevailing assumption that they cannot complete these assessments in a given content class. ESL students are set adrift frequently to catch what they can either from the instructor, or their peers. The support they need is unavailable for the most part as teachers try to meet the heavy demands of too many students and too much administrative paperwork.

Is it language that makes such a difference? Since many teachers have many languages represented in their ESL classroom that they don't know and their students still achieve—knowing the student's language cannot be the sole reason for a student's success. Educators who seem more adept at working with ESL students in the regular classroom accept all languages and cultures as rich vehicles for learning. They bridge the "intellectual legacy" students bring to the subject and link this understanding to new ideas and perspectives. For example, a teacher using *House on Mango Street* (Cisneros, 1984) found his Hispanic girls in awe over the story of their everyday lives. They were amazed that a writer would write about sandals, kids chipping their teeth on parking meters and eating in the lunch room, especially about kids with names like their own: Rafaela, Alicia and Elenita.

As in all instructional planning, instruction and assessment should complement each other. Ongoing assessment through observation, talking to students, and taking anecdotal notes are immensely helpful in studying how students are progressing, which parts of the lesson are understood and which aren't. The following activity includes many solid instructional tasks that can also provide performance assessment data. The tasks require more than simple recall, and they require students to perform at the application level.

Reading Comprehension Strategy: 3-2-1

TABLE 11

INSTRUCTIONAL SUMMARY OF 3-2-1

Literacy Strategy	3-2-1
Primary Focus	Informal Assessment
Learning Principles	❑ Active Involvement ❑ Organizing Information ❑ Thought-demanding Activity
When to Use	During Unit Plan
Goals: ESL National or State Literacy Standards	❑ Use English to interact in the classroom ❑ Use English to achieve academically in all content areas
Materials	Teacher developed materials
Time	Unit time interval

Dresseler & Kamil, 2006 National Literacy Panel

Koelsch (2006) in her study of secondary ELL students writes "For English language learners, the introduction to the ways of making meaning, to the specialized ways of reasoning and using language in different disciplines is a critical component of developing literacy in English." Furthermore, English language learners need to develop text-level literacy that develops their ability to use their background knowledge, make inferences and build meaning.

The following strategy is designed to give students an opportunity to explore meaning by summarizing key ideas, focusing on those they are most interested in and posing a question. Students are asked to respond to the following directions:

Jones (2006)

Reading Comprehension Strategy: 3-2-1

After reading an assigned text write about:
   3   Things you found out
   2   Interesting things
   1   Question
Note: Please write in complete sentences.

This strategy reflects students' own interests, curiosities and inquiries and builds skills in using the unique language and reasoning of the subject area. It can be an instructional activity or serve as an informal diagnostic tool. It provides the teacher with feedback on the semantic skills, the cognitive abilities and the level of understanding the English language learner has from the assigned reading. It is also a versatile strategy in that the actvities students do can be changed to reflect particular topics. For example, if students are studying current history the directions can be extended and specified to include locating 3 similarities and 3 differences between the wars in Vietnam and Iraq. Most importantly, it provides a jumping-off point for continuing the conversation as the teacher and students respond to the questions raised.

Is this process difficult for the ESL student? For some it will be. Our own experiences bear this out. One of the authors had a Spanish teacher who taught primarily with questions. As students, we had to come to class prepared with questions on a given topic, deliver the question to the class, and listen carefully to the response. A major part of the class consisted of listening and responding activities related to our questions. Our oral language skills grew tremendously along with our vocabulary, as well as our use of syntax and semantics. Similarly, with time, students become quite proficient at raising questions. We have observed classes where students' questions listed in vibrant colors on charts hanging around the classroom guide the development of the entire lesson. Students seem to sit a little taller, and participate more animatedly when it is their questions that guide the learning.

See the following example of a 3-2-1 Lesson Plan as an example of weaving instruction together with assessment. In this lesson, an authentic problem is addressed. The students have an opportunity to think through their questions about the environmental issues addressed in the problem and, furthermore, have an opportunity to seriously engage in confronting a government agency directly. The teacher guides their activity through the various steps of the 3-2-1 activity, however, the students provide the direction for their inquiry through their questions.

Finally, performance assessment is built into the instruction. The performance task that the students complete can be used to assess a variety of forms of knowledge: i.e., specific information on Old Growth Forests, how decisions about habitat affects the community, and process information like taking a position on an issue.

In conclusion, we have designed assessment activities that are instructional and still provide insight into students' progress. They are also activities which can be used with the mainstream student as well. In addition, we would advocate encouraging students to work in their native languages at times. By observing students using their native language, the teacher can determine their collaborative skills, their explanations and clarifications of assignments. It is an opportunity for a teacher to observe the fullest measure of capabilities students bring to an instructional task.

TEACHER TALK

Why do I assess the way I do? There are some formal assessments that I have to use, but overall I think any opportunity to get the student talking about or writing about their reading is the most effective. Retelling requires that students not just be able to reconstruct the plot, but also make inferences and notice details (Reutzel and Cooter, 2003). These are the very skills that my students have identified as ones they desire to learn.

Am I really making instructional decisions based on what kids do and can do? I am definitiely learning as I go....

FIGURE 8.17. READING COMPREHENSION STRATEGY: 3–2–1 LESSON PLAN

Lesson Plan: Science

Grade: 6–8

Topic: Old Growth Forest

Purpose: To help students gain knowledge of Old Growth Forests and the controversy surrounding them.

State Content/Literacy Standards: 1) Identify a system's inputs and outputs; 2) To explain the effects of changing the system's components; 3) To use process skills to question, infer, hypothesize and communicate information

Student Objectives:
1. Students will be able to identify the elements of an Old Growth Forest by writing questions and sharing information.
2. Students will be able to draw conclusions based on changes made to the Old Growth Forest by writing a summary or drawing a picture.
3. Students will be able to communicate their understanding by writing a letter or e-mail taking a position regarding the logging of Old Growth Forest to their local Forest Service representative.

Introduction:
1. Ask students to brainstorm the topic, "Forest." (1 minute)
2. Summarize students' ideas with a concept map. (2 minutes)
3. Introduce topic of a particular forest, the Old Growth Forest. (1 minute)
4. Show video of Old Growth Forests. (5 minutes)

Learning Activity:
1. Distribute handout describing Strategies for Reading Comprehension: 3–2–1. (3 minutes)
2. Direct students through steps of 3-2-1. (20 minutes)
3. Check students' responses. (10 minutes)

Closure:
Students draft a letter or prepare an e-mail to the Bureau of Land Management (BLM) taking a position to continue or to halt the clearcutting of Old Growth Forest acreage. Encourage students to refer back to the details in their responses to their questions. Include such details as clearcutting 's effects on the trees, the animal and plant life the trees support, the effect on the water supply, and the effect on the community.

Address e-mail to: OR100MB@or.blm.gov (e.g., if referring to an Oregon timber harvest). Access this site for an address if students wish to send their letters.

See the website http://www.umpqua-watersheds.org for information about the BLM.

Evaluation:
After students have revised their writing, it is assessed for: a) accurate understanding of significant supporting details, b) interconnectedness of habitat and the community, c) integration of concept, "Old Growth Forest," and d) communication of a position.

What difference does it make? I think that assessments are a critical part of my curriculum. I am able to create a classroom environment for my students that is very individualized based on their needs. My students also seem to be growing in confidence and independence.

Academic Literacy Teacher, Grade 9 & 10, 2006

Endings: A Summary

In this chapter, we have presented issues and strategies of assessment. We have selected techniques that will enable you to make instructional decisions about the students you teach as well as the materials you use.

As teachers, we begin with preassessment practices to see where students are starting. Then we implement instruction based on our perceptions as well as data. Meanwhile, both ongoing and final assessment measures help us monitor and make informed decisions on where to proceed next.

We have offered some of the more common informal diagnostic reading tests. Most classroom teachers will use these either as diagnostic tools to get a quick picture of their students' reading abilities with their content material or as an instructional strategy to enhance their students' learning.

Many diagnostic measures can be adapted for instructional use.

Many of the strategies are suggested to exemplify our definition of assessment as a "sitting-down-with" experience, one that is engaging and worthwhile for the student and her teacher. Informal measures such as self-assessment strategies, informal inventories, and checklists demonstrate how to provide this instructional environment.

Finally, we have included in our conversation assessment practices for students with special needs as well as ESL learners. Our writing on this issue stems from our belief that any well-developed assessment practice is potentially suitable for most learners.

Expanding Understandings through Discussion

Directions Follow the directions for each section. Your group will be asked to report on your decisions. Be prepared to support your responses as a group.

Literal Level

Directions: In your small group, come to consensus in your discussion. Check those statements that you agree were made explicitly by the authors.

_____ 1. Teachers find standardized tests valuable.

_____ 2. Informal assessment includes student self-reports, inventories, checklists, teacher-made tests, observations and student conferences.

_____ 3. If developed early in a student's experience, self-assessment helps cultivate lifelong learning skills.

_____ 4. Informal inventories address interest, attitude or skills involved in learning the specialized subject area.

_____ 5. Assessment instruments need not be tailored exclusively for able or disabled readers.

Interpretive Level

Directions: Come to consensus with members of your group. Check those statements that you agree were made implicitly by the authors.

_____ 1. Assessment experiences should be learning experiences.
_____ 2. Learners have a critical role in the assessment process.
_____ 3. Students' ability to read and their desire to read do not always operate in tandem.
_____ 4. Assessment is an instrument for instructional decision-making.

Applied Level

Directions: Come to consensus with members of your group. Use your own experiences as well as ideas in this chapter to justify your choice.

_____ 1. The secret of education lies in respecting the student.
_____ 2. One very important ingredient of success is a wide-awake, persistent learner.
_____ 3. Action to be effective must be directed to clearly conceived ends.

In the Field Applications

A. Create a cloze test and administer to your class or to at least three students. Use a piece of content area text for this exercise, e.g., a history text, a science text, etc. Write up a professional summary on your procedures, results, and conclusions.

B. Develop a diagnostic profile of a high-achieving student in your content area and a student at risk in your class. Include a sampling from the following measures: an interest survey, results of a standardized reading test, self-assessment freewrite, samples from the student's learning log, Textbook Activity Guide, anecdotal material or observational checklists. Write up a professional report including your data sources, results and recommendations for both students' instruction. Add a conclusion to the report, responding to the question 'Was it helpful examining two different students' performance levels?" Support your response.

References ❏ ❏ ❏

Alvermann, D., & Phelps, S. (1994). *Content reading and literacy: Succeeding in today's diverse classrooms.* Boston: Allyn and Bacon.

Arick, J., & Nave, G., et al. (1999). An evaluation study: Executive summary. *Oregon English Journal 21*(2): 41–43.

Arick, J., & Nave, G., et al. (1999). Example performance task. *Oregon English Journal 21*(3): 45–47.

Atwell, N. (1990). *Writing and reading from the inside out.* Portsmouth, NH: Heinemann.

Baer, A. L. (2005). Do you hear voices? A study of the Symbolic Reading Inventory. *Journal of Adolescent & Adult Literacy, 49*(3), 215–225.

Board of Directors (1999). *High stakes assessment in reading.* International Reading Association. Retrieved April 12, 2007 from http://www.reading.org/downloads/positions/ps1035_high_stakes.pdf

Bormuth, J. (1966). Readability: A new approach. *Reading Research Quarterly,* 79–132.

Boud, D. (1989). The role of self-assessment in student grading procedures. *Assessment and Evaluation in Higher Education, 14*(1), 101–111.

Bussert-Webb, K. (1999). To test or to teach: Reflections from a holistic teacher-researcher in south Texas. *Journal of Adolescent & Adult Literacy 42*(7): 582–585.

Calkins, L., Montgomery, K., Santman, D., & Falk, B. W. (1998). *A teacher's guide to standardized reading tests: Knowledge is power.* Portsmouth, NH: Heinemann.

Cisneros, S. (1984). *The house on mango street.* NY: Vintage Books.

Cross, K., & Angelo, T. (1988). *Classroom assessment techniques.* Ann Arbor, MI: National Center of Research to Improve Postsecondary Education Teaching and Learning, University of Michigan.

Cruz, M. (2005). Do our students really speak the language of the test? *English Journal, 94*(6), 15–17.

Cullinan, B., & Fitzgerald, S. (1985). IRA, NCTE take stand on readability formula. *Reading Today,* 1(January).

Davenport, R. (2002). *Miscues not mistakes: Reading assessment in the classroom.* Portsmouth, NH: Heinemann.

Delpit, L. (1995). *Other people's children: Cultural conflict in the classroom.* NY: New Press.

Deshler, D. (2002). Above and beyond: Effective teaching involves more than checklists and mnemonics. *Stratenotes.* Lawrence, KS: Center for Research on Learning.

Dresseler, C. W., & Kamil, K. (2006). First- and second-language literacy. In D. August & T. Shanahan (Eds.), *Developing literacy in second-language learners. Report of the National Literacy Panel on Language-Minority children and Youth.* Mahwah, NJ: Lawrence Erlbaum Associates.

Edmiston, P. E. (1990). *The nature of engagement in reading: Profiles of three fifth graders' engagement strategies and stances.* Unpublished manuscript.

Eisner, E. W. (1999). The uses and limits of performance assessment. *Phi Delta Kappan 80*(9): 658–660.

Forgan, H., & Mangrum, C. (1976). *Teaching content area reading inservice programs.* Columbus, OH: Charles E. Merrill Publishing Co.

Fox, M. (1993). Radical reflections: Passionate opinions on teaching, learning and living. NY: Harcourt, Brace & Company.

Fry, E. (December 1977). Fry's Readability graph: Clarifications, validity and extensions to level 17. *Journal of Reading,* 249.

Fulwiler, T. (December 1980). Journals across disciplines. *English Journal,* 14–19.

Gallagher, K. (2004). *Deeper reading: Comprehending challenging texts,* 4–12. Portland, ME: Stenhouse Publishers.

Graham, K., & Robinson, A. (1984). *Study skills handbook: A guide for all teachers.* Newark, DE: International Reading Association.

Hansen, J. (1994). Literacy portfolios: Windows on potential. In *Authentic reading assessment: Practices and possibilities.* S. W. Valencia, E. H. Hiebert and P. P. Afflerrback (Eds.). Newark, DE: International Reading Association.

Johnston, P. (1992). *Constructive evaluation of literate activity.* NY: Longman.

Jones, R. (2006). *Strategies for Reading Comprehension: 3-2-1.* Retrieved January 14, 2007, from http://www.readingquest.org/strat/321.html

Kajder, S. B. (2006). *Bringing the outside in: Visual ways to engage students.* Portland, ME: Stenhouse.

Karre, I. ((1994). Cooperative learning tools in the college classroom. Greeley, CO: University of Northern Colorado.

Koelsch, N. (2006). *Improving literacy outcomes for English Language learners in high school: Considerations for states & districts in developing a coherent policy framework.* National High School Center. Retrieved April 11, 2007 from http://www.betterhighschools.org/docs/NHSC_AdolescentS_110806.pdf

Kohn, A. (2006). The trouble with rubrics. *English Journal, 95*(4), 12–15.

Lane, B. (1999). *The reviser's toolbox.* VT: Discover Writing Press.

McCutcheon, R. (1985). *Get off my brain: A survival guide for lazy students.* Minneapolis, MN: Free Spirit Publishing Inc.

Murray, D. (2004). *A writer teaches writing, 2nd ed.* Boston: Houghton Miiflin.

National Council of Teachers of & English. (1998–2006). *NCTE Guidelines Standards for the assessment of reading and writing.* Retrieved January 7, 2007, from http:/www.ncte.org/about/over/positions/category/assess/107609.htm

Nelson, J. (1978). Readability: Some cautions for the content area teacher. *Journal of Reading, 21,* 620–625.

Nelson, M., & Lardy, P. I. (2006). *A wreathe for Emmett Till.* NY: Houghton Mifflin.

Newman, B. (1991). Risking to learn, learning to risk. *Portfolio News,* p. 3, 9–10.

Perkins, D. (1999). The many faces of constructivism. *Educational Leadership, 57*(3), 6–11.

Ransom, K. A., & Santa, C. M., et al. (1999). High-stakes assessments in reading: A position statement of the International Reading Association. *Journal of Adolescent & Adult Literacy 43*(3): 305–312.

Rhodes, L., & Nathenson-Mejia, S. (1992). Anecdotal records: A powerful tool for ongoing literacy assessment. *The Reading Teacher, 45,* 502–506.

Rogers, C. (1969). *Freedom to learn.* Columbus, OH: Merrill.

Routman, R. (1991). *Invitations: Changing as teachers and learners K-12.* Portsmouth, NH: Heinemann.

Schallert, D. &. Roser, N., (1989). The role of reading in content area instruction. In D. Lapp, J. Flood, & N. Farnan (Eds.), *Content area reading and learning.* Englewood Cliffs, NJ: Prentice-Hall.

Scherer, M. (1997). The understanding pathway: A conversation with Howard Gardner. Educational Leadership, 57(3), 12–16.

Sewall, G. (1988). American history textbooks: Where do we go from here? *Phi Delta Kappan 69,* 553–558.

Shufton, V. (1994). *Real kids, real inclusion: An ethnography in four parts.* Unpublished manuscript, Portland State University, OR.

Spandel, V. (2006). In defense of rubrics. *English Journal, 96*(l),19–22.

Stevens, D. D., & Levi, A. J. (2005). *Introduction to rubrics: An assessment tool to save grading time, convey effective feedback and promote student learning.* Sterling, VA: Stylus Publishing.

Strong, R. Beaverton School District In-Service Materials: Hanson Silvet Strong Associates, Inc (Box 402, Moorestown, NJ 08057).

Sui–Runyan, Y. (1991). Holistic assessment in intermediate classes: Techniques for informing our teaching. In B. Harp (Ed.). *Assessment and evaluation in whole language programs*. Norwood, MA: Christopher-Gordon, 109–136.

Taylor,W. (1953). Cloze procedures: A new tool for measuring readability. *Journalism Quarterly 30,* 414–438.

Tonjes, M., & Zintz, M. (1981). *Teaching reading/thinking/study skills in content classrooms*. Dubuque, IA: Wm. C. Brown.

Vacca, R., & Vacca, J. (1996). *Content area reading* (5th ed.). NY: Harper-Collins.

Warlik, K. R. (2000). Alternative assessment forum speech, Large Scale Assessment Conference, Council of Chief State School Officers.

Wilhelm, J. (2004). Reading is seeing: Using visual response to improve the literary reading of reluctant readers. *Journal of Reading Behavior*, 27, 467–503.

Wilson, M. (2006). *Rethinking rubrics in writing assessment*. Portsmouth: Heinemann.

Wolf, K. (1993). From informal to informed assessment: Recognizing the role of the classroom teacher. *Journal of Reading 36*(7): 518–523.

Wood, K., Lapp, D., Flood, J. (1992). Guiding readers through text: A review of study guides. Newark, DE: International Reading Association.

Zemelman, S., & Daniels, H. (1988). *A community of writers: Teaching writing in the junior and senior high school*. Portsmouth, NH: Heinemann.

Real World Literacy

9

The basis of our government being the opinion of the people, the very first object should be to keep that right; and were it left to me to decide whether we should have a government without newspapers, or newspapers without government, I should not hesitate a moment to prefer the latter.

Thomas Jefferson

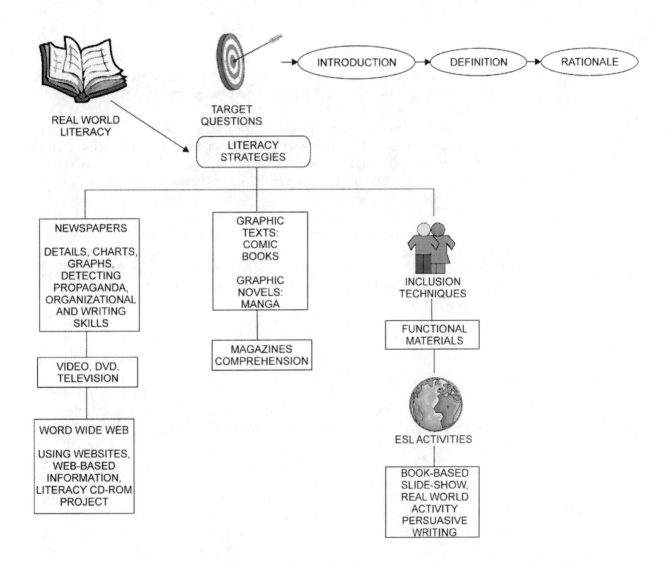

Target Questions

Target Questions

Consider the following questions before reading this chapter. Discuss these with a colleague. Continue writing notes and develop specific questions regarding real world literacy options that you want to explore.

1. How can you integrate technology, newspapers, television, DVDs, video, magazines, graphic texts and survival print materials into your classroom?
2. How can you provide students with strategies to capitalize on multimedia resources?
3. How can the Internet help you and your students to better comprehend a particular content area of study?
4. Is it worth the investment to order newspapers for your classroom? Why?
5. How can you better serve second language learners using a multimedia approach in your classroom?
6. How will the implementation of multimedia resources help your students with special needs?

Introduction

In order to survive in today's world students need to be aware of functional literacy. However, to function in the 21st century students need to be exposed a variety of literacy demands.

"The texts that students interact with have rapidly expanded from the days when the only definition of a text was a print-based book or magazine. While students interact with a range of print, visual, and sound texts, they do not always recognize that these many documents are texts. By creating an inventory of personal texts, students begin to consciously recognize the many literacy demands in contemporary society. With this start, they create a working definition of literacy that they refine and explore as they continue their investigation of the texts that they interact with at home, at school, and in other settings" (Gardner, 2006, p. 1).

Students face highly different literacy demands compared to ten years ago. In the past, teachers depended on books, commonly known as texts. Due to technology, texts in the classroom today" include a wider range of modalities—systems that people use to make meaning" (NCTE, 2006, p. 3).

Media-savvy students today read texts that include typical alphabetic print, still images, video, and sound. "They listen to podcasts, watch animations on the Internet, film their own videos, and compose visual arguments on paper and online. Reading and composing for these students includes such features as visual design, nonlinear organizational structures, and oral storytelling techniques" (NCTE, 2006, p. 3).

Students and teachers need to understand literacy in the digital age. In updating this text, the authors do not purport to be experts in the field of technology and certainly recognize that as teachers we need to continually update our skills so we feel comfortable working with students to develop and continue to refine a definition of literacy—especially in the area of technological communication. We will present a number of strategies that expose students to a variety of functional or day-to-day life coping literacy skills in the areas of newspapers, magazines, DVD's, television, graphic texts, and technology.

Definition

We believe that functional literacy is the appreciation and application of basic educational skills to life-coping demands. One of the best ways to develop literacy is through the use of real world resources: technology, newspapers, television, DVDs, video, magazines, graphic texts and survival print materials (multimedia). In this chapter we are defining literacy as "the minimal ability to read and write in a designated language" (Harris & Hodges, 1995, p.142). Alvermann and Hagood (2000) suggest that we need to engage students by developing their critical media literacy. Luke (1999) defines critical media literacy as the ability to reflect on the pleasures derived from mass media and popular culture practices (e.g., radio, TV, DVDs, video, movies, CDs, the Internet, gang graffiti and cyberpunk culture). Thus, we need to engage those 3 million students in the United States taking a portion of their instruction over the Internet by accommodating to the diversity of mass media (Bennett, 1998).

What is functional literacy?

Rationale

In this section we will discuss the rationale of implementing newspapers, DVDs, video, television, graphic texts and technology as major components to integrate into your content area.

The newspaper, unlike a textbook, is a learning resource that the student does not leave behind after graduation. It will always be available and will be relatively inexpensive. The use of the newspaper in the content area classroom could instill an attitude that can bring wealth even to a poverty stricken family—a wealth of information in all areas of intellectual challenge.

The use of newspapers in the classroom helps students to become more aware of themselves, the community, the nation and the world.

Rhoades & Rhoades (1980)

TEACHER TALK ————————————————————————————————

I have found that a daily subscription to a newspaper is one of the most valuable resources in my classroom. All students can find something of interest. Even one of my most recalcitrant students heads for the sports page as soon as he spots the papers on the news table.

The newspaper is one of the most comprehensive curriculum resources available. All content area teachers can and should draw from its information. The imaginable uses of the newspaper are many and varied. A resource you might want to consider is *Classline: USA Today's education program.* This is a series of teaching guides designed to help teachers use *USA Today* as a tool for teaching language arts and reading. Also included is a handbook for educators.

Rawlings & Schlosberg (1989)

How can students use television, DVDs, and video as a positive learning tool? Can they become selective and separate the good from the bad?

Educators and parents do not need to complain about television. Instead, it should be thought of as a medium for communication. Most people seem to believe that when students watch television, it is something they do alone. Viewing an enjoyable program in the classroom could prove to be a very valuable and educational experience which could develop vocabulary and comprehension. Television exposes students to a tremendous number of experiences which they might never otherwise have had.

There is a positive aspect to television. Take advantage of excellent television programs.

Hatchett (1990)

We believe that teachers should use television to help teach comprehension and critical thinking skills and use it as a motivating bridge between learning and entertainment.

TEACHER TALK

As a teacher I try to find books in my content area that could be related to specific television programs. I then put all of those books on a shelf and put a sign above them that reads "If you like to watch _____, you might want to try one of these books!" E.g., students who like to watch Superman may choose from superheroes such as those found in mythical tales like Hercules, Paul Bunyan or Ged in the *Earthsea trilogy* (Le Guin).

Supplement television programs with good books.

There are many television programs of educational value. Especially helpful for teachers are two publications. The first, "Teacher's Guides to Television" (PO Box 4, Lenox Hill Station, NY, NY, 10021), is published twice yearly. Each issue explains the content and objectives of selected programs, when the programs will be aired and on what channel. Besides a synopsis of each program, suggestions are given before and after viewing each selected program. A bibliography of related books and films is included.

Identify television programs that are suited to your content area.

The second publication is "Television Most Worth Watching" (Television Resources, Inc., Box 6712, Chicago, IL, 60680). This weekly newsletter for educators includes previews of programs and suggests classroom applications and related resources.

It is time that educators "cash in" on prime time and take advantage of the tremendous number of excellent programs, DVDs, and videos available.

Hogan (1997)

Thousands of students are using electronic communications. It is exciting to envision students linking with others worldwide. Students, via computers, have their papers reviewed by scientists, historians, artists, etc. As they prepare for AP exams, they seek out the latest information via the web.

Schools are the one place where all students come together no matter the diversity of their backgrounds. It should be an environment where technology resources are easily accessed, updated and required for classwork. These students are transitioning into the 21st century. How well will they be prepared?

STUDENT TALK

I love the classes where my teachers let us work on computers. Sometimes I just like to play around on the computer. Other times I need the teacher to tell me how to use the computer, like the web sites, to get stuff I need for a report. It's fun and doesn't seem like work! With the click of a mouse, I can be in Cancun.

"Properly produced and used, new multimedia technology enables students to better visualize, empathize with, and understand historical events like the Holocaust, the incarceration of Japanese Americans during World War II, or even more ordinary instances of racism and prejudice" (Hammer & Kellner, 1999, p. 522). The authors continue by describing the Shoah Visual History Foundation founded by Steven Spielberg and designed to document the impact of the Holocaust through innovative 21st century multimedia technology. Like the Shoah project UCLA has produced Executive Order 9006 which documents the incarceration of Japanese Americans during World War II through a CD-ROM that provides students with the realities of resisting political oppression, persecution and racism.

Alvermann and Hagood (2000) rationalize the need to use diverse media literacy by stating:

> "...there is a need for including critical media literacy as a regular component of school curricula in the United States. We also wanted to make the argument that the present discourse of schooling in this country is ill-equipped to support the incorporation of critical media literacy in such curricula. The binaries of in-school and out-of-school literacies will need to be blurred if we are to move beyond the current discourse and to begin to learn about, and to meet, the changing literacy competencies. To ignore the importance of doing so in these new times is to short-change adolescents destined to live out their lives, literate or otherwise, in a highly technical and global 21st century" (Alvermann & Hagood, 2000, p. 203).

Word processing has been used by some to teach sequencing when students revise stories in order to successfully make their stories flow from a beginning through a middle and to an end. Main idea evolves when one must create the best title for a story. Most important, however, is the fact that the computer allows students to cut and paste, edit, revise, etc. in an engaging format that elicits interest and limits frustration.

The following strategies will help you and your students to implement and integrate the use of multimedia in your classroom. In this case, multimedia refers to the use of the newspaper, video, DVDs, television, magazines, graphic texts and technology.

Strategies to Promote Real World Literacy

Newspapers

The wealth of strategies available for using the newspaper as a resource are as numerous as the number of creative teachers. What is important is that content area teachers have an avalanche of ideas to be able to select what is most appropriate for any given situation. The procedures for the following strategies can be used across all content areas:

Details, Charts and Graphs in Newspapers

TABLE 1

INSTRUCTIONAL SUMMARY OF DETAILS, CHARTS AND GRAPHS IN NEWSPAPERS

Literacy Strategy	Details, Charts and Graphs in Newspapers
Primary Focus	Details using charts and graphs
Learning Principles	❑ Activate Involvement ❑ Variety of Thought-demanding Activities
When to Use	After reading a newspaper article
Goals: National or State Literacy Standards	❑ Use a variety of reading strategies to increase comprehension and learning ❑ Identify details ❑ Use a variety of written forms ❑ Locate information using graphs and charts
Materials	Newspapers
Time	30 minutes

After reading a selection have students discuss answers to the typical newspaper questions of who, where, what, why and how. Once they have sufficient factual details ask them to design and or complete a matrix giving specific details. Student comprehension will likely increase when the student can make a concrete representation of information. Figure 9.1 should help students to learn how a matrix chart can help them to organize their information. Once the chart has been completed you may want to ask different groups of students to graph the information using a variety of graph models such as a bar or a pie graph. In Figure 9.1 we used information from the sports page for students in physical education. Finding details could also be done using photos in the news, maps, comic strips, or any other news formats.

Once the matrix information is assembled, encourage students to graph the results. Use different types of graphs. Questions such as "Do you see any trends?" or "Can you make any predictions?" help students synthesize and summarize information. This could also be used in a basic mathematics classroom.

FIGURE 9.1.   MATRIX INFORMATION

Attendance at various stadiums	Capacity of stadium	% of occupied seats	% of unoccupied seats
North Stadium 46,000	46,500	99%	1%
East Stadium 29,000	32,000	90%	10%
South Stadium 53,000	53,000	100%	0
West Stadium 33,000	34,000	97%	3%

Detecting Propaganda Techniques in the News

TABLE 2

INSTRUCTIONAL SUMMARY FOR DETECTING BIASES IN THE NEWS

Literacy Strategy	Detecting Propaganda Techniques in the News
Primary Focus	Critical Thinking
Learning Principles	❑ Talk Time ❑ Thought-demanding Activities
When to Use	After reading a newspaper article
Goals: National or State Literacy Standards	❑ Analyze and evaluate information ❑ Recognize persuasive writing
Materials	Newspapers
Time	30 minutes

Students should develop reading attitudes that cause them to question what they read. Propaganda techniques are used to influence someone to think in a certain way that would influence their decision-making abilities. Billion-dollar corporations depend on these advertising techniques for selling their wares and services.

Miller & Allan (1989)

Why do students need to pay attention to propaganda techniques?

Students need to understand the various propaganda techniques and to critically question what they mean. Since these techniques employ the use or misuse of vocabulary and its connotations, the teacher should help students to identify words used by the propagandist.

❏ **Personal Endorsement or Testimonial**
A famous person says a product is good.
"Mitch Gymlord recommends that you eat Gymnastic Crunch."

❏ **Statistics**
A comparably high number is used to endorse the product.
"Four out of five dentists recommend Sparkle toothpaste.

❏ **Bandwagon**
The theme is to encourage the consumer to realize that the value of the product is due to the fact that everybody thinks it's good.
"Join the _____ . Everyone is doing it."

❏ **Name Calling**
The product is made to look good by using unpopular descriptions of the competition.
"Dentists do not recommend Sparkle toothpaste. Glisten will make your teeth shine more."

❏ **Plain Folks**
The endorsers of the product are average, typical people.
"He's country-like and down-home. You'll agree with his ideas."

❏ **Loaded Words**
A promise is implied by using such phrases as virtually, usually, help, or if you're lucky.
"Chances are you will write more legibly if you use a Clear-Write pen."

How can carefully chosen language affect or influence us? Loaded language is designed to manipulate one's thinking. Gallagher (2004) suggests using euphemisms with students in order to show them how their thinking is manipulated. For example, give students a list of real world euphemisms and ask them to come up with the actual word or phrase substituted—beauty mark for "mole"; or nail technician for "manicurist, frugal for "cheap." To study euphemisms in depth, see websites and dictionaries that provide meanings such as Rawson's (1981) *Dictionary of Euphemisms and other Doubletalk*.

Explore key concepts like "death," that has a huge amount of euphemisms to describe this phenomenon. Allow students to generate their own. ELL students particularly benefit from this study. Fluency in English depends on students understanding these. To study manipulative language in other places one not need to look beyond the mailbox! Weekly, we receive envelopes each with a misleading message intended to tempt us to open it. For example, "Urgent Documents—Your Membership Has Lapsed," inside is a plea to send money to a political party and, incidentally, you have never had a membership with them!

To avoid taking such communication items at face value, the use of these examples of manipulative language helps students become more critical in their reading. Give them practice finding this language and there is no better place to start than with advertising. By the way, do not overlook the advertising that appears on food labels or email SPAM that has a subject line that encourages you to open the email.

Have students explain how words in an ad have been used effectively or ineffectively to increase their desire for an item or service. In the following Your Turn, use loaded language or propaganda vocabulary to create newspaper ads that deal with your content area.

What is loaded language?

Across the content areas teachers should encourage the use of newspapers to generate critical thinking from their students. For example, in the theater arts a teacher could have students read a review of a play and decide how much of the article is the opinion of the reviewer as opposed to what actually occurred. This same idea could be projected in science by differentiating fact from opinion in articles on such topics as AIDS, the environment, or others. In the social studies classroom students could discuss the persuasive arguments used in editorial cartoons or the pros and cons used to present a current debate, altercation, etc.

Organizational and Writing Skills

TABLE 3

INSTRUCTIONAL SUMMARY FOR ORGANIZING AND WRITING INFORMATION

Literacy Strategy	Organizing and Writing Information
Primary Focus	Organizing information
Learning Principles	❑ Organize Information ❑ Thought-demanding Activities
When to Use	Writing for a class newspaper
Goals: National or State Literacy Standards	❑ Use a variety of written forms ❑ Use a multi-step writing process: plan and draft, revise, publish
Materials	Newspapers
Time	30 minutes

When students can organize information into specific categories they are more likely to comprehend more effectively. Students could learn to do this using the physical format of the layout of a newspaper.

Have students create a newspaper for a topic in your content area.

Using the front page of a newspaper, trace the outline of columns, photos and headlines onto butcher paper. A skeletal layout is now ready for students to organize their writing. This can be used for a subject area book report or to organize information gathered in small groups as a content area survey of information. Use catchy headlines, a few pictures, and advertisements. Appointing students to

Notes

Your Turn

Name _____ Date _____ Subject Area _____

Directions: Write ads related to your content area for the following categories:

❑ Personal endorsement or testimonial:

❑ Statistics:

❑ Bandwagon:

❑ Name calling:

❑ Plain folks:

❑ Loaded words:

different tasks helps move this activity along. Appoint one person as the editor, one or two students are reporters, one student designs layout, and so forth. See Figure 9.2.

In the first example, students reporting on *The Hobbit* (Tolkien) create a newspaper using the columns for various book-related events. In the second example, the Roman Tabloid, a group of students respond on their reading in similar fashion.

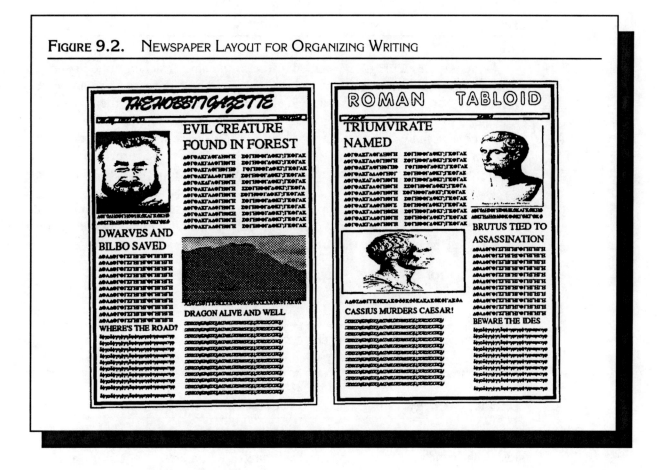

FIGURE 9.2.   NEWSPAPER LAYOUT FOR ORGANIZING WRITING

Video, DVDs and Television

Viewing for Answers

TABLE 4

INSTRUCTIONAL SUMMARY FOR VIEWING FOR ANSWERS

Literacy Strategy	Viewing for Answers
Primary Focus	Comprehension
Learning Principles	❏ Background Knowledge ❏ Talk Time

When to Use	Critiquing of a television program or a video related to a content area
Goal: National or State Literacy Standards	❑ Make predictions to extend and deepen understanding of a topic ❑ Distinguish main idea from supporting details ❑ Analyze and evaluate information
Materials	Television program or video
Time	30 minutes

Provide students with activities that encourage them to think while viewing television.

Before viewing a program assigned by the content area teacher, students should be encouraged to write questions to be answered. These questions should be developed at the various levels—literal, interpretive and applied, thereby giving students a purpose for watching the program. "Teacher's Guides to Television" would be especially helpful here. Students should preview the related books or films and develop questions in areas where they want more information, then watch the assigned program to answer their questions. You might even consider the use of a K-W-L PLUS.

Figure 9.3 contains topics for discussion of video or television programs. You may want to refer to Chapter 5 regarding the organization of discussion groups for the implementation of these topics.

Detecting for Bias and Propaganda Techniques

TABLE 5

INSTRUCTIONAL SUMMARY FOR DETECTING BIAS AND PROPAGANDA TECHNIQUES

Literacy Strategy	Detecting for Bias and Propaganda Techniques
Primary Focus	Comprehension
Learning Principles	❑ Searching for Meaning ❑ Thought-demanding Activities
When to Use	Critiquing of a television program or a video related to a content area
Goals: National or State Literacy Standards	❑ Identify facts from opinions ❑ Analyze and evaluate information ❑ Recognize persuasive language
Materials	Television program or video
Time	30 minutes

Students need to recognize bias in order to critically think about a topic. When watching the news, a talk show or other related programs, decide if equal time is given to both sides of the issue. Assign students to view different news programs. Plot the lead stories on a matrix. Decide if different television stations stressed different lead stories. Is the lead representative of a bias held by the television station? See Figure 9.4.

Many times opinions are expressed on a variety of programs. In particular, encourage students to watch talk shows, the news, commentaries, and interviews. To distinguish facts from opinions, have students gather factual information. Factual information should answer who, what, where, when, why and how. If there were two sides to an issue, can students determine if both of these were represented in an interview or presentation?

Becker (1973)

FIGURE 9.3.   IDEAS FOR VIEWING FOR ANSWERS

Language Arts/Social Studies
How characters dressed.
How characters talked.

Geography
Details of land and water formation.
Specific notations of the climate.

Science
Particular behaviors of animals.
Details related to major medical achievements.
How to prune shrubs or trees.

Physical Education
Specific details in a field strategy such as the instant replay that includes tracing the play with a line drawing.

Vocational Education
How to repair an appliance.
How to attach the siding to a house structure.

FIGURE 9.4.   LEAD STORIES

Becker (1973)

CBS	ABC	PBS
The accused murderer was caught in the cafeteria.	The suspect was accused of murdering the victims.	The suspect is accused of shooting the teens.

Opinions, judgments and expressing someone's point of view on a topic are not facts and most likely cannot answer the six question words listed above. Many times commentators, reporters or talk show hosts care very much about a topic and find it difficult to keep opinion out of their report. It is up to the student to decide if facts and opinions are both present and to distinguish one from the other.

Assign students to watch a program germane to a specific content area. Have them keep track of what they thought were facts or opinions. Compare these in class. This would also give students a purpose for watching a program.

Have students watch the news and list words that express an opinion, such as the following:

The <u>handsome</u> firefighter <u>bravely</u> rescued
the child from the <u>uncontrollable</u> fire.

Have students differentiate programs according to their use of fact and opinion.

Furthermore, listen for opinion through tone of voice, or non-verbal expressions and gestures. Have students write reports based on a guest speaker. Compare reports. Were the words who, where, when, what, why and how included? Were any words expressions of opinions? Discuss why one report was different from another. Finally, consider the source of the information. What sources do you trust to be the most accurate? There are five basic sources for information:
1. the main source,
2. people close to the main source,
3. a reporter,
4. other media, or
5. experts in the field of topic.

As students analyze a variety of reports, have them identify the source and judge the authenticity of the source. They need to be constantly reminded to keep an open and questioning mind.

To summarize a television program, students must learn to find the main idea and the most important supporting details. After comparing one another's summaries, compare them to what appeared in the "TV Guide." Was the professionally written summary accurate? Why or why not?

To criticize a program students will need to express an opinion. They will need to discuss their opinion of the program, how it could have been improved and whether they would recommend it to others. Their opinion is as valuable as that of the next person. However, the opinion should be substantiated.

The classroom teacher should collect critical reviews of programs and movies related to a particular content area. Assign the student to watch a program and write a critical review. Compare their criticism to the professionally written one. Discuss the important features of each. Discuss the components of a good critical review.

Students should realize that television commercials and programs can have an effect on how they think and feel. Television, like newspapers, can be very persuasive agents for young audiences. Students should be aware of and understand the propaganda techniques.

Tape videotape clips from popular TV commercials. Have students analyze the persuasive language or techniques used. Since actual application of a strategy is probably the best way for the student to learn a principle, have students design their own commercial for a product they have invented. Share their advertisements and discuss the propaganda techniques used. In a marketing class these could be projects for contests and business-partnered exhibits. Besides the use of the six propaganda techniques used in newspapers, discuss other strategies used in television, such as the following:

❏ **Size**
The scale or size can be made to look bigger on TV.

❏ **Speed**
The pacing of the advertisement can create a more desirous image of a product.

❏ **Voice**
The voice heard in the advertisement can help to sell a product. A striking voice will be remembered. Note how commercials usually are louder than the regular programming.

❏ **Casting**
The actors chosen for commercials are specifically selected so they represent a positive image for the product.

❏ **Tone or mood**
The mood of the commercial will determine whether the viewer can be persuaded by "hard-sell" versus "soft-sell."

Students could write television commercials for products designed in a class project.

Have students watch a content-related program or commercial. Discuss how the character persuaded another character or the viewer to make a certain decision. What convincing strategies and/or techniques were used?

In the following Your Turn, analyze and detect bias in a reported news story.

Notes

Your Turn

Name _____ Date _____ Subject Area _____

Directions: Watch the news on an early news report; then later in the evening, watch the news again, but on a different station. Compare the information reported using a Venn Diagram so you are able to distinguish what was similar and what was different. Also, decide if you detected any reported biases.

Station A   Station B

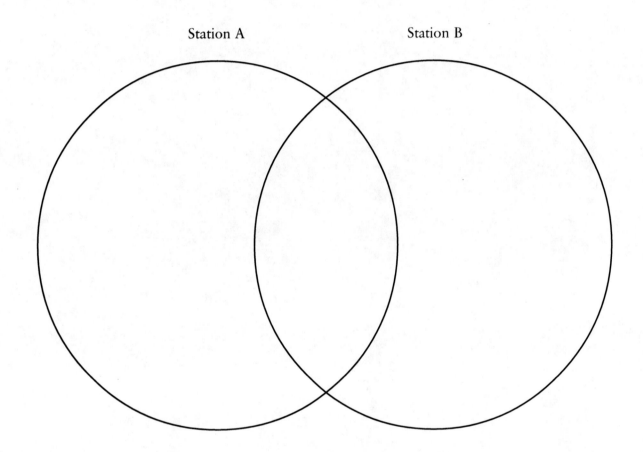

❏   List here any loaded language that indicated to you that bias was reported:

Viewing Skills

TABLE 6

INSTRUCTIONAL SUMMARY FOR VIEWING SKILLS

Literacy Strategy	Study Skills
Primary Focus	Comprehension
Learning Principles	Organize Information
When to Use	❏ During a video, DVDs or television program
Goals: National or State Literacy Standards	❏ Demonstrate organization of thoughts ❏ Convey clear, focused main ideas and supporting details
Materials	Television program, DVDs or video
Time	30 minutes

A number of study skills can be used while viewing television. As students watch a program have them take notes for specific details. For example, if a made-for-TV film has been assigned for a social studies classroom, have some students take notes on the dress of the characters. Have others take notes on how the characters talked. Still others could take notes on the cultural reflections, such as architecture, transportation and values.

The notes taken from a program could be used in class to write outlines. The outlines then could be used to write summaries. Maps could be used to locate the locales depicted. Students could use other references to verify the authenticity of the program.

Have students practice taking notes while viewing a program.

Graphic Texts

Comic Books

There are a number of graphic texts published today—comics, graphic novels, and manga.

In an article in the USA Today Web Site (5/3/2005), Greg Toppo reported that the American Library Association invited Jeff Smith, famous artist of comic books, and three other comic book artists to its annual meeting in 2002. The librarians were thrilled because their books were helping kids to learn to read—especially boys. Teachers, as well, are finding comics to be motivational for reading for recreational or instructional purposes.

"They're using the caped crusader *Batman* to explore mythology and Art Spiegelman's *Maus*, a Holocaust memoir, as well as other titles, to teach history" (Toppo, 2005). He writes further that in a comic book project where students can have their own comic books published, kids are writing about AIDS, Tibet and other issues. In Maryland some schools are using *Dignifying Science*, a comic about women scientists. Sales of comic books are rising and they are becoming a national movement. An Austin, Texas librarian and author, Michele Gorman, has developed a graphic-novel collection in one of the Austin libraries. It has become one of the most popular collections in the system. The graphic novels of today are not the remembered *Batman, Superman* or *Donald Duck*. Rather, they are much more sophisticated. However, not all teachers consider comic books as part of instructional materials. Are we creating a two-level system when we assign comic books to lower level readers and assign heavier books in the English class? Advocates hope to revive comic books after a 50-year hiatus.

Rocco Versaci, (2001) asks his students to read comic book excerpts by analyzing life experiences through popular cultural representations. His students were unaware that comic books address mature subject matter. His primary goal for using comic books in class is to provoke students to think more deeply about particular comic books that have an artistic value. Versaci also sees comic books as affording the teacher to "enact a powerful lesson for students about the dangers of literary presumption, to not make assumptions based on the appearance or popular conception of certain works. We agree with Versaci that "if more students enjoy going to their English classes in order to be surprised and challenged to think more deeply, and if they become more involved in the creation of their own opinions about literary merit, then we, as teachers of English, are fulfilling our implicit promise to make the world a place where readers, writers, and artists can flourish" (pp. 66–67).

What role do comics play in the secondary classroom?

Graphic Novels

The graphic novel is a longer more artful version of a comic book. Lev Grossman (2003) states that "graphic novels appeal to various readers, offer all kinds of genres, help students develop critical thinking, and encourage literacy" (p. 18).

Greg Toppo of USA Today recommends the following titles taken from Michele Gorman (2005) as some of the best graphic novels available for teens:

Ages 12-14

Azumanga Daioh, Volume 1, by Kiohiko Azuma
Ultimate Spider-Man, Volume 1: Power and Responsibility by Brian Bendis, Mark Bagley and Bill James
The Barefoot Serpent by Scott Morse
Usagi Yojimbo: Grasscutter by Stan Sakai
Kare Kano by Masami Tsuda
Ranma, Volume 1 by Rumiko Takahashi
Fruits Basket, Volume 1 by Natsuki Takaya

Ages 15-18

Sandman: The Doll's House by Neil Gaiman. Mike Dringenberg, Malcom iones III and Michael Zulli
The Ultimates, Volume 1: Super-Human by Mark Millar and Bryan Hitch
Strangers in Paradise: High School by Terry Moore
Blankets by Craig Thompson
Fray by Joss Whedon
Flight, Volume 1 by various artists

As teachers we seek out ways to motivate students, our mantra: "If they don't learn the way you teach, teach the way they learn." Jacquie McTaggart (2006) suggests that comics should supplement a balanced reading program, not supplant it. She suggests that teachers keep a collection of comic books with the classroom library, she reminds us that comic books have many of the same themes and topics as do traditional books, and encourages reviews of comics along with traditional book reviews. For lesson plans using comic books, art activities, lists of appropriate comics, and for student writing of comic books see the following Websites:

www.tascorp.org/mediacenter/media coverage/ 061504comic. Thinking Outside the Box, Inside the Panel

http://sidekicks.noflyingnotights.com. Sidekicks: A Website Reviewing Graphic Novels for Kids

http:/ /my.voyager.net/ ~sraiteri/ graphicnovels.htm. Recommended Graphic Novels for Public Libraries

Gretchen Schwarz (2006) suggests that the graphic novel lends itself to critical media literacy which affirms diversity, gives everyone a voice, and "helps students examine ideas and practices that promulgate inequity"… (p. 63).

What is the relationship of graphic novels to critical media literacy?

Graphic novels are increasing in number, quality, variety, and availability. They offer a new kind of text for the classroom and they demand new reading abilities. They tend to appeal to diverse students, including reluctant readers, and they offer both great stories and informational topics.

In addition, manga, a type of graphic novel, is popular with middle school students and includes elements of Chinese mythology. A different form of manga has to be read from back to front, and offers a comparison of Japanese and American culture.

Manga

What is manga? It should not be confused with anime. Japanese animators base anime frequently on manga which is roughly translated as "comic books." Anime is simply any animation often released as TV shows, movies or Original Video Animation. Derrik Quenzer (2006) defines manga as Japanese comics that have been around for a long time. Manga accounts for 75% of all graphic novels sold in the U.S.

What is the difference between anime and manga?

> Those who love flashy, colorful superhero comic books will not find them in manga. The stories are fun, quick to read and character-driven, but they are black-and-white and—because they're imports from Japan—most are read from right to left, which can cause American readers some initial confusion. But don't let that stop you. Although the pacing tends to be slow at the beginning, the tales end with great payoffs. Each digest gives you a complete story, so you don't have to wait a months to see what happens next (Quenzer, p. 42).

Genres of manga vary from science-fiction to Westerns, to romance to fantasy. Readers need to literally fish through dozens of titles. Teachers and parents need to be alert to the range of manga publications. Some are great stories fit for students. Others contain explicit nudity and sex.

The following interview with a middle school fan of manga highlights what this age group finds appealing about the genre.

STUDENT TALK

1. *What was it about manga that got you interested and keeps you reading manga?*

   I got my first manga comic from a friend for my birthday. I like manga because the pictures give you good insight into the characters. You know their personality right away. Pictures tell the story, you can follow the story easily.

2. *In reading about it, one author said that manga, unlike many American comics or stories for young people, are more realistic: Characters in manga die, they lose the one they love to another, they fail at what they are trying to do. Characters are more complex, the villain can change their ways, heroes can show the bad side of themselves and even commit horrid acts. Do you agree? What examples can you tell us about that show some of these characteristics?*

   Yes, the characters in manga have fantasy characteristics but they are not heroes, like Superman or Batman. They are not fighting evil, or to save the world from something bad. They have many sides like my favorite Naruto, a character in a top-selling comic, written by Masashi Kishimotcy. He is in training to become a ninja. As a child, he had a Kyuubi (nine-tailed fox demon) sealed in him. Because of this, the villagers avoided him, he grows up an orphan. He gets attention through pranks and mischief. However after graduating from the Ninja academy, he finds out why people avoid him and that his sensei Umino Iruke cares about him. Upon graduation he changes and begins the rest of his journey.

3. *Are boys more interested in manga than girls? Why?*

   Not necessarily, my best friend is and a girl in my class reads Naruto also.

4. *A writer compared manga to Shakespeare's writing. It is common in serious manga stories for a comic moment to occur or vice versa—tragic moment occurs in normally humorous manga. Would you agree with this? Again do any examples come to mind?*

   I don't know much about Shakespeare but, yes, Naruto plays pranks . For example, he is supposed to transform himself. Instead of becoming the important guy in the village, he turns himself into an ugly person.

5. *Are manga used in your classroom in language arts/English or in Social Studies?*

   No! In fact, I have a feeling that my teacher would rather have me read something else.

6. *If not, do you think that using manga would encourage more reading among your classmates?*

   Yes, I think it would be very good for creative writing and kids could draw the characters. I like to draw manga characters and bought a book on how to draw these. Now I keep a notebook of my drawings, but I create my own ideas about a manga character rather than use the book. In addition, the chapters of Naruto continue to be created, kids could write their own version of the next chapter.

7. *Yes, I saw that there were many books on drawing manga characters. What about Social Studies?*

   Yeah! You could learn a lot about Japan from Naruto. Naruto is a city in Japan known for its Naruto whirlpools (Uzumaki). Naruto's first name is Uzmaki. It is also home to two temples that the Japanese visit on pilgrimage. There is also a suspension bridge, one of the largest in the world across the Naruto Straits.

8. *Are there times that reading manga becomes difficult? If you don't get the manga story, what do you do to make the story clearer?*

   Yes, it is easier to follow Naruto on the cartoon channel. In the comics, sometimes the action moves so quickly and it is hard to see in the frames. To make it clearer, I reread the comic frames.

9. *Do you ever write manga yourself? What are other manga that your friends might like?*

No, I just draw pictures. *Sailor Moon, Inu-Yasha: a feudal fairy tale, Ranma, How to draw manga: Getting started, Nausicaa of the Valley of the Wind, Hikaru no Go,* and *Fushigi Yugi.*

Max Chvilicek, 8th grade

In this interview with Max, it is exciting to note how involved kids can get with alternative media. In addition, to the comics themselves, there are sufficient relevant websites to warrant a web-based curriculum.

Students could read for the usual elements of fiction as well as figurative language used. In addition, they can write: contributing their ideas to forums, adding factoids to the Naruto link, creating ongoing Naruto chapters, participating in Naruto art contests. They can also compare and contrast manga comics and their characters with characters from assigned classroom readings.

> Why not bring out into the open, interests of kids that presently are "relegated to the drawings on their notebook pages, the covers of assignment folders and the sheaves of drawings in their backbacks" (Frey & Fisher, 2004).

Schwartz and Rubinstein-Avila (2006) report that "several scholars have claimed that manga require multimodal reading skills and a sharp critical inquiry stance. For example, recent studies have reported on how manga have been used as both a teaching tool and a subject of cultural study (Allen & Ingulsrud, 2003; Frey & Fisher, 2004). Ultimately, like any cultural texts, manga provides a way for youths to negotiate alternative identities. By engaging with a wide range of manga characters, dynamic plots, and storyboards, children and young adults make connections between these popular texts and their own life experiences.

Allender (2004); Frey & Fisher (2004)

Dallas Middaugh (2006) in his article called *Reading Manga: Or How I Learned to Stop Worrying and Just Love Reading* discusses how he learned to read using comics and made the transfer to a variety of genres. But it was the comics that motivated him and caused him to love reading; it was comics that became his passion.

Magazines

Comprehension in Magazines

TABLE 7

INSTRUCTIONAL SUMMARY FOR COMPREHENSION

Literacy Strategy	Comprehension
Primary Focus	Comprehension
Learning Principles	❏ Metacognitive Experience ❏ Thought-demanding Activity
When to Use	❏ Anytime

Goals: National or State Literacy Standards	❏ Read for enjoyment
	❏ Assessing interest about topics to guide instruction and to motivate students
	❏ Extend and deepen comprehension by relating text to other texts
Materials	Magazines for a specific content area
Time	Varies

Cronin & Hines (1990)

As teachers of content area subjects we need to assess the availability of magazines related to our specific fields. It is important that you survey your library and make appropriate assignments which target the magazines available. The use of periodical literature is appropriate with all of the activities given in the newspaper section of this chapter. As with newspapers, magazines are also popular due to the variety of topics, the length of articles and the up-to-date information available.

Stoll (1997)

Content area teachers need to make periodical literature accessible to their students and keep a good variety of magazines in the classroom.

There are a number of magazines that will print articles written by students. This opportunity is very motivating and teachers should encourage their students to submit their writing for publication.

Encourage your students to submit their work for publication.

TEACHER TALK

I once had a student who had submitted an article and when the notice arrived in the mail that it had been accepted the student ran into my room yelling, "Look, Mrs. M., I'm published! I just got a postcard telling me that my article will appear in the next issue of *Young Voices!*"

See the reference section for a listing of magazines by content area and for those that exclusively or regularly print student writing.

World Wide Web

As you and your students become proficient at using the Internet and computers, you will want to consider how you could use any of the strategies presented in this book by integrating the computer and/or Internet. For example, a note-taking chart could be used for navigating the World Wide Web. You would give the students a Web site for your content area and ask them to complete a skeletal chart of main ideas and details from the assigned site. Another idea would be the integration of a Feature Matrix. The vertical column might list a number of Web sites and the features across the top would encourage students to compare Web sites such as number of links, use of graphics, etc. For writing consider the use of e-mail in your classroom (Ryder & Graves, 1998).

Martha Rekrut (1999) suggests that before moving directly into strategies for using the computer in the classroom, it is imperative that we first consider some basic guidelines for creating lessons using the Internet. First, you must decide whether the use of the Internet is the best resource to use in order to meet your lesson goals. If the World Wide Web is to be the research tool of choice then you will need to make certain that your students are given ample instruction on how to use it. Second, you should have done some initial research on the topic to be certain the task is possible. This basic background should also include vocabulary instruction so students are not confused regarding basic Internet language. Each time students use the Internet you will need a specific objective and a time frame that will allow them to accomplish the goal. Block periods are usually better than shorter periods. At the end of an Internet lesson it would be helpful if students are accountable to submit a written component of their accomplishments. This might be a downloaded document or as simple as a completed worksheet. Organizing information in a graphic organizer is also an efficient and effective strategy. See specific web sites for graphic organizers in the reference section of this chapter. Last, ask students to evaluate their Internet experience. Their comments should help you to improve a future lesson on the World Wide Web.

Using Websites

TABLE 8

INSTRUCTIONAL SUMMARY FOR USING WEBSITES

Literacy Strategy	Using Websites
Primary Focus	Comprehension
Learning Principles	❑ Background Knowledge ❑ Searching for Meaning ❑ Thought-demanding Activity
When to Use	❑ When appropriate
Goals: National or State Literacy Standards	❑ Extending and deepening understanding of a topic ❑ Acquire information from electronic sources ❑ Record and store data ❑ Demonstrate skill with a variety of electronic tools, including word processing ❑ Use appropriate citations and adhere to copyright regulations
Materials	Computer access to the Internet
Time	Varies

Deirdre Kelly (2000) suggests that too much online research could be a wild goose chase. What can we do to turn that around? She further suggests that students be taught the use of specific search engines and that teachers find valuable Web sites in their content areas. Students then need to understand how information is stored on Web sites so they can be better sleuths! Students should never go to the Internet empty handed! At the least they should be prepared to take notes. Thus, they will need paper and pencil and the knowledge that Web site information is stored and structured differently from books. Students may need to take notes from a variety of electronic branches on a single Web site. "Having students do research online is productive and necessary. And making sure that the process is organized around a logical set of parameters is vital to the success of the project. Providing a structure such as a graphic organizer for decision-making, note-taking, and application is a good way to approach online research in the classroom and ensure that it is a true learning experience for your students" (Kelly, 2000. p. 6).

Web-based Information

How do we show students how to determine what is fact and what is not in their reading?

Nicholas Lemann (2006) writes in the *New Yorker* that journalism is a "perfect vehicle for theories about conspiracies by the powerful, and this year has brought an efflorescence of them" (p. 96). There is a Web-resident called Loose Change that often refutes the mainstream media. The Web site opens with frames that convey "the thrill of the revelation of concealed truths" (p. 98). The main thesis is that the September 11, 2001 attacks were staged. Likewise, there are Web sites that state the Holocaust never occurred. Thus, it is necessary that our students understand propaganda techniques, how to recognize them and become critical consumers and critical readers of information—if it is in print or on the Web does not mean that the information is the truth.

When searching for information on the Web we need to teach students to be as discerning as possible. Critical reading is imperative—constantly question the information. One way to do this is to have students use a Web Page Evaluation Sheet (Haley, 2005) as described in Figure 9.5.

The following web sites can be used to take a cyber trip to the ever-open library for authenticated information:

American History: American Memory: Historical Collections for the National Digital Library www.memory.loc. gov / ammem / ammemhome.html

Prehistory and medieval to 20th century: Best of History Web Sites www.besthistorysites.net

Facts in General: Fact Monster www.factmonster.com / index.html

Factual and Statistical Information: Gary Price's Fast Facts www.freepint.com/gary/handbook.htm

General Resources: HomeworkSpot.com www.homeworkspot. com

General References: iTools www.itools.com; Ready Reference on the Internet www.mcls.org/webpublic/refcenter: NoodleTools: Smart Tools for Smart Research www.noodletools.com; My Virtual Reference Desk-My Homework Helper www.refdesk.com/homework.html.

FIGURE 9.5.   WEB PAGE EVALUATION SHEET

Name: _____ Date: _____

Directions: Please complete this evaluation sheet for each Web page that you want to use as a source for any assignments.

Name of page: _____

URL: _____

Author: _____

1. If the Web page has an author, what are his/her qualifications to write on this topic?
2. Does the page have a link to his/her homepage and/or provide a way to contact him/her?
3. If the page does not list an author, what is the domain name in the address? (edu, gov, etc.).

Currency:

1. When was the page last updated?
2. How current are the links?

Objectivity:

1. What is the purpose of this page? (to persuade?, to inform?)

Mechanics:

1. Is the page free of spelling and grammatical errors?
2. Do all the links work?

Recommendation: Based upon your response to the above, do you recommend this Web page as a credible source of information for your topic? Explain.

Adapted from Haley, K.W. (2005) Web Page Evaluation Sheet retrieved December 21, 2006 from http: / / kwhaley.20m.com / studenteval.htm.

The following lesson plan is designed to introduce students to the World Wide Web by defining literacy in a digital world.

FIGURE 9.6. LESSON PLAN: DEFINING LITERACY IN A DIGITAL WORLD

Grade: 9-12

Topic: Changing Definition of Literacy

Purpose: To explore different literacies through popular culture and technology

Topic: Explore Multimodal Literacies through Popular Culture and Technology

State Content/Literacy Standards: 1) To extend understanding of a topic through research, 2) To acquire information from electronic resources, 3) To comprehend, evaluate and appreciate texts, 4) To conduct research on issues and interests by generating ideas, questions, and problems.

Student Objectives:

Students will:
1. expand definitions or texts.
2. identify different kinds of texts: print, visual, audio.
3. compile a list of strategies needed to read and write texts.
4. develop and continue to refine a definition of literacy.

Introduction:
1. Choose a text such as a poster, film clip or music video.
2. Review web sites which are used in "Defining Literacy in a Digital World Interactive," http:/ /interactives.mped.org/view interactive.aspx?id=739&title=to make certain they are appropriate for your classroom.
3. Test the "Defining Literacy in a Digital World Interactive" on your computers to familiarize yourself with the tools and ensure that you have the Flash plug-in installed. You can download the plug-in from the technical support page.

Learning Activity:
1. Assign students to work in small groups (3 minutes)
2. Ask students to brainstorm items that combine different ways of expressing ideas. To get them started try the following:
   a. Select a poster and discuss how ideas are expressed such as in the text, the image, the use of color, and the visual layout.
   b. Point out Web sites, PowerPoint presentations, videos, etc. (15 minutes)
3. Share all the group ideas and record on chart paper under "Texts." (10 minutes)
4. Explore with students the changing definition of "texts." Examples: audio texts, video texts, etc. as well as the skills needed to interact with the list of texts. The interaction should be guided by verbs such as "view, listen or analyze." (10 minutes)
5. The students should also be aware of how the texts were created by brainstorming a list of verbs such as "compose, draw, design." (10 minutes)

FIGURE 9.6.   LESSON PLAN: DEFINING LITERACY IN A DIGITAL WORLD (CONT.)

6. Now that the students have their list of texts and the interactions necessary to work through the texts demonstrate the "Defining Literacy in a Digital World Interactive" and discuss any questions the students may have. (20 minutes)
7. Ask students to explore all ten sites, or put them in groups to explore one site for each group. Ask them to use the Web Site Analysis Worksheet located: http:/ / www.readwritethink.org/lesson images/lesson915/WebSiteAnalysisWorksheet.pdf (30 minutes)
8. Once they have done the Web site analyses ask them to brainstorm as many strategies as possible needed to interact with the sites.

Closure:
Based on student findings make additions or changes to the class definition of literacy and appropriate list of verbs. (7 minutes)

Evaluation:
To indicate that they have gained a deeper understanding of their own literacy skills have the students reflect in their journals about their literacy strengths in using specific "texts."

Web Resources:
Media Literacy Clearinghouse http:/ / medialit.med.sc.edu/

❑ This site is for K-12 teachers to learn about media literacy and its integration into the classroom. 21st Century Literacies http://www.kn.pacbell.com / wired/ 21stcent/ index.html
❑ This site concentrates on information, media, multicultural, and visual and explores the ways teachers can use these new literacies in their instruction.

Adapted from Gardner, T. (2006). ReadWriteThink Lesson plan: Defining literacy in a digital world. Retrieved December 21, 2006 from http:/ /wvvw.readwritethink.org/lessons/lesson view printer friendly.asp?id=915.

CD-ROM Project: Myst

TABLE 9

INSTRUCTIONAL SUMMARY OF MYST

Literacy Strategies	Myst
Primary Focus	Language Arts: Writing, Reading, Speaking, Listening
Learning Principles	❑ Active Involvement ❑ Thought-demanding Activities
When to Use	Before, during, after reading
Goals: National or State Literacy Standards	❑ Use a variety of modes (e.g., narrative, imaginative) in appropriate contexts ❑ Identifies relationships, images, patterns or symbols ❑ Uses technology to communicate information.
Materials	❑ Myst CD ❑ Writing, & art materials

CD-Roms like the Myst game are excellent instructional additions to the language arts curriculum. Myst and its more recent sister, Riven CD-ROM, provide awesome visuals and a storyline that can be interpreted in myriad ways and adapted to most English curricula. An English teacher, Megan Owens (personal communication, November 30, 2000), shared with us a unit she has designed that uses this CD game imaginatively and creatively. As a result of completing this unit, most students will have completed a portfolio that includes:

1. Journal—Daily entries exploring the island and collecting clues.
2. An Illustrated 5-sense Poem—Students locate the "coolest" place on the island and describe it by creating a 5-sense poem and illustrate it.
3. Burned Book Story—After seeing and reading some of the burned books found in the Library in Myst, students create a story following the style found in the stories they have read on the CD. Students dye and "burn" the edges of their stories to make them look more authentic.
4. Travel Brochure. Students create a travel brochure to lead other students to places in Myst. This includes a clever title, an illustration on the cover of the brochure, a description of the destination, a step-by-step procedure of how to get to their destination from the dock, and a description of the highlights to see along the way. After these are completed they are given to the school's Media Center. Other students who want to play Myst can use the Media Center's computers and read these travel brochures to get to a certain destination.

5. Story Pyramid. See Chapter 7 for a description of this poem.
6. Students complete this as a way of summarizing a story they have written or read about an experience on Myst.
7. Scoring Guide—Criteria

A sample of a student's work from her travel brochure, *The Mystical Land of the Mechanical Age: A Resort on the Water* reads:

> *Getting from Myst island to the Mechanical Age is very simple. At the dock go straight and make a left. Go up the stairs and then make a right up another flight of stairs. You should be at a big sunken gear. Next to it there is a marker switch. Flip it up. Go back down one flight of stairs and then go straight. You should be on a platform. Go all the way straight and then make a right and go all the way up the stairs...*
>
> Christina W., 1996

Christina's use of italics, unique font, and her visuals—all connote the flavor and the adventure that surrounds Myst. Writing and communicating directions are some of the many literacy skills students develop as they complete their project. It has proven a failsafe unit.

Over the years, Megan has added to this unit. As a highlight of all the work her students have done, their final activity is participation in a Myst Fair, where they display and present their projects. Aspiring musicians, video directors, historians, artisans, webmasters, scientists and mathematicians introduce their audiences, other classes who visit the Fair, to the world of Myst viewed through their particular intelligence (Gardner, 1999). Samples of students' work can be viewed on her website: http://www.grammarface.com.

From *Using CD-ROM Technology in the Language Arts Classroom—A Classroom Guide.* By Megan Owens, Beaverton, OR, 2001.

Inclusion Techniques

As necessary, the content area classroom teacher must monitor and adjust for the student with special needs. This might involve an adaptation of the planned activity for using the newspaper, television, magazines, functional reading materials or technology resources. It might also demand that the teacher design alternative lessons for these students. These decisions will be based on several variables, such as the amount of time the student participates in your classroom, the availability of resource teachers and the availability of instructional assistants. Nevertheless, what specific uses of real world literacy might be used for such students?

Elkins (1986)

Comprehension for Inclusion Students

Table 10

Instructional Summary for Comprehension	
Literacy Strategy	**Comprehension**
Primary Focus	Comprehension
Learning Principles	❏ Megacognitive Experiences ❏ Thought-demanding Activities
When to Use	During reading
Goals: National or State Literacy Standards	❏ Determine the meanings of words ❏ Demonstrate literal comprehension ❏ Demonstrate inferential comprehension
Materials	Functional reading materials
Time	30 minutes

The following gives you a variety of ways to teach details and main ideas as facets of comprehension, in general.

Using Functional Materials to Teach Main Idea and Details

According to Nancy Patterson (2005) "...exceptional students thrive in the same rich learning environments that "regular" students thrive in" (p. 62). We need to provide special needs students with digital and online resources. The curriculum for inclusive students should not be an easier textbook but rather a flexible use of real world literacy that is authentic for them. The following lesson plan serves as such as an example:

Internet

Because of the availability of a tremendous number of resources on the Internet a broad spectrum of lessons, resources and teaching ideas can be found which could be used to modify the existing curriculum. Students could use software designed for less capable readers and learn to use the Internet through a scavenger hunt. See the reference section of this chapter. They could browse a Web site and list new vocabulary words, new ideas that need clarification, etc. The teacher would then re-teach that information, assign a partner to help the student or whatever means is necessary for the inclusive student to comprehend the content information.

Newspapers

Ciani (1981)

Because a high number of newspapers are written at a fairly easy reading level (grades 6–8), this resource can be easily adapted for the student with special needs. Specific words can be circled in an article related to a content topic. Large print advertisements can be used for students with visual problems. For students who need to work on basic mathematics problems, newspaper ads can be used to

FIGURE 9.7.   BOOK REPORT VIA A SLIDE-SHOW

Lesson Plan for Inclusion Students: Using a Slide-Show to Report on a Book

Grade 8

Topic: Technology-based activities that allow students to create a slide-show.

Purpose: Give students ability to use technology, to control the use of a computer and to be creative rather than just writing a review of the book.

State Content/Literacy Standards:

Students will:
1. Read to perform a task
2. Understand and explain the use of technology by following technical directions.

Student Objectives:
1. Using slide-show software students will manipulate ideas, graphics, color and sound.
2. Students will create a slide-show that shows their response to the book.

Introduction:
1. Introduce students to slide show software.
2. Establish a minimum number of slides they are to create.

Learning Activity:
1. Provide guidance for creating each slide.
2. Guide students to realize that each slide should include ideas about characters, the setting, the plot, the background of the author, etc.
3. Allow students to choose the sequence of the slides and to control the color, images and content.
4. Show students a slide show that has been created by the teacher or a past student.
5. Students create their slide shows.

Closure: Students present their slide shows.

Evaluation: Distribute slips of paper and ask students to provide a sentence or two on what they liked about each student's presentation. Encourage them to use comments referring to color, images and content used in the presentation. Then, direct them to give these to the presenter.

Web sites:
Center for Applied Special Technology: http/ / www.cast.org
Council for Exceptional Children: http/ / www.cec.sped.org/
Universal Design for Learning: http/ / www.cast.org/udl/
Special Education Resources on the Web: http/ /seriweb.com/

calculate daily needs and expenditures. Pictures in the news can be discussed. Basic articles can be used to teach comprehension and critical thinking skills. In general, the easy-to-read basic news articles related to specific content areas should be one of your considerations. Many newspapers include a weekly high-interest, easy-reading supplement.

Television

Television programs are well-suited for the student with special needs who is unable to read content area material. There are television programs available regarding almost any content area. Educational videos and DVDs can also be used to supplement content for the student who cannot read. It may be that television will serve as the most important teaching resource used to impart content area knowledge and concepts. Consult your local television station for adaptive programming, e.g., closed caption viewing.

Magazines

Reed (1988)

Magazines for diverse populations could be selected from those available. Easy-to read magazines are available in most content areas. The classroom teacher could use the pictures and photographs in these magazines as a major resource for the student who has special needs.

Functional Reading Resources

Functional reading resources for the special student should be quite similar to those discussed earlier for use in the regular content area classroom. Develop work samples/units around billboards, advertisements, menus, and bus schedules, to name a few. It is the mainstreamed student who might rely on these much more than other students. The severity of the handicapping condition of the student will determine which functional resources are best to use and how to relate them to a particular class.

Real World Literacy for English Language Learners

The use of the Internet has helped to make the acquisition of a second language more attractive to second language learners. The Internet is widespread in a great variety of fields and domains. It carries great potential for educational use, especially for second and foreign language education (Signal, 1997). E-mail conversations can be intensely social and attract students' interests. They serve as a means for students to put into practice structures they have learned in the classroom (Kuang-wu, 2000). Besides the Internet, survival reading resources can also be used for English language acquisition.

What is survival reading?

Some students prefer not to read and tend to look for information by listening to television or the radio. However, in our society most citizens are going to need to read for functional purposes. This kind of survival reading can be taught in the content classrooms. We suggest that by using real-world reading material, students can be motivated to the point where they eventually can move into more sophisticated resources.

Harris & Hodges (1995)

We must not overlook the fact that English language learners need as much writing instruction as reading instruction. The following lesson plan is designed for ELL students to use persuasive writing:

FIGURE 9.8.   REAL WORLD PERSUASIVE WRITING

Lesson Plan for ELL Students: Persuasive Writing for "Eat At McDonald's"

Grade 9

Topic: Eating at McDonald's

Purpose: To help students to understand the power of persuasion through writing on why one should frequent McDonald's.

State Content/Literacy Standards:
1. Extend and deepen understanding of propaganda techniques, in particular persuasion.
2. Recognize the components of a well-written paragraph.

Student Objectives:

Students will:
1. use persuasive words to write about McDonald's.
2. organize their ideas using a graphic organizer, 3) review the important components for writing a paragraph. 4) write a persuasive paragraph.

Introduction:
1. Ask students to brainstorm what they like about McDonald's.

Learning Activity
1. Ask students to review the menu choices at McDonald's. You can find this on the Webpage for McDonald's www.mcdonalds.com
2. Use these ideas to encourage students' brainstorming of McDonald's items to complete a graphic organizer such as beverages, paper products, meats, salads, potatoes, and desserts.
3. The students will outline their reasons to persuade someone to eat at McDonalds.
4. Share other students' work as models.
5. Assign students to write a paragraph based on the graphic organizer.
6. Remind students of the components of a persuasive paragraph.

Closure: Share student work.

Next Lesson: For a Daily Oral Language (DOL) lesson, the teacher projects a model paragraph on the screen. The students are asked to edit the writing, coming up to the overhead to share any corrections writing these on the transparency until the projected piece is correct. The students are responsible for writing the paragraph after the corrections are made in their writing journal.

Figure 9.9.   Outline for Persuasive Writing

Student Outline for Persuasive Writing

Restaurant: _____

Topic Sentence: _____

Supporting Details: (on the outline of pictures)

1. _____

2. _____

3. _____

4. _____

5. _____

Conclusion: _____

Parts of a persuasive paragraph: Check those parts of a persuasive paragraph you've written:

a. _____ It contains a strong opening sentence that hooks the reader.

b. _____ The writer tries to persuade the reader that his/her opinion is the best.

c. _____ The writer gives details and facts that prove, explain or support their opinion.

d. _____ The writer restates the main idea or opinion and summarizes the paragraph.

FIGURE 9.10.   ELL STUDENT SAMPLE OF PERSUASIVE WRITING

Restaurant: McDonald's

Topic Sentence: You can stuff your face.

Supporting Details: (on the outline of pictures)
1. Beverages: your beverages are so good; they got the best stuff you can drink.
2. Burgers: You can walk there, and the burger will fill you up.
3. On another hamburger: It is so good it will make your taste buds spin.
4. On another hamburger: There are a lot of $1 stuff and a lot of fries.

Conclusion: that's my reason for going there
5. Brainstorm the components of a persuasive paragraph:

    a. _X_ It contains a strong opening sentence that hooks the reader.

    b. _X_ The writer tries to persuade the reader that his/her opinion is the best.

    c. _X_ The writer gives details and facts that prove, explain or support their opinion.

    d. _X_ The writer restates the main idea or opinion and summarizes the paragraph.

Paragraph: McDonald's—It's a good place to stuff your face. You can walk there. It will fill you up. There are a lot of $1.00 menu stuff and lot of fries. It's so good that it will make your taste buds spin. Your beverages are so good! The best drinks are there. That's my reason for going there and you should too!!!

By Jeffrey Sanchez, 2006

Functional reading or *survival reading,* is defined as reading that is necessary for daily survival. Thus, reading materials such as menus, commercial signs, road signs, bus schedules, television schedules, the telephone book and the Internet are important resources.

Comparison/Contrast

TABLE 11

INSTRUCTIONAL SUMMARY FOR COMPARISON/CONTRAST

Literacy Strategy	Comparison/Contrast
Primary Focus	Comprehension
Learning Principles	❏ Thought-demanding Activities ❏ Searching for Meaning
When to Use	During reading
Goals: National or State Literacy Standards	❏ Determine the meanings of words ❏ Demonstrate inferential comprehension
Materials	Functional reading materials
Time	30 minutes

Many skills can be incorporated in the reading of functional materials. Such skills as comparison/contrast and analysis of the messages are described below.

Menus
Collect a variety of menus from diverse cultural restaurants. Compare various restaurant titles for similar dishes. Improve the menu listing by writing more specific details about the dish. Find recipes for various dishes and follow the directions to prepare these. Compare various recipes. Research the history of various culinary words.

Commercial signs
Commercial signs often become instantly recognized symbols analogous to words. The golden arches or "M" for McDonald's is more convenient as a symbol than to read the word, "McDonald's." Have students analyze the symbols for well-known commercial businesses. Which ones are effective and why?

LaSasso (1983)

Road signs
Many road sign symbols have become internationally recognized. Discuss the simplicity of such signs and the message conveyed. Have students design signs for functional activities, e.g. restrooms, cafeteria, offices, gym and lobby, for use in their high school. Compare their designs to those already being used.

Bus schedules
Collect bus schedules from a variety of cities—local, national and international. Compare the schedules. Analyze the schedules and decide which are most useful and why. How does the organization of a particular schedule make it easier to read and follow?

Audio tapes

It is not unusual for the content area teacher to have non-readers or students who refuse to read. Public libraries have a plethora of audio-taped books, fiction and non-fiction, poetry and professional literature, such as business topics.

Content area teachers need to consider providing "meaningful and appropriate content instruction for students needing instructional modifications..." (Vogt, 2000, p. 334). These are not "special needs" students; most have no learning disabilities, nor are they "slow" learners (Allington & Walmsley, 1995). We simply need to modify instruction for students who, other than a language barrier, are successful. These modifications might include extensive modeling, assigning a partner or buddy (mentor) to a student with limited English. Finding suitable texts for students in which you can point out new vocabulary, implement study guides, and apply study skill strategies (See Chapter 3) such as SQ3R will help to make the modifications necessary for these students to succeed (Vogt, 2000).

Endings: A Summary

Real-world literacy refers to the ability to read and write in a designated language using such learning resources as newspapers, television, video, magazines, and the Internet. All of these can be used to teach comprehension and critical thinking. In this chapter we discuss a number of strategies that we have found to be valuable for distinguishing fact from opinion, comparing and contrasting viewpoints, constructing support for a point of view, summarizing, using propaganda techniques, etc.

The most important point is that teachers be equipped with a wealth of activities to teach specific reading objectives through the use of these resources. A content area classroom that contains many newspapers, magazines, functional or survival reading materials, and has and promotes access to technology is a necessity in today's world. This area of technology is one of the most daunting yet most exciting developments in education today. How to use it for promoting literacy is described for the teacher interested in applying it to her day-to-day curriculum.

Teachers will also find that these materials are valuable tools for teaching a diverse population of students.

Expanding Understandings through Discussion

We want to introduce you to a strategy called the Group Reading Procedure (GRP) developed by Manzo (1980). It was created to help readers develop comprehension and recall and can be implemented in any of the content areas.

Directions: Form groups of five or six and appoint a group leader. The group leader will adhere to the following procedures:

1. Select a 250–500 word portion of this chapter you think is most important. After colleagues have read this portion, they close their books.
2. Ask colleagues to recall information read. The leader records it on the chalkboard.
3. Have colleagues go back to the text and make additions or changes to their list.

Manzo (1989)

4. Have colleagues make a semantic map or outline of the information.
5. Ask questions that will help colleagues to synthesize this information with their prior knowledge on this topic.
6. Give a short test to check short-term recall.
7. Later, give a second test to evaluate long-term recall.

Select a new group leader and have that person find another important portion in this chapter. Repeat the directions.

In the Field Applications

1. You will be teaching a class using computers in your content area. What reading skills will you need to teach students?
2. Go to the library where you are going to be an intern. Find all of the popular periodicals available in your content area.
3. Write a lesson plan in which you require students to watch a television program on a topic in your content area. It should include a comprehension or critical reading activity such as categorizing fact and opinion.
4. Will computers eventually replace teachers? Support your answer with current readings on the topic.
5. Maintain an electronic journal with your colleagues. Track the patterns of your conversation over a period of time. Discuss these patterns in small groups. Write your summary of these patterns.

References ❏ ❏ ❏

Allen, K., & Ingulsrud, J.E. (2003). Manga literacy: Popular culture and the reading habits of Japanese college students. *Journal of Adolescent & Adult Literacy, 46,* 674–683.

Allender, D. (2004). Popular culture in the classroom. *English Journal, 93*(3). 12–14.

Allington, R., & Walmsley, S. (1995). *No quick fix: Rethinking literacy in America's elementary schools.* Newark, DE: International Reading Association.

Alvermann, D., & Hagood, M. (2000). Critical media literacy: Research, theory, and practice in "new times." *Journal of Educational Research, 93*(3), 193–205.

Becker, G. (1973). *Television and the classroom reading program.* Newark, DE: International Reading Association.

Bennett, R. (1998). *Reinventing assessment.* Princeton, NJ: Educational Testing Service, Policy Information Center.

Ciani, A. (Ed.). (1981). *Motivating reluctant readers.* Newark, DE: International Reading Association.

Cronin, C., & Hines, J. (1990). Integrating computers, reading and writing across the curriculum. *Educational Leadership, 48,* 57–62.

Elkins, R. (1986). Attitudes of special education personnel toward computers. *Educational Technology, 26*(7), 3121–3134.

Frey, N., & Fisher, D. (2004). Using graphic novels, anime, and the Internet in an urban high school. *English Journal, 93*(3), 19–25.

Gallagher, K. (2004). *Deeper reading: Comprehending challenging texts 4–12.* Portland, ME: Stenhouse Publishers.

Gardner, H. (1999). Intelligence reframed: Multiple intelligences for the 21st century. NY: Basic Books.

Gardner, T. (2006). ReadWriteThink Lesson plan: Defining literacy in a digital world. Retrieved December 21, 2006 from http://www.readwritethink.org/lessons/lesson view printer friendly.asp?id=915.

Grossman, L. (August, 2003). Singing a new toon. *Time, 25,* 162.

Haley,K.W. (2005) Web page evaluation sheet. Retrieved December 21, 2006 from http://kwhaley.20m.com/studenteval.htm.

Hammer, R., & Kellner, D. (1999). Multimedia pedagogy for the new millennium. *Journal of Adolescent & Adult Literacy, 42*(7), 522–526.

Harris, T., & Hodges, R. (Eds.). (1995). *The literacy dictionary: The vocabulary of reading and writing.* Newark, DE: International Reading Association.

Hatchett, E. (1990). Cashing in on prime time, *Instructor,* 57–60.

Hogan, J. (1997). Wired: Educator success story. *Classroom CONNECT, 3*(9), 14.

Isaak, T., & Hamilton, J. (1989). Authoring software and teaching reading. *Reading Technology, 43,* 254–255.

Kelly, D. (2000). Online research skills for students. *Classroom CONNECT. 7* (2), 4–6.

Kuang-wu, L. (2000). Energizing the ESL/EFL classroom through internet activities. *The Internet TESL Journal, 6*(4), 1–5.

LaSasso, C. (1983). Using the National Enquirer with unmotivated or language handicapped readers. *Journal of Reading, 26,* 526–548.

Lemann, N. (October 16, 2006). Paranoid style. *The New Yorker.*

Luke, C. (1999). Media and cultural studies in Australia. *Journal of Adolescent and Adult Literacy, 42*(8), 622–626.

Manzo, A. (1989). ReQuest procedure. *Journal of Reading 13,* 123–126.

McTaggart. M. (October/ November 2006). Using comics and graphic novels to encourage reluctant readers. *Reading Today* 23(2), International Reading Association.

Middaugh, D. (2006). Reading manga: Or how I learned to stop worrying and just love reading. *RHInc*. VI (1), p. 70–76. Retrieved December 20, 2006 from http: // www.randomhouse.com /' highschool / RHI magazine/ RH106.pdf.

Miller, S., & Allan, K. (1989). *Reading the newspaper*. Providence, RI: Jamestown Publishers.

Myst. CD-ROM. Mead, Washington: Cyan, Inc., 1993.

NCTE (2006). Engaging media-savvy students: exploring multimodal literacies through popular culture and technology. Urbana, IL.

Patterson, Nancy. Technology and the exceptional learner. *Voices from the Middle*, 1 (4) 2005.

Quenzer, D. (2006). Understanding manga. *The Oregonian. A & E*. Friday, February 24, 2006.

Rawlings, K., & Schlosberg, D. (1989). Newspapers in education: Their time has come! *Reading Today, 6*(5), 1.

Rawson, H. (1981). A dictionary of euphemisms and other doubletalk. NY: Crown Publishers, Inc.

Reed, A. (1988). *Comics to classics*. Newark, DE: International Reading Association.

Rekrut, M. (1999). Using the Internet in classroom instruction: A primer for teachers. *Journal of Adolescent & Adult Literacy, 42*(7), 546–555.

Rhoades, L., & Rhoades, G. (1980). *Teaching with newspapers: The living curriculum*. Bloomington, IN: Phi Delta Kappa Educational Foundation.

Ryder, R., & Graves, M. (1998). *Reading and learning in content areas*. Upper Saddle River, NJ: Prentice-Hall.

Scharwz, A., & Rubinstein-Avila (2006). Understanding the manga hype: Uncovering the multimodality of comic-book literacies. *Journal of Adolescent & Adult Literacy. 50* (1), 40–49.

Schwarz, G. (2006). Expanding literacies through graphic novels. *English Journal, 95*(6), 58–63.

Signal, M. (1997). The internet and foreign languages education: Benefits and challenges. *The Internet TESL Journal, 3*(6).

Stoll, D. (1997). *Magazines for children*. Newark, DE: International Reading Association.

Teacher's guides to television. PO Box 264, Lenox Hill Station, NY, NY 10021.

Television most worth watching. (no date). Television Resources, Inc. Box 6712, Chicago, IL 60680.

Tolkien, J. (1938). *The Hobbit*. Boston: Houghton Mifflin.

Toppo, Greg. (2005). Teachers are getting graphic. *USA Today*.

Versaci, Rocco. (2001). How comic books can change the way our students see literature: One teacher's perspective. *English Journal. 91*(2), 66–69.

Vogt, M. (2000). Content learning for students needing modifications: An issue of access. In *Creativity and innovation in content area teaching*. McLaughlin & Vogt, (Eds.), Norwood, MA: Christopher-Gordon.

Magazines for Content Areas ❏ ❏ ❏

Arts and Music
Listen
Popular photography
Rolling Stone
Dramatics
Hit Parader
Images Doc
In 2 Print

Language Arts
Atlantic
ByLine
Travel
Vital Speeches
Scholastic Sprint
Claremont Review, The
Scholastic Scope

Scholastic Art
Plays, The Drama Magazine
  for Young People

Writing
Literary Cavalcade

Science and Math
Audubon
Aviation Weekly
Bio Science
BYTE
Environment
Bulletin Atomic Science
National Wildlife
Popular Science
Sky and Telescope
The Maihai Club Newsletter
Okapi
Quantum

Physical Education and Health
Aging
Current Health II
Field and Stream
Health
Sports Illustrated
Outdoor Life
Prevention
Skiing
Sport
Sail
Soccer Jr.
Surfer

Social Studies
Cobblestones
American Heritage
Business Weekly
Current History
Education Digest
Smithsonian
Forbes
Fortune
Futurist
Life
Money
Psychology Today
Journal of the West
Wild West
Phosphore
G-Geschichte mit
Pfiff (History with Pizzazz)

General
Car and Driver
Consumer Reports
Ebony
Esquire
Glamour
Good Housekeeping
Home Mechanic
Newsweek
New Yorker
Scholastic Up-Date
YM (Young and Modern)
YES Magazine
Teen Beat
Scholastic Action
Scholastic Choices
TG Magazine (Voices of Today's Generation)
Auto Week

Careers
American Careers
Career World
First Opportunity
Black Collegian, The

College
Careers and Colleges
Talents
College Bound
College PreView

Multicultural
AIM-America's Intercultural
  Magazine
Teen Voices Magazine

Foreign Languages
Ahora (Spanish)
Aktuell (German)
Bonjour (French)

Exclusive Use of Student Writing

Regular Use of Student Writing

How on Earth! Youth Supporting
Compassionate, Ecologically Sound
Living
    Vegetarian Education Network
    P.O. Box 339
    Oxford, PA 19363–0339
In 2 Print
    P.O. Box 102
    Port Colborne, ON
    Canada L3K 517
Merlyn's Pen Senior Edition
Grades 9–12
    Merlyn's Pen, Inc.
    4 King Street
    P.O. Box 910
    East Greenwich, RI 02818
Merlyn's Pen: The National Magazine
of Student Writing—Middle School
Edition Grades 6–9
    Merlyn's Pen, Inc.
    4 King Street
    P.O. Box 910
    East Greenwich, RI 02818
360 Magazine
    2625 Connecticut Avenue
    NW, #400
    P.O. Box 25356
    Washington, DC 20007
The 21st Century—Teen Views
    Teen Views
    P.O. Box 30
    Newton, MA 02161
Virginia Writing
    Longwood College
    201 High Street
    Farmville, VA 23909
Young Voices
    P.O. Box 2321
    Olympia, WA 98507

American Careers
    Career Communications, Inc.
    6701 W. 64th Street   Suite 304
    Overland Park, KS 66202
The Acorn
    1530 Seventh Street
    Rock Island, IL 61201
The Claremont Review
    The Claremont Review Publishers
    4980 Wesley Road
    Victoria, BC   Canada V8Y 1Y9
For Seniors Only
    Campus Communications, Inc.
    339 N. Main Street
    New City, NY 10956

Circle K
    3636 Woodview Trace
    Indianapolis, IN 46268–3196
Soccer JR.
    Triplepoint, Inc.
    27 Unquowa Road
    Fairfield, CT 06430
FFA New Horizons
    National FFA Organization
    5632 Mt. Vernon
    Memorial Highway
    Alexandria, VA 22309
Keynoter
    Key Club Internat'l
    3636 Woodview Trace
    Indianapolis, IN 46268
Scholastic Art
    Scholastic Inc.
    555 Broadway
    New York, NY 10012
Teen Magazine
    8490 Sunset Blvd.
    Los Angeles, CA 90069
Writing!
    Weekly Reader Corp.
    P.O. Box 2791
    Middletown, CT 06457–9291
Young Scholar
    Scholar Communications, Inc.
    4905 Pine Cone Dr.
    Suite 1
    Durham, NC 27707

Contests for Student Writing ❑ ❑ ❑

Library of Congress Student Writing Contest—Cash Prize
    www.loc.gov/letters
Olive Garden Student Writing Contest—Cash Prize
    www.olivegarden.com/ourcommunity/pastatales.asp
National Book Scholarship Fund—Cash Prize
    www.nbsf.org
Reader's Digest Word Power Challenge—Cash Prize
    www.wordpowerchallenge.com

Regular Use of Student Writing ❑ ❑ ❑

Skipping Stones
    www.SkippingStones.org

Electronic Sources ❑ ❑ ❑

Art
Art in general: http://occ.awlonline.com/bookbind/pubbooks/vacca_awl
Art on the Net: http://www.art.net/welcome.htlm
Links to Foreign Language Educators http://www.erols.com/jbrennan/flteachers.htm

Literature
Children's Literature Web Guide: http://www.ucalgary.ca/~dkbrown/index.html
Cyberguides: http://www.sdcoe.k12.ca.us/score/cyberguide.html
Electric Library: http://www.k12.elibrary.com
International Reading Association: http://www.reading.org
Nancy Keane's Booktalk Site: http://rms.concord.k12.nh.us/booktalks
National Council of Teachers of English: www.ncte.org
Pride and Prejudice: http://uts.cc.utexas.edu/~churchh/pridprej.html
StoryBook Park: http://www.planetzoom.com/Storybook.htm
Susie's Place: Word Lover's Paradise: http://www.primenet.com/~hodges/susplace.html
The Complete Works of William Shakespeare:
    http://thetech.mit.edu/Shakespeare/works.html
The Virtual Bookshelf: http://www.islandmm.com/
To Kill a Mockingbird: http://pwnetwork.pwcs.edu

Science (General)
Eisenhower National Clearinghouse: http://www.enc.org:80/classroom/index.htm
National Wildlife Federation: http://www/nwf.org/nwt/
Science Learning Network: http://forum.swarthmore.edu/
ScienceMaster: http://www.sciencemaster.com/

Math
Canada's SchoolNet: Mathematics:
    http://www.schoolnet.ca/home/e/resources/mathematics/
Coolmath4kids: http://coolmath4kids.com/
Eisenhower National Clearinghouse: http://www.enc.org:80/classroom/index.htm
Fun Mathematics Lessons: http://math.rice.edu/~lanius/Lessons/
Interactive Mathematics: http://www.cut-the-knot.com/content.html

DAU Math Refresher: http://www.cne.gmu.edu/odules/dau/math/index.html
Fun mathematics lessons: http://math.rice.edu/~lanius/Lessons/
Math-abundance:http://www.ping.be/~ping1339/hp.htm
Web Math, step-by-step tutorials: http://www.webmath.com/index.html

Social Studies (General)

American Memory: http://memory.loc.gov/ammem/amhome.html
History/Social Studies Web Site for K-12:
    http://www.execpc.com/~dboals/boals.html
National Council for Social Studies Links: http://www.socialstudies.org/links/
Nebraska Department of Education Social Science Resource HomePage:
    http://www.nde.state.ne.us/SS/ss.html
People Past and Present: http://www.ala.org/parentspage/greatsites/peopole.html#b

Multicultural Resources

Cultures of the World: http://www..ala.org/parentspage/greatsites/people.html#b
Diversity: http://www.execpc.com/~dboals/diversit.html
Multicultural Pavilion: http://curry.edschool.Virginia.EDU:80/go/multicultural/

Students with Special Needs

Council for Exceptional Children: http://www/cec.sped.org/home.htm
ERIC Clearinghouse on Disabilities & Gifted Education
    http://www.cec.sped.org/er~menu.htm
Learning Disabilities Association of America: http://www.Idanatl.org

Appendix A

La Hija Del Torreo

Veracruz es el puerto más importante de la costa oriental de México. La ciudad fue fundada en 1519 por Hernán Cortés quien le dió el nombre de la Villa Rica de la Vera Cruz. Generalmente hace buen tiempo en Veracruz, pero en ciertas estaciones hay huracanes y tempestades terribles.

La isla de Sacrificios está cerca del Puerto de Veracruz. En esta pequeña isla se halla un faro que ha salvado la vida de muchos marineros durante los cuatro siglos de su existencia.

En la primera parte del siglo diecinueve había un torrero que se encargó de faro. Se llamaba Felipe. Era un hombre joven y valiente, muy dedico a su trabajo. Vivía felizmente en el faro con su esposa Catalina y su hijita Teresa. Las queriá muchísimo.

Una mañana, Catalina le dijo a su hija que tenía diez años: -Para celebrar tu día de santo, Teresa, puedes acompañar a tu papacito a Veracruz ¿Quieres ir, hijita mía? -¡Ay, sí, mamacita, con mucho gusto!—respondió la niña.

Asi Felipe y su hija salieron en un bote pequeño para Veracruz. Cuatro horas más tarde, cuando se prepararon para volver a la isla, una gitana vieja vino al bote —Buenas tardes—dijo la gitana. —Con su permiso, señor, voy a decir la fortuna a su hija.

— Muy bien, si la niña quiere saberla—respondió el torrero.

— ¡Oh, si, deseo saber si algún día voy a casarme con un príncipe! Los tres rieron.

— Dame tu manecita, niña—dijo la gitana.

Después de mirar la mano por unos minutos, la gitana dijo:—Veo solamente una estatua, nada más. Creo que es una estatua de una persona valiente, cerca de la costa.

— ¿Es una estatua de un príncipe?—preguntó la niña Teresa.

— Creo que no—respondió la gitana.

— Pues,¿qué significa una estatua?—dijo el torrero que dió unos centavos a la gitana.

— Significa buena suerte, señor, y gracias por el dinero. ¡Que Diós los bendiga! Adiós—respondió la gitana.

Todo iba bien con el torrero y su familia hasta la próxima semana cuando una tarde la esposa, Catalina, se puso enferma.

— Voy al pueblo por medicina, pero vuelvo pronto porque vamos a tener una tempestad, según las nubes negras. Tú, Teresa, favor de ser una enfemera buena y una torrera valiente—dijo Felipe que iba corriendo a su bote.

El viaje al pueblo era difícil para el torrero. Hacía mucho viento, estaba lloviendo y las olas eran immensas.

473

Al llegar a la costa, tres piratas salieron detrás de unas rocas grandes, prendieron a Felipe, le ataron las manos y los pies y lo pusieron entre dos rocas immensas. Estos hombres iban a robar muchos barcos que ahora no podrían llegar a la costa sin la luz del faro.

Cuando el torrero no llegó a casa, su familia se puso nerviosa.

— !Ay, tu pobre papá y los pobres marineros que no pueden ver sin la luz del faro!

— Dijo Catalina. —Yo no puedo encender la luz porque estoy tan enferma.

— No se apure, mamá, voy a encender la luz-respondió la niña

— Es imposible, Teresa, eres tan pequeña.

La niña no oyó las palabras de su madre. Con fósforos en la mano, subió la vieja escalera hasta la torre, pero no pudo alcanzar la farola.

Teresa llevó una silla pequeña, varias cajas de madera y libros grandes a la torre. Con estas cosas construyó una escalera con la que pudo alcanzar la farola y encender la mecha.

Un rayo de luz iluminó el océano. Ya, aunque había una furiosa tempestad, todos los marineros en sus barcos llegaron a la costa sanos y salvos. Al ver la luz, los piratas se fueron sin robar a nadie.

A la mañana siguiente, dos marineros encontraron a Felipe y le desataron las cuerdas de las manos y los pies. También le contaron de la luz de la farola de la noche anterior.

Después de comprar la medicina para su esposa, el torrero volvió al faro para una reunión feliz con su familia. Entre lágrimas y besos, gozaron de estar reunidos otra vez.

Algún tiempo después, el pueblo entero, demostrando su gratitud a la niña torrera, erigió una linda estatua de Teresa Valiente en la costa de Veracruz.

APPENDIX B

Little Red Riding Hood (Spanish version)

Había una vez una niña muy bonita. Su madre le había hecho una capa roja y la muchachita la llevaba tan a menudo que todo el mundo la llamaba Caperucita Roja.

Un día, su madre le pidió que llevase unos pasteles a su abuela que vivía al otro lado del bosque, recomendándole que no se entretuviese por el camino, pues cruzar el bosque era muy peligroso, ya que siempre andaba acechando por allí el lobo.

Caperucita Roja recogió la cesta con los pasteles y se puso en camino. La niña tenía que atravesar el bosque para llegar a casa de la abuelita, pero no le daba miedo porque allí siempre se encontraba con muchos amigos: los pájaros, las ardillas listadas, los ciervos.

De repente vió al lobo, que era enorme, delante de ella.

— ¿Adónde vas, niña bonita? — le preguntó el lobo con su voz ronca.

— A casa de mi abuelita — le dijo Caperucita.

— No está lejos — pensó el lobo para sí, dándose media vuelta.

Caperucita puso su cesta en la hierba y se entretuvo cogiendo flores: — El lobo se ha ido — pensó — no tengo nada que temer.

La abuela se pondrá muy contenta cuando le lleve un hermoso ramo de flores además de los pasteles.

Mientras tanto, el lobo se fue a casa de la abuelita, llamó suavemente a la puerta y la anciana le abrió pensando que era Caperucita. Un cazador que pasaba por allí había observado la llegada del lobo.

El lobo devoró a la abuelita y se puso el gorro rosa de la desdichada, se metió en la cama y cerró los ojos. No tuvo que esperar mucho, pues Caperucita Roja llegó enseguida, toda contenta.

La niña se acercó a la cama y vió que su abuela estaba muy cambiada.

— Abuelita, abuelita, ¡qué ojos más grandes tienes!

— Son para verte mejor— dijo el lobo tratando de imitar la voz de la abuela.

— Abuelita, abuelita, ¡qué orejas más grandes tienes!

— Son para oírte mejor — siguió diciendo el lobo.

— Abuelita, abuelita, ¡qué dientes más grandes tienes!

— Son para… ¡comerte mejor! —y diciendo esto, el lobo malvado se abalanzó sobre la niñita y la devoró, lo mismo que había hecho con la abuelita.

Mientras tanto, el cazador se había quedado preocupado y creyendo adivinar las malas intenciones del lobo, decidió echar un vistazo a ver si todo iba bien en la casa de la abuelita. Pidió ayuda a un segador y los dos juntos llegaron al lugar. Vieron la puerta de la casa abierta y al lobo tumbado en la cama, dormido de tan harto que estaba.

El cazador sacó su cuchillo y rajó el vientre del lobo. La abuelita y Caperucita estaban allí, ¡vivas!

Para castigar al lobo malo, el cazador le llenó el vientre de piedras y luego lo volvió a cerrar. Cuando el lobo despertó de su pesado sueño, sintió muchísima sed y se dirigió a una charca próxima para beber. Como las piedras pesaban mucho, cayó en la charca de cabeza y se ahogó.

En cuanto a Caperucita y su abuela, no sufrieron más que un gran susto, pero Caperucita Roja había aprendido la lección. Prometió a su abuelita no hablar con ningún desconocido que se encontrara en el camino. De ahora en adelante, seguirá las juiciosas recomendaciones de su abuelita y de su mamá.

http://spanish.about.com/cs/vocabulary/a/caperucita_roja.htm

AUTHOR INDEX

Subject Index

Page numbers followed by *t* indicate tables and those followed by *f* indicate figures.